Mist on the North Sea
Beach, 1955. Photo by Ad
Windig / MAI, Amsterdam

2003

Published by the

The Low Countries

ARTS AND SOCIETY IN FLANDERS AND THE NETHERLANDS

11

Flemish-Netherlands Foundation 'Stichting Ons Erfdeel'

Contents

Chronicle

Film and Theatre

History

Language

Literature

Music

Philosophy and Science

Society

Visual Arts

Always
the Same H₂O

Queen Wilhelmina of the Netherlands hovers above the water, with a little help from her subjects, during the floods in Gelderland, 1926. Photo courtesy of Spaarnestad Fotoarchief.

Luigem (West Flanders), 28 September 1918. Photo by Antony / © SOFAM Belgium 2003.

Foreword

ἄριστον μὲν ὕδωρ - *Water is best.*
(Pindar)

Water. There's too much of it, or too little. It's too salty, or too sweet. It wells up from the ground, carves itself a way through the land, and then it's called a river or a stream. It descends from the heavens in a variety of forms – as dew or hail, to mention just the extremes. And then, of course, there is the all-encompassing water which we call the sea, and which reminds us of the beginning of all things.

The English once labelled the Netherlands across the North Sea '*this indigested vomit of the sea*'. But the Dutch went to work on that vomit, systematically and stubbornly: '*... their tireless hands manufactured this land, / drained it and trained it and planed it and planned*' (James Brockway). As God's subcontractors they gradually became experts in living apart together.

Look carefully at the first photo. The water has struck again. We're talking 1926. Gelderland. The small, stocky woman visiting the stricken province is Queen Wilhelmina. Without turning a hair she allows herself to be carried over the waters. She is the embodiment of the stubborn Netherlands, the country that knows how to keep its feet dry.

And look at the other photo, taken in '*that sullen swamp*' that was Flanders between 1914 and 1918. The horses are going up to the front. The wounded are coming back. The eternal movement to which mankind appears to be condemned. There is a fatalistic serenity about this photo. These men have learned to live with water. Do they still notice it? The sky seems to repeat itself in the mud.

The theme of this book, then, is water. In all its forms it keeps turning up where you don't expect it. Can you paint water? Flemish painters have tried it with a modest river, the Leie. Can you live on water? In the Netherlands they've specialised in that, from houseboats to floating brothels and new neighbourhoods and whole towns wrested from the sea or built defiantly next to or on it. The Dutch East India Company was a sea-borne multinational that wasn't too strict with its employees. Amsterdam's ring of canals at last gives up its secrets. The epic of the Frisian Elfstedentocht and other heroic deeds are paraded before you. In the poems it is freezing, snowing or foggy. In the prose the storm is apocalyptic.

But there is more than water in this book. It overflows with writers and painters, with Johan Cruyff and Eddy Merckx, the Greens in the Belgian and Flemish governments, conductors, musicians, architects and organs, airports and slave-traders, cabaret, and English that is actually Dutch.

All this and much more you can read in this eleventh edition of *The Low Countries*. They haven't yet been swallowed up like Atlantis. Come and see.

The Editors

God's

Subcontractors

The Dutch and Water

On 1 September 1996 the radio discontinued its daily reports on water levels. Shipmasters and bargemen could get the necessary information better and more quickly via other channels. No consideration whatsoever was given to their numerous compatriots for whom the daily ritual of an arcane dance of figures, attached to exotically named river villages, gave them something with which to cheerfully face another day: '*Lobith 919... minus 20; Eefde aan de IJssel 383 ... minus 6; Grave 499 ...no change.*'

The wide range of numbers lent the whole proceedings that mythic incomprehensibility required by all rituals. Furthermore, tension was built up by a pause of a couple of seconds before the announcement of yet another surprising final result – usually a minus to my recollection, but very occasionally a plus and sometimes a very disappointing '*no change*'. That run-up followed by a short silence was absolutely essential. When asked about this, one of its readers explained: '*You had to introduce that gap, that silence. You had the idea that if you rattled off the water levels too quickly a boat would run aground at Lobith.*'

This comforting ritual of secular prayer, now so sadly missed, is just one example of the many things that, for better or worse, we Dutch owe to the water. Almost everything that we think or do has its roots in the water. And it's not just a matter of the Delta Works, but also our remarkable predilection for boring parliaments, our raising ordinariness to the level of a lifestyle and our ability, by suggesting a 'sandwich lunch', to destroy any expectation of something decent to eat or drink.

Nowadays, any speculation about – let alone praise for – the history of our settlement in the region, or our common language and form of government, is not particularly popular. This reflects a pragmatic attitude that has much to do with a collective mentality forced upon us by our water management. Which seems a good enough reason to ask how it is possible that so many of our national traits, in our own eyes as well as in those of others, all seem to be linked directly to the water that surrounds us.

The floodgates of the dam near Grave, one of those *'exotically named river villages'* whose names figured in the daily radio reports on water levels.

The Rhine enters the Netherlands in Lobith. The sign shows the highest known water level on this spot (19.93 m) and the height of the dike (19.10 m).

Busy beavers

It was in this marshy delta that one of the greatest discoveries of the Middle Ages was made. Nowadays nobody is much interested in it and, more to the point, hardly anybody is even remotely aware of it. The discovery in question was that an artificially low water level could be created by digging parallel drainage ditches, and could be maintained by building dikes. So throughout the Middle Ages our ancestors were constantly hard at work, in a way reminiscent of busy beavers; the difference being that beavers always build the same kind of dam while we have now progressed to the Delta Works.

All that ceaseless toil produced another equally forgotten monument, namely the West-Frisian Ring Dike, about 115 kilometres long, many parts of which can still be seen and even touched. Not only did the work on this dike take longer than that on the pyramids, the cathedrals or the Chinese Wall, but during those centuries it gave rise to more disputes than any other construction project in the world.

But in the Netherlands, *'lieux-de-mémoire'* are not in fashion, even though we have plenty of them: Heiligerlee, Mokerhei, Bartlehiem, the perfectly preserved States Chamber in Dordrecht where the Holland Estates for the first time met freely in 1572 in what was effectively the birth of the Dutch state. Compared with the theatre in Philadelphia, a reconstructed building full of shop-window dummies, by which Americans commemorate

Salomon van Ruysdael,
*River Landscape with
a Ferry*. 1656.
Canvas, 105.4 x 134.6 cm.
The Minneapolis Institute
of Arts.

their Constitution of 1779, it demonstrates straightaway that the Dutch will have nothing to do with that kind of show.

Neither do many people have any interest in the stream that runs past my garden in Bussum through the Naardermeer in the direction of Muiden, the Karnemelksesloot (Buttermilk Ditch). It is not difficult to find where in this ditch the nobles murdered Count Floris v in 1296 as the peasants from the Gooi were about to rescue him. But though it is not surprising that no one now knows much about the event, some token to mark a memorable moment of Holland's history would not have gone amiss.

This indifference also extends to our appreciation of the landscape. It is striking how defensive even our poets become when the beauty of our countryside is involved. Our back-up national anthem 'Holland', by the nineteenth-century E.J. Potgieter, illustrates this well. He starts by mentioning the grey sky, the stormy beaches, bare dunes and monotonous landscape, but after acknowledging the shortcomings of the landscape he then goes on to glorify it because quite obviously God could have had little or no hand in its creation: *'You created nature with a stepmother's hand / And yet I love you deeply, O my land!'*.

But why? *'All that thou art is our forefathers' work / Wrought from a marshland through heroic toil …'*

And so on.

Actually this reveals not just pride but a high degree of arrogance. We, in contrast to the rest of the world, have created our own land.

Vomit of the sea

The rest of the world has also shown little appreciation of the Dutch land-scape, which has always been associated with the state of mind that it evidently generates in its madcap inhabitants. The Roman historian Tacitus repeatedly warned against the stinking marshes on the other side of the Rhine ('*brushwood-choked forests and rotting swamps*'), where the soil conditions contaminated the minds of the Germanic natives with rebellious and fractious attitudes. His contemporary Pliny simply described the Low Countries as a kind of cheese with holes, congealed along the banks of the numerous river channels on their way to the sea.

This perception continued to prevail. Even Napoleon could do no better than famously to dismiss Holland as alluvium deposited by a number of great rivers that originated in his France. The English poet Andrew Marvell, during the bitter Anglo-Dutch struggle for hegemony in Europe, went somewhat over the top in 1653 when he described the Dutch as slime dwellers:

Holland, that scarce deserves the name of land,
As but th' off-scouring of the British sand;
… And so much earth as was contributed
Of shipwrack'd cockle and the mussel-shell;
This indigested vomit of the sea
Fell to the Dutch by just propriety.

Holland, said another Englishman, was never intended by the Creator for human habitation. After all, the first condition that land should meet is to provide bread to eat and wood and stone for building. So whoever lives there must be a profiteer who wants to rob fish of their habitat. Or frogs, as someone else added.

Here you are pitilessly forced to wade through mud in continuous wind and rain, complained Erasmus's friend Cuthbert Tunstall in 1517 when he

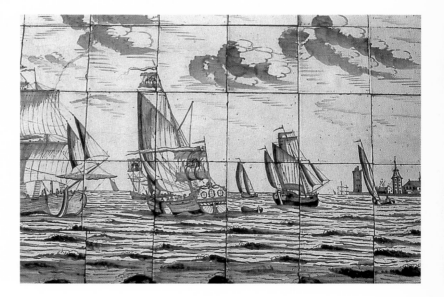

A 17th-century tile picture of ships in the Texel roadstead. Maritiem en Juttersmuseum, Oudeschild (Texel).

reluctantly found himself on the island of Walcheren. His complaint appears to have become the model on which all later complaints about and criticisms of the Dutch countryside and its abominable weather were based. He began with the all-pervasive smoke of burning peat in the towns that attacked the nose, head and chest. Which is why he went looking for some fresh air: '*But if you go walking in the country, you immediately sink in the mud since the lightest shower makes walking difficult. And you can't walk in the meadows because, wherever you go, your way is blocked by ditches. You can only walk comfortably along the sea dikes, except that it's almost impossible to*

Master of the St Elisabeth Panel, *The St Elisabeth's Day Flood* (right panel). c.1500.
Panel, 127 x 110 cm.
Rijksmuseum, Amsterdam.

reach them. To reach them, you have to cross hundreds of flax pools, where the rotting flax creates a stench far worse than the worst sewer. Furthermore, you always have to retrace your steps so that any pleasure you might have experienced is undone on the way back. So you return as bored and depressed as when you set out.'

The miserable conditions of the land and weather are consistently associated with a corresponding state of mind. Surely only flattened spirits could live in such a flat country. Moreover, the inhabitants of this apology for a country, stolen from the fish and the frogs, must be incorrigible profiteers. After all, they could only survive through trade since they had no alternative. And the almost exclusively negative connotations of the adjective 'Dutch' in the English language vividly illustrate how others chose to judge their activities: 'Dutch' usually means tight-fisted, greedy, frugal, grasping, slick, cunning and deceptive.

In the seventeenth century the relationship between land, weather and state of mind was considered to have been scientifically proved by the so-called theory of the humours. A person's physical and mental condition was believed to be determined by the balance between the four chief fluids, or humours, of the body. For Netherlanders this balance was upset from birth by an excess of water, both in the ground and falling from the sky. It made them develop spongy brains, a condition which was aggravated by their eager consumption of dairy products. As a result, a 'waterlander' could permanently absorb external impressions and images that were stored up in the 'sponge' in his head. When required, this sponge could be squeezed dry and deliver a true copy of what had been stored there. This explained scientifically how the Low Countries could produce such excellent painters. After all, the essence of painting was to be able to produce exact replicas of daily life. At the same time, it explained why our literature attracted virtually no international interest. Literature involves a level of abstract conceptualisation for which such spongy brains were inherently unsuitable!

Tinkering with creation

The concept of objective beauty in one's own landscape is illusory. Such a leap in perception is brought about by the discovery that we are here talking of a human creation, which in a sense turns us immediately into God's subcontractors. This idea was very popular in the seventeenth century but it had deep medieval roots. God had deliberately left Creation incomplete. As one of His chosen people, we had a duty to finish His work, especially since this muddy, marshy delta was so obviously unfinished. That this was God's intention was manifest from the fact that we survived so many floods, a familiar instrument of God's wrath ever since the time of Noah. There were many indications that this was part of the divine plan, for after every flood there were reports of babies floating in baskets who presumably would grow up to be a new Moses.

This theology of superiority served as propaganda for the great drainage works of the seventeenth century. The Netherlands, under an exclusive commission from God, was to be created by its inhabitants. As a result, the Netherlanders have had an obvious and irrepressible urge right up to the pre-

This flood inundated large parts of the Biesbosch and Land of Altena on 18-19 November 1421. Over sixty villages and thousands of people were engulfed overnight by the water of the Maas.

The great flood of 1 February 1953 resulted in 1853 casualties in the provinces of Zeeland and South-Holland. Photo from *The Disaster* (De ramp, 1953), a 'national edition' with a foreword by the Queen of the Netherlands.

During the winter of 1994-1995 the Dutch province of Limburg was under attack by the Maas.

sent day to keep tinkering with their own creation, to map it out and regulate it more closely. Any suspicion of wilderness, be it uncultivated land or freely running water, has to be tamed and cut back to create a garden, nature reserve, canal or pond. And in Madurodam we get a convenient overview of the way in which the Netherlands has been tamed and organised, in a replica that is deceptively close to the real thing.

This almost obsessive orderliness has, since the earliest times, also produced forms of democratic self-government. Drainage and land reclamation (impoldering) required constant consultation. Nobody could undertake such work only for his own plot of land because his neighbours would immediately find themselves up to their knees in water. So from all that local consultation arose the dike reeve, not a nobleman as his name in Dutch suggests ('*dijkgraaf*' – dike count), but an officer appointed to carry out a function that has continued for some seven centuries.

Furthermore, the structure of the land prevented the establishment or development of a powerful noble or ecclesiastical authority. There are no large uninterrupted stretches of land. Everywhere one can find a ditch, a canal, a river, or a waterway to form an easily defensible boundary. Similarly, there is neither the space nor indeed the ambience for large hunting parties; it is almost impossible to ride out without getting wet. Business and trade were the obvious strategies for survival, and that is how it has been from the early Middle Ages. So instead of great palaces and abbeys one got numerous little towns with merchants' houses and canals.

For the same reason, there was no place for barricade-storming on matters of principle because that was no way to keep the commercial pot boiling. Trade requires good will, understanding, genuine and pragmatic toleration; in short, what is generally meant nowadays by the term '*poldermodel*' in Dutch politics. Its origins go back to the urban guild structure of the late Middle Ages, which was most widespread and popular in the Low Countries. Employers and employees developed a strong feeling of solidarity within a particular craft, and resolved any problems themselves.

Perfectly ordinary people

Outline of a polder, with at the top a pumping station (r.) and a discharging sluice (l.). It also shows the circular canal and the enclosing dike around the drained lake. Drawing from *The Dutch and their Dikes* (Amsterdam, 1956).

That is why we are not fond of heroes and leaders. After all, we are all equal and dependent upon each other, with forms of administration that prefer to give responsibility to a consultative board, usually with a spokesperson rather than a leader. This means that any 'leader' should not claim in public to have superior knowledge or insight to the rest. The painter Karel Appel is a master of this approach, describing his artistic work as '*just messing around*'. After which we knew in our hearts that he was an incomparably great painter.

In the Netherlands we like to hear that kind of language from the truly great. We know full well that they are exceptional, but for us the important thing is the ritual of ordinariness that has developed over the centuries from a self-image that is now unshakeably rooted in our collective consciousness. And it is precisely those who are most prominent amongst us, whether artist, scientist, politician or even prince, who are subjected to the closest scrutiny. In the Netherlands, 'ordinary' is certainly not 'common'; 'ordinary' is no more and no less than how it should be.

So if you want to be admired in the Netherlands, you cannot be ordinary enough. In fact, even the most talented receive recognition only to the extent that they are able to appear most ordinary. That is why the 1998 businesswoman of the year, a far from ordinary person in most people's eyes, exclaimed to the TV cameras immediately after her award: '*I'm a very ordinary person, you know!*' Of course, we know better. And more to the point, so does she. But we still like to hear her affirm the opposite. And she was well aware of this.

Politicians in particular excel in declarations of ordinariness. And obviously the prime minister takes the lead. So former Prime Minister Wim Kok, an extremely exceptional person, regularly let it be known that he enjoyed camping and, of course, in a pup tent, a lowly shelter tent that one rarely sees nowadays but which expresses the height of humility in the face of the modern family caravan. The tone had been set by one of his predecessors, the late Joop den Uyl, who is probably the only political leader in the world to have made an official state visit from a camping site – in Portugal I believe. Heroes and heroines are not very fashionable here. At most they live on, so long as it's from long ago, in the name of a waterbus, a neglected street or a messy square. Usually the hero's name will no longer be recognised, as is the case with Willem Park in Amsterdam.

KLM (the Royal Dutch Airlines) names its larger aeroplanes after exotic rivers. In fact, the less Dutch you appear to be, the greater the impact on your own circle. None of our national heroes, starting with Floris V, can expect commemorations, national feast days, rituals or other expressions of warmth and solidarity. On the other hand, one detects a certain degree of sympathy for prominent lame ducks from the past, people who meant well and usually paid for it, somewhat clumsily, with their lives. One thinks of Jan van Schaffelaar, who for no good reason jumped off a tower and is now forever remembered in popular and children's rhymes. And the same applies to the poor orphan child Jan van Speyk, who blew himself up when the Belgians threatened to take over his ship in 1831.

We also like to remember how irresistibly ordinary these so-called heroes actually were. So Floris v lives on primarily as '*der keerlen Go*d' or in other words, a peasant king. We learn in school that Vondel, one of our greatest writers, sold stockings; that Admiral Michiel de Ruyter originally earned his living on the treadmill in a rope factory; that Multatuli (the author of the famous *Max Havelaar*), as a minor civil servant who couldn't count, cut corners; and that Vincent van Gogh was just mad and therefore went to live in France. That these simple men attracted attention because they had extraordinary talents was taken as read and something which it was embarrassing to mention. Even the well-known song about Admiral Piet Heyn, who famously captured Spain's Mexican treasure fleet, begins by mentioning that his name is rather short, before going on to celebrate his achievements. And even here the use of a 'folksy' vocabulary serves to emphasise that his audacious 'pranks' were after all really quite ordinary.

This all has to do with our lowlands bourgeois society of merchants and farmers, who from the late Middle Ages conducted their own little affairs (note the use of the word 'little') with the help of an impenetrable network of committees, councils and boards. In this, there was no place for the vertical hierarchy of powerful leadership in Church and State. From the outset, we were able to do without emperors and cardinals. Furthermore, our national past has been carved up by a long history of the bizarre but harmonious system of 'pillarisation', which is lubricated by a readiness to compromise. It therefore could not tolerate the divisive triumphalism of different religious and social groups celebrating their own heroes.

The Dutch are always sure that they know best, and sometimes even better, which tends to give rise to scornful comments by foreigners about our finger-wagging. There may be something in that, but it's a price we gladly pay for having embraced super-democratism, together with its companion, the spirit of equality. No country in the world has such a relatively large number of organised and recognised amateur practitioners of the arts and sciences. One out of every fifty Netherlanders takes part in amateur dramatics. And a recent survey revealed that these amateurs do not believe that they are any worse than professional actors. Illustrative of this know-it-all confidence in one's talents is the popularity of the quiz show. Unlike in America where the main figures are generally exceptional all-knowing enthusiasts in a specialist area, here it is always an ordinary man who glories in being asked questions about the world in general. His appearance suggests that, in principle, everything can be known by everyone, since in the sitting room we can always get the better of him. After all, aren't we all supposed, in principle, to be equally learned? And although these rituals of ordinariness and democratised erudition give an impression of naivety, there is surely a direct link between this and the absence of the usual bloodbaths when Protestants and Catholics meet and which continue to this day, even in a corner of Europe.

Only sports heroes and heroines are eagerly locked into our hearts, and we have no problem in loudly worshipping them. But here it is still emphatically all about the triumph and veneration of ordinariness. After all, we're talking about boys and girls from down the street; hence the friendly use of first names, preferably in the diminutive. Above all we recall their humble origins, but the sluice gates of emotion are only fully opened if, after their sporting career, they return to an ordinary life.

The Zaandam Canoe Club on a trip to the Loosdrechtse Plassen, Whitsun 1931. Photo collection J. Huysman.

For instance, there have been a few skating world champions, male and female, who on retirement expressed a desire to become, or remain, postmen. We are told *ad nauseam* that football whiz Johan Cruijff came from Betondorp, a concrete suburb in east Amsterdam, and that Evert van Benthem, several-times winner of the Elfstedentocht, a prestigious skating marathon, has returned to farming, while it appears that the last winner of that heroic race, Henk Angenent, is now engaged in that most Dutch of occupations, growing Brussels sprouts. Even the winner of the Tour de France, Joop Zoetemelk, has touched us with his assertion that he only wants to be a gardener at the French hotel which his wife runs.

Most recently, the unprecedentedly successful swimming champions, Inge de Bruijn and Pieter van den Hoogenband, have been subjected to the compulsory ordinariness treatment. Inge is now better known for having coined the expression '*oppie-toppie*' to signify a sense of well-being, while Pieter (referred to as 'Pietje' – Pete – by many) after his first gold medal was immediately reminded by TV news of his unspectacular schooldays. To this end, a reporter went to his secondary school in Eindhoven and naturally interviewed not the headmaster but the caretaker who assured us all that 'Pietje' had been a very ordinary lad who shuffled anonymously through the school corridors. That's what we like to hear. And we admire our 'Pietje' all the more for it: so ordinary, and yet all those medals won against the awesome Australians and Americans!

Water dominates everything in the Netherlands, from the earliest times until now. And it does not look as if that will ever change. Managing and exploiting the water involves a visible struggle that resonates in the most basic parts of our collective consciousness. And although our relationship with the water is always shifting, our state of mind changes with it. Whoever wants to know what Dutch society finds important and what we might think of a future in Europe and the world, would be well advised to consider the history and the ambitions of our national water management.

HERMAN PLEIJ
Translated by Chris Emery.

xcerpts

from a Log Book on the Scheldt and Maas

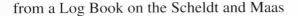

In Autumn 2000 I sailed the length of the Scheldt from source to estuary. In Spring 2001 I did the Maas ('La Meuse' in French), which is twice as long. Both rivers rise in France, flow through French-speaking Belgium and Flanders (though to be honest, as far as the Maas is concerned, only just in Belgian Limburg) and out into the sea in the Netherlands.

Each time it took me three boats to reach the estuary, three boats that got bigger each time. But to be completely honest, one never sails from the source, and the exact estuary of the Maas is endlessly debatable. Rivers are made by people and names can be misleading. As Heraclitus knew, '*everything is in a state of flux, nothing stays the same*'.

Here are excerpts from the log that I kept on board. Although even that is not quite correct, because travel stories are written at home. Besides, do rivers tell us anything about the landscapes they pass through? Not much, probably. The landscape does look different, though, when you see it gliding past. For a moment it seems as though we are standing still.

In the realm of the nymphs

My brief was simple, to sail the river from source to estuary, to take note, as I travelled, of what I saw as well as what I did not see, but which is there nonetheless: the story of the river, and the landscapes and towns along it. But at the source of the Scheldt, in the unprepossessing French village of Gouy, above St Quentin, the plan no longer seems so simple. Of course the source looks idyllic – a pool a few metres across, confined between walls. Clear, almost still water fed by a few springs that have made their way to the surface on the plateau here. There is a flowery Latin inscription, a statue of a child playing with a dolphin. This fitting symbol stands for the '*fertilité, prudence et sagesse du fleuve*'. The Scheldt can certainly use prudence and wisdom, as the river basin's $21,800 \text{ km}^2$ (8,417 square miles) are some of the most densely populated and industrialised in the world. A brave and still innocent sign hangs on a tree: '*Défense sous peine d'amende de jeter des ordures dans l'Escaut et de détériorer l'ouvrage*' – persons throwing rubbish into the Scheldt or causing damage to the structure will be fined.

It is impossible to sail on the brook in Gouy as it twists its way through the undergrowth, and it will be like that for a while. I travel not on the Scheldt but on the St Quentin Canal, which was constructed under Napoleon I, until past Cambrai. So, will I be able to travel on the Scheldt when the three metre wide stream flows into the Canal de l'Escaut? At the source it says that the river has lost a lot of its identity beyond Cambrai, but what is its identity? The one it had five hundred or five thousand years ago? The one it had before human intervention or afterwards?

Close to the source are the ruins of St Martin's Abbey, which have been converted into a farm now. This holy man probably Christianised a heathen place of worship, perhaps even the spring itself? Myth has it that the spring shares its identity with the nymph that lives in it, indeed the spring *is* the nymph. Where it rises, Nature displays her mysterious power and fertility. People who live in a web of myths make the incomprehensible comprehensible by proclaiming the spring a nymph and venerating it. Christianity transferred the mystery to the creator and then the creator was dispensed with, as was St Martin's Abbey. The French revolution turned it into a castle, in which the diplomat and statesman Talleyrand and the Duke of Wellington lodged. The First World War destroyed it, and now it is a farm overgrown with ivy.

I come across the young Scheldt a couple of times between Gouy and

The source of the Scheldt in Gouy (France). Photo by Philippe Debeerst / © SABAM Belgium 2003.

Vauxelles, but on the whole it winds a hidden path amidst the undergrowth. I have an appointment with a boatman at the Abbey of Vauxelles. We will spend five days together travelling from here to Ghent. His boat, sailing under the French flag, is waiting for me one bridge further up the St Quentin Canal.

(…)

A dragon exploring its prison (Oudenaarde – Ghent)

We leave Oudenaarde at first light. By eight we are bobbing around in the lock, the next to last one before Ghent. At the railway bridge, just outside the town, we pass the site of Ename. But even from the roof of the boat I can see none of the excavated foundations, neither the abbey nor the massive fortress founded here by the German Emperor Otto II round 975. There were, of course, three fortifications on the right bank of the Scheldt, in Valenciennes, Ename and Antwerp, to defend the Holy Roman Empire against the Counts of Flanders, vassals of the French Crown.

We glide along the wide and slowly meandering river, hemmed in by tall poplars, passed only by barges that forge ahead, with cars on the forward deck, to meet commercial goals and deadlines. Today they are called *Carmen* and *Interballast*. They travel so fast and we so slowly – our engine was overheating – that we are alone most of the time with the herons that stand like statues on the banks, scrutinising the Scheldt, guarding it, and then rise, cleaving the sky with curved necks, to return again in a great arc. Then there are the inevitable ducks, croaking ravens and joggers, muffled up, passing us on the towpath. It is hard to believe, in this green corridor with ears only for itself, that we are moving through densely populated Flanders. The first seagulls appear beyond Gavere. It is not far to Ghent now. We leave the old Scheldt on the right, as it veers off to the East on its way to join the Ring Canal further up. This part of the Scheldt, closed as it is to traffic, has a clear function. It is a tidal arm whose purpose is to keep floodwaters from Antwerp out of Ghent city centre. Beyond Ghent, of course, the Upper Scheldt becomes the Sea Scheldt and is tidal. At the end of the nineteenth century, some areas of the city were regularly flooded. The Ring Canal, into which the Leie and Scheldt disappear now, and the locks have tamed these vagaries.

With the Castle of Zwijnaarde on the left bank the idyll is over, Fabelta's chemicals loom. We sail under the Brussels-Ostend motorway and cut across the Ring Canal to dive into an open lock. Just before the lock we travel under the New Scheldt bridge. The graffito here is laconic: '*Long live nature*'. I look behind me, and see a seething motorway encased in concrete, factories, and cows grazing in a meadow that lies, imperturbable, in the midst of it all. So how new is this bit of the Scheldt? But let us stay with the part that makes its way to the city. The dome of St Peter's Church and the abbey towers, the tower of the university library and, a little later, the cathedral point the way. More motorways and intersecting railway lines follow. An enormous cinema complex with a red carpet goes by, and then St Peter's Abbey. We sail past the majestic back wall of Vooruit, formerly a People's Palace, a temple of culture now, and swing into a pool where the Scheldt disappears under a wall. I step out of the boat – I have no choice – and go on foot to

The Geeraard de Duivel-steen in Ghent in the 19th century. Stadsarchief, Ghent.

the Reep via a section of the Scheldt that is vaulted over. We are in the heart of the city, behind the cathedral. A bit of the Scheldt has been preserved here, a square pool, flanked on the left by the Geeraard de Duivelsteen, a Romanesque fortress from the early thirteenth century (c.1245) in darkly mildewed Doornik limestone. Geeraard Vilain (*nomen est omen*), a savage-looking knight who owed his nickname to his dark skin and black hair, was in reality very devout. The building has been a prison, convent, school, insane asylum, arsenal and fire station. Nowadays the public archives are there and it must accommodate all the memories of the city, its rivers and canals. Further up, the Reep has been filled in, and another five hundred metres on there is the Leie, which used to flow into the Scheldt here. But today just the opposite seems true, the Leie outshines a castrated Scheldt. Which river flows into which is apparently convention, too.

At the Duivelsteen, however, I remain faithful to the Scheldt. In spring 2000 there was a copper-coloured dragon out on the river. Had the proud dragon at the top of the bell-tower been tamed at last? No, it was a work of art that had been dropped into the pool during the art-in-the-city exhibition *Over the Edge*s. The work was called *Amphibian*, but it was actually the Scheldt itself, disarmed, and bobbing up and down, that had been given the freedom to explore its prison.

Ebb and flow (Ghent – Antwerp)

From Ghent onwards the Scheldt gets steadily wider and flows in broad curves through territory which it dominates more and more. It no longer lends itself to canalisation. The banks become muddy, more wooded. Here and there, at low water, silt and marshland appear, the influence of tides and current increases. The river endures no more locks, but acquires ferries. Bridges become scarcer and are eventually replaced by tunnels. But we are not there yet. This morning I am at the lock in Merelbeke, on the Ghent Ring Canal, where the *Eddy* is moored, a river barge that will bring sacks of grain – and me – from Deinze to Antwerp.

In Melle the Ring Canal flows into the Scheldt on its way out of Ghent. But the first surprise of the day is on the right bank between Kwatrecht and Wetteren, a huge twin-engine passenger plane (*République populaire du...*) which has miraculously landed here, never to leave again. In Wetteren a lanky, narrow church shows its backside to the river. The Schellebelle ferry, the first on the river, is true to its name. There are bells on either side that must be rung to summon the ferryman from the café. On one side there are two cafés, on the other a church with a graveyard full of chrysanthemums: Flanders writ small. The river winds more, the first flood plains appear. '*We won't pass any more ships now*', my new skipper predicts, '*They left Antwerp on the high tide this morning.*' He turns out to be right. I see a campsite at Zele, the first along the river since the solitary houseboat floating on drums I saw in France. A little further there is a charming villa on the dike. An empty sunlounger adorns the veranda, a ringside seat from which to watch the Scheldt: a show that burbles along with no need for an ingenious plot or moments of suspense, but slow undercurrents and recurring rhythms. On the right, Dendermonde's towers loom, but it no longer lives up to its name ('*monde*' = 'mouth', 'estuary'). The old Dender, which is still there in the town, cannot flow out into the Scheldt these days. A canal with a lock does instead. Only a few posts on the bank before the bridge mark the confluence.

Beyond Dendermonde, halfway between Ghent and Antwerp, the river becomes really wide. The bollards get higher, the distance between the bank and the dike gets bigger. In the wide S-bend at Kockham, between Moerzeke and Baasrode – which I now declare the most idyllic since the source – the ship is alone with the water, marsh and woods. A weeping willow with its yellow veil bows elegantly before the sovereign Scheldt. At Baasrode, the first – abandoned – shipyards appear. They will not be the last. An old woman with a bicycle waits for the ferry. In Sint-Amands a bronze ferryman greets us from the bank, a tribute to the French-speaking poet Emile Verhaeren, who was born here and sang the praises of the Scheldt in broad meandering verses. He is buried on the bank in a black marble tomb on a broad stone plinth. From my vessel, it looks like a container on a solid boat, about to be lowered into the water.

The great shipyard at Temse has been dismantled. All but one of the machines and cranes have been sold to countries where ships are made more cheaply, though not better. The metal bridge – the last over the Scheldt – will never again open up to let an ocean giant sail to Antwerp. At Rupelmonde, a tower is a reminder of the Counts of Flanders' buttressed fort, one of the oldest fortifications on the eastern border of the County. The roof of the last remaining tide-mill along the Scheldt glides past, but a monumental rusting warship at the quayside steals the show. A massive power station,

A detail of the Hypsos map of Antwerp (made especially for the World Fair in Ghent, 1913): the Antwerp port including Kattendijk dock, dry docks, Grote Bik and Noorderpershuis. Nationaal Scheepvaartmuseum, Antwerp.

The tomb of the poet Emile Verhaeren (1855-1916) on the bank of the Scheldt in Sint-Amands.

casting its high tension wires across the river from the other bank, stands watch at the estuary of the Rupel, which has acquired a sea lock alongside it here. The power station heralds a right bank built up with industries that will keep us company from here to Antwerp. Only the restored St Bernard's Abbey in Hemiksem does its best to survive between the factories. Monks from the abbey at Vremde, which was founded by Bernard of Clairvaux, built it here in the thirteenth century. At Hoboken I pass the Métallurgie, one of the dirtiest factories in Flanders. They turn lead into gold here, my skipper remarks, literally and metaphorically. Instead of ships, the Cockerill Yards now build container cranes for the Port of Antwerp, whose proximity is evident in everything now. In the misty afternoon light the tower of the Cathedral of Our Lady rises from behind *Dutch Faith*, the first sea-going vessel that I have seen on this trip. From here, I can see that a single tower looks more beautiful than the two that were planned. Gradually the Antwerp docks come into view. Cars drive into the belly of an immense car-transporter. An *Amerigo Vespucci* beside it is worthy of its name. The houses and apartments gliding past along the quay betray a rich and flamboyant city, populated by self-aware '*sinjoren*' who think they know it all.

As expected, Antwerp wins the prize for most impressive city on this river. But still the city shrinks from the Scheldt. It was too powerful, too capricious, and had to be kept at a distance behind embankments and a high wall. In the city, too, the water was kept at bay. The South Docks were filled in. The real port has been banished to the north of the city. Meanwhile, the lacelike masonry of the cathedral glides past and the Steen, which still stands on the spot where the German Emperor Otto II built his fort against France a little before 980. Here they refer to the other side of the Scheldt as 'Flemish head'.

27

After about six hours sailing I take my leave of the *Eddy* and climb a rickety ladder to a deserted quay in the old port, past the pilot service's impressive building. In Antwerp the river will change its identity one last time.

Water and air (Antwerp-Vlissingen)

I look out of a window in Antwerp's pilotage office at a fast-flowing Scheldt. This is the Eilandje, or Little Island. The bargemen's quarter with its ladies of the night is behind me. Commemorative plaques unite pilots from Antwerp and Vlissingen, '*morts pour la patrie*' in two world wars. I wait for a pilot and a ship that will take me to Vlissingen. It turns out to be the *Geo Milev*, a 23 by 158 metre Bulgarian container ship that is waiting in the Berendrecht lock north of the city, on the border with the Netherlands. A car takes us there, along a Scheldt that curves majestically away to the north. We drive for half an hour through a world-class port, past factories, refineries, docks and locks, cranes that hang above the river like giant spiders and handle containers as though they were matchboxes. On the other side of the river, huge cooling towers thrust upwards from the power station in Doel, enormous, well-formed bottle necks, a miracle of the potter's craft on this glorious day. Their contours will guide me to Vlissingen. In front of the power station I see the church towers and mill of that besieged and threatened polder village, Doel. It has become a symbol of the struggle between port and village, quality of life and economics. The outcome is certain, but it has been stubbornly resisted. I went there early this morning to see the truth behind the gloomy reports vented in newspapers and books about the village. The trip there is an experience on its own. The fort of Liefkenshoek was built by Marnix of St Aldegonde, the mayor of Antwerp, a couple of years before the fall of the city in 1585, and was rebuilt by Napoleon to give him control of the Scheldt. Now it is a peaceful oasis on the left bank – Waasland, East Flanders – where the port has long since put out its greedy tentacles. I came across the huge Deurganckdok, a tidal dock which ships will be able to sail straight into and out of, without locks – because time is money. Concrete mixers drive in and out. Access prohibited for unauthorised persons. We make a detour along the Doeldok, which is further inland, where signs on the heaped up embankment say, '*Warning: quicksand*'. Doel welcomed me with another sign, but houses stand empty in the village. Others sport black flags and still more signs that say '*Doel must stay*', '*Doel will stay*', and '*No deportation*'. '*The church is not a museum*' hangs militantly in the church. That was Doel then, a village laid out like a chessboard behind the high Scheldt dike, squeezed in between the river, the power station and the advancing docks, still alive under the rumble of the port and factories. You could see ocean-going giants pass here as if they were sailing above the village. I saw the town hall where a 'social mediator', who offers counselling to a dying village, is based. Those who have stayed sneer bitterly at those who have left. Property prices slumped long ago. At the newsagent's they looked at me with distrust: '*Everyone comes and pokes their nose in here. I don't come to your town, do I?*' Doel is turning inwards on itself. The quicksand is moving in. I had to leave.

The *Geo Milev* is in the Berendrecht lock. A tired captain, in jeans and un-

Neeltje Jans: the flood barrier on the Eastern Scheldt.

buttoned shirt, stands on the bridge. It was a long night. He arrived yesterday, unloaded half his cargo and took on as much again. The containers are piled up on the deck. The captain wants to sail again immediately. He has to be in Le Havre by evening. The ladies of the night did not get a look at this crew. The lock gates swing open and the pilot starts his word game of mysterious numbers and orders, which are repeated ritualistically by the helmsman. The common language is English. The Belgian flag, way out in front, is replaced by a Dutch one, '*out of courtesy*' to the country we are sailing through, says the helmsman. In the Bath bend the ship turns to the left on the current. The engines do not have to work so hard now. Until about 1500 the Scheldt still flowed northwards here, turning westwards towards the sea at Bergen-op-Zoom. Only then did the sea finally break through between Vlissingen and Breskens, so that the Honte became the Western Scheldt, which we are sailing on now. The original outlet became the Eastern Scheldt, which has been brought under control in recent decades with bridges and flood defences. The Western Scheldt has still not been tamed.

On the right bank a succession of windmills glides past, a row of propellers lined up on top of high masts. One of the largest wetland areas in Europe appears on the left bank, the submerged land of Saeftinghe. The Counts of Flanders had a fortress there, but everything – villages and fortress too – was devastated, first of all by the great flood of 1570 and then by the people of Antwerp who finished the job a few years later when they breached the dike to keep the Spaniards out of the city. Their efforts turned out to be futile, but the area remained in the grip of the river. After the Belgian revolution in 1831 it became, once and for all, Dutch territory, which probably saved it from the Antwerp Port expansion.

Hidden behind the dikes lie the fertile polders the dikes have reclaimed from the silt and marshes. In Zeeuws-Vlaanderen, however, calls to breach the dikes and allow the polders to return to their original state – to '*give the land back to nature*' – are getting steadily stronger. Under frontal attack by the port's bosses, the farmers of the Flemish Waasland find their flanks threatened too, now, by Greens from the Netherlands. With concrete on one side and swamp on the other, they are caught between economics and ecology. Just try explaining to a farmer that the most fertile land in Europe is to be allowed to become silt and marsh again.

As Terneuzen and Dow Chemicals pass on the left, and a platform in the middle of the river on which Scheldt sand is being heaped up, the captain talks about Varna, on the Black Sea, the home port of this ship that makes the trip to Hamburg, Felixtowe, Naples, Heraklion and Alexandria twice every two months. I do not get to hear what is in the containers, just that the cargo can vary from scrap metal to Porsches, loaded in Hamburg and bound for Beirut. An explanation follows on the loading of containers, a careful juggling of weights and balance, and the increasing levels of stress captains suffer. You do not live beyond sixty in this job.

So who was Geo Milev? The answer is: a Bulgarian communist poet shot by the fascists in 1923. The captain pushes aside the charts and points proudly to a silhouette scratched into the shining metal, a *poète maudit* with a lock of long hair arranged in front of his glass right eye. Meanwhile, the ship that bears his name is fast moving up the estuary. Vlissingen comes into view on the right and Breskens on the left. In front of us is the busiest sea in the world and there are two world-class ports nearby. The engines fall still: a tanker in the estuary is blocking the shipping lane. Courteous phone calls are made about priority. The river pilot stays on the bridge until the sea pilot relieves him. He will guide the *Geo Milev* some thirty miles through the southward channel, and then be taken ashore by helicopter. We are taken ashore by the *Pieter de Coninck*, a low-lying tug, which first drops the pilot at a ship that is waiting for him to bring it back to Antwerp. I am taken, with other pilots collected along the way, to Vlissingen and dropped near the statue of Michiel Adriaenszoon de Ruyter. The hero of Chatham was born here, and went off to sea as an eleven-year-old cabin boy to die a legendary admiral at Syracuse in 1676. At the statue, with its Latin inscription, flanked by two of De Ruyter's cannons fished up from the sea at Messina, my journey ended. This journey that began with a Latin inscription in Gouy and took me through '*nobile Belgium*', the 'noble Netherlands', past towns that are bathed, enriched, caressed by the river, on vessels that got steadily bigger, as the river itself did. Only here do I realise the futility of asking where the river ends and the sea begins. '*Gravius Thetidem intras*' was the self-assured inscription in Gouy. Does the Scheldt enter the sea goddess solemnly here? There is only the grandeur of sea and air, grey and blue. And in between there are warships, tankers, car transporters, container ships, dredgers, tugs and ferry boats. The nymph hiding at the source does not know what she is missing.

The Maas in a drunken boat

'*Watershed*', says the sign to the right of the road. On the right all the water from the Plateau de Langres flows to the Mediterranean, on the left it goes to the Atlantic, the Channel and the North Sea. In March 2001 there is more than enough water on this plateau, it is one huge, saturated sponge. A glance at the map reveals the sources of the Sâone, the Marne and the Maas (or 'Meuse' in French) here. The hot springs of Bourbonne-les-Bains are nearby. To the North are Vittel, Contrexéville, and Grand, the Celtic sanctuary dedicated to Grannus, the god of healing water whom the Romans identified with Apollo. But I needed to be in Pouilly-en-Bassigny. The only thing painted in this forsaken village in the Vosges, in the department of Haute-Marne, is, strangely enough, the memorial to the fallen from the two world wars, on the square. I count sixteen dead in the First World War and two in the Second. The village itself looks abandoned, like a village in the Balkans when the tanks from some unidentified army roll in. There are hopelessly dilapidated farms, their windows boarded up.

In a boggy meadow outside the village, a weathered stone stands amidst grazing carthorses. I clamber over a wire fence and sink into the squelchy mud as I make my way to the source of the Maas. The stone says '*LA MEUSE FONTAINE*'. Back in the village, the only man in the street seems to be the mayor. Have I seen the source? The official – somewhat higher – one is actually on the other side of the village. There has been a sign there since an abbot from Flémalle walked up there in the sixties and convinced the locals that this trickle of northward-flowing water has produced an impressive delta, less than a thousand kilometres away, with the biggest port

A sluice on the Maas in the French Ardennes. Photo by Luc Devoldere.

One of the sources of the Maas. Photo by Luc Devoldere.

in the world. Pouilly itself has no priest, no post office, no school and no shop any more.

Above the official source with its picnic table there is a rainbow. The sun is shining and it is drizzling – carnival in Hell they call it in Dutch. I decide to interpret it as a good omen for this journey from source to mouth. '*Liberté-Egalité-Fraternité*' (France) with Roman fasces, '*L'Union fait la Force*' (Belgium) and '*Je Maintiendrai*' (the Netherlands) appear together fraternally on the memorial plaque. The water is sludgy brown. It runs away in a gutter that disappears into a pipe under the village. When I find the stream again beyond the village it has been reinforced by more water, and at the first bridge over the Maas another waterfall flings itself into the rushing torrent. Could it be the spring from the boggy meadow? A weathered plaque is illegible. In Malroy, I stand on the second bridge above the substantial brook that the Maas has turned into, bolstered yet again by a tributary. In Meuse village, on the third bridge over the Maas – I will stop counting now - the Bar-Hotel-Restaurant *Aux sources de la Meuse* tries to exploit what is, as yet, only a promise.

(…)

The land of Maas and Waal

When I wake next morning the *Frama* is already on its way. The Waal turns out to be a wider river than the Maas, the traffic heavier. Pusher tugs each with four huge barges head upstream past us on a twenty-hour, non-stop journey between Rotterdam and the Ruhr. Meanwhile, one of Hendrik Marsman's poems unfurls along the bank:

Landscape

In the pastures the peaceable
beasts are grazing;
the herons sail
over glittering lakes,
the bitterns stand
by pools of dark water;
and out in the meadows
the horses are running
with rippling tails
over rippling grass.

(Translated by Tanis Guest)

We travel into that great alliance of air and water, the land of Maas and Waal, which has been subject since time immemorial to frequent flooding, as well as to military operations and sieges, and is therefore thinly populated. For centuries battles have been fought at this natural border. Fortresses, strongholds, redoubts and land designed to be flooded for defence bear witness to this. Grave aan de Maas (whose name means 'fortifications on the Maas') was once one of the most fought-over cities in the Netherlands, captured and recaptured by Spanish troops and soldiers of the States General, and then by the French in the catastrophic year of 1672 and again in 1794.

At Rossum aan de Waal, the Maas and the Waal come to within just one

French guns at Grave.
Photo by J. Houttekier.

kilometre of each other. It is amazing that the two rivers did not meet years ago! The Batavians erected an encampment at this strategic spot and the Romans built a fortification there. Now I can see a lock and the beginning of the St Andries Canal, which connects the two rivers.

Maastricht: St Servaas Bridge (l.) and the Bonnefanten Museum (r.). Photo courtesy of Gemeente Maastricht.

Now the *Frama* can see Zaltbommel's bridges: the metal railway bridge and, behind it, the new bridge, named after the poet Martinus Nijhoff. Only as you sail underneath do you notice that the disused bridge from Nijhoff's poem is still there between the two. The poet went off to 'Bommel' to have a look at the 'new bridge'. The year is 1933:

The Bridge at Bommel

I went to look at the new bridge at Bommel.
I saw the bridge. Two facing banks there were,
which once seemed each of them to shun the other,
now neighbours once again. Lying there idle
for a while in the grass, after I'd drunk my tea,
my mind filled with the landscape all around –
let me from that infinity perceive a sound,
a voice filling my ears which spoke to me.

It was a woman. The boat that carried her
came downstream through the bridge, steady and calm.
She was alone on deck, stood at the tiller,

and what she sang, I heard then, was a psalm.
Oh, I thought, oh, that there went my mother.
Praise God, she sang, He'll keep you from all harm.

(Translated by Tanis Guest)

Nearly seventy years later I see ships pass called *Deo confidentes*, in God we trust, and *Deo favente*, God willing. There is no singing any more, though.

During the Eighty Years' War Zaltbommel was the farthest outpost of the United Netherlands. But the last bit of the Dutch defences can be found at 'drielandenpunt', where three towns and three provinces meet, Gorinchem (Holland), Woudrichem (Brabant) and Slot Loevestein (Gelderland). I find the Maas again here. Until 1904 it flowed out into the Waal between Woudrichem and Loevestein. Then it was dammed and the Bergse Maas, which brings the water from the Maas to the Hollands Diep and through the Haringvliet into the North Sea, was opened, drastically reducing the risk of flooding in this water-rich area. Slot Loevestein, built on the strip of land between the old dammed-up Maas and the Waal, glides past. The Spanish and the troops of the States General fought over the castle till the *Watergeuzen* (irregular Dutch water-borne forces) took it in 1572. Prince Maurice turned it into a state prison, where he incarcerated the great scholar and jurist Hugo de Groot, who escaped to Paris in a book crate two years later.

Here, between Loevestein and Woudrichem, I declare the river up which the *Frama* is steaming indomitably, to be the pre-1904 Maas-Waal. On the other side, however, a sign appears and informs me that I am now leaving the Waal and sailing up the Upper Merwede. It is the beginning of the great confusion of tongues. The delta is close now, as you can see from the frenzied rail traffic between Amsterdam and Antwerp, that races over the bridge past Gorinchem. My skipper talks about his strict Reformed colleagues from Gorinchem, Werkendam and Sliedrecht, hard-working people who have lots of children and never sail, load or unload on Sundays. Often they do not insure their boats, as they can always rely on close communities and churches that will have a word with the banks. *Deo favente. Deo confidentes.* At Werkendam the Frama chooses again. It is the Lower Merwede this time, straight to Dordrecht.

(…)

Private vice, public benefit

The *Frama* chooses the North, drawn thither by Rotterdam. At the confluence with the Lek the city skyline appears. A new dredger with a Japanese name lies in a shipyard, dreaming of the Orient. Architects make tentative efforts to imitate bridges in their buildings. Then there are the bridges themselves, the Willemsbrug, the Koninginnebrug or the 'Hef', from which the Rotterdammers could not bear to be parted and which now hangs pointlessly in the air – a bit of history in this town without a past. But all bridges pale before the Erasmusbrug, the soaring 'Swan' visible from afar. It is, without doubt, the most beautiful on the whole Maas, mirrored by those in Huy and Liège. It quivers proudly across the river between the town and Kop van Zuid, flanked by Renzo Piano's tower block which, in my opinion, takes the prize for the most beautiful new building along this river, this stretch of which is called the New Maas. Green buds make specks of light dance across its glass walls. The bridge and tower form an alliance of abstract beauty that reconciles me to this city.

On the Erasmus bridge I think of the first bridge across the Maas in Pouilly-en-Bassigny (they have nothing in common except that my wife leaned over the railings on both of them), and of Rimbaud who – as he predicted in 'The Drunken Boat' ('Le Bateau Ivre') – would long for *'Europe's ancient parapets'* when he reached the end of his wanderings. I think back to the parapets in France at Dun and Monthermé, which American armies and German tanks crossed in two wars.

Rotterdam is, more than it is Erasmus' city, Pierre Bayle's. He lived there from at least 1681 until his death in 1706. After Louis XIV closed the Protestant university in Sedan Bayle was appointed as a lecturer in Rotterdam. In the late seventeenth century the city became a market place for books and ideas. It was here that the link between morals and religion was severed and atheists could become respectable citizens. A philosophical society, *De Lantaarn*, was active in the riverside house of the Quaker banker, Furley. There Bayle, too, must have looked out across the Maas to what was, in those days, still the idyllic island of Feyenoord. The Frisian, Bernard Mandeville, went even further in the discussions in *De Lantaarn*. According to him, public well-being and economic prosperity depended on individual egoism and greed. In exile in England, he was to develop his thesis in the *Fable of the Bees* (1714) as '*Private vice, public benefit*'.

Rotterdam has proved his thesis. Its inhabitants work hard and drive tough bargains, buy and sell ruthlessly. Here, a covered shopping street is called, quite simply, 'Koopgoot', or 'sales gutter'. The bombing of 14 May 1940 reinforced this characteristic, it excised the heart but not the soul of Rotterdam. The soul re-established itself in an impersonal American-type inner city. On the roof of an insurance bank it says, ironically, '*Everything valuable is vulnerable*', a line from the poet Lucebert. A few places offer resistance though, the elderly river barges bobbing up and down in the grave of the old harbour. And beyond Rotterdam, of course, there is Delfshaven, where Delft's canal flows into the Maas, the legendary Admiral Piet Heyn was born, and the Pilgrim Fathers left to build America.

Cabin trunks

At Kop van Zuid the office building of the collapsed Holland-America Line has been converted into the Hotel New York. Where thousands of down and outs once congregated to try their luck in the New World, you can now eat oysters in a cluttered and cosy restaurant, where binoculars for looking out across the water hang on chains. To the left and in front of me thirty kilo-

Rotterdam, 1923: a ship of the Holland-America line. In the background is the office building of the old Holland-America Line, now Hotel New York. Photo by Henri Berssenbrugge.

metres of port, docks and industry stretch right to the North Sea, to the right is the centre of Rotterdam. The peninsula is well on its way to becoming the kind of Manhattan on the Maas that is planned. The hotel, banished to the farthest point of the pier, is already overshadowed by oppressive skyscrapers, and there are more to come. The new Luxor Theatre has just opened, but Las Palmas' windows are still boarded up, and there are still the warehouses, and the splendour of the air and water. I have come across this place at just the right moment – before it is finished.

The Haringvliet Dam, where most of the Maas water reaches the North Sea.
Photo by J. Houttekier.

The hotel is crammed with memories of its origins. There are clocks that show the time in Bombay and New York, and cabin trunks that remind me of Rimbaud's cabin trunk in the Vieux Moulin of Charleville on the French Meuse, now the Musée Rimbaud. The knife, spoon, fork and mug that he used in Harrar are on display there too. Rimbaud's America eventually turned out to be Africa. There were still blank spaces, empty holes there, that he could fill with his yearnings. He had left poetry behind. He had exhausted it, reached its limits too fast. Travelling, receding horizons, the whole empty world took its place. On the old warehouses at Kop van Zuid it says *Celebes, Borneo, Java*. Rimbaud was in Java for a while as well. He went via Brussels and Rotterdam to Harderwijk, and on 19 May 1876 he signed up at the barracks there for six years in the Dutch colonial army. Three weeks after his arrival in Java, having pocketed his bounty, he deserted and returned to Europe on a British sailing ship. He was back in Charleville on 9 December. By the end of his short life '*the man with the wind in his heels*' had explored the walls of his prison. No landscape pleased him, nothing he did satisfied him. '*All moons are atrocious, all suns bitter*' declared 'The Drunken Boat' prophetically. He lost more than a leg. His last words, dictated in feverish delirium, on the eve of his death in Marseilles, and addressed to the Directeur des Messageries Maritimes, were: '*Tell me what time I am to be transported on board.*'

'Oh, go to hell you rivers, / Flow where the old folks go' (HH ter Balkt)

After the marshlands of Pouilly and Bassigny, the squelchy mud on the Plateau de Langres from which water flows to three seas… After more than forty locks (automatic, unmanned ones, with radar and sliding gates; mechanical ones with a lockkeeper manning the gates from high in the lockhouse; and the manual ones with a lockkeeper whose house and garden are on a little island in the Maas, and who divides his time between the lock and the barrage, routine and danger. At the barrage he tames the water by becoming its accomplice, at the lock he carries out routine manoeuvres, opens a gate, walks round the lock, opens the other gate, jacks up the sluices, lets them down again and repeats the ritualistic circumambulation in reverse)… After the yellow broom in the Ardennes, the herons in France, Belgium and the Netherlands, the swans begging arrogantly in Monthermé, and the one near Dinant who sailed into the lock… After the Maas that rocked, teased, laughed, and carved itself a course through the earth, after three drunken boats that have staggered down the river… After all of that I am at the Hook of Holland. This trip has to end somewhere – it was a choice. At the end of

its course the Maas loses itself in a muddle of names, diversions, canalisations, dams and newly constructed beds. Eventually, the river disappears into a delta. In a delta you have to decide on an estuary to the sea. I could have stood on the sluices of the Haringvliet Dam, where most of the Maas water reaches the North Sea. The dam, which was completed in 1970, has turned what was an inlet of the sea into a freshwater lake. I chose the place where water is wiped out by sea, although I knew only too well that other things had made the choice for me: a boat, the compulsive power of towns and ports, history and lies. But above all, it was the plain and simple Dutch name 'Hoek van Holland' (Hook of Holland). On the map it is an angle of 90°, formed by the coastline and the Nieuwe Waterweg, a direct link cut between Rotterdam and the North Sea, which is connected to Het Scheur, and into which both the 'New' and the 'Old' Maas have flowed. These names are a source of confusion to the end, but it does not bother me any more, I want to follow this thing through to its conclusion. That is why I took the train from Rotterdam. I saw the ships on the quay getting bigger and got out at Hook of Holland beach, the end of the line. It seems the ninety-degree angle is non-existent, because a pier sticks out into the water. Even here the Dutch could not resist reclaiming land from the sea. At the end of the pier I was stopped by a prohibition sign, even though the causeway runs for another kilometre. For a moment I thought of ignoring it, but the heavy rocks that the causeway is made of were too big and too off-putting.

So here I am, with the sea, sand, wind and salt at last. The breath knocked out of me at last. An ocean giant glides silently out to sea. A three-master dancing before the wind seeks the harbour channel. At my feet a flock of swans drifts up and down, miscast at this farthest border of land and water. On the other side of the Nieuwe Waterweg loom the abstract contours of the Maasvlakte, a desert of cylinder silos, fickle cranes and lonely chimneys heaped up in the sea. There the biggest port in the world rumbles away, here on the beach at Hook of Holland walkers relax. The Netherlands lives with both, brings them together, and puts water between them. This is a tidy Dutch beach, with a row of shining blue rubbish bins and a sign from the Rijkswaterstaat (the Department of Public Works), that draws my attention to the fact that they ensure the sea lane is deep enough for tankers with a depth of 22 metres. There is art, too, art on the beach – for the cultural consumer at leisure. You can give artwork X a name yourself. Apparently a sloop, run aground in the sand and buried under orange rope, is a work of art, too. I can tell that from the sign, 'Little Boat'. So this is it, then, my Drunken Boat. And here, for the last time, is Rimbaud. After all the seas in the world his Drunken Boat finally chooses ...a dark pool in his native Ardennes:

If I want Europe, it's a dark cold pond
Where a small child plunged in sadness crouches
One fragrant evening at dusk, and launches
A boat, frail as a butterfly in May.

NOTE

All Rimbaud translations taken from *Collected Poems* (tr. Martin Sorrel). Oxford, 2001.

LUC DEVOLDERE
Translated by Lindsay Edwards.

D

ordrecht,

City of Living Water

There may be no spot so typical of Dordrecht as the Groothoofd, the forti-fied landing stage at the northernmost point of this Dutch city that marks the confluence of three rivers: the Oude Maas, the Noord and the Merwede. From the restaurant of the Hotel Bellevue you have an unparalleled panora-ma of the water and the busy river traffic. But for the most famous views of Dordrecht – those executed by Jan van Goyen, Albert Cuyp and other artists – one has to cross to the far side of the water. By positioning himself in Zwijndrecht the painter could take advantage of the full breadth of the Oude Maas as a dramatic foreground for a scenic cityscape in which the Great Church, with its well-known truncated tower, and the Groothoofdspoort rarely failed to feature. The Groothoofd was constructed and fortified well before the Saint Elisabeth's Day Flood of 1421 to keep the city from crum-bling away. It was the most important entrance to the city on the Merwede, the place where so many eminent visitors came ashore, from Emperor Sigis-mund of Germany and Charles V to practically all the Stadholders of the

Groothoofd Bridge on the land side, with the Hotel Bellevue.

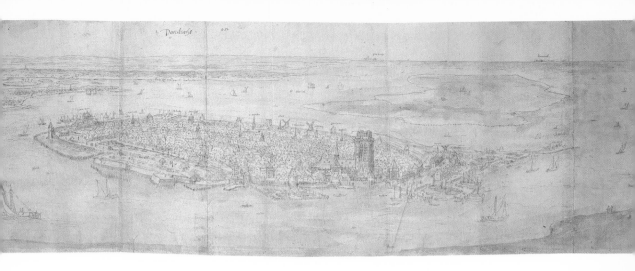

House of Orange and King William II. Their first glimpse of the city was the Groothoofdspoort, built between 1440 and 1450, given a face-lift in the seventeenth century and restored between 1968 and 1971. The red stone facade is graced by the Maiden of Dordt seated in a garden. She's surrounded by the coats of arms of fifteen cities of Holland, all of whom looked to Dordrecht as their 'mother city' for administrative justice in business affairs and water rights. Indeed, during the Middle Ages Dordrecht was the only city in Holland with a District Water Board.

Anthonis van Wijngaerde, *A Panorama of Dordrecht.* c.1544-1545. Ashmolean Museum, Oxford.

Key to Holland and Zeeland

Dordrecht was long regarded as 'the key to Holland and Zeeland', and although it was permanently outstripped as a mercantile town by Amsterdam and Rotterdam in the seventeenth century, it still managed to retain its place

View of Dordrecht from the river.

among the leading cities for quite some time. Dordrecht owed its position mainly to its good relations with a number of successive counts of Holland. The first to become connected with Dordrecht was not so fortunate: his name was Dirk IV, and in 1049 he was killed *apud Thuredrech*. A statue was erected to him in the twentieth century, something of a belated peace offering. Thuredrech(t), Thuredricht or Thuredrith literally means 'through' (thure) 'stream' (drecht). It was the name of a small stream that had become a connecting channel by around 1150 as a result of heavy flooding. Up until then the inhabitants of the local settlement had been mainly involved in peat extraction, but this stimulated them to embark on more substantial commercial activities. A further boost came from Count Floris III, who in 1179 was given a free hand by the German emperor to collect tolls throughout the region. Floris III saw the settlement of Thuredricht as a suitable centre for his toll system, which consisted of striking a good balance between toll collection and exemption so as to generate the maximum amount of income without discouraging trade.

Dordrecht willingly complied with the Count's wishes and reaped the reward of its labours: after being granted a charter in 1220, Dordrecht was granted exemption from tolls by William II with the exception of lucrative products such as wine, steel and iron. Count Floris V granted the faithful townspeople even more privileges in 1284; not the least of these specified that all goods transported along the Lek and the Merwede were to be brought to market in Dordrecht. Foreign merchants were thereby assured that they could sell their goods and purchase return cargo at a single location. This regulation turned Dordrecht into a centre of commercial activities from which both the city and the count profited handsomely. In 1294, Floris V entered into a trade agreement with England that did even more to stimulate Dordrecht's trade. In 1299, Count Jan I granted the city staple rights, the most important being the wine, grain and wood staples. This to all intents and purposes gave Dordrecht the monopoly on the Rhine wine trade; all wine coming up out of Germany had to be unloaded in Dordrecht and brought to market there. The Zeeland cities of Middelburg and Zierikzee were less than pleased with this arrangement, but were placated by being allowed to import wine for private consumption outside the Dordrecht staple. It was the South Holland city of Schoonhoven that finally rose in revolt. Schoonhoven managed to gain the support of the cities of North Holland and succeeded in supplanting Dordrecht for a short time in 1326. But Count William III had too much to gain from the Dordrecht staple to let this situation continue. In 1330 the wine staple was re-established, followed by the salt staple in 1335, and by 1336 everything was as it had been.

Under Count Willem IV Dordrecht also obtained Maas rights in 1338, which meant that all ships from Oostland (Germany) that sailed up the Maas had to sell their goods in Dordrecht. In 1355, Count William V issued a charter extending the staple even further: in addition to the Lek, the Merwede and the Maas, now the Rhine, the Waal and the Hollandsche IJssel were also specifically mentioned. This meant that henceforth no goods could be transported on any river in Holland that had not first been taken to market in Dordrecht. Only Middelburg and Zierikzee were compensated with exemption for a few important products. The Burgundian Duke Philip the Good even allowed Dordrecht to station armed vessels at various points in order

A view of Dordrecht, dominated by the truncated tower of the Great Church. Drawing by Paul Constantijn la Fargue, 1771.

to ensure compliance with the staple right. That the second half of the fourteenth century was Dordrecht's 'Golden Age' is hardly surprising. With its unique combination of wholesale market, transit port and retail market, Dordrecht became the commercial centre of Holland.

The Dordrecht staple continued until 1795, but after 1540 and 1541 in a somewhat reduced form. In those years Emperor Charles V listened to the protests of upcoming Rotterdam and other Holland cities, and issued several ordinances by which the absolute monopoly that had obtained until then was drastically cut back. The river area to which the staple right applied was reduced, and products coming downstream that were needed by the cities of Holland for private consumption were exempted. From now on the staple would apply to only a number of well-defined goods, which still included certain major products: grain, wine, salt, wood, lime, coal, steel, iron and hops.

Water management and the growth of the city

The decision taken by the counts of Holland to make Dordrecht the hub of interregional trade had to do with a decisive intervention in water management. Between 1270 and 1280 a drastic change had been brought on by the damming of the Maas near Heusden in Brabant. Water from both the Rhine and the Maas was thereby drained off by the Merwede between Gorinchem and Dordrecht, so that the Thuredricht lost its Maas function because of the greatly reduced flow of water. In 1282 a new watercourse to the west was dug in the city itself, which emptied into the Oude Maas south of the Great Church. This waterway still runs between Groenmarkt and Voorstraat and is

Timber rafts on the Wantij.
Drawing by Abraham van
Strij, 1810.

known as the Voorstraatshaven. This new harbour joined the old Thuredricht
near the Visbrug. It was a busy part of the city where vegetables (Groenmarkt) and fish (Visstraat) were sold.

In 1383 a Late Gothic building was erected across the Voorstraatshaven
to serve as a hall for Flemish merchants. It was mainly intended for the wool
cloth trade, but in that same year the wool staple was established in Middelburg. The trading hall had its main entrance on the short side across from the
Groenmarkt. A great many Hanseatic merchants had started fleeing from
Flanders in 1382 when the count turned against Bruges and Ghent. In 1389
even the Bruges Hanseatic office was moved to Dordrecht, but in 1393 it
was returned to Bruges. The Flemish trading hall continued operating in
Dordrecht until 1544, when it was put to use as the city hall. The main entrance was moved to the long side, which in 1835 was given a neo-classical
facade. The building is still used for ceremonial functions such as weddings
and receptions. Every now and then there's talk of restoring the building to
its Late Gothic splendour. This would be a definite plus for tourists, who in
recent years have been able to view the city from the deck of an electric-
powered boat that takes them through the inner harbours.

Moving eastward along the waterway we still have Voorstraat on the
right, the backbone of the city which is in fact a dike. On the left there's the
extension of Groenmarkt: Wijnstraat. Wine merchants were already living
in Wijnstraat in the Middle Ages, when they fitted out the lower floors of
their mansions to serve as wine cellars. The wine trade was known as '*the
principal means of prosperity for the exemplary city of Dordrecht*'. Both the
wine merchants and the timber merchants became the patricians of the city.
The family of the famous Dordrecht citizen Johan de Witt (1625-1672),
Grand Pensionary of Holland, owned a timber yard located on a parcel of

land that ran from Groenmarkt to the Houttuinen. The timber trade flourished in Dordrecht well into the nineteenth century and so did shipbuilding, of which certain street names are still a reminder: Hellingen (slipways) and Kromhout (curved timber; named after the curved ribs for ships that were made there). The wood was transported down the Rhine in enormous rafts made of tree trunks all lashed together, sometimes three layers thick or more. The rafts were moored in the Nieuwe Haven, which was dug in 1409 on a sandbar in front of the city because the Oudehaven and the Voorstraatshaven could no longer cope with the growing commercial traffic. Additional proof of the city's prosperity could be seen in the digging of new harbours: the Bomhaven (1540), the Wolwevershaven (1607), the Lijnbaanshaven (1643), the Maartensgat (1647) and the Kalkhaven (1655). In 1655 the harbour area in the centre of Dordrecht assumed its final form.

The function of the city underwent quite a change after its staple rights were reduced. After 1541 (the ordinance of Emperor Charles v), north-south river traffic was free to bypass the city. Dordrecht did manage to hold onto the lucrative wine and grain trade. Although pure trading was reduced, all the other activities that went with trading, fishing and shipbuilding actually increased. The city was able to recover from the loss of its role as international seaport by developing into a vital provincial centre. In 1543 a new ordinance was issued which may have been intended as a salve for the city's wounds, requiring that any fish caught in the inland waterways of South Holland be brought to market in Dordrecht. The people of Dordrecht themselves fished in the surrounding region for certain migratory fish: salmon, shad and sturgeon.

We have yet to discuss the area beyond the current city centre. When we speak of Dordrecht and the water, it's not only the harbours and the timber industry that deserve our attention. There's the Biesbosch as well, a swampy area formed after a series of dikes gave way in 1421. The disaster is known as the Saint Elisabeth's Day Flood, named after the saint whose feast day is 8 November. The bursting of the dikes was the fault of excavations that had been carried out as part of peat and salt extraction (called '*moernering*'). The cities of Dordrecht and Geertruidenberg had begun urging that the dikes be maintained and improved in as early as 1377 – while at the same time granting peat permits that undermined the dikes elsewhere! The action taken after the first dikes gave way in November 1421 was not vigorous enough, due to political disagreements among the city authorities. So when a much more disastrous flood occurred three years later, practically all the countryside surrounding Dordrecht found itself under water. The city became an island, with the city wall as its dam. It became more difficult to monitor shipping traffic after the Saint Elisabeth's Day Flood, but in the end the disaster also resulted in new activities. The leasing of fishing grounds in the Biesbosch brought in almost as much revenue as the farmlands that had existed there earlier. It was more than a century before a project to drain the area got under way. In 1602 shipyards were created on the reclaimed land near the city wall for building and repairing flat- and round-bottomed boats.

Dordrecht continued to thrive even during the Spanish Revolt, a fact confirmed by its purchase of the Merwede manor in 1604. The city council also contributed to various drainage projects that had been commissioned by the lords of Dubbeldam and De Mijl. By 1659 the draining of four very large

A creek in the Biesbosch, a swampy area formed after a series of dikes gave way in 1421 during the Saint Elisabeth's Day Flood. Photo by J. Houttekier.

polders was completed, and in 1748 all four decided to merge permanently. A few smaller polders were created in the eighteenth century, and the Dordtse Biesbosch was drained during the twentieth. At De Biesbosch visitors' centre, the twenty-first-century tourist can steep himself in the history of this unique marshland and follow a nature trail that leads across a piece of preserved withy-land. Since the annexation of the village of Dubbeldam in 1970, the entire Island of Dordrecht has come under municipal authority.

From commercial gateway to centre for inland shipping, industry and culture

According to some historians Dordrecht was eclipsed by Rotterdam after 1620, but we can safely assume that the demographic and economic centre of Holland had moved north long before then. Even though the city had lost its significance as a seaport, it did continue as a centre for inland shipping. More than half the goods exported from the regions of Dordrecht and Gorinchem went to the Rhineland, and a third went to England and Scotland. The English trade had always been important, as we can see from the presence of typical Dordrecht facades in Norwich, the capital of East Anglia. In around 1656 a group of 'Merchant Adventurers' established itself in Dordrecht. This was an association of English merchants specialising in the woollen cloth trade and manufacturing. These gentlemen of the 'English Court', as they were known, had been enticed by all sorts of special advantages, but the English wars did the Court little good and Rotterdam managed to get the agreement nullified by the States General in 1674. English trade went into a steep decline as a result, and in 1839 the English church on the Wijnstraat closed its doors. The city was able to develop a much more lasting relationship with the Walloons, Protestants who for the most part had fled from Liège and its surroundings and who included many wealthy merchants. They had their own Walloon church and acquired a permanent clergyman in 1586. A new wave of immigrants from Liège, many of whom worked in the iron trade, settled on the 'Nieuwe Werck', the district created in 1620 on the north side of the Wolwevershaven. The names Buitenwalevest (Outer Walloon Street) and Binnenwalevest (Inner Walloon Street) still refer to these Walloon immigrants. In 1681 the Liège wine merchant and banker Hubert Borret moved to the city. Borret was a fiery Catholic who made his sizeable house on the Kuipershaven available for religious services and contributed a great deal to the growth of Catholic self-awareness in an overwhelmingly Calvinist city.

At the beginning of the nineteenth century Dordrecht was still an important commercial port for Holland, but some of the accents had shifted. The economic situation in agriculture had taken an upward swing after 1740, making Dordrecht a regional market for agrarian products. The early nineteenth century was marked by an economic malaise throughout the Netherlands. In Dordrecht the situation in shipbuilding gradually picked up after 1824, the year the Dutch Trading Company was set up. For the timber industry, however, the glory days were over. Dordrecht became a city in isolation, its residents closed and withdrawn. All this changed with the coming of the Industrial Revolution. From 1850 onwards, more and more steamboats moored in Dordrecht's harbours. A gasworks was built, a railway bridge constructed over the Oude Maas (1866), and a railway station opened (1872). By around 1900 Dordrecht had become primarily an industrial city rather than a commercial centre. Companies were established that had nothing to do with the flow of merchandise, and large manufacturing companies built proper mechanised factories. Even so, Dordrecht remained a transit port for various products, and Rhine traffic and inland shipping continued to be important. At the same time, banks and insurance companies of national consequence established themselves in the city. Among the important factories that made their home in Dordrecht were the Victoria biscuit factory (1904), the Lips key factory (1910) and the Du Pont de Nemours synthetic fibre factory (1959). As the years passed all the companies of Dordrecht were absorbed by larger associations, and more and more residents of Dordrecht became commuters. In 1994, 18,800 of Dordrecht's inhabitants were employed in the Rijnmond area or in the industrial growth centres of Zwijndrecht and Papendrecht.

Dordrecht's days as an island are long over. The water connects more than it isolates. In the past it was ferryboats that went back and forth between Dordrecht and the villages on the other side, but in recent years it's been a waterbus: a high-speed ferry whose regular route includes two landing points in Dordrecht as well as Zwijndrecht, Papendrecht and Sliedrecht. There are also waterbuses to Rotterdam and (in summer) to Gorinchem. In 1997, Dordrecht – with its 130,000 inhabitants – was placed on the big city list, which means it can benefit from a subsidy from the Ministry of Urban and Integration Policy. In 2002 the subsidy was extended to the surrounding 'Drecht' cities: Zwijndrecht, Alblasserdam, Heerjansdam, Sliedrecht, Papendrecht and 's-Gravendeel. In May 2002, an agreement was signed on board the tour boat *De Zilvermeeuw* between Minister R. van Boxtel, Dordrecht and the Drecht cities to engage in more cooperation in the areas of housing, urban renewal, infrastructure and safety. If the experiment is successful it will be adopted in other urban areas of the Netherlands as well.

Dordrecht also promotes itself as a city of history and culture. The bien-

Inner and Outer Kalk
(=lime) Docks.

Modern buildings on Spui Dock.

nial event *Dordt in stoom* (Dordrecht under Steam), which takes place in and around the historic harbours, is a must for lovers of steamships, steam loco-motives and other steam-driven machines. In 2002 it attracted 250,000 vis-itors. There are also plans to convert the Hof (where the first assembly of the United Provinces took place in 1572) and the surrounding area into a centre for culture, art, history and science. The fact that Dordrecht is thriving is largely thanks to the water, of course. But there's more to it than that.

KEES SNOEK
Translated by Nancy Forest-Flier.

BIBLIOGRAPHY

FRIJHOFF, WILLEM, HUBERT NUSTELING and MARIJKE SPIES (eds.), *Geschiedenis van Dordrecht van 1572 tot 1813*. Hilversum, 1998.

HERWAARDEN, JAN VAN, DICK DE BOER, FRED VAN KAM and GERRIT VERHOEVEN (eds.), *Geschiedenis van Dordrecht tot 1572*. Hilversum, 1996.

KOOIJ, PIM and VINCENT SLEEBE (eds.), *Geschiedenis van Dordrecht van 1813 tot 2000*. Hilversum, 2000.

LIPS, C.J.P., *Wandelingen door Oud-Dordrecht*. Zaltbommel, 1974.

MOLENDIJK, AD *et al.* (eds.), *Dordrecht 1650-1850*. Zwolle, 1992.

ature

between Ebb and Flood

The Zwin: from Sea-Inlet to Nature Reserve

At the entrance to the Zwin there is a bust of Count Léon Lippens, who founded this nature reserve, the first of its kind in Belgium, in 1952. Lippens was one of the great pioneers of nature conservation in Belgium, and it is no wonder that he turned his special attention to the Zwin. The Zwin is a remarkable reserve from the point of view of natural history, but also in the pure historical sense. Centuries of silting and reclamation have reduced the area to its present size.

In fact, it is a relic of a sea-inlet which once extended to Bruges. On the Dutch border one can still find the remains of the enormous creek that was

Aerial view of the Zwin.

once 5 kilometres wide, and is now no more than 3 metres at low tide, and 60 metres at high tide. The mud flats of the Zwin are still submerged by every tide, the Zwinschorre, salt-marsh, only by spring and/or storm tides. Indeed it is to this regular direct contact with salt water that the exceptional natural historical value of the reserve can be attributed.

The sea moves inland

In the course of the fifth century Sincfal, as the Zwin was then called, came about as a result of severe floods, which in their turn were to be blamed upon a gradual sinking of the ground. The sea drove 30 kilometres inland, destroying everything in its path. In the sixth and seventh centuries Vikings sailed up this broad inlet and established a settlement they called 'Bryggia', the later Bruges.

Under the influence of currents and tidal movements a degree of stabilisation occurred. Thus an easterly, fairly deep channel was formed, which gave access to sizeable sea-going vessels. The people of Bruges built an outport and constructed a dam: Ten Damme, the later Damme. They were not to lose by this; Bruges' greatest period of prosperity was in the eleventh century and the first half of the twelfth. From the second half of the twelfth century onwards the Zwin began to silt up very rapidly. After the economic decline of Bruges, first Monnikenrede, then Damme, Hoeke, Muiden and finally Sluis in turn became important ports along the entrance to the Zwin. But they too lost their importance because of the silting.

From 1590 on Sluis and the Zwin mouth were cut off from Bruges as the result of the rapid sequence of skirmishes between the United Provinces and the Southern Netherlands, which were under the rule of the Spaniards. After the end of the Eighty-Years' War (1648) there followed a series of enclosures and land reclamations. Polders were gained from the sea in this way. The area around the Zwin itself has been fairly well preserved. Some dikes have remained intact, such as, for instance, the beautiful Krinkeldijk. This is an eleventh-century tideway dike, that winds its way from Hoeke to Oostkerke. The dike that leads to the entrance to the reserve is the Hazegrasdijk, a polder development of 1784. The last reclamation took place in 1872, when the International Dike was built. The reclamation of the Willem-Leopold Polder was the very last, and signified, once and for all, the end of the Zwin as a navigable waterway.

In 1950 the Zwingeul (Zwin channel) itself, which is on Dutch territory, was closed off as part of the Dutch Water Board's Delta Plan. At the instigation of Léon Lippens the International Zwin Committee was established, because, among other things, this closure would mean the end of the intertidal area. After endless meetings it was decided that the Dutch must reconnect the Zwingeul to the sea: for their part, the Belgians must raise the International Dike to Delta level. As it happened, the famous storm of 1953 restored this channel by natural means.

And so we have the Zwin of today. Not only is it the foremost nature reserve in Belgium, it also covers 150 hectares, of which 125 are in Belgium and 25 in Holland. A bit of nature which, thanks to a private initiative, became a major tourist attraction and a site of great scientific and educational value.

On border-defying broods and the beauty of a sparrow

In the educational bird park in the Zwin, a former wooded area of 7 hectares in the dunes, there is a collection of living birds, all of species indigenous to the area. All the cages and ponds have signs with interesting educational information, pictures of every species, where the birds are to be found (breeding and overwintering areas), general information about long-legged waders, songbirds, birds of prey etc.

The bird park has successfully reintroduced a number of species, among others greylag geese, night herons and storks. This latter project, in particular, has been an important and instructive success, so much so even that foreign storks came to call on the native population. In 2002 four Dutch storks and one French female (from Marquenterre, on the coast near the Somme estuary) and two birds originating from the Plankendael zoo (near Mechelen) bred here. A nice detail is that one of the Dutch males managed to seduce the beautiful French female; they produced two offspring. Up until a few years ago we were also cooperating on a reintroduction project for eagle owls in the Eifel, right by the German-Belgian border. Birds born in captivity in the Zwin were released in this area. From there the eagle owls came back over the border, and at present more than 30 pairs are breeding in the Ardennes. This species had not bred in Belgium since the beginning of the twentieth century.

All these 'collections' also provide useful study material for scientists. Thus there have been studies, among other things, of the display behaviour of the various kinds of duck, the mating behaviour of herons and others. But, at the Zwin, the uninitiated visitor too learns to really *look* at birds. In very many cases, it is their first acquaintance with birds in the wild, where they can look at them and work out what they are while walking and watching. I once heard a woman telling her family about a handsome bird that is quite common here in the Zwin: black bib, reddish brown head, lovely dark wings with a double white wing-stripe. When I told these nice people that they were talking about a lovely house sparrow, they looked most surprised: they had come all the way to the Zwin to discover the beauty of a sparrow!

Strange visitors and regular guests

'Zwin' is a Dutch word meaning a tideway, or creek, in land outside the dikes. In other words, it is an area directly connected to the sea. Thus the small pools left on the beach when the tide ebbs are 'zwin's in the strict sense of the word.

Mud flats are areas that the sea covers every day, twice a day – with the tide. A beach is also covered with every tide, yet no sedimentation of the minute mud particles occurs. But this can, and does, happen where the tide can come and go in the shelter of an island, a sand bank, or a row of dunes. In such places the minuscule grains of mud are able to sink. On the beach the tide is too turbulent and the mud particles are washed away by the water as it ebbs. Salt-marsh, however, is only covered by spring and/or storm tides. In theory that can happen twice a month, namely with the full and new moon.

The softness of the ground makes these mud flats difficult to walk on. One easily sinks in. In the twenty or so years that I have been warden in the Zwin, I have witnessed one or two rather funny sights on guided walks. Particularly in the seventies, when society was somewhat more rigidly divided. The people who came in those days tended to be from the upper classes, and were rather spoilt by my predecessor. In the best scenario they would be wearing expensive rubber boots, but for the rest they would be in all their finery. Now it was, and still is my belief that such a visit to the Zwin must be a real exploration into nature. That was also the opinion of Count Léon Lippens, the active founder, who often came along too: indeed, it is no accident that his bust shows him wearing a sturdy, warm hat. Let me put it like this: visiting the mud flats of the Zwin in an expensive fur coat is not really a very good idea!

You don't go to the mud flats to be seen, but to feast your own eyes. Mud flats are an unimaginably rich biotope. A mud flat can hold as many as 25,000 marine organisms per square metre. The abundance of bird-life in such an area is directly proportional to this profusion of food. Four species of summer visitors very closely connected to mud flats are the avocet, the redshank, the oystercatcher, and the shelduck. The avocet is a dazzling, black and white, long-legged wader. Its chief characteristic is its long, black, up-turned beak. There are tactile nerves in the tip of the beak, a sixth sense in the true meaning of the word. With these it can sweep the soft mud for all kinds of small worms, minute crustaceans and molluscs. The parents of young avocets behave in a most remarkable way if one approaches a nest. As a decoy manoeuvre they sink down on their long legs and move forward as if they have damaged their wings.

The black and white oystercatcher is another bird generally to be found wherever you have mud flats. It has a long red beak, which is flattened along the sides. The oystercatcher forces his beak between the two halves of the shell of a mussel, a cockle or some other mollusc. He then slices through the sphincter and polishes off the tasty contents. Lugworms and ragworms are also on the menu of this beautiful long-legged wader. But the redshank has long legs too. It owes its English name to the colour of its legs, while its Dutch name – *tureluur* – comes from its melodious call. As with so many Dutch bird names it is onomatopoeic. Like most long-legged waders redshanks are tireless migrants. In winter they even go as far as South Africa. The ones we see visiting the Zwin at migration time often come from Siberia, Iceland and even Greenland.

The shelduck adorns the Zwin logo. This dazzling duck breeds mainly in rabbit burrows. It is a true coastal bird that hides its nest. On the mud flats you can also find a whole range of birds that are hardly ever to be seen in any other biotope. They pass through the Zwin as they migrate, or stay there as winter visitors – birds like the curlew sandpiper, the knot, the grey plover, the bar-tailed godwit, brent goose, and others. The only thing you *don't* find in mud-flat areas is vegetation. This is chiefly because such places are covered by the sea twice a day, so that any seeds that fall there cannot get a hold.

The avocet lives on the mud flats of the Zwin. As a decoy manoeuvre he sinks down on his long legs and moves forward as if he has damaged his wings. Photo courtesy of the Zwin, Knokke-Heist.

The salt-marsh in bloom: from the middle of July to the end of August the sea lavender – or '*zwinneblom-me*' – covers vast areas of the Zwin salt-marsh with a marvellous carpet of purple. Photo courtesy of the Zwin, Knokke-Heist.

The 'dry' plants of the salt-marsh

As has been mentioned already, the salt-marsh is only covered by the sea in the case of spring or storm tides. Unlike the mud flats, the salt-marsh has its own, very special, vegetation. This consists of plants that are able to withstand direct contact with salt water: the so-called halophytes or salt-loving plants.

Because the spring tides are not so high in summer as in spring and autumn the salt-marsh can sometimes remain dry for quite long periods, so that at times these plants are growing in an extremely dry environment. Moreover, their excessive concentration of salts means that they are less able to absorb useful nutrients from the salt water. So 'physiologically' they are dry plants, comparable to desert plants. Succulents, in particular, are frequently to be found on the salt-marsh. They have fleshy stems and leaves which function as a sort of water reservoir. A good example of this is glasswort. Others such as common orache or sea purslane have hairy leaves or are covered in scales. These retain a layer of air, thus greatly reducing evaporation. In addition, in the Zwin the rapid proliferation of sea purslane is becoming more and more apparent. This is a direct result of the silting of the Zwin salt-marsh, where this plant has optimal conditions for growth.

The vegetation of a salt-marsh develops step by step, as it were, depending on the length of time it is under salt water. Each species develops best at a particular level, directly related to the amount of contact with salt water that it can tolerate. The pioneer in this process is the glasswort. The moment you reach a point on the edge of the mud which is not covered daily by the tide, you will see these lovely fleshy plants popping up. It is glasswort that is sometimes eaten as a vegetable with sea-food platters or fish dishes. But without doubt the best known plant is sea lavender. From the middle of July to the end of August this stunning plant covers vast areas of the Zwin salt-marsh with a beautiful, almost uninterrupted carpet of purple. Insects are also greatly attracted to sea lavender. It is exceptionally rich in nectar, and so a favourite landing-site for butterflies, hoverflies and over thirty kinds of bees, including the honey bee.

To be in the salt-marsh in the breeding season is quite an experience. The

Vegetation along the tidemarks: the grass-leaved orache thrives in this environment which is abundant in nitrogen. Photo courtesy of the Zwin, Knokke-Heist.

long-legged waders that feed on the mud flats use the salt-marsh as a breeding place. In the late summer and autumn the seeds of the faded sea lavender, common seablite and other plants form an important source of food for a whole range of seed-eating birds, such as the linnet, twite, shorelark, lapland and snow bunting. September is also the time when the sea aster is in bloom. This plant has been increasing fast in recent years, and covers large areas of the reserve. Like the sea lavender, it is both rich in nectar and a home to species-dependent insects. Some fly and bee species can only be found close to sea asters.

Sea fish inland

Finally, we find a very specific vegetation along the so-called tidemarks. These are the places where the highest spring or storm tides have deposited dead branches and marsh plants during the winter months, or heaped up rabbit droppings and other waste. In spring there is a lot of nitrogen in this tightly-packed humus, so we also find there a few nitrogen-loving plant species, such as grass-leaved orache, hastote orache and sea beet. In winter you sometimes see hundreds of seed-eaters such as linnets, greenfinches, bramblings and chaffinches in this area which is so rich in seeds.

On the south-west side of the reserve there is a lake, a kind of salt-water lagoon, on the site of old workings from 1956. The excavated material (sand and clay) was used to raise the International Dike to the so-called Delta level. The pools are quite deep (some eight metres) and extremely rich in fish. To date we have identified some 30 species of sea fish in the Zwin. Naturally

this makes it a fine biotope for a whole range of fish-eating birds. In winter you can sometimes find the five different kinds of European grebe. The cormorants stay right through the year, and grey herons and little egrets are enthusiastic visitors to this part of the Zwin. Indeed, both these species have their breeding grounds in the nearby woods on the downs. In December, in particular, this water is packed unimaginably tight with birds. Every evening some 30,000 birds come to pass the night around these ponds. These include, among others, lapwing, hundreds of grey plover and golden plover, more than 1,500 curlews, a few thousand (maybe as many as 15,000) gulls of different species, and sometimes more than 10,000 white-fronted geese.

A rare phenomenon during a cold winter in the Zwin: the accumulation of ice floes as a result of spring tides. Photo courtesy of the Zwin, Knokke-Heist.

Choking and change ....or maintenance?

Birds, insects, fish, plants: the Zwin is an exceptional place, particularly as far as natural history is concerned. But in addition to this there is also the beauty of the landscape, partly thanks to a rich and extensive buffer zone. If in the next few years a permanent solution can be found for the problems of silting which threaten to choke it, the Zwin will remain extremely valuable. Failing that, there will be an enormous change, and among other things a completely new biotope will be created. It will undoubtedly be fascinating to observe such an evolution; but none the less, in my opinion the maintenance of such a valuable inter-tidal area remains paramount.

GUIDO BURGGRAEVE
Translated by Sheila M. Dale.

The Zwin: Graaf Léon Lippenslaan 8 / 8300 Knokke-Heist / Belgium tel. +32 50 60 70 86 / fax +32 50 62 20 00 / www.zwin.be

New Atlantis

The Geometric Ideal and Amsterdam's Ring of Canals

Dutch historiography has a strong tradition of respect for hard facts and an aversion to speculation. Unfortunately, this also means that ideological concepts and metaphysical speculations of earlier generations are often overlooked as subjects for serious historical research. A good example of this is the debate about the ring of canals in the centre of Amsterdam. The Amsterdam canals are so engrained in our consciousness and so obviously 'beauti-

Lijnbaansgracht,
Amsterdam, Winter 1963.
Photo by Frits Weeda /
Gemeentearchief,
Amsterdam.

ful', that hardly anybody stops to wonder about the thinking behind their powerful visual impact. Certainly, the three main canals are spacious and wide, they present a picturesque succession of handsome gables, water and trees, and they are attractively old with no evidence of decay. But there is nothing to suggest that they form part of an original broadly-conceived city plan.

A generation ago, the Italian Leonardo Benevolo investigated the aesthetic principles behind the canal plan and attempted to analyse the secret of their spatial charm. In awe-struck terms he described the plan as a single, coherent masterpiece of dimension, proportion, and scale. But Benevolo was laughed out of court by some of his Dutch colleagues, for whom the ring of canals was no more than the fortunate outcome of a series of chance decisions by the town council, stimulated by some underhand dealings in real estate by an exclusive club of money-grubbing regents.

Now it is true that there is little in the Amsterdam archives that points directly to any explanation other than practical considerations in a gradual process of decision-making. Nevertheless, in recent years it has become apparent that there certainly existed a single very ambitious project that was carried out in two phases of about four years each. The first phase was between 1610 and 1614, the second exactly half a century later between 1660 and 1664. But there is even more to it than that: the Amsterdam ring of canals was the realisation of an ancient ideal of city architecture.

The most important task facing the town council around 1600 was to find a solution to the population explosion. Amsterdam had been flooded with immigrants from the Southern Netherlands, especially after the fall of Antwerp in 1585. As well as the need for more dwellings and business premises, there was also a military problem. For as Amsterdam became economically more powerful, so its strategic importance also grew, creating an urgent need for a strong and modern ring of defences.

Population pressure and gunpowder

The problem was not entirely new. The military use of gunpowder had dramatically changed the face of warfare. Because traditional stone-built walls were unable to withstand bombardment by cannon Italian engineers had developed a totally new defensive technique in which walls and towers were replaced by massive ramparts and bastions. This new system spread rapidly throughout Europe, and particularly in the Dutch provinces during the revolt against Spain. As early as 1542-1543 the Italian Donato de' Boni Pellizuoli had designed fortifications for the poorly-defended eastern side of Amsterdam, although the plan was not implemented. In 1566 – the year of the iconoclastic riots – the Brussels engineer Christiaen Sgrooten designed a ring of defensive ramparts for the entire city to replace the brick walls and towers. But because of the prevailing unrest and acute danger, Stadholder William of Orange, at the time still a loyal servant of the Spanish King Philip II, advised against Sgrooten's plan.

Twelve years later, in 1578, Amsterdam finally joined the revolt. Whereupon William of Orange, now the leader of the revolution, immediately sent his fortifications advisor, Adriaen Anthoniszoon, to Amsterdam to discuss a new ring of fortifications for the city. Under his guidance, work began on a broad rampart with bastions, outside the old town wall. But only after the fall of Antwerp in 1585 was it finally extended around the whole city, more or less following the line of today's Herengracht. Scarcely had it been completed when it became clear that it was too small. So a second considerably larger expansion was immediately begun, consisting of a complex of large rectangular islands and canals at right-angles to each other between the IJ and Amstel rivers on the east side of the city.

Not only the rampart with its bastions, but also the straight canals and rectangular islands were completely new to Amsterdam. Previously, any expansion of the town had always retained the original surrounding canal and the existing irregular plots of land. This time, however, as well as Adriaen Anthonisz, the famous surveyor and town planner, Joost Jansz Bilhamer alias Beeldsnijder, was specially engaged to draw up plans for the new areas. Nothing was left to chance. Each new urban area was turned into a regular geometric pattern of rectangular islands or peninsulas, criss-crossed by canals and harbours, and all pre-designed on the drawing boards of Bilhamer and his successor, the city surveyor Adriaen Ockers.

Within fifteen years, as a result of this phased expansion, the city had more than doubled in size, but even this was not enough. So in February 1610, before all the plots of land in the 'Nieuwe Stad' (New Town) had even been allocated, the burgomasters laid before the council '*a number of maps touching on the enlargement and expansion of this city*'. This master plan, drawn up by the city carpenter, Hendrick Jacobsz Staets, envisaged an enormous circular fortification around the existing city. Two years later, after Prince Maurice had also given his opinion, the council decided to accept the expansion in principle, but on the basis of a considerably modified plan submitted by the surveyor Mr Lucas Jansz Sinck, which now also showed the canals. Meanwhile, construction work had already commenced, starting from the northwest, though it was decided for the time being only to build the section between the IJ and today's Leidsegracht. This area alone was enormous, but by 1616 most of it was completed.

But the plan was still not yet finished. The first phase had brought so much new land into the city that it was not until 1660 that the ring of canals was extended round to the IJ on the east of the city. Amsterdam was now so large that it would be another two hundred years before any thought was given to further expansion. A supplementary plan in 1660, which followed up Sinck's scheme of 1612, was largely the work of the city surveyor Cornelis Dankertsz de Rij. Presumably the city architect, Daniel Stalpaert, also played an important part, just as the city carpenter Staets had done in his master plan for the ramparts of 1610. As well as these professional master builders and surveyors, there will also have been city councillors with an interest in such matters who had a hand in formulating the main ideas behind the plan.

A semi-circular disc

But what were those ideas? After all, the question is whether the designers of this historic expansion merely proceeded step by step, reacting to the practical demands of the moment, or whether they were also influenced by certain architectural traditions, rules, norms or ideals. The council minutes contain no record of the discussions about the submitted plans, let alone any written explanation. Furthermore, any drawings relating to the master plan of 1610 and the ring of canals were lost when the old town hall went up in flames in 1652. All that remains are a few scattered observations in the minutes and a series of extremely sketchy printed maps that were used to illustrate official and semi-official publications between 1610 and 1614.

Nevertheless, it is precisely these simple little maps that enable us to trace the formal principles underlying the project. For they show in brief the development from the original idea of ramparts in principle – Staets' plans of 1610 – to the final placement of the rampart in the first phase. The first map – from the north-east – shows the situation as it existed in 1610 with the 1585-95 ramparts. Far outside them an almost circular rampart with bastions has been sketched, with a couple of bastions drawn in detail. On the final map one can see what remained of this scheme at the moment that the town council decided to embark on the first stage. The layout of canals and streets in Sinck's design is not yet shown. But it is clear that the committee had not yet abandoned the idea of a circular rampart, since traces of the original circle have not been erased.

On a plan of the city drawn in about 1625, one can see that the new ring is dominated by three concentric principal canals: Herengracht, Keizersgracht and Prinsengracht. The Jordaan district beyond – between Prinsengracht and the ramparts – is laid out in a grid pattern, and the western islands are modelled on the islands of the 'New Town' of the 1590s. The continuation of the ramparts is also shown, though this has been modified in the meantime; the main circular shape has been abandoned and in its place is a strictly symmetrical horseshoe outline with 24 bastions, of which the eastern half is still unfinished. That would have to wait until 1660-1664, and the result is shown on Stalpaert's map of 1662, which reflects the present situation fairly precisely.

That map also reveals a couple of other important deviations from the manuscript plan. The newly enclosed area is much larger than was originally intended, thereby changing its entire shape. Most striking, however, is that the contours and layout of the second stage are in fact a consistent extension of the first. Even the substantial sea dike, which ran straight across the new area, has been levelled and moved to fit into a pattern of regular blocks. So in the end, after all the modifications and adjustments, the total effect is still that of a semi-circular disc – exactly what had been proposed in Staets' original plan. The semi-circular area is broken up into segments by concentric canals, which are crossed by a number of radial streets. The map shows a ring of church squares along the partially completed Prinsengracht. The present-day Noorderkerk, Westerkerk, Amstelkerk and Oosterkerk are the surviving remains of these. If we study the map more carefully, it is evident that the guiding principle must have been symmetry, not only in its broad outline but also down to the smallest detail. The districts on either side of the Amstel, for instance, virtually reflect each other, and the area between the Amstel and the Leidsegracht – the boundary between the first and second stages – creates a perfect triptych. Furthermore, the artificial islands and peninsulas have been laid out symmetrically, as have the plots of land between the canals in the Jordaan district. All in all, there is sufficient reason to assume that successive planners and committees were following certain clearly established aesthetic principles. But what were those principles?

Plan of Amsterdam,
showing the fortifications
designed by Hendrick
Jacobsz Staets (1611).
Gemeentearchief,
Amsterdam.

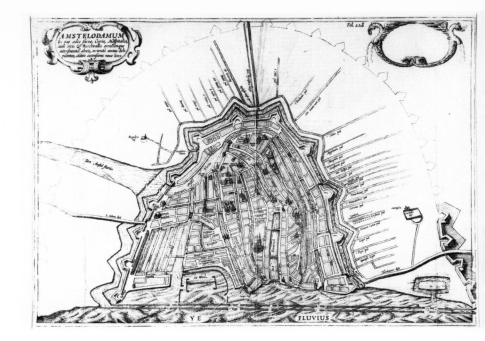

Plan of Amsterdam with
Staets' adapted design
(1614). Gemeentearchief,
Amsterdam.

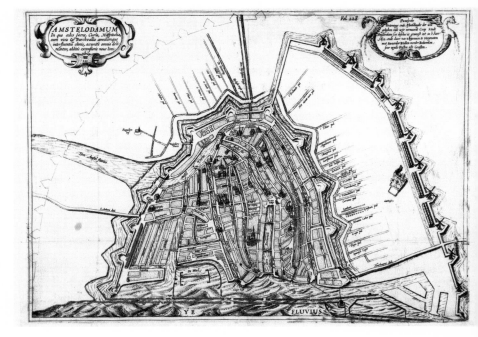

Plan with the first stage of
the great extension and a
design for a consistently
symmetrical completion
(c.1625). Gemeentearchief,
Amsterdam.

Plan of Amsterdam by
Daniel Stalpaert, showing
the completed great
extension (1662).
Gemeentearchief,
Amsterdam.

It is well known that from the beginning of the Renaissance, thinkers and artists in Italy were preoccupied with the concept of the '*città ideale*' – the ideal city. The number of designs for the ideal city described or drawn in publications or manuscripts between 1450 and 1650 is well-nigh incalculable. The remarkable thing is that they are all based on two basic forms, or combinations of them, namely the circle and the square. Writers on aesthetics considered these forms to be the divine foundation for every architectural object in the widest sense, for they believed that God had structured the universe along mathematical principles. It was an ancient belief, already elaborated by Pythagoras and his school in the fifth century before Christ. However, there were also practical reasons for choosing these two forms as the basis for town design. The circle creates the shortest line of defence for the greatest area and also has other military advantages; the square, on the other hand, is the simplest shape for creating a new settlement and dividing it up into spatial units and building plots.

The Roman military camp, as described by Polybius, was rectangular and divided into a grid of squares. This was certainly one of the reasons why Prince Maurice's councillors, Justus Lipsius and Simon Stevin, both thoroughly versed in the classics, opted for the latticed rectangle as the model for a defensible city.

Most Italian designers, however, fell back on the *Ten Books on the Art of Building* by the Roman writer Vitruvius, the only classical work on the subject to have survived. Vitruvius was considered to be the absolute authority. His work is set out like an encyclopaedic reference manual in which every aspect of building is discussed. In the first book he deals with the character of a master builder and the aesthetic principles of the art of building, after which he focuses chiefly on the layout of a city. Vitruvius adopts a highly practical approach. He starts with the walls, which should be more or less circular because that makes them more difficult to attack. The towers should be placed within arrowshot of each other so that each can be defended from adjacent towers. Once the wall is completed, one should begin by laying out the streets in relation to the prevailing wind, since that is most important for the health of the inhabitants. The most powerful winds should not blow straight down the main streets, but should strike the walls at an angle. Vitruvius pays particular attention to this, but unfortunately this section especially is difficult to interpret. What is clear, however, is that he recommends using a pair of compasses to draw a large circle around the centre within which an octagon is drawn to correspond to the eight main compass-points: '*Then comes the moment to lay out the main roads and streets in straight lines along the dividing lines between two compass points. This method of division ensures that excessively strong winds will be kept out of the buildings and streets.*'

These brief and rather cryptic recommendations by a fairly obscure classical author have been responsible for every conceivable construction, all based on a circular or polygonal outline. Some designers opted to fill the circle with a grid or lattice. Most, however, preferred the so-called 'radial city', with a number of lines fanning out from the centre to the equal sides, or corners, of the perimeter.

For both the outer ramparts and the internal layout it was normal to make use of 'beautiful' numbers, reflecting, for instance, the Holy Trinity, the

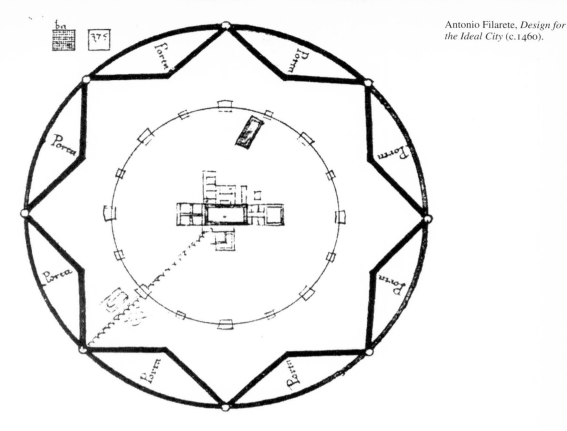

four points of the compass, or the twelve gates of ancient Jerusalem. A very early Italian example of such an ideal city, based on the theories of Vitruvius, was designed in 1460 by the Florentine Antonio Filarete. His design, for a city that he called Sforzinda, consists of a circle within which are two intersecting squares. Defensive towers stand on the eight corners; the city gates at the eight intersections. The palace and the main square are in the centre and the principal streets follow the radius of the circle. They lead from the centre directly towards the towers and are intersected halfway by a concentric main street with rectangular squares. Most Italian designs for an ideal city follow this pattern.

During the High Renaissance no serious attempts were made actually to build an ideal city, in any shape or form. But that began to change in the course of the sixteenth century. The ring-shaped formula was ideal for constructing fortified towns with a ring of five-sided bastions designed to withstand modern gunpowder. The perimeter could then be filled in either radially or as a grid. The biggest problem in practice was not so much the building of an entirely new city as the expansion of existing fortified cities that had grown organically and not geometrically.

Dozens of writers addressed themselves to this problem. They hawked themselves and their treatises on fortress construction around every European court and university. One of them was Donato de' Boni Pellizuoli, another was Francesco de Marchi, who like Pellizuoli, made a study of Amsterdam's fortifications. In 1599 he published his *Della architettura militare*

Daniel Speckle, *Plan of the Ideal Fortified Town* (1589).

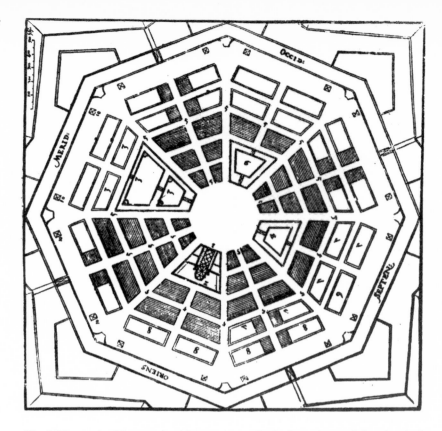

(On Military Architecture) with many practical adaptations of the classical radial city that included cities standing next to a large stretch of water or on either side of a river.

Sometimes an entirely new city was designed according to the theories of the military engineers. The best known is Palmanova in Veneto, which was completed in 1599. The town plan of Palmanova was known in the Netherlands; it shows a striking similarity to the ideal fortified city that had been published ten years earlier by the German Daniel Speckle. The best example of a radial fortified city in the Northern Netherlands is undoubtedly Coevorden, which was built under the direction of the same Adriaen Anthonisz who had supervised Amsterdam's new fortifications after 1578.

Both Palmanova and Coevorden were considered in their time to be textbook examples of the military art of building fortified towns. Characteristic of both is that the administration is housed in the centre and the roads radiate out from there to the bastions, intersected by concentric streets with smaller squares. In this context, it is interesting to note that Prince Maurice, who had advised Amsterdam on the plans of 1610, possessed an extensive library that included two publications by Vitruvius, various Italian manuals on fortress construction as well as the aforementioned work by Daniel Speckle.

Other sources reveal that there was great interest in the Netherlands not only in the modern theories of fortification but also in theories of urban construction in general. Furthermore, the division of rural and urban land into geometrical patterns, far from being an Italian import, was a long-established tradition in the Netherlands. Not only had it been applied to the layout of medieval polders along the coast and in marshland but also in the construction of villages, towns and fortifications. So the modern theories of fortress building fell on fertile and long-prepared soil. One might even question whether it was a new Renaissance concept at all, since throughout the Middle Ages the work of Vitruvius could be found in every important monastic library. The mathematical approach reflected in his handbook and the consistent application of straight lines, rectangles and circles presumably contributed in some way to the geometric arrangement of land and towns in the Netherlands during the Middle Ages.

One of the most important elements in the theory of town and fortification building was the concept of symmetry. Vitruvius refers to *symmetria* as one of the fundamental principles of architecture; for him it means something like 'balanced proportion'. He himself explains it as 'the proper harmony between the sections of the structure itself and the interaction, on the basis of fixed units of measure, between its separate parts and the visual impact of the form as a whole'. In architectural practice this symmetry often implied equilateralism, in the sense of a mirror image. However, in the strongly mathematically-oriented theories of Renaissance builders and designers, this element acquired such importance that in practice symmetry came to mean a preference for 'multiple equilateralism'.

'Symmetry' in this sense must not only have exercised a fascination but have even been seen as an aesthetic imperative. That applied not only to theorists but also to the men on the battlefield. Prince Maurice, in a conversation with Simon Stevin, once confessed that if he was forced to deviate from formal symmetry when designing a city's defences, it caused him actual physical pain even though he could not explain why.

If we look again at the first plan by Staets and Stalpaert's map, we can find all the elements of the ideal city which have been discussed above. The broad layout of Amsterdam turns out to be the realisation of everything of which the idealistic city-builders had dreamed – though admittedly adapted to the geographic location and economic needs of the city. And by 'the' idealistic city builders, I mean not only the Dutch masters of surveying, masonry and stonework, but also to some extent the man who nearly two thousand years earlier had put their dream into words, namely Plato.

The only dialogue of Plato's that was available in Latin translation throughout the Middle Ages was the *Timaeus*. In its opening pages, Socrates refers to the ideal society, which had been discussed in an earlier dialogue, and wonders whether it had ever existed. His companions immediately suggest early Athens and the legendary Atlantis as possible examples. After that the *Timaeus* moves on to the creation of the world and its organisation by the Divine Creator. However, there is a kind of appendix, amounting to a second volume, in which Socrates' pupil Critias talks at much greater length about the mythical state of Atlantis. Atlantis, so the story goes, was an elongated island in the Ocean with, on the south side, a long plain running parallel to the sea. The inhabitants of Atlantis had cultivated this fertile plain and laid it out as an enormous rectangular agricultural area measuring 2,000 by 3,000 *stadia* (a Greek *stadium* was about 180 metres). This agricultural area was surrounded by a wide, similarly rectangular canal and criss-crossed by a network of smaller irrigation canals; they served to transport agricultural produce and wood from the hills to the actual city of Atlantis, which lay precisely half way between the agricultural area and the sea. The agricultural area and the sea were connected by a canal that ran from the middle of the southern section of the outer canal straight through the city to the sea, where it opened out into a wide harbour.

It is interesting to consider that the ideal defensible settlement according to Simon Stevin was also rectangular with a grid pattern of canals and streets, and that the ratio of the external dimensions was also two to three. But it is particularly the form and the organisation of the city between the agricultural area and the sea that makes Critias' account so absorbing. For the city is completely round with a diameter of a hundred *stadia* (nearly two kilometres) and exactly in the centre is a circular island in the form of a citadel incorporating the royal palace and the temple of Poseidon. This citadel is surrounded by three concentric canals separated in effect by two ring-shaped islands; the canals are respectively one, two and three *stadia* wide. Beyond the third canal lies a third and by far the widest ring of land. This in turn is enclosed by a massive wall and finally by the outermost canal which protects the whole city. The concentric canals are linked to each other by canopied connecting canals, while a main street runs from the central citadel via bridges over the principal canals, connecting all the ring-shaped residential areas with the outer canal and the harbour.

Even without a map, it is clear that this mythical city of Atlantis shows, in broad outline, fascinating similarities to Amsterdam. The pursuit of circularity, the three principal canals, the canal running from the fertile hinterland through the city to the sea, combine to make Atlantis an idealised image of Amsterdam. Plato's Atlantis never existed, certainly not in this form. Its exaggerated dimensions alone show that he never intended Atlantis to be an example to be realised in practice, but rather as the image of an idea, that of the ideal society. But images too can inspire imitation. From the fifteenth century on the texts of most of Plato's dialogues became available in Italy, and from the sixteenth century throughout Western Europe, in the original Greek as well as in Latin translation.

Could something of Plato's description of the ideal city have filtered through, directly or indirectly, to the ambitious governors and craftsmen of Amsterdam?

BOUDEWIJN BAKKER
Translated by Chris Emery.

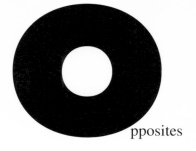

Opposites

Attract

Living on the Water

For centuries the Dutch have done their best to keep their feet dry. The simplest solution has always been to live above the NAP: the '*Normaal Amsterdams Peil*', or the zero Amsterdam ordnance datum. Yet as early as 600 BC people were making their homes in areas that were regularly under water.

Floating houses on the Maas near Roermond.

Bathhouse on the Amstel, Amsterdam, c.1900.

Carving out an existence under these damp conditions couldn't have been easy, a fact confirmed in a letter from the Roman soldier Pliny the Younger to Emperor Trajan in around AD 50: *'One vast area is flooded by the ocean twice a day, so that those involved in this eternal battle with the forces of nature come to doubt whether the ground belongs to the mainland or to the sea. The place is inhabited by a miserable race of poor people living in huts on naturally-formed high grounds or self-made elevations. They resemble seamen when the water covers the area, and survivors of a shipwreck when the water has receded. In the area around their huts they hunt for fish, which are carried back on the ebb. They have no cattle and no milk, like the other people in their area. They cannot even struggle against the wild animals, because there are no bushes to be seen. They braid ropes from seaweed and rushes, from which they make knotted fishnets. They grab up handfuls of mud, which is dried more by the wind than the sun. With this they cook their food and warm their limbs, stiffened by the northern winds. Their only drink is rainwater, collected in pits at the entrance to their houses.'*

At first these terps, or man-made mounds, were sufficient for the small number of people living in the lowlands, but population growth made it necessary to keep more of the land permanently dry for agriculture. A chain of dikes resulted in a fertile man-made landscape, although in large parts of the Netherlands the water remained a threat. The development of new techniques in the seventeenth and eighteenth centuries made it possible to drain inland bodies of water. In the mid-nineteenth century the Haarlemmermeer was drained, and other polders quickly followed. The twentieth century saw the construction of the Afsluitdijk, the reclamation of the North-East Polder, a new province – Flevoland – and, after the great flood of 1953, the Delta Works in Zeeland and South Holland.

The Netherlands is renowned for its inventive attempts to exploit and control water by means of dikes, sluices, ditches and pumps. A famous example, of course, is the Afsluitdijk. There are other plans that were never carried out and are therefore less well-known, such as the plan to connect the Waddenzee islands. Way back in 1667, Hendric Stevin came up with a plan to construct dams between the Waddenzee islands, and from Ameland to the Frisian coast. The scheme was not technically feasible, however. In 1876 the NV Friesche Landaanwinningsmaatschappij (Frisian Land Reclamation Company) did succeed in building a dam from Friesland to Ameland, but it was so expensive to maintain that the intended plan to drain and reclaim a large part of the Waddenzee came to naught. The dike was never taken down, and parts of it can still be seen at low tide. The Netherlands is a land of plans, and the number of plans that have been carried out to control the water just about equals the number of plans that bit the dust.

Besides being a threat, water was also an important means of production. The VOC (the Dutch East India Company) owed its existence to the benevolence of water, and the Dutch spirit of commerce was kept alive back home in the harbours of Rotterdam. Unorthodox attempts were made to keep one step ahead of the competition. A well-known example is the Maasvlakte, which was constructed near Rotterdam harbour between 1970 and 1985 by building up a sandbank just off the coast using 170 million cubic metres of sand. A lesser known example is the endless struggle with the Belgians. Access to the harbour of Antwerp is dependent on the Western Scheldt, which flows through Dutch territory. This fact has led to squabbles ever since the separation of the Netherlands and Belgium in 1830. The recent deepening of the Scheldt, despite the Water Treaties, became a sensitive topic. A compromise guaranteed that Antwerp would also be kept accessible to the most modern container ships.

The part of the country that lies below sea level has become the most densely populated part of the Netherlands. The increasingly urbanised Nether-

The Eilandenbuurt ('Islands Quarter') in Almere.

lands found the room it needed for homes in the new polders, making it possible to maintain and protect what is left of the natural landscape in the Randstad, the large western conurbation. Both Almere and Lelystad are new cities below sea level. Since 1976, 150,000 people have made their home in Almere and almost 80,000 in Lelystad. And although no one lives at Schiphol, each year more than 40 million passengers are put on planes there.

After the completion of the Delta Works, it was believed that the Netherlands had 'finished' and that the battle with the water had nearly been won. Today people think otherwise. Changes in the climate and a rising sea level have already led to many dike improvements, along the rivers as well as around the polders and along the seacoast. When will the limit be reached? It is expected that by the year 2050 sea level will be half a metre higher than it is now. On the one hand, the constant draining of the polders is a big expense that will only get bigger. On the other hand, the continuous removal of water causes the land to keep sinking.

The 'advances in understanding' of the last few decades have produced a different, more cautious look at the way the Netherlands is laid out. It has led to solutions that go beyond the mere separation of water and land. One striking reminder of the age of absolute faith in the ability to create an engineered landscape is the dike that connects Lelystad with Enkhuizen. This was supposed to have been the dike of the Markerwaard, which was never reclaimed. It's a plan that appears with a certain regularity on the political agenda, only to be scrapped once again under the protest of environmental activists and lovers of the landscape.

High water levels, such as those that occurred in 1993 and 1995 in the Dutch river regions, resulted in substantial improvements to the dike systems, but apart from that rigorous interventions in the water and the landscape rarely take place these days. Instead, ways are being sought to bend with the water, as it were. As a result of the appeal to develop more nature reserves in the Netherlands, in certain wildlife areas the dikes have been intentionally lowered to allow flooding at high tide. This produces a kind of controlled freedom of water movement so the wildlife areas can develop in a 'natural' way. Under the constant pressure of the water on the river dikes, thinly populated areas have been designated as buffer zones in the event of flooding. These measures have had some critical feedback, especially from the German states along the border. Wherever the Germans have raised the dikes, the water quickly returns 'through the back door' via the Netherlands.

In 2000, the province of South Holland held a competition on the theme of housing under the name 'Amphibious Living': *'Amphibious Living is a plea to abandon the compulsive need to control water and to make room in our residential environment for the influence of the weather, the tides and the seasons. It is a plea for a new housing mentality. Controlling the natural environment is not a matter of imposing our own will on the landscape, but of taking maximum advantage of the qualities inherent in a dynamic relationship between land and water. This also means that living conditions cannot be predicted. So Amphibious Living requires an adventurous mentality and a higher degree of self-reliance than we are accustomed to in the Netherlands, where everything is regulated down to the smallest detail...'*

Home is where the water is

Floating brothels in Utrecht. Photo courtesy of Daniël Depenbrock.

Prototype for 220 water homes in IJburg (Amsterdam), to be built in an unsinkable combination of wood and aluminium.

A few forms of living on the water did already exist before the term 'Amphibious Living' came into fashion. Living in houseboats, for instance, is a more or less a distinct lifestyle. This form of housing is mainly to be found in cities that have a historic ring of canals such as Amsterdam and Utrecht, and it enables people to live near the city centre with limited costs and a certain nomadic sense of freedom. The disadvantage of this way of life is often a lack of space and comfort. Houseboats are not only used as homes, by the way, but also for commercial purposes. In several cities we find the unique combination of a pancake restaurant in a ship. Utrecht has gone one step further in a move that typifies the way the Dutch make practical use of the water and the way the Netherlands deals with the grey sectors of society: at the edge of the city, in a spot where there's least likely to be any trouble, prostitutes ply their trade on houseboats.

Amphibious Living is no longer limited to incidental cases. Amsterdam was faced with the problem of building thousands of dwellings without sufficient available land. The result is IJburg, a new residential area located entirely in the water: part of it on newly created islands, and part of it afloat. Discussions of the IJburg project go all the way back to 1965, when a study appeared entitled *City on the Pampus* (a sandbank in the IJsselmeer east of Amsterdam), proposing the construction of an entire city where 350,000 inhabitants could live and work. In the period that followed, policy turned against further expansion of large cities and the idea disappeared from the agenda. In the late 1970s Amsterdam adopted the 'Compact City Policy': keeping urban expansion as close to the existing city as possible in order to maintain quality facilities and to preserve the countryside. In the 1980s the idea of building in the IJmeer gained momentum once again and a variety of studies were carried out. The 1990s were taken up with realising the plans. This was accompanied by the predicted social protest. The loss of the area's natural elements was seen as a major disadvantage. This will be alleviated by the development of 'new' natural areas in the immediate surroundings. The current decade promises a large amount of construction, although the 350,000 inhabitants originally projected have been reduced to 45,000. A total of 18,000 dwellings will have to be built by 2012. A special part of IJburg

is the Waterbuurt, located on Steigereiland, with experimental housing on the water for about 1,000 inhabitants. In 2001 an article in *Algemeen Dagblad* reported that '*buyers are given a concrete barge that has a temporary hut for cooking, eating and sleeping. The rest they can build themselves*'.

The fact that dwelling on the water is becoming less unusual in the Netherlands is evident from the folders featuring a selection of fully-equipped floating homes ready to moor at the owner's spot of choice. Idyllic living on the river dike is hampered by the necessary raising of the dikes, and living in the river forelands is being prevented as much as possible. Symbolic of the Netherlands' changing relationship with the water are the floating houses on the Maas near Roermond. They adapt to the river's water level and make it possible to return to the romance of living on the water.

Interestingly enough, living on the water has been going on for decades in the United States and Canada. Examples are Lake Union and Portage Bay in Seattle. Floating neighbourhoods can be found in other cities as well, such as Portland, Vancouver (Marina Wes-Del, Canoe Pass), New Jersey (Sea-Village Marina) and San Francisco (Sausalito Floating Community). At first attempts were made to outlaw these places, most of which were populated by students and artists. The film *Sleepless in Seattle*, however, did a great deal to popularise them and drive up the prices. Today's city councils have a much friendlier attitude to the mostly well-to-do water dwellers who inhabit these neighbourhoods.

Clearly, the Netherlands and water are inextricably linked in a kind of love-hate relationship. It's an exciting relationship that is never in danger of becoming routine, as recent developments have shown. Complete control over the water is just not going to happen, nor does anyone today really desire it. Using the water cleverly and taking full advantage of its unpredictability are what give the relationship that special something. And as they say, opposites attract.

DANIËL DEPENBROCK
Translated by Nancy Forest-Flier.

Herman Hertzberger's design for eight interlinked water homes for the Ypenburg development (1999-2001).

Amphibious Living:
www.amfibischwonen.nl
Projectbureau IJburg:
www.ijburg.nl

ow

to Paint Water

The Leie as a Stream of Inspiration

Lovely indeed is the Leie, that on the happiest of days
Reflects the taut repose of my count'nance…
The evening will be tranquil again, and bear boats
In which a square light of calm love dwells.

Karel van de Woestijne (1878-1929)

'*This part of the country has hilly woods on one side and on the other grassy meadows watered by the Leie, that are uncommonly pleasant in the summer*', wrote Sanderus in *In Praise of Flanders* (Verheerlijkt Vlaandre, 1735) about the countryside around the river Leie, to the south of Ghent. Evidently, locals and visitors have been impressed by the beauty of the river valley between the various villages along the banks since time immemorial, '*so that for one who loves the great outdoors it is impossible to imagine anything more agreeable*'.

Arcadia-on-the-Leie

The bucolic nature of the area between Deinze and Ghent, with Sint-Martens-Latem as its spiritual centre, has long remained unspoiled. Besides this, its attraction lies in its refreshing variety, the contrast between pine woods and sandy hills, wide open fields stretching as far as the eye can see, and green meadows and orchards surrounded by hawthorn hedges. But most of all there is the Leie, out of sight one minute only to reappear again suddenly, slow pale green water meandering lazily, with grass along its banks and rows of tall poplars. The river threads its way through the different features of the landscape, drawing them together into a lively whole. At every turn the view imposes itself like a set of diverging lines, that disappear behind the crest of a dune or a cluster of houses and clumps of trees here, to continue their course undisturbed again over there. This scenery is charming rather than majestic, and conceals places where one loves to linger, that urge reflection or offer creative spirits inspiration. So, with the meanders of the Leie as the thread, nature here strings together an endless variety of fascinating views that will, in the course of time, attract the artist's attention. With their sensitive antennae, painters and sculptors, writers and poets, hermits and apostles of nature find their way to this favourite place. One could even say that there was an artistic exodus to the Leie valley towards the turn of the century. Some artists, especially the earlier ones, are fascinated by the captivating prettiness of the landscape and give expression there to their objections to the sterile academicism of the late nineteenth century. Others, round 1900, find more than anything peace, solitude and originality, an existence far removed from the expanding city where the atmosphere is full of smoke from the factories and social turmoil. They are seeking life in its authentic state – in the inspiring company of colleagues and soul-mates. Still others, the later ones that is, are attracted not only by the countryside, but also by the strange, indefinable pull of a place where art is born, where artists live and work. The result is that, in many respects, the Leie draws its own curve through Belgian art history in the first quarter of the twentieth century.

From left to right:
Alfons Dessenis, Gustave
van de Woestijne, Valerius
de Saedeleer and Maurice
Sijs on the Leie. Sint-
Martens-Woluwe, c.1905.

Emile Claus,
Girl by the Leie. 1892.
Canvas, 56 x 46 cm.
Galerie Oscar De Vos,
Sint-Martens-Latem.

Sunshine House

Any artist of the Latem School put the Leie on his agenda at least once, with Emile Claus at the top of the list. He discovered the art of painting light in Paris, and from 1890 a closer acquaintance with paintings by Renoir, Monet and Pisarro leads to looser, more spontaneous brushstrokes. Gradually, the representation of atmosphere and light gains in importance. The painting *Girl by the Leie* (1892) is a striking example. The palette acquires great clarity here, light filters, as it were, into the canvas. Over the years the focus is transferred from the figure to the landscape, to nature in an ever-changing light. That does not mean, however, that the figure disappears from the scene completely. Mostly it remains as decoration in a sun-drenched view of nature. But for all that, his drawing retains a remarkable solidity, his forms do not blur to vague shadows under the all-dissipating power of the light, as do those of the French artists.

In the nineties, with unshakeable conviction, Claus continues down his chosen path, secluded in his country home, Sunshine House, whose name sums up his artistic programme. His perception is influenced more and more by a lyricism of light that controls form and colour. He paints the sunny side of life in the Leie valley, with a general sentiment of joy. He sees the quivering summer light reflecting in the calm water, fishermen emptying their nets on a thin winter morning, or spotted cows wading through the blue-splashing Leie. Claus continues to be the painter of joyful reverberating light, of sun along the water and the paths through the fields, of the sun on roofs and cornfields, of the sun that shimmers on white walls.

Around 1905, when Impressionism has lost most of its impetus in France, Emile Claus is widely acclaimed in Belgium. His form of painting light becomes, for the first time, very fashionable. Some fall permanently under its spell, others are side-tracked for a while by this late blossoming. Valerius de Saedeleer, who is *the* landscape artist, only relinquishes Impressionism in 1904, with the realisation that the only way to create durable, timeless art is with restraint. In this process he seems, increasingly, to emulate the example of his medieval colleagues, who, after all, experienced the secret of art as the fruit of lengthy study. Through patient, silent, sustained research of the landscape around Latem, De Saedeleer becomes thoroughly familiar with the particular characteristics of the area. Now that the spell of Impressionism is broken, he tries to explore the intrinsic significance of his subject more deeply. What he conveys now is the result not of an optical impression, but of essential experience.

It goes without saying that an artist, for whom knowledge of his subject is an absolute prerequisite, prefers to seek inspiration in his immediate environment. That is one of the reasons why the Leie near Sint-Martens-Latem features prominently in De Saedeleer's works. Year after year he has the image of the river and its surroundings in his mind. He can observe it continually straight from his atelier. There on the bank he will look conscientiously for the intrinsic poetry, the spirit of his environment. The painting *Leie on a Grey Day* (1904) is a convincing example of the results of this process. The contrast with his earlier paintings is striking. The casual haste of his earlier years is tamed. The reward is a landscape that combines clarity and purity with simplicity. Displays of sheer cleverness are alien to the artist now,

Valerius de Saedeleer,
Leie on a Grey Day. 1904.
Canvas, 79 x 107 cm.
Museum Oud Hospitaal,
Aalst.

his artistic vision has evolved. The way he balances his composition, with the cloudless sky as the dominant element, contributes to an atmosphere of desolation and boundlessness – a dreamy, rather wistful mood which the mirror effect of the water reinforces. Despite the flat stylisation of the painting, it draws the viewer into its depths, to the horizon far away. By stressing the horizontal lines of the river-banks and their convergence on the horizon the artist gives an impression of calm and space. The localised glitter of light and colour has also largely disappeared. What else is striking is the fine finish of the surface compared to the meagre subject matter. This embodies very succinctly the break with Impressionism which, after all, imbued the autonomous character of the paint-skin with its own significance. The colours are applied to the painting in thin, smooth layers. Eventually the canvas is so carefully finished that the surface betrays no traces of the artist's natural, spontaneous activity. This is the reinstatement of the medieval attitude towards painting as craftsmanship.

The artist Gustave de Smet, who belongs to the so-called 'second Latem group', is engaged for a while in the second wave of Impressionism in this village on the Leie. Emile Claus and, in particular, his reputation and success steer him in that direction. De Smet's preference is for more modest moments: the soft, sometimes mysterious light under an apple tree, a forgotten corner of a flower garden, sunset by the water. That does not mean, though, that Gustave de Smet did not paint broad panoramas bathed in sunlight. From a technical point of view, the study of light is paramount in these canvases, as it interprets the ever-changing intensity of the hazy atmosphere

Gustave de Smet,
Leie in the Summer. 1911.
Canvas, 49.5 x 68.5 cm.
Private collection.
© SABAM Belgium 2003.

above the water. The openness of the Leie countryside, which at the same time so inspired De Saedeleer's broad panoramas, is at its best in *Leie in the Summer* (1911). It is the bend in the Leie near Latem on a summer day, radiant with light, painted with the trusty dab and dash brush technique. Nonetheless, the picture is spacious and solidly constructed. Above the semi-circular receding lines of the river-banks a sharp horizontal line separates the areas of earth and sky. Behind a row of tall poplars, which draw the eye towards the horizon, a deep blue sky with clear white clouds stands out. The water of the Leie provides an identical mirror image. In this way, the lavish strokes of paint do not distract attention from the elements of the composition. At the beginning of the 1920s Gustave de Smet would underline the shortcomings of Impressionism when asked: '*I understood clearly how unsatisfactory the means of expression afforded by the style were and I constantly looked beyond it.*' Indeed, just before the First World War the artist ceases to express himself exclusively in the language of Impressionism. But for the time being, the technique barely changes. The big change only comes during the years of exile abroad.

The river as scenery

After a long stay in the Netherlands (1914-1922) Frits van den Berghe and Gustave de Smet return to the Leie, as do other artists, refreshed and enriched with new insights. Both have surfaced again from their adventure

75

Frits van den Berghe,
The River-Banks. 1926.
Canvas, 94.5 x 121 cm.
Private collection.

with Impressionism as artists with a personal, recognisable idiom. The Leie has now lost its status as the pictorial objective of their canvases. Henceforth it forms the backdrop in which people prove their – sometimes tragic – existence. In Van den Berghe's exquisite painting *The River-Banks* (1926) grace, lightheartedness and luxury dominate. The scene is playful and composed with casual ease, unfolding like a colourful fan. The empathy is perfect. Day trippers are gathered around a central open space, seeking recreation along the Leie. The scene is serenely peaceful, there are no bold gestures to spoil the enchantment, no signs of commotion. At the most one could point to lazy excess, an atmosphere of worldly lightheartedness in which the tramp on the bank to the right seems to sound a wrong note. Each couple tries to strike a pose for their short, intimate meeting, sometimes rather shy, sometimes blasé. In a picture which remorselessly casts aside the trusty old ballast in front and behind, above and below, the artist has portrayed the playfulness of the subject effectively and freely. In any case, in the spirit of Giorgio de Chirico, objects like boats and the arches of bridges have erotic significance.

The scene of *Summer* (1926), by Gustave de Smet, also breathes an atmosphere of paradise. In a tranquil spot on the banks of the Leie, a fisherman catches a fish on his hook, apparently absent-mindedly. With a well-chosen gesture the artist has drawn the curve of the waterway and divided

Gustave de Smet,
Summer. 1926. Canvas,
120 x 135 cm. Stedelijke
Musea, Bruges. © SABAM
Belgium 2003.

the water from the land – a strip of land seems to float on a sleepy lake. In the foreground, the soft blue of the fisherman forms a contrast with the pink-white of the naked woman. Further on, the eye is drawn to the open living room, which is set like a strange theatre décor along the waterside. The scene is serenely peaceful. The artist has apparently consciously sought the fullness of human existence. Nevertheless, the scene is not drained of all tension, it is quite clearly the intimacy between man and woman which creates the intrigue. The cool, feminine nakedness lacks, as usual, any kind of erotic charge. A sense of happiness bursts through in the clear, pure forms and subtly nuanced palette. Linked to this wealth of peaceful joy and intrinsic calm is a profound longing for a harmonious world. Meanwhile, the Leie has taken second place to all of this and is merely a useful element in a carefully constructed picture.

PIET BOYENS
Translated by Lindsay Edwards.

Valour

on Ice

The Elfstedentocht in Friesland

In the Netherlands, finishing the Elfstedentocht (Eleven Towns Tour), the skating route that takes in eleven Frisian towns, is considered the ultimate sporting achievement. The nice thing about it is that it is not restricted to the several hundred real athletes, but about 16,000 amateur skaters can join in too. This means it is not only a contest but has also become an event for would-be popular heroes. Since mega-spectacles and great physical achievements score highly in the publicity stakes, the whole of the Netherlands is already in a state of high excitement in the days preceding the event. On the day itself the province of Friesland (now officially Fryslân), where it takes place, comes to a standstill and hundreds of thousands line the route to cheer on the participants. A large proportion of the Dutch population is glued to the box so as not to miss a thing. Membership of the club that provides the right to participation is so restricted that it is almost fought over. This, despite the fact that, for finishing the route in the given time, one wins no more than a silver medal in the shape of a cross. It is a distinction that many value more highly than a knighthood.

When it freezes hard, the Frisians thaw

Although the precise route may vary, the Elfstedentocht is always about 200 kilometres long. This fivefold marathon goes from Leeuwarden to Sneek, on to IJlst, Sloten, Stavoren, Hindeloopen, Workum, Bolsward, Harlingen, Franeker and then back to Leeuwarden by the long and most troublesome part through Dokkum. The official skating contest has existed for a little less than a century, and has been imitated in other sports. The cycling Elfstedentocht is very old too, and the walking tour of several days has also built up a solid tradition, while several other sports have now established courses round the eleven Frisian towns.

But the only true Elfstedentocht is the skating race. It can only be held if the natural ice in the canals and waterways, ponds and lakes is thick enough to take the weight. The saying in Friesland is '*When it freezes hard, the Frisians thaw*'. When the frost is so hard that it is possible to skate on the waterways and lakes it is as if a virus strikes, resulting in an epidemic of Elfstedentocht fever. The decision of the committee of 'De Friesche Elf Steden' association is awaited with bated breath; forecasts are made every other minute; weather men and the 'ice master' with his area supervisors who check the ice are suddenly the most popular people in the world. If it has been freezing hard for quite a few days and the forecasts are reasonably reliable, the words '*It sil hewe*' or '*It giet oan*' ('It's on!') may suddenly be heard from the lips of the chairman of the organising club and everything is in uproar. Everything has to be prepared in the local areas, and an army of volunteers sets to work.

The ice has to be got into the best possible condition; for recent contests ice transplants have even been carried out at the weaker spots, such as under bridges. At places that remain unreliable or other parts where skating is impossible, the participants have to '*klune*', which means run across land in their skates. Carpet or straw is usually laid on these '*kluneplakken*', to keep damage to the skates to a minimum. This is because not every corner of Friesland gets the same degree of frost; the nearby sea has an influence here, and not all waterways that have frozen over are just lying there waiting for more frost.

The first tours

It goes without saying that the most important thing is the sporting achievement and the popular festivities that have gradually grown up around it, but the magic of the tour was already associated with these eleven Frisian towns in the eighteenth century. In 1763, for instance, Johann Hermann Knoop, of German origin, wrote that the waters of Friesland, '*are not only useful, but also provide entertainment in the winter, when they are frozen by the cold and covered with ice. Then the people enjoy themselves incredibly, especially the young, by skating. Foreigners who come from mountainous and dry countries are astonished when they see this skating, and are almost of the opinion that it is sorcery*'. He continues, '*It has also occurred more than once that good skaters have passed through and seen all XI towns of Friesland in one winter's day: but they must not stay anywhere very long and the ice has to be good and strong.*'

The first recorded skater to have completed the run on his own took no less than 22 hours to do it: '*though,*' said a 1862 newspaper report, '*according to records of his arrivals and departures in his notebook, made by trustworthy people in the various towns, he was not skating for more than 15½ hours, including about 2 hours when he took the wrong route as a result of faulty directions. The painter and drawer Willem Troost, who lives in Leeuwarden, has provided us with a rare example of both will-power and physical strength,*' wrote the reporter. On the morning of 22 January 1862 '*he left entirely alone, in a fierce north-east wind, to visit the eleven towns of this province... and arrived back at his home fresh and healthy.*' Troost was a real skating enthusiast and in 1855 did a lithographic print of the speed-skating behind the Prinsentuin and at the Oldehove in Leeuwarden, the place that was so often to be the finish of the Elfstedentocht.

The first contest

Over the years this skating tour of the eleven towns attracted increasing numbers of sportsmen. In the harsh winter of 1890 there were actually several hundred who, in small groups, collected the signatures of innkeepers in the eleven towns as proof of their having completed the run. In that same winter the Frisian Pim Mulier completed his own elfstedentocht. As a sport propagandist Mulier introduced many sports, including cricket and football, to the Netherlands and organised them into leagues. After his own tour he continued to cherish the idea of an organised *Elfsteden* competition. But it was only in the late autumn of 1908 that another truly hard winter set in. Pim Mulier was able to persuade the newly established (by himself) Dutch Federation of Physical Education and the Frisian Ice League to organise the competition on 2 January 1909. A thaw set in and the ice was no good at all. Only nine of the 23 skaters completed the course. The fastest in this first official Elfstedentocht was Minne Hoekstra, a theology student from Wergea near Leeuwarden. It took him almost 14 hours.

Twelve days afterwards, Mindert Hepkema founded the 'De Friesche Elf Steden' association. He became its president, a post he held for many years. This new association got its first chance for a competition in 1912. It too was plagued by thawing ice. President Hepkema, the chairman, came ninth; the winner was Coen de Koning, in 11 hours 40 minutes. This was also the first

Skating contest for couples in Leeuwarden. The print is by Willem Troost, who in 1862 '*left entirely alone, in a fierce north-east wind, to visit the eleven towns of this province... and arrived back at his home fresh and healthy*'. Photo courtesy of *Friesch Dagblad* & Peter Karstkarel.

Karst Leemburg (see arrow), the winner in 1929, arrives at Willemskade in Leeuwarden. Photo from *De Elfstedentocht 1909-1997* (Leeuwarden, 1997).

time that non-competing skaters took part, not for glory, but for the experience. Only four of the 22 reached the finishing line.

Coen de Koning, winner in 11 hours 40 minutes in 1912. Photo from *De Elfstedentocht 1909-1997* (Leeuwarden, 1997).

Hard tours and popular heroes

In 1917 De Koning won again, in splendidly settled weather, in almost two hours less; furthermore, he was in the lead all round the course and almost entirely alone. Then for a number of winters it stubbornly refused to freeze, but in 1929 conditions were right again, to say the least: when the 98 competitors and 206 others started off on 12 February the temperature was 18° below zero. It turned into a heroic struggle, with tragic cases of frostbite. Even so, 54 competitors and 103 enthusiasts crossed the finishing line in Leeuwarden. The winner of this rigorous contest was Karst Leemburg, who, wearing traditional skates, was initially several minutes behind the skaters using modern racing skates. In 1933 the conditions were ideal for a record: Abe de Vries and Sipke Castelein went round in 9 hours 5 minutes, and 230 skaters finished the course.

The run was organised again in early 1940 when there was a severe frost. Only 93 of almost 700 competitors completed the course, accompanied by exactly 1% of the 2700 enthusiasts. The weather allowed this feast of skating to take place again in the next two years, war or no war. In 1941 the conditions were marvellous, and a great many participants in what was by now a mass event reached the finishing line, with Auke Adema from Franeker winning for the second time. Conditions were also reasonable in 1942. Plenty of participants finished and Sietze de Groot set a new record of 8 hours 44 minutes.

No records emerged from the next run in 1947, however. The weather and the state of the ice were so poor that outside Friesland people cried out against it: it would be irresponsible to skate in such conditions. But all Friesland knows that risks and heroism are inseparably linked to the contest and so the party went ahead. Only 10% of at least 3000 participants finished. And at the finish there were a good many protests and disqualifications because several good skaters had accepted help. Jan van den Hoorn was declared the winner. In 1954 conditions were superb once again, allowing Jeen van den Berg to set a new record of 7 hours 35 minutes. In the 1956 Elfstedentocht (now written with a capital 'E' for the first time), five skaters crossed the finishing line together after 8 hours 48 minutes and were promptly disqualified. The rules no longer allowed it. Such display of brotherliness no longer paid off: the struggle had to go on to the end.

A severe frost, bitter wind and lots of drifting snow made the 1963 tour probably the most testing in history. The winner, Reinier Paping, became a true popular hero whose name has still not been forgotten in the Netherlands. It was as if after these horrors everything first had to quieten down again, but it turned out to be a very long interval. In 1979 Friesland was cut off for some time by a tremendous snowfall, but you cannot skate on snow. There was no Elfstedentocht and so alternative tours were organised in Finland and Austria; the real stars of the tour wanted to maintain their affinity with natural ice.

But in 1985 things looked good again. Many people were a little taken aback by it all. No fewer than 13,000 non-competitors were able to complete the course. The contest itself was won by Evert van Benthem in a record time of 6 hours 46 minutes. Among the non-competitors was a special guest, Crown Prince Willem-Alexander, incognito, who was greeted at the finish by his mother Queen Beatrix. Conditions were again favourable the following year. The event, covered in full on television, turned into a popular festival that was only just kept under control. Almost 15,000 skaters completed the course, with Evert van Benthem again the fastest of all.

After a last-minute cancellation of the event in 1996, the fifteenth tour, and the last to date, was organised in 1997. Conditions were reasonable and

Auke Adema from Franeker winning for the second time in 1941. Photo from *De Elfstedentocht 1909-1997* (Leeuwarden, 1997).

Elfstedentocht 1997. Photo by Tjerk de Jong.

Henk Angenent won in a contest that attracted overwhelming interest. Many tens of thousands of spectators encouraged the participants from the sidelines and 11.2 million viewers followed the race on TV.

Ice carnival and 'mop bands'

A 'mop band' at the 1997 edition of the Elfstedentocht. Photo by Jacob van Essen (*Het Hoge Noorden*).

The sporting performance of the participants in the Elfstedentocht is so highly regarded that the warm-hearted attention and encouragement from people along the route have become a tradition. The association has gradually been professionalised, but everyone from the members of the board to the humblest helper does everything voluntarily. There is support from all sides, but up to now the organisation has succeeded in resisting commercial sponsorship. This has led to an atmosphere whose motto is '*we'll get down and do it ourselves*' and the Frisians are not a little proud of this. In addition, on the last three occasions, major festivities have taken place around the Elfstedentocht, a sort of carnival with snacks and drinks, banners and crazy hats and lots of small brass bands, nicknamed '*dweilorkesten*' (mop bands) – the ice is kept in condition by mopping and sweeping. The idea has caught on, too: the short and medium circuit contests and the European and World Championships in the Thialf ice stadium in Heerenveen in Friesland are the friendliest in the world. This atmosphere has also transferred to the cultural 'Slachtemarathon' first organised in Summer 2000, a running race for 800 athletes and a recreational walk for 9,200 on an age-old 42-kilometre dike complex in Friesland known as the Slachte. A little less sport, perhaps, but more culture, with many hundreds of volunteers and 42 brass bands, dance groups, stage shows, artists, and so on. More than forty nearby villages each assume responsibility for a particular section of dike and show off the pride of their cultural history there. It may be that the richness of the cultural history of these eleven fine old towns and of a splendid old dike complex unconsciously provides the solid basis for these remarkable events.

PETER KARSTKAREL
Translated by Gregory Ball.

Solid

and Volatile

Twelve Poems Selected by Jozef Deleu

Bernlef (1937-)

Skater

Ripples frozen solid
right through to spring
till lumps and bumps melt and
skates go to sleep

Ripples congealed in the
middle of the deserted lake
where you let a pin drop
and stare after your labouring breath

Puckered wavelets you feel
in your very bones
in the pounding pulses
under the mittens on your back

Crosswise over ridges
pushing on regardless
like an obstinate ship
a sweating figurehead

Your eyes focused on snow
that clads the far side
you hear movement
feel frozen in space.

Schaatser

Rimpeling bevroren tot
aan de lente toe
tot hobbels smelten en
schaatsen slapen gaan

Rimpeling midden op
het verlaten meer gestold
waar je een speld laat vallen
en je stokkende adem nastaart

Gefronste golfjes die je
tot in je botten voelt
tot in de kloppende polsen
onder de wanten op je rug

Dwars gericht op ribbels
voetstoots verder
als een halsstarrig schip
een zwetend boegbeeld

Je blik gefixeerd op sneeuw
die de overkant blindeert
hoor je beweging
voel je stilstand.

From *Over and Done With. Poems 1960-1990* (Achter de rug.
Gedichten 1960-1990). Amsterdam: Querido, 1997.
Translated by Tanis Guest.

Martinus Nijhoff (1894-1953)

The Clouds

I still wore boy's clothes and lay side by side
Outstretched with mother in the heath's warm lair;
Above us shifting clouds were drifting by
And mother asked me what I saw up there.

And I cried: Scandinavia, and: swans,
A lady, and: a shepherd with his sheep –
The wonders were made word and drifted on,
But I saw mother, smiling, start to weep.

Then came the time I kept the earth in sight,
Although up in the sky the clouds were rife;
I did not seek to try to catch in flight
The strange thing's shadow as it grazed my life.

– Now on the heath my lad lies next to me
And points out what in new clouds he can spy;
I'm crying now, for far off I can see
The distant clouds that made my mother cry -

From *Collected Works* (Verzameld werk). Amsterdam: Bert Bakker, 1982.
Translated by John Irons.

De wolken

Ik droeg nog kleine kleeren, en ik lag
Lang-uit met moeder in de warme hei,
De wolken schoven boven ons voorbij
En moeder vroeg wat 'k in de wolken zag.

En ik riep: Scandinavië, en: eenden,
Daar gaat een dame, schapen met een herder –
De wond'ren werden woord en dreven verder,
Maar 'k zag dat moeder met een glimlach weende.

Toen kwam de tijd dat 'k niet naar boven keek,
Ofschoon de hemel vol van wolken hing,
Ik greep niet naar de vlucht van 't vreemde ding
Dat met zijn schaduw langs mijn leven streek.

– Nu ligt mijn jongen naast mij in de heide
En wijst me wat hij in de wolken ziet,
Nu schrei ik zelf, en zie in het verschiet
De verre wolken waarom moeder schreide –

Hendrik Marsman (1899-1940)

Holland

Heaven high vaulted and grey.
below, the mighty lowland with marshy pools;
green-houses and steeples, trees and mills,
squared into patches by the dikes, silver-grey.

this is my people, my country;
here is the land where I shall sing.
let me gaze into pools an evening,
then may I like a cloud go away.

From *Collected Works* (Verzameld werk). Amsterdam: Querido, 1960.
Translated by E.D. Blodgett.

Holland

De hemel groots en grauw.
daaronder het geweldig laagland met de plassen;
bomen en molens, kerktorens en kassen,
verkaveld door de sloten, zilvergrauw.

dit is mijn land, mijn volk;
dit is de ruimte waarin ik wil klinken.
laat mij éen avond in de plassen blinken
daarna mag ik verdampen als een wolk.

Richard Minne (1891-1965)

Resisting Winter

Oh land of snow and biting ice,
what have you in store for me?
Above the wood the white moon starts
her voyaging through all the nights
and the silence seems to creak.
In your soil, beneath the sod,
shivering my good dead lie,
while my sick soul reaches out
to every dream, oh, Abishag!
who rest there under the canopy
in the pink glimmer of the dawn.
Why, oh land of biting ice,
do you perplex your son like this,
and do I always yearn for spring?

From *Open House and Other Poems* (In den zoeten inval en andere
gedichten). Amsterdam: Van Oorschot, 1955.
Translated by Tanis Guest.

Verweer tegen den winter

Gij land van sneeuw en snerpend ijs,
wat heb ik van u te verwachten?
Boven het bos begint de reis
der witte maan door al de nachten
en 't is alsof de stilte kraakt.
In uwen grond, onder de zoden,
liggen huivrend mijn goede doden,
terwijl mijn zieke ziele haakt
aan iedren droom, o, Abisag!
gij die daar rust onder de tente,
in 't roze gloren van den dag.
Waarom, gij land van snerpend ijs,
brengt gij uw zoon zo van de wijs
en zucht ik altijd naar de lente?

Anna Enquist (1945-)

Winter's Day

My son was seven years old; his skates
were much too big. We saw fishes and
a frog under ice, whooshed by reeds,
past eleven imagined towns, ate freezing cold
chocolate and sat on the bank. In the peat
we found a potsherd. All the world
lay bright and dry at our feet.

From *Poems 1991-2000* (De Gedichten 1991-2000). Amsterdam:
De Arbeiderspers, 2000.
Translated by Tanis Guest.

Winterdag

Mijn zoon was zeven jaar; zijn schaatsen
waren veel te groot. Wij zagen vissen en
een kikker onder ijs, suisden langs riet,
langs elf verzonnen steden, aten bevroren
chocola en zaten op de wal. Wij vonden
in het veen een potscherf. Heel de wereld
lag helder en droog aan onze voeten.

J.A. dèr Mouw (1862-1919)

Dull violet is the west and purplish grey.
Still I walk through the thickly frosted grass,
hear on the waterway beside me the thin whine
of skates over the hollow-ringing ice:

It feels as if I, on the frozen glass
circling, gliding, wheeling skilfully,
with flexing upper body sink and rise:
it's in my back, as though I too were skating.

Just so I hope that he past whom my verses glide,
singly, in pairs, or linked into long trains,
swinging to rhyme and rhythm of Dutch steel,

that he too hears the wind that bore me blowing,
and the fine skimming and the glorious broad swaying
of his own spirit in my words can feel.

From *Complete Poetic Works* (Volledig dichtwerk). Amsterdam: Van
Oorschot, 1986.
Translated by Tanis Guest.

Dof violet is 't west en paarsig grijs.
Nog wandel 'k door het zwaar berijpte gras,
en hoor naast me op de vaart het fijn gekras
van schaatsen over 't hol rinkelend ijs:

ik heb 't gevoel, of 'k op 't bevroren glas
cirklend, zwevend, zwenkend op kunst'ge wijs,
met 't buigend bovenlichaam daal en rijs:
't is in mijn rug, of 'k zelf op schaatsen was.

Zo hoop 'k dat, langs wiens geest mijn verzen glijen,
alleen, in paren, of in lange rijen,
schomm'lend op maat en rijm van hollands staal,

dat hij de wind, die mij droeg, zelf hoort waaien,
en 't fijn slieren en 't heerlijk brede zwaaien
voelt van zijn eigen stemming in mijn taal.

Hendrick Avercamp,
*Winter Scene with Skaters
near a Town.* c.1620.

Canvas, 47 x 89 cm.
Private collection.

Willem de Mérode (1887-1939)

Evening Rain

There was a gentle dripping in the leaves
As if the summer rain would now begin.
And lazily the twilights glided in
Of showers borne menacingly on the breeze.

The smell of flowers and dampness merged and then
It drifted round the paths like wisps of mist,
Through steam the gable's red was faintly guessed,
Huge rain-drops dashed against the window pane.

And you: with life there's nothing can contend.
The shower is heavy in its headstrong fall
Fortunate what's been saved and stowed away,

But I: see how each rose stands calm and tall,
Sustains the cruel assuagement heaven sends.
Endures and lives to flower at break of day.

From *Collected Poems* (Verzamelde gedichten). Amsterdam:
Bosch & Keuning, 1987.
Translated by John Irons.

Avondregen

Er was een zacht gedruppel in de blâren
Of nu de zomerregen zou beginnen.
En traag gleden de schemeringen binnen
Van buien, die ons dreigend overvaren.

De geur van vocht en bloemen vloeide samen
En dreef de paden rond als lichte nevel.
Bleek uit den damp hief zich de roode gevel.
Toen kletsten groote druppels aan de ramen.

En gij: het leven is niet te vertragen.
De bui komt zwaar en driftig nederslaan
Gelukkig wat gered is en geborgen.

Maar ik: zie hoe gerust de rozen staan,
En hemels wreede lafenis verdragen.
Zij dulden sterk en bloeien tegen morgen.

Roland Jooris (1936-)

Density

Haze. Now don't
speak.
Much is kept silent.
Little is much.
Barely the
word barely moves
in the wind
which is nowhere.

Now don't speak.
Don't erase anything.
On the same plane
of evening. Against which
scarcely and nowhere.

From *Still-Leave* (Bladstil). Revolver, 1977.
Translated by Theo Hermans.

Density

Nevel. Zeg
nu niets.
Veel is verzwegen.
Weinig is veel.
Amper beweegt
het woord amper
in de wind
die nergens is.

Zeg nu niets.
Veeg niets uit.
In hetzelfde vlak
van de avond. Waartegen
nauwelijks en nergens.

Lucebert (1924-1994)
Fisherman from Ma Yuan

under clouds birds sail
under waves fly fish
but in between rests the fisherman

waves become high clouds
clouds become high waves
but in the meantime rests the fisherman

From *About the Abyss and the Air Man* (Van de afgrond en de luchtmens).
Amsterdam: De Bezige Bij, 1978
Translated by Peter van de Kamp.

Visser van Ma Yuan

onder wolken vogels varen
onder golven vliegen vissen
maar daartussen rust de visser

golven worden hoge wolken
wolken worden hoge golven
maar intussen rust de visser

Adriaan Morriën (1912-2002)
Snow

The snow's too white for walking in.
Only an animal, with light step
and delicate hooves, should tread there,
under the heavy-laden trees
picking its way over the buried ground.
That would just enhance the stillness.

Only a bird whose raucous screech
prevents the winter sinking down
into the purest innocence,
flying up out of the stillness,
should, now the heavens rest after their bleeding,
make this whole expanse re-echo.

From *Collected Poems* (Verzamelde gedichten). Amsterdam:
Van Oorschot, 1992.
Translated by Tanis Guest.

Sneeuw

De sneeuw is te wit om in te lopen.
Alleen een dier, met fijne hoeven
en lichte tred, zou 't mogen,
om onder de beladen bomen
op de bedolven grond zijn weg te zoeken.
Het zou de stilte nog verhogen.

Alleen een vogel die de winter
verhindert met zijn hese schreeuw
in louter onschuld te verzinken,
opvliegend uit het hart der stilte,
zou nu de hemel uitrust van het bloeden,
de ruimte mogen laten klinken.

Paul van Ostaijen (1896-1928)

Autumn Landscape

An ox and an oxcart move slowly in the mist
stepping through the mist an ox
of the oxcart unfailing its pace
Lost in mist emerging from the mist
on the jerking cart of the driver's slumber
does not lose itself in traceless sleep

Behind the cart a dangling lantern
drives a slight wedge of light into the deep-dark street

From *Collected Works. Poetry 2* (Verzameld werk. Poëzie 2).
Amsterdam: Bert Bakker, 1974.
Translated by Theo Hermans.

Herfstlandschap

In de mist is trage een os met een ossewagen
stappend naast de mist nooit mist zijn maat
de os van de ossewagen
Uit de mist in de mist met de hortende wagen
dut de wagenvoerder zich niet vast
in een spoorloze slaap

Achter aan de wagen drijft lantaarnlicht
een geringe wig van klaarte in de donkerdiepstraat

Erik Spinoy (1960-)

Seascape

It dwells in icecold seas, amongst the flounders,
kelp and shrimp. It sings of icebergs,
frost, the deep cold in a waterfall.
It hides in clothes or skin, with scales
of silvery white. It hankers shyly
to be touched.

Night falls and goes on falling.
No net or hook or elbow moves.
No fin cuts through the surface.

A shiver runs where no one
seems to lie.

From *Whimsies* (Fratsen). Amsterdam: De Arbeiderspers, 1993.
Translated by Tanis Guest.

Marine

In koude zeeën woont het, onder wier
garnaal en bot. Bezingt de ijsberg en
de vorst, de vrieskou in een waterval.
Sluipt in een kleed of huid, van schubben
zilverwit. Verlangt linkshandig naar
een aanraking.

De nacht breekt aan, maar daalt niet neer.
Geen net of haak of arm beweegt.
Geen vin klieft door het oppervlak.

Een rilling loopt, waar nooit
een lichaam was.

ailing

along the Wagenspoor

On the Sea-Road with the Dutch East India Company

Between 1595 – when four ships from Amsterdam sailed around the Cape of Good Hope to Asia – and 1794 – when the last flotilla of ships under the flag of the VOC, the Dutch East India Company, sailed to the East Indies – some 4700 vessels set course for the Orient, while only 3300 ships returned. Considering the discrepancy between these two numbers, and looking at the fate of the first and last ships that left for the East, we might presume that these were hazardous expeditions. Only 87 members of the original crew of 240 sailors of the first fleet returned two years later. Of the last fleet of eight ships only one ship reached its destination, Batavia. The English and French confiscated the others *en route*, except for one ship that was wrecked on the French coast. These bare facts, however, paint a false picture. The first navigation of the Dutch was after all a veritable expedition of discovery, while the last navigation to the Indies under the VOC flag was disrupted by war conditions with England and France. The vast discrepancy in numbers between the outward-bound and homeward-bound ships in the two hundred years of the Company's existence can be explained easily. Many ships were built for use in Asian waters and so remained there until they were finally dismantled.

If we take a closer look at the regular traffic between the ports of Holland and Zeeland in Europe and Batavia, the Company's general *rendezvous* in Asia, over a period of two hundred years, it becomes clear that the navigation to and from the Indies was in fact a very well managed enterprise with – given the ways and means of that period – relatively few shipwrecks and generally speaking a high survival rate of those on board. Exactly such a closer look was taken in the 1970s by a team of historians from Leiden University, when computer-based quantitative analysis of historical research became feasible for the first time. In a three-volume study, which contains a general analysis of the collected data and a detailed survey of all the outward-bound and homeward-bound voyages from the Netherlands to Asia and the Cape of Good Hope, the authors reached the conclusion that, bearing in mind the limitations of sea transport three hundred years ago, a well-organised and basically safe transport link existed between Holland and Java. Notwithstanding its long elaborate lists of data on ship tonnage,

Crew members of the *Peter and Paul*, the Dutch East Indiaman which Czar Peter the Great helped to build – as an anonymous carpenter – during his stay in Holland (detail of a painting by A. Storck, 1698). Nederlands Scheepvaartmuseum, Amsterdam.

departure and arrival dates, numbers of crew and passengers and so on, *Dutch-Asiatic Shipping in the 17th and 18th Centuries* offers fascinating reading for today's armchair traveller who tries to make sense of those numbers with the help of the introductory volume.

Sailing on cockle shells

Another interesting source about the navigation of the ships of the voc is the *Beschryvinge van de Oostindische Compagnie*, a detailed account of the organisation of the Dutch East India Company in five volumes written by the executive director (*advocaat*) Pieter van Dam and presented to the Company management in 1701. The *Beschryvinge* also devotes several chapters to the navigation to and from the Indies. The Institute for Dutch History (ING) has recently republished this originally highly secret manuscript, which was not published until the late 1920s.

But in order to get a true 'historical sensation' of what a trip to the East

The replica of the *Batavia* in Lelystad.

must have been like, a visit to one of the two existing replicas of Dutch East Indiamen that are open to the public in Lelystad and Amsterdam is an absolute must. The landlubber's imagination is fired when he or she crosses the gangplank to the *Batavia*, a colourful, curvy seventeenth-century sea fortress, or for that matter the more austere and functional looking replica of the *Amsterdam*, an eighteenth-century VOC ship. To the traveller who bridges the distance between Schiphol Airport and Soekarno-Hatta Airport in only 14 hours by 400-passenger Boeing 747, the duration of a sea journey from Holland to Java may seem to have taken an age. It took on average two hundred days to reach Java, with a short sojourn at the Cape of Good Hope. Yet three hundred years ago people lived at a much slower pace and thought differently about long distances. Already by the middle of the seventeenth century the navigation of the long voyage to Asia had become so regular, that the sailing route was known as the *karrespoor* or *wagenspoor,* the cart track.

Romantic writers have likened the sailing ships of the past to cockleshells compared with today's container vessels and oil tankers, but while the latter tend to overawe us by their sheer size and businesslike appearance, a wooden sailing ship with its towering masts and rigging emanates a sense of adventure. Indeed, as soon as the visitor to the *Batavia* has stepped on board this sturdy, well-built seventeenth-century square rigger, and peers up at its stout masts and yards and looks down from the railing of the high poop deck at the water some thirty feet below, he or she cannot but feel admiration for the shipwrights and sailors of yore who built and sailed those ships across the oceans. So well organised were the shipyards of the Company that on average one ship was launched every six months on the wharves of Amsterdam and Middelburg. Although there were several types of ships – varying from the heavily built and armed *schip* to the lightly armed *fluit* or the smaller *yacht* , which was often used for patrol missions in Asia, all were built to special qualifications or *charters.* The well-built East Indiamen were the object of everybody's admiration. No wonder sailors used to speak about their ship as if she were a female companion that had to be cared for and steered but which at the same time took care of them in times of distress.

This said, it is still very hard for someone visiting a museum replica to project himself into the travel conditions of the passenger of three hundred years ago, and perhaps even more difficult to put oneself in the wet shoes, or should we say the bare feet, of the sailor of those days. The museum ship lies safely moored in a harbour occasionally stirred slightly by the wake of a passing barge; groups of tourists meekly follow the guides who explain to them a particular feature of the vessel. How different it must have been for those passengers who sailed on a small vessel from Amsterdam all the way to the northern Wadden island of Texel, where the East Indiamen anchored before their departure. Well-sheltered from western winds, the East Indiamen would gather at the Koopvaardersrede (Merchantmen's Roadstead), and wait for a fair easterly wind to blow them safely out to sea, pushing them Godspeed all the way along the white cliffs through the English Channel as far as the wide space of the Atlantic Ocean. In the seventeenth century a large Dutch East Indiaman of 700 tons carried apart from its cargo between 250 and 300 people, i.e. about 140 sailors, 120 soldiers and a dozen passengers. The majority of the sailors came from the Dutch provinces and Scandinavia, but most of the soldiers originated from the German kingdoms. The passengers were generally speaking high officials, the *gequalificeerden*, with their wives and occasionally their children.

Square-rigged sailing ships were notorious for their bad windward capabilities. While a modern sailing yacht can sail as close as 30 degrees to the wind, the windjammers of yore were fortunate if they came as close as 60 degrees. If we take into account that they also drifted considerably and thus made considerable leeway, and needed some thirty minutes to go about when approaching the shore, then it becomes understandable that no captain dared to leave the Dutch estuaries while headwinds were blowing. Woe betide the captain who got caught in a south-westerly gale in the English Channel. If he didn't bear away and run before the storm back to where he came from he ran the risk of wrecking his vessel on the French or English coast, as indeed happened to the skipper of the *Amsterdam* who beached his ship at Hastings, where now, some 250 years later, the ribs of the wooden wreck can occasionally still be seen sticking out of the sands at low tide. Sometimes ship's captains who faced adverse conditions shortly after leaving Holland would gather and decide to sail right round Great Britain by following the island's eastern coast as far as the Shetland Islands and there enter the Atlantic Ocean.

The hazards of travel

It will by now be clear why the navigation of ships heading for the East Indies with large crews of sailors, soldiers and passengers and costly cargoes of silver and gold bullion soon became a highly regulated affair. Generally speaking, three fleets left the Dutch shores annually, respectively around Christmas, Easter, and finally around the time when the September fair was held, this last fleet being appropriately named the *Kermis* or 'Fair' fleet. These fleets always sailed in convoy under a flag admiral who, the weather permitting, frequently held council *en route* with officers of the oth-

The mutiny of the crew of the *Batavia*, which ran amuck after the ship stranded on the Abrolhos, west of Australia, in 1627 (plate from *Voyagie van 't schip Batavia*. Amsterdam, 1647). Nederlands Scheepvaartmuseum, Amsterdam.

er ships to decide on the course to be taken. Often the outward-bound fleets of five to ten East Indiamen were even escorted by warships as far as the Atlantic to make sure that they could reach its deep blue waters.

Vessels were issued with excellent maps, rutters and coastal descriptions which featured beautifully drawn prospects of the coastal promontories together with instructions for sailing routes from Holland to Java, indicating the prevailing winds and currents along the way throughout the seasons, and the ship's officers were ordered to follow these routes unless extraordinary weather conditions forced them to take a different course. On arrival the logbooks would be checked and any deviation from the beaten path had to be accounted for.

These same instructions also detailed the dangers that awaited the ships on the way. First of all there were the navigational hazards, rocks, shallow waters, gales, but also mistakes in the dead reckoning of the position of the ship. The wrecking of the *Batavia* in 1627 at the Abrolhos Islands off the south-western tip of the Australian continent is a case in point. Because it was very difficult to calculate the exact longitudinal position of a vessel at sea as late as the eighteenth century, ships crossing the Indian Ocean in an easterly direction had to be very careful that they did not come to grief off the Australian coast while *en route* to Java. Only after John Harrison had devised a trustworthy chronometer was this navigational conundrum solved.

Another danger that threatened the crew was of course the onslaught of epidemic diseases. One disease which frequently struck sailors when they had to do without fresh food for long periods was scurvy, a nutritional disorder caused by a deficiency of vitamin C and characterised by bleeding gums with loosened teeth, bleeding under the skin and stiffness of the joints.

VOC ships near the Cape of Good Hope (anonymous drawing, late 18th century). Nederlands Scheepvaart-museum, Amsterdam.

Crew members on the deck of an East Indiaman. This sketch was made by Jan Brandes during his return trip from Batavia, where he spent a few years as a Lutheran minister. Rijksmuseum, Amsterdam.

No wonder the Company's management eagerly sought refreshment stations along the route until they took the weighty decision to establish such a settlement at the Cape of Good Hope in 1652.

The pleasant aspect of the Cape Town settlement with its agreeable climate, vegetable gardens and wine farms in the hinterland region of Stellenbosch was noted by many voyagers, including Nicolaus de Graaff, a ship's surgeon who made many journeys to the East. When he visited Table Bay for the first time, however, in 1639, he described it as a *'wild and inhospitable land … without any fruit trees or cultivated acres, but inhabited by wild, heathen, dirty and stinking people'*. Nonetheless, he noted that even then no words could describe the pleasure and joy among the crew when the landfall was sighted: *'the lame, the crippled and those who were able to leave their sickbed came on deck to see the land'*. De Graaff lived long enough to witness the transformation of the settlement in later years. There can be no doubt that the presence of this *'Indische Zeeherberg'* ('Indian sea tavern') saved the lives of many sick sailors. Yet there were also other deadly illnesses for which there was no cure. Typhus and various forms of dysentery led to violent outbreaks of epidemics on board ship for which the ship's surgeons had no treatment.

A third hazard on board the heavily crowded ships was, of course, discipline. So called *ziekentroosters*, comforters of the sick, took care of the religious duties, reading sermons or texts from the Bible to the crew who would frequently gather on the main deck and listen and pray with bowed heads. As the term implies, the comforters of the sick also helped the ship's surgeon in comforting the sick people on board and would direct the last farewell ritual when a dead crew member would be sent overboard in a tarpaulin bag weighted with stones, with the final salute: *'een, twee, drie in Godsnaam!'* ('One, two, three in the name of God!').

But occasionally religious admonition was not enough to keep all the sailors 'straight'. Individual fights might lead to riots, and on occasion even to mutiny. Insubordination occurred quite frequently, most often among crew members of foreign nationality. There were basically two kinds of rebellion: refusal to carry out the daily chores or outright insubordination and seizure of control. The case of the mutiny of the crew of the *Batavia*, which ran amuck after the ship stranded on the Abrolhos, west of Australia, is well known. Mutinies also could occur unexpectedly: at Christmas 1783 the crew of the *Java*, a large East Indiamen, was startled by a mutiny of Asian crew members who tried to subdue the ship's officers who had collected at the poop. There were some 25 Chinese and 25 Javanese crewmen among the 143 sailors on board, roughly one third of the crew. In the skirmish that followed several people, among them the Councillor of the Indies Jacob Radermacher, were killed before the mutineers were dealt with. The *Java* was undoubtedly an unlucky ship. On the way to Java it had already lost 185 of its crew of 289 men to epidemic diseases.

En route

Now that we have reviewed in passing the hazards aboard, let us briefly recapitulate what the route of the average outward-bound trip to the Indies looked like. The first short stop after passing the often stormy Bay of Biscay and Cape Finisterre on the Portuguese coast (Cape Finis Terrae, the end of the world) was at the Cape Verde Islands off the African coast, where fresh water and victuals such as cattle and poultry for consumption on board could be loaded. During the ship's council, which was held while the ships were at anchor waiting for all the ships to reassemble, the decision was taken what

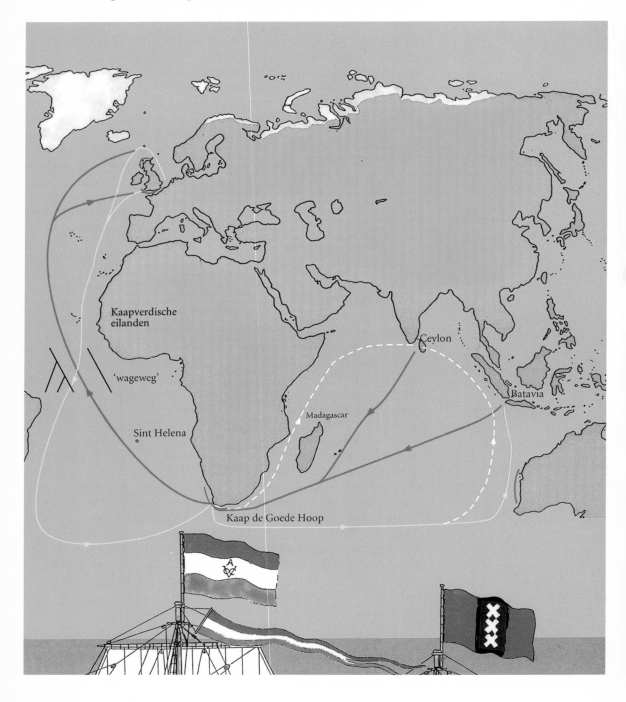

course to steer to reach the next destination, Table Bay at the Cape of Good Hope. Following a north-easterly trade wind as far as the island of Fernando Po off the Brazilian coast, the ships would continue their journey after a shorter or longer pause in the Doldrums – a belt of converging winds along the equator where ships often lay becalmed for days – until they picked up the westerly winds of the southern hemisphere which conducted them close by the islands of Tristan da Cunha towards Cape Town. The journey from Holland to the Cape took on average about four months. After a stop of two or three weeks in which fresh provisions were loaded and infirm crew members were taken ashore to recuperate, the ships would put out to sea again and embark on the last stretch across the Indian Ocean to the Sunda Straits, the thoroughfare between the islands of Sumatra and Java in the Indonesian archipelago.

On the sea-road with the VOC (yellow = route to Batavia; red = return to Holland; green = dangerous spots for wreckage; dotted line = direct routes to Ceylon).

From the Cape the ships of the Dutch East India Company took a quite different route towards Asia than the Portuguese or for that matter the English. While the latter headed for the Indian subcontinent and therefore either followed the eastern coast of Africa or set course for the island of Mauritius in a northerly direction, the VOC ships set out in an easterly direction picking up the 'Brave Westerlies', strong trade winds which took them along the tiny Amsterdam archipelago as far eastward as Australia, where they altered course northwards so as to reach the Sunda Straits with favourable winds and currents. This stretch took on average three months. The first landmark to be sighted was generally the formidable Krakatoa volcano, in the middle of the approaches to the Sunda Strait. Shortly afterwards messages would be exchanged with the VOC watch post of Anjer on the Western tip of Java. From there the Bay of Batavia with its Thousand Islands could be easily reached within a few days. These islands made the bay in front of the city a well-sheltered roadstead and anchorage. Ironically, almost every arrival on the Batavian roadstead brought a few more deaths. Here we are not speaking of those sick people who were already on their deathbeds, but of relatively healthy crew members, who literally stuffed themselves to death with tropical fruit. They could not withstand the temptation of the tasty tropical fruits, which were handed to them by Javanese peddlers who steered their little boats to the newly arrived East Indiaman. Eating a lot of fruit after several months of vitamin deficiency meant instant death.

Of course, for most sailors the voyage did not end at Batavia. They had only just arrived. From the *Generaal Rendez-vous*, as the headquarters of the VOC in Asia were called, they would proceed to other destinations: to Persia or the ports of India to the west, to the many islands of the archipelago itself or northeast to China and Japan, where the redoubtable typhoons were waiting for them. How the sailors felt about their own plight it is hard to know. We have seen that there were occasional mutinies, but some adventurers have also left us their memoirs. Those were the lucky ones who made it back to Europe, and their stories often make wonderful reading. I have already mentioned Nicolaus de Graaff, but he is only one of the writers who wrote up their adventures in the Orient The best way to find out how the sailors felt when they returned home is by listening to the songs they belted out, like this one which was sung on the safe return of 21 East Indiemen in the year 1718:

The 'Lord of Six Weeks': VOC sailors, when they returned home, could afford all kinds of entertainment. When their money was spent, it was time to sign on again (plate by C. Dusart, late 17th century). Nederlands Scheepvaartmuseum, Amsterdam.

Gelyk van aart, is wel gepaart.

C. Dufart inv.   J Gole Exc Amftelodami cum Privilegy.

Hurrah all you young ladies
And good-time girls and whores
Who love to paint the town red
With rough and rowdy boys:
This is your lucky day;
Now you should all be gay,
Get a-swinging and a-singing:
Throw care away!

This happy song of twelve verses in which all the pleasures of coming home and the delights of soft welcoming embraces are described, ends with the sailor inevitably heaving a sigh when he realises that he has spent all his money and that it is time to sign on again and embark on another voyage along the *wagenspoor*.

LEONARD BLUSSÉ

FURTHER READING

BOXER, J.R., *The Dutch Seaborne Empire, 1600-1800*. London, 1965.

BRUIJN, J.R., F.S. GAASTRA and I. SCHÖFFER (eds.), *Dutch-Asiatic Shipping in the 17th and 18th Centuries* (3 vols.). The Hague, 1979-1987.

DAM, PIETER VAN, *Beschryvinge van de Oostindische Compagnie. 7 vols*. Reprint The Hague, 1976.

DASH, MIKE, *Batavia's Graveyard*. Crown Publ., 2002.

GLAMANN, K., *Dutch-Asiatic Trade, 1620-1740*. Copenhagen / The Hague, 1958.

tormy

Weather

Anne Provoost's Ark and Jeroen Brouwers' Houseboat

The floodgates of the heavens are opened

(From *Voyagers on the Ark* by Anne Provoost. In-press Arthur A. Levine Books, an imprint of Scholastic Press, a division of Scholastic Inc. Copyright by Anne Provoost. Reprinted by permission.)

It was the seventeenth day of the second month. All the fountains of the deep broke open. To the sound of howling winds, solid curtains of water came down. There was not only rain, but also hail. The wind raged over the land. Trees bent, chickens were plucked alive on their roosts, tents broke loose, planks and boards were hurled around. The dead floated from the caves where they had been buried.

Our shelter tore apart. The section that was left was just large enough to keep me dry, but my father sat in the rain. From where we were fighting the wind, we could see what was happening to the others. The large group waiting at the base of the ship were taken unawares by the tempest. The gangplank was still out, but guarded by so many warriors with long swords that anyone who set foot on it was immediately beaten back. Many were killed, pushed onto the gangplank by the mass of people and instantly impaled on the spears. Even at that stage, they might appear to be victims of an accident, and most of them still seemed to expect the hatch to be opened soon. There were some who had armed themselves, and practised an assault in the hills. Now they, too, arrived, forming small groups and going around the ship with ladders and ropes to attack it from its unguarded side. But already the chaos was too great. Even armed groups with careful plans were scattered. The hulk they wanted to climb was tall, and the wind against them. Together with hordes of others, they fled up the cliff. They assumed the water could never rise to that height. To be able to overlook the land made them feel certain they would not be taken by surprise. But they were troubled by the wind. They had to lie down to stop themselves being blown into space.

We saw how Zedebab's twin sister was led away from the ship by warriors. And we saw Ham coming up the cliff! We had been waiting for him for a long time. The light was failing and the landscape changing. We had

Jacob van Ruisdael,
Rough Sea. c.1650-1655.
Canvas, 98 x 132 cm.
The Kimbell Art Museum,
Fort Worth (TX).

worried about how he would find the path in this storm, and now we thought he was coming for us. But we were wrong, it was the brushwood a long way below us that he was heading for. Groping around he found a tree stump to which he tied the dog. The animal was sodden with rain and hung its head. I jumped up, my father following me quickly to protect me, and shouted, 'Come on, Ham, come on! The calamity has arrived! What's keeping you?' (…)

And what had to happen happened. With a few slashes at the ropes, the gangplank was cast off. It scraped along the bow, I heard it fall and the screaming of the warriors shook me out of the stupor I had been in through-out the embarkation. With a strength I had not suspected was in me, I kicked the front panel of my cage loose. In his hurry, Ham had not shut the barred door of the pen properly and it swung open as soon as I pushed against it. I searched for a way up. I climbed stairs and ramps. I got to the deck via one of the trapdoors, probably not the normal way, but the ship was shaking too much to look for anything else. I could barely stay upright out there, the wind tugged at my body and I had to use both hands to hang on to the edge of barrels full of rain water.

Under the gangplank lay warriors. Many had been killed by the fall. Of those that had stood below, some died because the storm hurled rocks against their heads or drove sharp pieces of wood through their bodies. They were the lucky ones: they perished quickly and from a cause they could, in their final moments, comprehend. Those who were still alive now were gripped by despair. The notable, the distinguished, the warriors, the tradesmen, they all rushed the ship. They hit its sides with their fists, they shouted curses which could be heard deep inside the ship, they pressed against the bow like dogs. And the children, all those boys and girls who used to hang around the ship hoping to be given a pitch doll, they screeched like animals.

When the ship was lifted off the ground, the hold resounded, even more than before, with the screams of creatures in terror of death. Never before had they felt the ground move under their legs. They were not used to their bleating, bellowing, barking and twittering reverberating against the inner wall of the ship. And the thunderclaps now followed each other so rapidly they were like their own echoes. The wake of the ark caused small boats to break their moorings and drift. They either took in water or capsized. All around floated rafts with people hanging on.

The Builder shouted at them, 'The Unnameable, who knows no regret, has been driven to regret. He regrets that it had to come to this.' And the hatch closed.

Then the god of the Builder opened the floodgates of the heavens. The land which he had divided from the water when he created the world, was now joined to it once more. The water came from the east and the west, from the south and the north. Whirlpools and eddies formed, there were clouds of spume, masses of silt and foam rolled towards us. The air became briny. Far away, tempestuously rising rivers broke their banks. The water smashed stones and rocks. The sea came rolling inland. The ark yawed and listed. The people were washed off the cliff. Everything that was outside the ship disappeared.

I could not see anything any more because I was enclosed by spume. I knew that another tidal wave would wash me off the deck. I had to go back. I did not have time to go down the ladder, and plunged into the depths through the well-hole. Crawling on my belly, I reached the pen. I wanted to get back inside the hutch, it was, all things considered, the best place. But the ark was pitching and yawing so hard that I found it impossible to get through the small opening. As soon as I attempted to, I rolled against my fellow inmates, who screeched and beat their wings tumultuously and wounded me with their beaks and claws. If only I had the cushion, I thought, but I could not reach it. My head and shoulders hit the wall, now to starboard, now to port.

The tempest went on endlessly. Whenever the roar subsided momentarily, there was still a continuous dull rumbling. Then you could hear people shouting, 'Here! Over here!' They all drowned, those people who thought they would fare differently, who did not realise that exceptions are not always possible. No matter how talented, how skilled, how determined in their thinking, they drowned. I managed to get a firm hold by hooking my hands and arms in the bars. The water smashed against the hull, shaking the planks of its outer skin. With my feet braced against a rafter I experienced the way the water gathered its force, exhausted it, gathered it again and exhausted it again, in a rhythm of effortless patience.

The rumbling and the lightning ceased. A shaken silence remained, together with the sour smell of vomit. I heard nothing but the raging of the wind and the thundering of the waves against the bow. My first sorrow was not for my father or Put. I was convinced they were in the ark. My first sorrow was for Camia, the little, dancing girl who now floated somewhere in the water. With much pain and effort, I got up and went back to the deck. It was night, but because burning particles were still falling out of the sky, I was able to see. There were animals that could swim and followed the ship for a long time: dogs, beavers, geese, hippopotamuses, crocodiles. Of people able to swim there were none, there were only those who had got a hold on the small boats that floated here and there. The rich had the best boats. They were made out of sound timber and had partitions to stop the water streaming in. They were leaking all the same, and sink they did in the end. The parents jumped overboard to save the children. But even that weight was too much for the boats. And so the last ones to float on the surface of the water were mainly children, wearing well-made woollen clothes and pearl ornaments round their wrists.

ANNE PROVOOST

From *Voyagers on the Ark* (De arkvaarders). Amsterdam: Querido, 2001, pp. 207-208 / 213-215.
Translation © John Nieuwenhuizen.

Zuiderparkbad, The Hague, 1938. Photo © Henk van der Horst / Nederlands Fotoarchief, Rotterdam.

Sloops full of seawater

Five or six sheets of the month-to-a-page calendar ('Windmills in the Dutch Landscape') further. Late summer, yet all the trees stood bare and shivering in the latest of countless storms rolling in from the sea.

All year such storms had raged periodically throughout Europe, breaking suddenly, lasting for days or even weeks. The result was traffic and other types of chaos: the hurricane-force winds hoisted cars up bodily and flung them down some distance away like dinky toys. Pedestrians, cyclists, roofs, entire public gardens sailed through the sky, while on the other hand planes plummeted from it. Stricken birds – rudders out of action, navigation equipment disabled, compasses gone haywire – propelled through the air like

scraps of paper, encountered congregations of fish. Even though it did not rain constantly, broad lakes of water swept across the landscape, as if scooped up, bathtubs at a time, from the sea and other liquid-retaining basins and launched through the air with living denizens and all. In this coastal region the salt liquid clung like silvery posters the colour of snail slime to the houses and trees, the surface of the road and the flat fields outside my windows, so that one seemed to be living in a dream landscape as sinister as it was foul-smelling.

Everything had happened before and been described or represented in some other way. There was nothing left to imagine that had not happened and was not related to hundreds of other events that had either taken place previously or would occur in the future.

For instance, in a sensational article in *National Geographic* lavishly illustrated with colour photographs, my old university contemporary, Professor Sibelijn, had furnished proof that subterranean cave drawings, unimaginable aeons old, depict flying saucers and extraterrestrials equipped with antennae. After this his glorious reputation as a great scientist seemed established once and for all in the international annals of his subject. First that celebrated Stone, which he had unearthed in his youth, and now Martians in prehistoric caves. Nico's double whammy: his glasses slid down his nose too often, so that he did not always see things clearly. Poor pitiable Nico.

In the paper I read an essay, translated from French, about the constantly lurking storms, together with the incidental catastrophes they provoked, earthquakes, dike bursts, floods, apocalyptic gales, by another authority – some kind of scientific theologian from the school of Teilhard de Chardin. Using statistics on the phases of the moon and spring tides, the writer demonstrated that such stormy conditions always prevailed around the turn of a century and that the face of the earth was thus periodically renewed, in accordance with God's intention, just as a housewife sets to work with a feather duster and bucketfuls of suds with an analogous passion reminiscent of storms at the approach of spring.

My eyes nearly popped out of my head.

With the presently prevailing natural phenomenon, claimed the essayist, an ex-member of the Society of Jesus, the environment was functioning as a sponge that wiped clean all the slates of the preceding hundred years, so that the century now dawning, like a new school year, could start afresh, blown clean, washed by rain, laundered, cleansed, etcetera. Examples of tempests, deluges, celestial fires from 1897, 1780, 1692 and even further back. Now that we were taking leave not only of a century but of a millennium, according to this Nostradamus based at the university of Lille, the storms were occurring with tenfold force, as had also happened in 999 and 1089.

Absolutely fascinating.

Bored, I folded the newspaper and thought for a quarter of a second of J.J.J. Möser.

The connection between the accession in the last year of the first millennium of Pope Silvester the Second, the prototype of Doctor Faustus, and the evaporation of the ozone layer at the end of the second, discussed in relation to the St Elisabeth's Day Flood.

Those were the kinds of question he asked. Preferably me.

In the view of the psychiatrist Dr. A. Weldon it was here that the concrete foundation was laid under my uncertainties and anxieties. Again he prescribes me a pound of pills, which I do not take. The drivel people talk!

Personally, the storms did not bother me at all, the boat was stuck immovably in the bed of the canal, through which, it was true, the water gushed slightly more turbulently than usually, sweeping ducks and other waterfowl along with it like items on a conveyor belt. On the roof, onto which the rains and buckets of liquid transported from elsewhere clattered noisily, the mast of the television aerial bent submissively with the pushing and tugging of the gusts of wind, having been expertly rigged. Everything remained firmly in place, as did the ship itself, the taut metal cables with which it was moored to both banks, albeit unnecessarily, sang like Aeolian harps. The wooden outer skin, which I had painted only last spring, green, to distract myself with manual work from the pain of faded dreams of love, showed the salty patches that shone like enamel, more and more of which appeared as the wind transported ever more sloops full of seawater through. Gradually our abode took on the aspect of a shell.

Outside the dog and I prevented each other from being blown away by staying linked by the lead. One could lean into the wind, just as one can lean on hope and illusions in a depression. When there was no gale blowing and there was no danger of her being carried into space like a kite, the dog was let off the lead, as she had been used to being all her life. Once she came back from the fields that seemed covered with sperm with a still thrashing plaice in her jaws.

Apart from that nothing happened. Black four on red five, red ten on black jack, the seven of diamonds that has been hiding for ages can go on the eight of clubs so that the six of clubs can finally change places and is no longer blocking progress. There are days when you can't finish a single game. Which is not the slightest bit different from days when you can.

I was back in the vacuum of Nico Sibelijn's inaugural lecture – there was nothing but howling emptiness, both outside me and within.

JEROEN BROUWERS

From *Secret Rooms* (Geheime Kamers). Amsterdam: Atlas, 2000, pp. 151-155.
Translated by Paul Vincent.

lose

the Sluices!

So you think we've told you everything about the Low

Countries and Water?

Water may be '*best*', as Pindar observed around 500 BC, but against that one has to set W.C. Fields' riposte that '*fish fuck in it*'. For there are some who hold the view that, as a rule, water should only be drunk in moderation and that any other contact with it should be limited to what is hygienically necessary. I too am a bit of a hydrophobe. Or perhaps it's just that water and I do not mix. Even as a child, geography lessons on sluices, polders and dams were guaranteed to make my attention wander. Boating? Wasted on me. Swimming? It just gave you nasty wrinkly fingers. Do I need to tell you that as a child I was not exactly keen on trips to the seaside? People belong on land, not in water, which is the domain of all kinds of weird fishes and other unearthly creatures. Furthermore, they can move around in it far more quickly and gracefully than you or I.

Perhaps it's because I'm Flemish. For, and let's be clear about this, stories about the Low Countries and water are in fact almost always stories about the Netherlands and water. Flanders, the region of Belgium that con-

Children swimming in the Zenne, near the Flemish village of Nieuwmolen, c.1900. Collection of G. Abeels.

tains the entire 67 kilometres of Belgium's short coastline, has an extremely modest maritime past. In *Ships Galore. Maritime Museums in the Netherlands and Belgium* (Schepen bij de vleet. Maritieme Musea in Nederland en België, 1966), we read: '*Apart from the three maritime museums described here, there are very few museums in Belgium that have any maritime objects of importance.*' This hurtful observation follows a survey of several dozen Dutch maritime museums ranging from the impressive Maritime Museum in Amsterdam to the tiny Fiskerhúske in the Frisian village of Moddergat.

Ordinary lads

There are other things that the Netherlands has in plenty that Flanders has not: naval heroes, for instance. Of course, this is played down, sometimes even denied, by the Dutch. It was no accident that an exhibition on four centuries of naval warfare held at Amsterdam's Maritime Museum in 2000 was entitled *What Do You Mean, Heroes?* (Helden, hoezo?). Romanticism gets short shrift from the down-to-earth Dutch. For although Michiel de Ruyter, Maarten Tromp and Piet Heyn lie entombed in stately marble, at heart they were just ordinary lads from 'back home'. According to an eyewitness De Ruyter, who became the hero of Chatham after sailing up the Medway in 1667 and making things rather difficult for the English, set aside some time after a naval victory to clean out his own cabin and feed his chickens. Tromp, who defeated the second Spanish Armada in 1639, began his career as a cabin boy and even languished for a time as a galley slave. And Piet Heyn, who captured the Spanish treasure fleet off the Cuban coast in 1628, was the son of a fisherman. Ordinary lads ... whose names are now given to streets and ships, and even grace the signboards of the now internationally notorious *coffeeshops*. Furthermore, De Ruyter was the first non-member of the Orange family to appear on a postage stamp, in 1907. Although Piet Heyn, for his part, had to wait a very long time to be honoured by a statue in his birthplace Delfshaven, he could always depend on a loyal body of fans. At dead of night on 8 January 1868, three men from Delfshaven built a statue of Piet in snow and ice to protest against the disgraceful neglect of their hero. It melted after 5 days, but the townspeople were so enthused that a real statue just had to follow.

And Flanders? Sheer knavery! Soon after being appointed commander of the fleet in 1629, Piet Heyn lost his life in a routine skirmish with Flemish pirates from Ostend. In Flanders even the most unlikely Dutchman became a hero. On 5 February 1831, during the conflict that followed Belgium's break from the Netherlands in 1830, a Dutch gunboat approaching Antwerp was blown aground in the Scheldt estuary by a sudden gust of wind making it possible for the Belgians to swarm aboard. The gunboat's commander, Jan Carel Josephus van Speyk, seeing that there was no escape ('*in that case, I'd rather be blown to bits*') plunged his cigar into a barrel of gunpowder. Only five of the crew of thirty-one survived the explosion and Van Speyk himself – a humble orphan from Amsterdam with a modest service record – became an instant hero, with a lighthouse in Egmond aan Zee as his personal monument. The solemn reburial of an '*identifiable piece of his anatomy*' in the Nieuwe Kerk in Amsterdam was a national event of unparalleled ceremony.

Waterlanders

The relationship between the Netherlands and water has also often been the subject of ridicule and disapproval. There is Andrew Marvell's well-known description of the Netherlands as '*this indigested vomit of the sea*'. James Boswell, whose father made him study law in Utrecht before setting out on the *Grand Tour*, noted in 1763: '*Consider Holland as the dark watery passage which leads to an enchanted and brilliant grotto*'. And when the Netherlands were ruled by Louis Bonaparte at the start of the nineteenth century, the French justified the annexation by claiming that the Low Countries were no more than an alluvial deposit of the great French rivers.

All of this has done nothing to discourage the Dutch from exploiting that water to typecast themselves. '*We, the Dutch, and water have something going between us*', declared the brochure for Children's Book Week 2002 during which the main theme was books on boats, under the slogan '*Aye, Aye Captain*'. That 'something' is an understatement. Just read what Amsterdam's burgomaster Cohen had to say on the occasion of Prince Willem-Alexander's wedding in February 2002: '*Water plays a major role in your life. You chose to do your national service with the Royal Marines and you have devoted the past few years to water management, both in this country and abroad (...) Not only does running water attract your interest, so in equal measure does frozen water. You completed the Frisian Elfstedentocht in 1986 and you still enjoy skating. Furthermore, and that is why we are all*

Jacobus Schoemaker Doyer, *Jan van Speyk Decides Whether or Not to Put the Spark to the Tinder*. c.1835. Canvas, 89 x 75 cm. Rijksmuseum, Amsterdam.

Seventeenth-century French print, showing skaters in Flanders ('*Exercice sur la glace en Flandres*'). Bibliothèque nationale de France, Paris.

here, you asked your princess to marry you on the slippery ice of the Huis Ten Bosch Palace. In short, you are a man of the water, and to underline that I have been told that today the stars are in the sign of Aquarius.' And for those who might still have doubts: being a waterlander, the heir to the throne is a true Dutchman. Furthermore, he is no mean skater and skating, according to a review of Wiebe Blauw's *Van glis tot klapschaats* (2001), is the number one popular entertainment in the Netherlands. Even though Blauw has to concede humbly in his exhaustive survey of 567 skate makers, manufacturers and brands in the Netherlands that the wooden skate was originally a Flemish invention. But after that – and the Frisians will also not enjoy this – it was the Hollanders who enthusiastically took it over to achieve well-known sporting success. Not for nothing does one find on the Royal Library's website in The Hague an extensive dossier devoted to the Netherlands and the Winter Olympics. Skating is such a serious business that since 2000 a '*literary periodical for skaters and readers*' has been published. Initially entitled *Glad IJs* (Thin Ice), the name had to be changed to *Zwart IJs* (Black Ice) because a commercial bureau had claimed the original name. Popular Entertainment Number One, indeed.

Skating also plays an important role in Mary Mapes Dodge's *Hans Brinker or the Silver Skates. A Story of Life in Holland* (1865). In this American children's book, Hans Brinker and his sisters set out to win a skating competition. But the book also contains a story within the story about Peter, the son of a lock-keeper from Haarlem, who saves the Netherlands from being flooded by putting his finger in a hole in the dike. Eventually, this Peter became confused with the chief protagonist of Dodge's tale so that for innumerable American readers Hans Brinker came to symbolise '*the spirit of the whole country*'. In the Netherlands itself the story was not particularly well-known, but to meet the expectations of American tourists a statue of 'Hans

Brinker' was erected in 1950 with the inscription: '*Dedicated to our youth, to honour the boy who symbolises the perpetual struggle of Holland against the water*'. And so yet another hero was created for a people who claim not to like heroes. Anyway, he is a more edifying example than that other little boy in Brussels, the Belgian icon Manneke Pis ('Little Peeing Man'), who emits a constant stream of water while excited tourists queue up to take photographs of this piece of bronze impudence. As a hydrophobe, one almost wishes that little Hans would return and put his finger against *that*.

Enemy and Ally

It is no coincidence that in 1995 Schokland, once an island in the reclaimed North-East Polder, was the first piece of the Netherlands to be added to UN-ESCO's World Heritage list. It is an archeological monument: land that has been defended strenuously against the water and is finally reclaimed from that same water. The prehistoric mounds, the medieval reclamations, the Afsluitdijk which turned the Zuiderzee into the IJsselmeer between 1927 and 1932 are all examples of the Dutch trying to improve on Creation. The showpiece of this struggle against water is the Delta Plan. In the wake of the disaster of 1 February 1953, this plan, which was only completed in 1997, was designed to defend the Dutch river deltas against storm surges from the North Sea. New sluices were built and the dikes were raised. But the most spectacular part of the Delta Plan is the storm surge barrier in the Eastern Scheldt, which can be opened and closed like a gigantic door to control the water during storms and unusually high tides. In spite of growing concerns about its ecological impact, the Delta Plan enjoys world renown as one of the largest examples of hydraulic engineering in the world and remains an object of national pride.

Velserbroek, the Bridge.
2000.
Photo by Ellen Kooi /
TORCH Gallery,
Amsterdam.

The same cannot be said of the Belgian Sigma Plan, of whose existence most Belgians are entirely ignorant. The February storm of 1953 also took about a dozen Flemish lives but that did not lead to any noteworthy defen-

The IJzer, South-West Flanders. Photo by Stephan Vanfleteren.

sive measures. Not until 1976, when a northwesterly storm drove a massive quantity of seawater up the Scheldt, did the Belgian government finally act. It set up the Sigma Plan, a *work in progress* that drew inspiration from the Delta Plan. Raised dikes and controlled flood areas are intended to prevent the North Sea from inflicting further damage along the Scheldt estuary.

Water must constantly be fought against, but it can also be a comrade-in-arms. In the mid-sixteenth century the idea occurred of using it to defend large parts of Holland. This led to the creation of the Old Holland Water Line. By inundating large stretches of land, the advance of any enemy force could be significantly impeded. Fortifications defended the points at which the water would be let in to the Line. In 1672 the Water Line did indeed prevent Louis XIV's army from advancing into Holland, but the water proved a fickle ally. A severe frost around Christmas turned the protecting waters into a solid floor of ice over which the French were able to launch an attack on Leiden and The Hague. A couple of days later, however, there was a sudden thaw which left the French soldiers not only surrounded by water and Dutch troops, but also cut off from reinforcements. But the water froze again in time for the next French assault. Between 1815 and 1940 work on the creation of an improved successor to the Old Holland Water Line was unceasing. The New Water Line ran for more than 85 kilometres east of Utrecht from the Zuiderzee to the Biesbosch. But unlike its predecessor its defensive qualities were never put to the test. In 1940 the Luftwaffe flew safely over the water and dropped their paratroops neatly behind the line.

The Belgians too have in the past used water against the enemy, though in a more improvised manner. At the outbreak of the First World War in 1914, the great rivers such as the Maas and the Scheldt did little to hamper the progress of the German army. But when the Belgian army was beaten back behind the much smaller river IJzer in South-West Flanders, the Belgian commanders hit on the idea – which was actually suggested by a lock-keeper, Karel Cogghe – of opening Nieuwpoort's sea sluices at high tide so as to flood the plain of the IJzer. The martial *Sturm und Drang* of the Germans simply got stuck in the mud.

The call of the briny deep

The dearest wish of the Dutch writer J. Slauerhoff was to go to sea. As a student in Amsterdam, he slept in a ship's bunk in his room. He treated his friends to 'shipwreck wine' that was supposed to have come from a ship that had run aground. From 1924 he sailed the world's oceans as a ship's doctor, a twentieth-century reincarnation of the Flying Dutchman, because, as he wrote, '*Holland's no place for me to live*'. In many cases, however, the hankering to sail away is very far from a romantic dream. Holland's whalers, who in the first half of the seventeenth century lived in the most appalling conditions on Jan Mayen Island and Spitsbergen, did so for the highly prized fat and oil of the 'floating florin-banks'. The fishermen from West Flanders who from 1849 until the 1930s went on six-month voyages to what the poet Guido Gezelle called '*Iceland's cold and barren shores*', were inspired solely by the compelling laws of supply and demand. And although seamen in the service of the East India Company may have made important botanical, geographical and technical discoveries, their motives too were primarily mercenary. The Company was the first Dutch multinational, and the first to introduce the homeland to the pleasures of nutmeg, coffee, tea and even slippers. When an Ostend Company was formed in Flanders in 1723 and succeeded in dominating the European tea trade for a number of years, the competing Netherlanders, helped by the equally annoyed English, made sure that the company was permanently banned in 1731. Clearly, the sea is not open to everyone.

Cornelis de Man, *The Whale-Oil Factory on Jan Mayen Island.* 1639. Canvas, 108 x 205 cm. Rijksmuseum, Amsterdam.

But although nowadays the great oceans may no longer constitute the 'fi-

nal frontier', and everything appears to have been mapped out, it is nevertheless primarily among our contemporaries that we must look for the true *aquanauts*, those who love water for water's sake. The industrial age's urge to explore has been completely replaced by a spirit of competition and achievement. In 1974, the Fleming Fons Oerlemans spent three weeks bobbing about on the Atlantic Ocean as a voluntary castaway. A year later he crossed the same ocean on a raft in 82 days, and in 1982 he attempted to beat the 32-year-old transatlantic speed record in a home-made hydrofoil that looked like a gigantic bottle. Between 1978 and 1985 the Dutchman Henk de Velde made his first voyage round the world in a Wharam catamaran. Later he set his sights on yet more records. In 1992 he set out in a bright yellow catamaran named *Zeeman* (nothing to do with the Dutch word for 'seaman'; that was the name of the clothing company that sponsored him). The Belgians Dixie Dansercoer and Alain Hubert have ventured onto the water in all its different manifestations. In 1998 they walked nearly 4,000 kilometres right across Antarctica. In 2002 they attempted to repeat the feat at the North Pole, but this time without success: drifting ice, thin ice, too much open water and bad-tempered polar bears combined to spoil the party.

In the twenty-first century we can of course still enjoy adventure, and in much greater safety. Through www.hollandsglorie.nl (named after Jan de Hartog's 1940 novel about heroism on seagoing tugboats) one can sign up for a day, a weekend, a week or longer on an old-fashioned sailing ship. The claim is that '*The proud days of the sailing ship have returned. Once again the sails of clippers, tjalks, schooners and barges billow on the horizon.*' No sailing experience needed, travel and cancellation insurance recommended...

The Fishermen's Monument in Ostend.

Epilogue

I am standing on the dike at Ostend, a Flemish resort with the somewhat off-putting attractiveness of faded glories. Behind me stands the Fishermen's Monument; in front of me is the sea, shrouded in a thick mist. As in Ad Windig's photograph on the cover of this book, you can only sense its presence. Well, not exactly. You can hear it and smell it too, of course. But that is more than enough. There is quite enough water in that bloody mist: condensed water vapour, but still it's always the same H_2O. I am reconciled to my hydrophobia. I get into the car and drive inland. As far as I am concerned, the sluices can all close now.

FILIP MATTHIJS
Translated by Chris Emery.

Hotel Normandie,
Oostduinkerke. Photo by
Stephan Vanfleteren.

ootballs,

Bikes and Heroes

Johan Cruijff and Eddy Merckx

In Belgium, and especially Flanders, football and cycling are the favourite sports, and the same goes for the Netherlands. Up in Northern Holland, though, there are times when skating manages to squeeze into first place. The Winter King Ard Schenk reigned over the icy Netherlands for a number of years. And the House of Orange's Prince Willem-Alexander even participated, more or less incognito, in the legendary Elfstedentocht skating marathon. Skating in winter and cycling in summer; though these activities are increasingly becoming spring and autumn affairs.

Cycling is a very popular sport throughout the Netherlands. In the old days cycle racing was mainly confined to the south and the Catholic enclaves in and around Amsterdam, with Gerrie Kneteman as the star. Hennie Kuiper, Jan Raas and the tour cyclist Joop Zoetemelk were all top athletes in their day, and each of them became world champion of the road at one time or another. A world title is the very highest distinction for a cyclist, an honour previously achieved also by Jan Janssen. In the field of track cycling, or cycling on the *piste*, comparable titles were also held by Gerrit Schulte, Arie van Vliet and Jan Derksen, all of whom were products of the war gen-

Johan Cruijff is about to score the opening goal for Ajax in the European Cup Final against Inter Milan in 1972.

eration. But none of them could be called 'the absolute king of cycling'. In other words, none of them became a living legend. Unlike Johan Cruijff, who did just that, and remained a legend even after his football career had ended. Cruijff, the football player without parallel, unsurpassed in all his feats on the football fields of the Netherlands and far beyond. Johan Cruijff, Holland's Glory in football boots, the undisputed number 1 (in shirt number 14!) of national football, the number 1 popular sport.

A cannibal in Belgium

We shall have more to say about Johan Cruijff, the phenomenon and role model, later on. First, though, let us cross the often imaginary border that separates the Netherlands and Belgium. Here we have more football, a lot of football, with a national team that is more truly 'Belgian' than any other group or movement in the country. With top figures from past and present all lined up: Jef Mermans, Rik Coppens, Paul van Himst, Wilfried van Moer, Jan Ceulemans, Jean-Marie Pfaff and now perhaps also Emile Mpenza.

As far as interest and number of players is concerned, here, in the bottommost of the Low Countries, football is clearly also the favourite sport. But has any Belgian footballer ever had the status of a Johan Cruijff? Not one! Van Himst comes fairly close, but as soon as we look beyond the country's borders he fades into insignificance. Rik Coppens was the brightest talent, but also a George Best *avant la lettre*. And when Bill Gormlie was coach, Jef Mermans paved the way for the later successes of Anderlecht and the national team in the early fifties; but he – unjustly – is almost forgotten today.

There is no Cruijff in Belgium, no footballer who became an icon for the entire nation, but instead, and in contrast to the Netherlands, there is a Belgian cyclist. And that, of course, is Eddy Merckx. The finest cyclist in the country, of all generations, all countries. Respectfully known as 'the cannibal' because of his unquenchable thirst for victory and his truly unsurpassed record: he won every race he ever wanted to win, not only once, but twice

A warrior's rest: Eddy Merckx makes himself comfortable after yet another success.

or more. When Belgians talk of the Big Three, Eddy Merckx, the unrivalled tour cyclist, easily outstrips the other two: Rik van Steenbergen and Rik van Looy. The lively battle they fought, sometimes against each other, and from generation to generation, made the three of them hugely popular. Enthusiasm developed into passion, and their supporters experienced a degree of excitement that Belgian football players never managed to arouse in their followers. Many see cycling as the sport that has penetrated the heart, some say the very soul, of the people far more deeply than any other. Because of his fighting spirit Rik van Looy in particular touched the heart of the Flemish underdog, so that the common people copied the popular cycling press and loudly proclaimed this product of the Kempen the 'Emperor of Herentals'. Until Eddy Merckx, who hailed from Brussels, established himself on the cycling throne. Eddy Merckx, the Belgian *par excellence*. Of Flemish extraction, he felt totally at home in Brussels and became the champion of all Belgians. Their icon.

Johan Cruijff and Eddy Merckx: the sporting icons of the Low Countries. And incontestably so, for there was no question of any choice or preference. They forced themselves upon us, both of them, on observers and fans alike. Their rivals, and those who preceded them and followed them, had to acknowledge it. However, it must be said that all this applies only to their own countries. For Cruijff, although one of the greatest players in Europe, on a par with figures such as Beckenbauer and Platini, close to being one of the top players in the world, was nevertheless outstripped by Pele, Di Stefano and Maradona. In the Netherlands Van Basten, Gullit and others ran him close, but he outdid Lenstra and Wilkes.

Merckx was the best in the world in his field, but then again his sport is not as widely practised internationally as football. Although in cycle racing there is less competition even at the top level, what is so phenomenal about Eddy Merckx is that he always saw himself as his own toughest competition. Winning was never enough; there always had to be more victories, with an even greater lead. Even in defeat he refused to submit to the tormentor within him, that other diabolical Merckx who could never be reconciled to losing. More than anything, Merckx was a tormented sportsman, always at war with himself and his doubts about winning and losing. Indeed, contentment was not part of his nature; in his own mind he could always have done better.

The footballer-saviour

Cruijff was different. He was not one to torture himself like Merckx. He acted out of his own self-confidence, challenging others and seeking conflict, only to emerge as the winner. It was something he did as a player; he even did it to his own team-mates with Ajax or the Dutch national team, where he more or less chased away such gentler characters as goalkeeper Jan van Beveren and the goal-scorer Van der Kuylen. Johan – the unshortened name by which the football world came to know him – had no great respect for referees either. Even before Ruud Gullit coined the word '*bobos*' to describe league and club managers, Johan had already spoken scathingly of these authority-figures and in one interview he said that he had never yet caught

Ajax chairman Jaap van Praag telling the truth. Later, as a coach, he was able to impose his own stubborn perceptions and ideas even on well-known players in such a way that some of them got sick of it and left. Like Frank Rijkaard, who nevertheless continued to respect Johan Cruijff for his opinions and as a person.

Cruijff's arrogant ideas and actions had their roots in his upbringing in Betondorp ('Concrete Town') on the outskirts of Amsterdam. A child of the streets who lost his father at a very early age, he moved with his mother to the Meer, which was home base to Ajax until well into the nineties. A skinny boy in the fifties, by the time he was 17 or 18 he was already playing in

Ajax's first team. He was full of suggestions and advice to other players, quick and skilled in evading the opposition, and had an incredible feeling, call it an instinct, for the use of space. And the wealth of comments too, the chattering on the pitch and the inimitable and incomprehensible explanations after the match. He never lost his youthful arrogance; it went with him from Amsterdam (Ajax) to (FC) Barcelona and back again. In every situation he remained the pure Amsterdammer, a contemporary of the protesting *provos* of yesteryear, but more working-class, lacking in education but certainly not in wisdom. In his own way he was a rebel, and looking back it would seem that 'Cruijffie', as he was known even to the so-called 'better-class' public, also helped to achieve a social breakthrough. Johan symbolised the grievances and desires of a rebellious younger generation. Armed with the ball, an outward show of flair and bluff and the free speech that went with it, he set out to achieve what he and his generation desired: money and status. In his case status and, who knows maybe even a statue. The Football Player. The Saviour; in Spanish, '*El Salvador*'. The problem with the statue was that it would have to be alive; as lively as Johan was in real life.

Cruijffese

If Johan lives to be hundred, he will still be a boy with a football. He is well into his fifties now, but we still see the street child in his face. Especially in his eyes. But the nervous tic that precedes or follows the rapid flow of words almost every second betrays his vitality. Although he no longer coaches and has no active involvement in the game, he is nevertheless wholly committed to it. He *is* football, and no matter what he imagines – and he claims he knows about everything – Johan Cruijff does know about football. His knowledge is based on two things: the speed with which he thinks and acts, in other words his ability in action or *Tatenkraft*, and his instinct; that nigh infallible feeling for using the space on a pitch. Being ahead of the others, avoiding problems or solving them, a step earlier or a step sideways. This is something that is part of him; he learned it very early on and honed it playing for Ajax and Barcelona, Ajax again and then very briefly for Feyenoord. And it won him cups and titles everywhere. But not with the national team, for in the 1974 World Cup Final they lost to the host country, West Germany. It was as if his football intelligence had briefly deserted him. Which must have also been the case in his farewell match for Ajax against Bayern Munich when they lost 8-0 (!). Once more it was the Germans who punished him. But they could not take away his three European Cup victories. Later, following in the footsteps of his former mentor Rinus Michels as coach for Barcelona, he again won national titles and the highest European trophy, though there were conflicts and defeats there too. Over the years his intuition has become mixed with a certain degree of rancour, which has helped the older Cruijff to keep his opinionated edge. You still notice this in his football commentaries, when he appears as a guest commentator on Dutch television. In both the Netherlands and Belgium, masses of viewers snort with enjoyment, or at times with irritation, though almost everyone admits to being won over, partly because of his unique, inimitable and sometimes

Bringing home the loot: Johan Cruijff (m.), Ruud Krol (r.) and Mayor Samkalden of Amsterdam lifting the European Cup for the Amsterdam people to see (1972).

incomprehensible use of language. *Cruijffese*. Cruijff, the inventor of a football language all his own.

The hidden force

And now we return to Eddy Merckx. In the first place, he is far more inhibited in his use of language, mixing up two of Belgian's three national languages, French and Dutch. He is the eldest child of Flemish, or rather Brabant, parents who were forced to move from their village to the – to them – foreign city of Brussels because of the war. At home the family spoke dialect and a smattering of French, and at school little Eddy spoke only French. The later cycling champion also inherited his father's reticence. Deeds not words, that was their motto. His was a quiet ambition, but all the stronger for that. Having started by becoming Belgian novices champion, he was then world amateur champion, three times world professional champion, winner of almost every classic race several times over, and five times overall winner of both the Tour de France and the Giro d'Italia, the two most prestigious stage competitions (or tours) in international cycle racing.

His unique record of achievement speaks volumes. It is generally accepted that Eddy Merckx is the greatest racing cyclist of all time. And indeed, he outdoes all others in his results and the way he achieved them. Above all, he had an irrepressible urge to surpass himself. Perhaps the illustrious Fausto Coppi, first a war hero then *campionissimo*, had a more magical aura and there was more tragedy to be seen in his martyr's face. Indeed, the fragile mechanism of his body, wasted by illness and fever, lasted no more than 40 years.

Eddy Merckx was consumed by racing fever. He broke almost every record there was, and in doing so taxed his body and soul to the utmost. Merckx was constantly extending his limits. Until he could go no further,

Eddy Merckx (left, of course) busy training.

The wedding of Eddy Merckx and Claudine Acou on 5 December 1967.

and gave up speed cycling at the age of 32. His spirit was no longer able to goad his body into performing great deeds. It was finished.

The young Merckx was born immediately after the war in 1945, barely two years before Cruijff (1947-). One grew up in Brussels, the other in Amsterdam. In some ways they were comparable, and in others completely different. The Merckx family joined the ranks of the self-employed, with the prospect of a better future for the children. Education was the way to that future, and the eldest son Eddy applied himself to his studies, only to abandon them fairly soon in favour of racing. The young Cruijff lost his father at an early age and came from a slightly lower social class. Study was not an option for him, and he grew up more familiar with the streets than with school – something which has plagued him all his life. Eddy did not have this problem. Consequently, he has always been more on his guard, far more reserved in his statements, and nobody has ever caught him bragging. Yet for all his greatness he has not always been universally understood, let alone believed or praised.

Pain and gain

Merckx went his own way at an early age, long before he became the Belgian from Brussels and the national symbol of '*Belgitude*'. His aim was to win, and he succeeded wonderfully well in this, though not without effort. Watched over by the former Flanders team member Félicien Vervaecke, and later under the wing of manager Jean van Buggenhout, he pushed his way to the top, dealing with his often rather older rivals on the way and challenging the dominion of Rik van Looy who, partly because of his temperament, was the most popular cyclist of his day. Eddy Merckx was different from Rik van Looy; he had the same fighting spirit but did not angle for the applause of the crowd. Merckx was there to win. No more and no less. Whatever else this might bring took second place. What drove him was not so much popular acclaim as his own boundless ambition. This resulted in so many victories that the crowd worshipped him anyway. Perhaps the first time this happened was when, aged barely 24, he was set to win the Tour of Italy for the second time, but was sent home prematurely for alleged doping. The people rose in revolt, eminent individuals became involved and the highest cycling authority, the UCI, lifted his suspension thus enabling the deeply offended champion to participate in the Tour de France. And on this, his first Tour, he immediately produced a crushing victory. It was 1969 and the first Belgian victory in 30 years. The last Belgian to win it, 30 years before, had been Sylvère Maes, in the last race before war broke out. On this day in 1969, the same day that the first man landed on the moon (the other Armstrong!), the country went wild. A government minister, no less, flew to Paris in a government plane to bring the new National Hero home.

All was forgiven and forgotten, the wretched business in Italy, and before that the rather painful controversy concerning his marriage, *in French,* to his partner Claudine Acou, daughter of an ex-cyclist. However, that same autumn fate struck yet another blow. During a track criterium paced by motorcycles, his pacesetter Fernand Wambst fell over a fallen colleague and was killed instantly. Eddy Merckx injured his back badly, after which he was dogged by excruciating pain for the remainder of his career. It affected him particularly when climbing, so that his superiority in the mountains deteriorated more quickly than on flat stretches of road.

That Eddy could keep going even when he was in the most dreadful pain became evident during his successful world endurance record run on the cycle track in Mexico City in 1977. He had never been so exhausted. Perhaps Eddy Merckx was the cyclist who suffered more than any other, both mentally and physically. But then he also won more than anyone else. No pain, no gain. And this was put into practice absolutely. He fought everything and everyone for as long as he could. In his own country, Roger de Vlaeminck and Freddy Maertens pressed hard, sometimes they beat and hurt him, but they could never make him give in.

'The Greatest' did not leave the scene until his time was well and truly over. The decision was his and his alone. He has a grown-up cyclist son, Axel, a bicycle factory and friends from the old days who now cycle way ahead of him. Eddy Merckx, once the divine cyclist, now sits like a Buddha on his bicycle.

JAN WAUTERS
Translated by Gregory Ball.

nglish = Dutch

A Dossier of Compelling Evidence

History has left many a Dutch mark on the English language. There is a sizeable English vocabulary of Dutch origin, such as *beer* (bier), *frolic* (vrolijk), *mate* (maat) and *pancake* (pannekoek); and borrowing from Dutch is an ongoing process, as witness recent additions like *apartheid, coffeeshop, lekker* and *gabber* music. But while these words are in frequent everyday use, their origin is largely unknown and forgotten today. '*We are not conscious that the words "brandy", "cruller", "golf", "duck" (light canvas), "isinglass", "measles", "selvage", "wagon", "uproar" are from the Dutch.*' (Baugh & Cable 1978, p. 9). It may therefore be of interest to consider in some more detail the historical background and development of this Dutch element in English.

Cultural and linguistic contacts across the North Sea

The Dutch loan words above reflect many centuries of cultural interaction and language contact across the North Sea. From the Norman Conquest onwards this traffic has brought many things and words from the Low Countries to the British isles – in trade and commerce, fishing and whaling, maritime and colonial rivalry, warfare and navigation, but also in water management, brewing and mining, agriculture and gardening, the textile industry, crafts, industries, art, science, printing and literature.

In 1066 William the Conqueror brought with him considerable numbers of Flemish troops and craftsmen. In the early twelfth century Flemish colonists who were '*highly skilled in the wool trade*' settled in many different areas, from the southern coast of Wales to the Scottish borders and East Anglia. Often the only trace they have left is a place name, such as Flemingston in Wales or Flemington near Glasgow. Elsewhere it may be a street name like *The Strand* in Central London, which reminds us that once upon a time – and really not so very long ago: it was still in use in 1952 – Londoners did have a beach (Dutch *strand*) along the north bank of the river Thames.

These settlers and colonists from the Low Countries brought new indus-

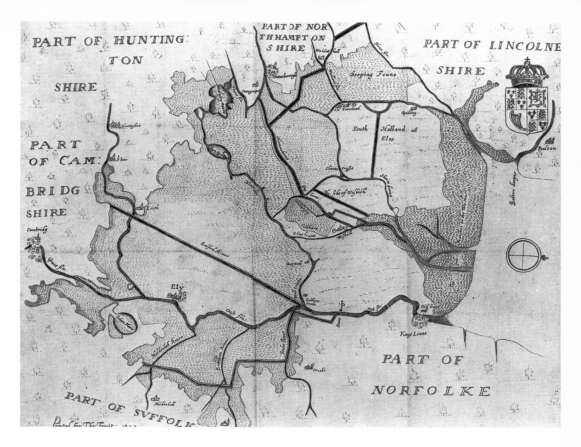

try and technology. The draining of the Fens in East Anglia, first by Flemish monks and later by Dutch engineers, brought with it words like *sluice* (sluis), *canal* (kanaal) and *morass* (moeras). In agriculture we find Dutch words like *hack* (hak), *yoke* (juk), *buckwheat* (boekweit) and *butter* (boter). Words like *clock* (klok), *drill* (drillen) and *besom* (bezem) were introduced by Dutch and Flemish craftsmen – clockmakers, glaziers, shoemakers, blacksmiths, joiners, coopers, pouchmakers, potters, surgeons and scriveners. And with the production and consumption of alcohol came words like *brewery* (brouwerij), *hop* (hop), *geneva* (jenever) which was later shortened to *gin, booze* (buizen) and *drunkard* (dronkaard).

In the seventeenth century the economic dominance of Amsterdam brought new financial institutions such as the Bank of England, and the so-called 'Dutch tax' of 1644 on meat, victuals, salt, starch, textile goods and other commodities. Here too we find words like *check* (strictly American) or *cheque, mint* (munt), *lottery* (loterij), *bluff* (bluffen) and *swindle* (zwendel), and words for money like *guilder* (gulden), *doit* (duit), *stiver* (stuiver), *dollar* (daalder) and, in American English, *dime*. The last word goes back to 1585, when the Flemish mathematician Simon Stevin, in his pioneering pamphlet *The Tenth* (De Thiende), proposed to introduce the decimal system in society, for '*Money-masters, Marchants, and Landmeaters*'. His French translation, *La Disme*, came out in the same year; and in 1608 Robert Norton's English translation, *Disme: the Art of Tenths; or, Decimall*

A map from Cornelis Vermuyden's *Discourse Touching the Drayning of the Great Fennes* (London, 1642). Folger Shakespeare Library, Washington, DC.

Arithmetike, was published in London. But Stevin's revolutionary proposal had to wait almost two hundred years before it was eventually adopted in the United States (in Great Britain it took another two centuries before the penny – or rather the shilling – finally dropped).

In 1648 the first substantial Dutch-English dictionary was published in Rotterdam, *A Copious English and Netherduytch Dictionarie*, compiled by the soldier, translator and scholar Henry Hexham. Through him and other English mercenaries in the Eighty Years War the English language acquired Dutch military words such as *booty* (buit), *beleaguer* (belegeren), *quartermaster* (kwartiermeester), *knapsack* (knapzak), *plunder* (plunderen), *tattoo* (taptoe) and *blunderbuss* (donderbus).

In naval and maritime terminology we find large numbers of Dutch loan words – for things related to ships such as *bowsprit* (boegspriet), *deck* (dek), *keel* (kiel), *ballast* (ballast), *freight* (vracht), and *wagoner* (a book of charts for nautical use); for the vessels themselves like *sloop* (sloep), *schooner* (schoener) and *hooker* (the common, not the happy variety); and for sailors' jobs like *gybe* (gijpen), *dock* (dok), *smuggle* (smokkelen), *splice* (splitsen), *steer* (sturen) and *aloof* (aan loef). At sea the Dutch language provided words for *buoy* (boei), *ebb* (eb), *lee* (lij), *maelstrom* (maalstroom), *reef* (rif) and *wrack* (wrak); and names for all kinds of sea creatures from *whiting* (wijting) to *walrus* (walrus). Ranks on board were known by their Dutch names as *skipper* (schipper) and *boatsman* (bootsman); and both *freebooter* and *filibuster* (via Spanish) derive from Dutch *vrijbuiter*. In all the harbours along the North Sea sailors used a common lingo, and this helps to explain how vulgar slang and taboo words from Dutch entered into English, such as *fucking* (fokkinge), *cunt* (conte), *crap* (krappe) and *shite* (schijten). Today it would seem the loan is being repaid with interest, as English *shit!* is now the most common and popular exclamation in Dutch.

The Dutch maritime expansion led to settlement in all continents – in South Africa, the Americas and Australasia – where the Dutch often lived and worked in close contact with English speakers. In the United States, at the time of independence, Dutch narrowly failed to be adopted as the national language; the Roosevelt dynasty was of Dutch descent; and New York in particular had a strong Dutch character. Dutch remained in use there till the early part of the twentieth century, and has left many traces – place names such as *Harlem* (Haarlem), *Wall Street* (Walstraat) and *Coney Island* (Konijne eiland); common words like *boss* (baas), *cookie* (koekie), *burgher* (burger), *coleslaw* (koolsla), *snoop* (snoepen), *spook* (spook) and *poppycock* (pappekak); the nickname *Yankee* (from Janke, Jantje); and the myth of *Santa Claus* (from Sinterklaas, i.e. St Nicholas, the maritime patron saint of the Dutch) and his *sleigh* (slee). In South African English too, there are many Dutch loan words such as *aardvark, springbok* and *wildebeest, boer, bush, trek, veld* and *outspan* (uitspannen).

In the Dutch East Indies (present-day Indonesia) Dutch acted as an intermediary for the adoption into English of words from Malay and other Oriental languages, like *amuck* (amok), *cockatoo* (kaketoe), *orang-outang* (orangoetan) and *tea* (from Dutch *thee* < Malay *teh* <Amoy Chinese *t'e*). The famous Hobson-Jobson dictionary of Anglo-Indian usage contains many examples of the linguistic adaptation processes that are at work here, involving the English speakers' talent for word play, pidginisation, mispro-

A COPIOUS ENGLISH
AND
NETHERDUYTCH
DICTIONARIE
Composed out of our best
English Authours.
With an APPENDIX *of the names of all kind of Beasts,
Fovvles, Birds, Fishes, Hunting, and Havvking.*
AS ALSO
A compendious GRAMMAR for the Instruction of the Learner.
―――――
HET GROOT
WOORDEN-BOECK
Gestelt in't ENGELSCH ende NEDERDUYTSCH.
Met een APPENDIX van de namen van alderley Beesten, Vogelen, Visschen, Jagerye, ende Valckerye, &c. Als oock,
Een korte Engelsche GRAMMATICA.
Alles met groote naersticheyt nyt de beste Engelsche Autheuren t'samen gevoeght, DOOR
HENRY HEXHAM.
Tot ROTTERDAM,
Gedruckt by AERNOFT LEERS, Anno 1648.

Title page of Henry Hexham's *A Copious English and Netherduytch Dictionarie* (Rotterdam, 1648). Koninklijke Bibliotheek Albert I, Brussels.

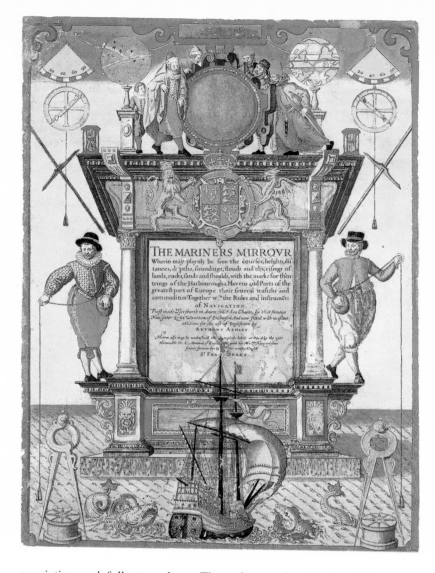

A *wagoner*: Title page of Lucas Jansz Waghenaer's *The Mariners Mirrour* (1588). Folger Shakespeare Library, Washington, DC.

nunciation and folk etymology. Thus, *decoy* miraculously derives from Dutch *eendekooi*, and *scorbut* from Dutch *scheurbuik* (scurvy).

In the field of art, painting and drawing many Dutch words were borrowed: *easel* (ezel), *sketch* (schets) and *maulstick* (maalstok), to name but three. Around 1800, if one wanted a masterpiece, one simply went and bought a *vandyke*. The case of *landscape* (landschap) is interesting in that its suffix *-scape* has become productive in modern English, witness words like *seascape, cloudscape* and – as C.S. Lewis has it – the '*great skyscapes of East Anglia*'. Today this is followed by further new formations like *artscape, soundscape, cityscape* and even *mindscape*.

In literature and the sciences we find a similar Dutch influence. If William Shakespeare was not actually a Fleming, it is not impossible that he visited the Low Countries as a soldier or an actor. Milton certainly knew Dutch and may have benefitted from Vondel's tragedy *Lucifer* (1654) when writing his

Paradise Lost (1667). Aphra Behn, Daniel Defoe, Jonathan Swift – they all knew and used Dutch models, and Gulliver spoke Dutch well enough to pass for a Dutchman. But then, he had been a student at the University of Leyden (now Leiden), where so many other English and Scottish students went in the seventeenth and eighteenth centuries to study medicine, law or theology. These students, and publishers like Elsevier, were instrumental in the exchange of ideas and knowledge and the dissemination in the British isles of disciplines like anatomy, botany and plant names such as *tulip* (tulp), *daffodil* and *nettle* (netel). Later on, however, much of this was forgotten, due to the intense linguistic rivalry that developed between the Dutch and the English in the late eighteenth century, and the ensuing dominance of English. This rivalry generated many strongly negative stereotypes and pejorative expressions such as Dutch cap (contraceptive diaphragm), Dutch courage (geneva), Dutch gold (cheap copper leaf), Dutch uncle (boring old pedant) and Dutch wife (guling, or sleeping pillow). A key element in this rivalry was the depiction of Dutch as Double Dutch (gibberish), or even, as James Boswell put it, *'a language fit only for horses'*.

Last but not least there is the domain of sport and games. *Cricket* goes back to a Flemish phrase, *'met de krik ketsen'*, literally 'to chase with a curved stick'. This was shortened to *krikets*, which finally became *cricket*, as John Eddowes relates in his *The Language of Cricket* (1997). The noble game of *golf*, first recorded in Scotland in 1457, was known in the Low Countries in 1360 as *kolf* – a game in which the players had to get a small, hard ball into a hole in the turf or lawn with as few strokes of their club as possible. In winter the game was played on ice, as one can see in the Golden Age paintings of Hendrick Avercamp. And today, in the age of football, we have the case of *Brooklyn* – the name David Beckham and his wife gave their first-born son, after the New York borough where he was conceived. But would the Beckhams know that this name goes back to the Dutch village of Breukelen – which also figures in the last name of one of Holland's most renowned goalkeepers, Jan van Breukelen?

A common ancestor: Ingvaeonic

The presence of so many words of Dutch origin in the English language reflects a shared past, a common North Sea culture, and a remarkable openness on the part of English speakers to new words adopted from abroad. However, much the same could be said for the presence of words from French, Latin and other, more exotic languages in English. That is, the history of contact and borrowing, though interesting and important, can tell us only so much, and it is only when we move beyond it that we discover a far more intimate connection between Dutch and English than between, say, English and French. For although the number of French and Latin loan words in English is quite substantial, they do not occur in the inner core of its grammatical system, amongst its pronouns, articles and demonstratives, its prepositions and conjunctions, in its inflections and its syntax. And it is precisely here that Dutch and English share a wide range of common elements.

There are many nouns that point to a deeper relationship between English and Dutch than we have seen so far. We find cognate words in the domain of family / kinship – *daughter* (dochter), *wife* (wijf) and *nephew* (neef); names for body parts – *lip* (lip), *tongue* (tong), *elbow* (elleboog), *thigh* (dij), *knee* (knie), *shin* (scheen) and *ankle* (enkel); for domestic animals - *cat* (kat), *hen* (hen), *sheep* (schaap), *cow* (koe), *swallow* (zwaluw) and *bee* (bij); plants and trees - *beech* (beuk), *oak* (eik), *birch* (berk) and *willow* (wilg); the seasons and the weather - *summer* (zomer), *winter* (winter), *day* (dag), *night* (nacht), *snow* (sneeuw), *rain* (regen), *wind* (wind) and *sunshine* (zonne-schijn).

We find similar close correspondences in other parts of the grammatical system. The two languages have in common not just weak verbs like *babble* (babbelen), *bake* (bakken), *hope* (hopen) and *knead* (kneden), but in particular also many strong verbs which are much older, such as *think-thought-thought* (denken-dacht-gedacht), *see-saw-seen* (zien-zag-gezien) and *swim-*

swam-swum (zwemmen-zwom-gezwommen). And there are common adverbs and adjectives such as *blue* (blauw), *naked* (naakt), *handy* (handig), *thick* (dik), *long* (lang), *gruff* (grof), *full* (vol), *cool* (koel), *tight* (dicht), *enough* (genoeg), *sickly* (ziekelijk), *manly* (mannelijk) and *openly* (openlijk).

Beyond this, the two languages have many other kinds of words in common. Common pronouns are *you* (jou), *me* (mij), *mine* (mijn), *him* (hem), *it* (het) and *himself* (hemzelf); common articles and demonstratives are *the* (de), *an* (een), *this* (deze), *that* (dat), *here* (hier) and *there* (daar); common numerals are *three* (drie), *seven* (zeven), *eleven* (elf), *twenty* (twintig) and *hundred* (honderd). Common prepositions are *in* (in), *over* (over), *for* (voor), *under* (onder), *to* (te/toe/tot) and *around* (rond); common conjunctions are *since* (sinds), *when* (wanneer), *than* (dan), *as* (als) and *while* (terwijl); common question words are *where* (waar) and *what* (wat); and common interjections are ahoy, *now* (nou), *well* (wel), *yea* (ja) and *Ach* (ach).

And then there are remarkable correspondences between the sounds, syntax and grammatical inflections of the two languages. We find regular sound change in the following pairs, where English *ou* corresponds to the vowel *ui* that is so typical of Dutch: *out* (uit), *clout* (kluit), *snout* (snuit), *spout* (spuit), *sprout* (spruit), *grout* (gruit), *loud* (luid), *south* (zuid), *mouth* (muide), *house* (huis), *louse* (luis), *mouse* (muis), *owl* (uil), *howl* (huilen), *foul* (vuil), *rough* (ruig), *thousand* (duizend), *brown* (bruin), *crown* (kruin), *down* (duin) and *town* (tuin). In inflection there are common affixes such as *be-* in *be-devil* (beduvelen) and *-er* in *baker*, but also the common plural ending *-s* for nouns (*baker-s*, bakker-s), the endings *-er* and *-est* in comparatives and superlatives (*great-er / great-est*, groter / grootst), and the *-ly / -lijk* endings we saw in the adverbs. In syntax, finally, we note that Dutch and English have very similar ways of stringing their words together in sentences. Shakespeare's English employs many Dutch constructions – a form of address like '*Min alderlefest sovereign*' (Mijn allerliefste soeverein), a greeting formula such as '*How now?*' (Hoe nu?), and questions like '*What think you, sailors?*' (Wat denken jullie, zeelui?) and '*How is it with you?*' (Hoe is het met jou?). Similar evidence is available from seventeenth-century polyglot conversation books intended for merchants travelling through Europe, where we find striking similarities between spoken English and Dutch sentences like '*Have you good wine?*' (Hebt u goede wijn?), '*Hath your horse droncke?*' (Heeft uw paard gedronken?) and '*How fare you?*' (Hoe vaart ge?). And today this is no different: an English sentence like '*Come here now, Peter, will yer, 'tis so cool here in the boat*' is almost literally the same as its Dutch equivalent 'Kom hier nou, Pieter, wil je, 't is zo koel hier in de boot'.

All these many different correspondences point to a connection between the two languages that goes far deeper than could be explained just by a history of contact and borrowing. So, instead, we must explore an alternative explanation, viz. that the two languages have a common origin and share a common ancestor. It is generally assumed today that this common ancestor language was the so-called Ingvaeonic or North Sea Germanic, which around AD 100-500 comprised the dialects of the Frisians, the Angles, the Jutes and the Saxons. Clear traces of this can be found on both sides of the North Sea – in place names such as *Norwich* (Noordwijk), *Bentham*

A Dutch ABC

The Dutch you know already – English words of Dutch origin, with dates of first recorded usage

A	*anchor* (1692)	< anker (1240)
B	*brandy* (1622)	< brandewyn (1300-1350)
C	*clock* (1664)	< klok (1237)
D	*dike* (chaucer)	< dijk (1035)
E	*etch* (1634)	< etsen (1573)
F	*furlough* (1625)	< verlof (1361)
G	*geneva* (1706)	< jenever (1606)
H	*hop* (1440)	< hoppe (1376-1400)
I	*iceberg* (1774)	< ijsberg (Middle Dutch)
K	*keelhaul* (1666)	< kielhalen (1590)
L	*landscape* (1598)	< landschap (1240)
M	*monkey* (1530)	< ?manneke (1498)
N	*nip* (1430)	< nijpen (1360)
O	*overall* (1596)	< overal (1240)
P	*pickle-herring* (1570)	< pekelharing (1500-1525)
Q	*quacksalver* (1579)	< kwakzalver (1390-1460)
R	*rack* (1305)	< rek (1287)
S	*skate* (1648)	< schaats (1567)
T	*tide* (1435)	< getijde (1236)
U	*uproar* (16th c)	< oproer (1537)
V	*vane* (1581)	< vaan (1170)
W	*waffle* (1808)	< wafel (1450)
Y	*yacht* (1557)	< jacht (1528)
Z	*zebra* (1600)	< zebra (1596)

Double Dutch

In 1994-1995 Dutch brewers Oranjeboom launched their beer on the London market with an eye-catching campaign of Double Dutch (It helps if you read it out loud in English).

1. Stuf de tur kei
   ei mof voor'aan
   Oranjeboom

2. Take uur tast buds
   voor aar rij de

3. U vil nijver hier
   aan ie tin negatief
   a bout de tast of
   Oranjeboom

4. Zeems lik dubbel Dutje?
   Wel, zuur prijs,
   zuur prijs, et ijs

(Benthem), *Plymouth* (Pleimuiden), *Amersham* (Amersfoort) and 'Nes' in *Skegness* (and Dutch Eemnes); and in shared words like *five* (vijf), *island* (eiland), *ladder* (ladder), *mare* (merrie), *bull* (bul), *wheel* (wiel) and *little* (luttel).

The original language is Dutch

The Ingvaeonic hypothesis is in line with what the printer William Caxton observed, back in the fifteenth century, viz. that Old English was much '*more like to Dutch than to English*' – something that is certainly true of Chaucer's work. Since then, however, it is English that has changed the most, for ...'*if that linguistic cataclysm, the Norman Conquest of 1066, had not occurred, the English today might speak a language not unlike modern Dutch*'' (McCrum et al. 1986, p. 58). It is therefore reasonable to suppose, not that the two languages share a common ancestor, but rather, quite simply, that Dutch is the older. The Dutch have known this for centuries. As the Antwerp humanist Joannes Goropius Becanus demonstrated in his *Origines Antverpianae* (1569), Dutch was actually the language spoken in Paradise. His argument was that, as a rule, older words are shorter, and since Dutch has more short words than either English, French, Latin, Greek or Hebrew, it clearly must be older. His younger contemporary, the mathematician Simon Stevin, added from a slightly different perspective that, of all the languages in the world, Dutch was best-suited to expressing ideas, because of its many mono-syllabic base words and the ease with which it can produce new word-combinations to express new ideas.

These insights are alive and well in the Netherlands today – for example in the recent claim of the *Duizenddichter* poet of Amsterdam, that all languages derive from Dutch – although this is still a bit contentious with the Frisians, who make the same claim for their own language in the epic *Oera Linda Bok* (1872). The *Duizenddichter* starts from the fact that Adam (< Dutch *adem,* breath) was the first human being to receive a Dutch name. He also reminds us of the fact that the Dutch are the only people in the world who give each other letters as presents each year on the fifth of December, when they celebrate St Nicholas' birthday. And he supports his theory with many striking examples of etymological derivation. Thus, English *teacher* obviously comes from 'Diets-heer' (= master of Dutch), *erudite* from 'eer-uw-Diets' (= honour your Dutch), and *alphabet* derives not from Greek 'alpha-beta' but from Dutch 'al-van-bute'-leren (= learning everything by heart).

Recently the Dutch linguist Hugo Brandt Corstius has taken this tradition into the twenty-first century by portraying Dutch as the natural world language of the future. In a flashback from the year 2099 he recalls the Nobel-prize winning invention by two Dutch scientists working in the field of advanced language technology, who discovered the so-called '*DNA of inanimate objects*', which assigns each and every object in the world its natural, generic name in a universal letter code. Take, for example, S-T-O-E-L. Though this happens to be Dutch for chair, what really matters is that this is now the one and only true name of this object, and therefore, inevitably, all resistance from other languages such as English and Spanish has proved futile.

And so, as we now see, Dutch truly is the once and future language. Take any of the basics – money, booze, sex, sports, the weather – and the Dutch have a word for it. This in turn helps to explain why all the other languages in the world - including English - are so easy for the Dutch and for those who know Dutch. So my modest proposal would be for the English to take Dutch as their first foreign language, and to follow the traditional Dutch recipe for successful language learning. The key is to start early, taking a language that is a close cognate, hence not too difficult. This will produce early success, which then breeds further success, and lays the foundation for learning other languages. So, the first foreign language to be learned by the English in school should not be the traditional bourgeois French, nor solid German, nor even popular Spanish, but simply Dutch, the mother of all mongrel languages (and also, it seems, an effective antidote to dyslexia). If the English were to follow this advice, who knows, one day they may become just as proficient in languages as the Dutch.

REINIER SALVERDA

BIBLIOGRAPHY

BARNOUW, A.J., *Monthly Letters on the Culture and History of the Netherlands*. Assen, 1969.
BAUGH, ALBERT C. and THOMAS CABLE, *A History of the English Language*. London, 1978.
BENSE, J.F., *A Dictionary of the Low-Dutch Element in the English Vocabulary*. The Hague, 1926.
BRANDT CORSTIUS, HUGO, '2000-2099; Neew Neelans'. In: Peter Burger & Jaap de Jong (red.), *Taalboek van de eeuw*. The Hague / Antwerp, 1999. pp. 227-231.
EDDOWES, JOHN, *The Language of Cricket*. Manchester, 1997.
HALEY, K.H.D., *The British & The Dutch. Political and Cultural Relations through the Ages*. London, 1988.
LLEWELLYN, E.C., *The Influence of the Low Dutch on the English Vocabulary*. Oxford / London, 1936.
MCARTHUR, TOM, *The Oxford Companion to the English Language*. Oxford, 1996.
MCCRUM, ROBERT, WILLIAM CRAN and ROBERT MACNEIL, *The Story of English*. London, 1986.
OSSELTON, N.E., *The Dumb Linguists. A Study of the Earliest English and Dutch Dictionaries*. Leiden / Oxford, 1973.
RIZZA, RICCARDO (ed.), *Colloquia, et Dictionariolum Octo Linguarum*. Viareggio / Lucca, 1996.
TOORIANS, LAURAN, 'Flemish in Wales.' In: Glanville Price (ed.), *Languages in Britain and Ireland*. Oxford, 2000. pp. 184-186.
VAN DER SIJS, NICOLINE, *Geleend en uitgeleend: Nederlandse woorden in andere talen en culturen*. Amsterdam, 1998.
VAN DER SIJS, NICOLINE, *Chronologisch woordenboek. De ouderdom en herkomst van onze woorden en betekenissen*. Amsterdam / Antwerpen, 2001.
WRENN, C.L., *The English Language*. London, 1966.

www.ucl.ac.uk/dutch: Study pack History of the Dutch Language

J oke

van Leeuwen's Light-Hearted Anarchy

For years now Joke van Leeuwen has occupied a special position in the Dutch cultural landscape. With such a versatile talent as hers this is hardly surprising. Central to all her work, whether in her early career in cabaret or her poetry readings today, her poetry for adults and for children, or more particularly her children's books, is a cheerful, sometimes unruly and slightly wistful light-heartedness coupled with a mild anarchy. In her books for young readers her intriguing characters observe the world through a perfect combination of illustrations and text, together with a disarming sense of humour and astonishing linguistic virtuosity. Over the years Magnus, Deesje, Viegeltje, Bobble and Kukel have become friends and allies of several generations of children and adults. Virtually every one of her children's books has been awarded a prestigious prize, while her poetry for adults is also greatly admired. Translations into English, French, Italian, German, even Japanese and Papiamentu have made her work popular far beyond the Dutch-speaking countries.

Controlled chaos

Joke van Leeuwen was born in The Hague in 1952. As a child she already wrote stories for the family newspaper produced in the parsonage in which she grew up. When she was fourteen the Van Leeuwens moved to Brussels, where she studied graphic design and history. Now she lives and works in Antwerp. As a result of her years in Belgium, Flanders and the Flemish are close to her heart. She once admitted that she sometimes finds the orderliness and determined trendiness of life in the Netherlands hard to take.

Joke van Leeuwen published her first book in 1978. *Apple Sauce Street Is Different* (De appelmoesstraat is anders) is a black-and-white picture book about a new resident who wants to shatter the uniformity of the street; at the time it was very unconventional.

Van Leeuwen deliberately chose not to join the ranks of the realistic problem-book writers of the 1970s who burdened children with serious social issues. Humour and cabaret-like fun have always been important ingredients in her work. She does not avoid injustice and sorrow, but gives them no undue emphasis. Recurrent subjects like loneliness and misunderstanding are treated as delicately as possible, and as a result their effect is even more telling. In her second book, *A House with Seven Rooms* (Een huis met zeven kamers, 1980), a girl goes on a voyage of discovery in her 'favourite Uncle's' house. Every room has its own appropriate amusing story. Interspersed among the stories are songs, rhymes, riddles and hand-written letters. The book is also richly illustrated with her characteristic pen and ink drawings, which form a playful complement to the text. Van Leeuwen says that some things are easier to draw and others easier to write about. Her squiggly drawings are often a very personal interpretation of the text, often even a substitute for it. The characters she draws do not belong in a cuddly children's world, like those seen in so many children's books. No rosy cheeks or sweet little snub noses here, but long or crooked noses, funny beady eyes and tousled spiky hair. In *A House with Seven Rooms* Van Leeuwen shows what she can do with language: since then word play, funny names for people and things, a totally personal approach to language and inimitable dialogues, together with an utterly original illustration technique, have become her unmistakable trademark.

Joke van Leeuwen (1952-)

Time and again Joke van Leeuwen succeeds in constructing perfectly composed stories from seemingly chaotic associations. In *Magnus' Metro* (De metro van Magnus, 1981), for example, eight Metro stations hold the story together. Magnus happens to find himself in an underground train that he has drawn himself. At every station he has to undergo a test, he has strange adventures and meets extraordinary people. At the last station he visits his grandma who lives in the old people's home 'Warm Waiting-room'. In almost every book Van Leeuwen makes her heroes go on a quest. Her characters are always on the way somewhere, in search of a safe haven for themselves. These journeys seem like lessons in living and are, it turns out, a reflection of life itself. Each journey is full of absurd encounters and funny coincidences. Despite their childish naivety her children are surprisingly emancipated and feisty. They observe the world around them in a receptive and independent fashion and cope boldly with bizarre situations. The adults usually play a less heroic role. They are often worn out, occupied by their own worries, and not much concerned with the children entrusted to their care. Only rather eccentric, a-social adults get more favourable treatment. They are usually unconventional dropouts whose non-conformity puts them on the same wave-length as the young heroes.

The virtue of lightheartedness

In *Deesje* (1985) a rather unworldly little girl called Deesje is sent to the town by her father to stay with her 'half-aunt'. This is another exciting trip, full of endless complications and strange encounters. Here too the recurring themes are isolation and lack of understanding. The same themes reappear in *The Story of Bobble who Wanted to Be Rich* (Het verhaal van Bobbel die in een bakfiets woonde en rijk wilde worden, 1987). Once more the heroine is out of the ordinary and not really capable of adapting to an ordered society.

The World Is Crooked but my Teeth Are Straight (De wereld is krom maar mijn tanden staan recht, 1995) is a kind of comic strip or cartoon about '*the light and dark sides of a budding young woman's life*'. A perfect combination of text and illustrations depicts that emerging life with a bubbly but often poignant humour. Every teenage girl will identify with this book about the many questions posed by a young girl who can't understand grownups.

At first *Eep* (Iep, 1995) simply seems a hilarious story, but it is more than that. It is a moving tale about loss, about an urge for freedom and emancipation, about loneliness and alienation. The small bird girl Viegeltje redraws reality for everyone she meets – the world seen and experienced from the air. The witty puns, the subtle and gentle observations of the human comedy which is the world of grownups, the unbridled imagination and disarming illustrations are all the epitome of light-heartedness. In *Eep* all Joke van Leeuwen's gifts as a writer and artist are united.

Kukel (1998) is yet another story of loneliness and lack of understanding cast in a form both droll and moving. The central character here is a little boy who is left to look after himself by his seven singing sisters. In his intense desire to belong to someone he makes a present of himself to the childless queen. The words Van Leeuwen puts in Her Majesty's mouth are particularly inspired and amusing.

In *Far Gone* (Wijd weg, 1991) and *This Book Has a Different Name* (Dit boek heet anders, 1992) Van Leeuwen experiments with symbolism. These are perhaps a little more serious, less straightforward, but certainly just as intriguing and skilfully written. *Visiting Years* (Bezoekjaren, 1998) is also intended for older readers. Stories told to her by Malika Blain from Morocco inspired Joke van Leeuwen to write this novel. Zima tells the story of what happened to her family during the political turmoil of the 1970s in Casablanca. The poverty-stricken but contented existence of a large family living on the outskirts of the city is totally disrupted when first the eldest son, then the second as well, are arrested and imprisoned for 'dissident activities'. The account of years of uncertainty, lengthy trials and endless visits to the prison is almost casually incorporated in the story of everyday life. Zima's naïve recital means that the reader can only guess at the political machinations concealed behind the events. As a result, rather than being a novel with a cause *Visiting Years* is a moving, amusing and informative story about a young girl growing up in a different culture. It also, but subtly, provides young readers with a clear insight into the causes of injustice and into the often relentless cruelty of some political regimes.

The little books for 'readers starting out' are also light-hearted and often hilarious. The restrictions that this sort of story imposes on language (short sentences with words of one syllable) usually make for dull and lacklustre reading. With *Sus and Jum* (Sus en Jum) and *Fien Wants a Flus* (Fien wil een flus) Van Leeuwen once more proved her boundless powers of invention and turned learning to read into an absolute treat.

Whatever genre she turns her hand to – from the above-mentioned little books for 'fresh' readers to poetry and novels (like her most recent *Free Forms* – Vrije vormen, 2002) for adults –, Joke van Leeuwen constantly surprises her readers with her uninhibited way of looking at people and things. She continues to hold the interest of fans of all ages and make them curious about what she is going to do next. In Joke van Leeuwen, the Low Countries have acquired a splendid successor to *grande dame* Annie M.G. Schmidt.[1]

ANNEMIE LEYSEN
Translated by Elizabeth Mollison.

NOTE

1. See *The Low Countries* 1994-95: 18-21.

TRANSLATION

The Story of Bobble who Wanted to Be Rich (Tr. Lance Salway). London, 1992.

A Poem and an Extract

by Joke van Leeuwen

Plaza

Not a breath of wind. Yet a man held on tight
to a woman, a woman to a child. Little legs
moved of themselves. Above on a string a balloon
like a fish. Above that the sun, blazing.

The child had let go of the fish. Watched it
rising, waved it goodbye. What – what's going on?
The man let go of the woman, dashed into the sky,
Stripped it absolutely bare.

From *Four Ways of Waiting for Somebody* (Vier manieren om op iemand te wachten). Querido, Amsterdam, 2001.
Translated by Tanis Guest.

Plaza

Nergens wind. Toch hield een man een vrouw
stevig beet, een vrouw een kind. De beenjes
bewogen zelf. Daarboven aan touw een ballon
als een vis. Daarboven de zon, laaiend.

Het kind hield de vis niet meer. Keek hoe hij
steeg, zwaaide hem na. Wat is er? Wat is er?
De man liet de vrouw los, holde de lucht in,
haalde die helemaal leeg.

Extract from *Eep*

Warre was later than usual getting home. There had been a lot of birds flying around that day, and a lot of other things too, like kites, model planes, and bits of fluff. Especially lots of fluff.

'I've had a busy day,' said Warre.

'So have I,' said Tine. 'I've been teaching Viegeltje to eat with a knife and fork – or a spoon, rather. I'll show you.'

She picked up a bowl and went outside with it. A little later she came back. On the bowl were a few earthworms, with a small spider by way of decoration.

'She likes these even better than peanuts,' Tine said, 'and at first I thought it was really horrid, but you have to make allowances, and I did, because after all we eat bits of cows' rump and fried wings and snails and things.'

She sat Viegeltje at the table and held her firmly. She pushed the extra-long spoon between Viegeltje's toes and put a worm on it. Viegeltje ate the worm with the spoon. But as soon as Tine let go of her she gobbled the rest down straight from the bowl.

'She *can* do it,' said Tine.

'Yes, but Tine,' said Warre, 'when Viegeltje eats like that, she's got her feet on the table the whole time. How can we go and eat decently with her in a restaurant if she sits with her feet on the table the whole time?'

'But she can't just sprawl there and gulp her food with her face in her plate, can she now?'

No, that was true. Eating was something you did sitting up straight at a table. Though it was quite possible to do it in other ways too.

In a high-speed way

or a messy way.

In a lazy way

or a careless way.

'Wait a minute,' said Warre. 'I'll make something that'll let her sit up nice and straight like a person and still eat like a little bird.'

He promptly disappeared into his shed. He stayed there working for a good two hours. Tine wasn't allowed in to get in his way. Nor to watch what he was doing. And certainly not to ask if it was ready yet because the soup was ready now.

Then Warre reappeared. Feeling very pleased with himself. He had made a flapping-powered feeding machine. 'Constructed,' he said, because that sounded better. He was quite sure that it was the first flapping-powered feeding machine in the whole world, though as yet he himself had only looked at two foreign countries.

They tried it at once to see if it worked. Viegeltje had to flutter and flap her wings without leaving the ground, and when she did that she made a wind. And that wind worked the machine.

It was hard on her wings, and sometimes she forgot to keep her head in the right place.

But all that wind-making did make her wings stronger. Before long they were wings any bird could be proud of.

From *Eep* (Iep). Amsterdam: Querido, 1995, pp. 35-39.

Translated by Tanis Guest

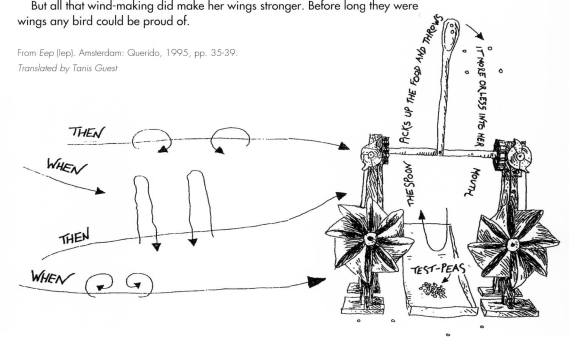

Enough

of Laughter?

The Unbridled Expansion of Dutch Cabaret

The death of Toon Hermans, the godfather of Dutch cabaret, on 22 April 2000, marked the end of '*le grand cabaret*' in the Netherlands in more than one respect: cabaret as a genre dominated by a few great names; cabaret which aimed to reach the widest possible audience; cabaret which was preferably presented in large-capacity theatres (see *The Low Countries* 1993-94: 248-253). From around the middle of the 1950s three major exponents of the art of cabaret, Toon Hermans (1916-2000), Wim Sonneveld (1917-1974) and Wim Kan (1911-1983) formed a triumvirate which dominated and shaped the Dutch entertainment world. Their acts drew capacity houses and the emergence of television helped to secure their reputation. Each of the three had their own loyal set of fans: those who liked political satire followed Wim Kan; Sonneveld was the favourite of those who liked show and glamour; while Hermans was appreciated primarily for his clowning and exuberant sense of the ridiculous.

Freek de Jonge (1944-).
Photo by Marc Mildner.

The last of the great names

Cabaret has now become so 'democratised' as a genre that there is little place for such monopolies. Freek de Jonge (1944-) and Youp van 't Hek (1954-) are perhaps the only two who could compete with each other for the prize of the top cabaret artist in the Netherlands, but both are now in the autumn of their careers. Just as Freek de Jonge expresses his admiration for Toon Hermans in just about every interview, it is striking that many newcomers in the field cite De Jonge as a source of inspiration.

There is a line that starts with the pre-war theatre clown Johan Buziau, runs via Hermans and De Jonge and ends with a large number of the latest talents in the world of cabaret. What binds the artists within this tradition is a natural urge to perform cabaret, to create entertainment through a huge investment of their own individuality. This does not mean that there are not also differences, for example in the social commitment of the artists. This is probably most pronounced in De Jonge, though the way in which he displays his engagement is by no means equally well received by everyone:

Youp van 't Hek (1954-).

some critics denounce his moralising, preaching tone and feel that the vicar's son – which he actually is – is too conspicuous a presence in his shows. And the young and talented artists of De Vliegende Panters do a striking parody of De Jonge's rather hazy moralism in their production *Hype* (1998).

Youp van 't Hek stands outside the above tradition, because he is much less of a natural talent and much less of a natural 'funny man'. Van 't Hek's current success in the world of cabaret is the result of almost thirty years of hard work, and in all his shows he has something of the tough guy who seeks to impress upon his audience that they should always be on their guard against dumbing-down and reduction to the lowest common denominator. As he himself has said: '*But I refuse to rest. I'll carry on fighting. When I die, my obituary will say: "He never stopped shaking people awake."*' (*Straatmagazine*, October-November 2001).

What is striking in this desire to be heard is that Van 't Hek directs his barbs mainly at the minor irritations in life – the curious paradox of alcohol-free beer, the pathetic quality of certain television programmes, the misplaced charity of the *nouveau riche* – and that he rarely gets worked up about the things that really matter. It is perhaps precisely this restraint, this avoidance of great themes which has made him the favourite of so many Dutch people, both young and old. With Van 't Hek, people rarely feel personally affronted; his criticisms can always be seen as directed towards the neighbours. In short, his shows offer the reassuring promise of an evening of pure entertainment, with no undue unpleasantness.

Gratuitous entertainment

The same also applies to the work of a number of other cabaret artists who have been around for some time, such as Herman Finkers (1954-), Hans Liberg (1954-) and Brigitte Kaandorp (1963-): striking talents who enjoy a large public following but who appear to concern themselves little if at all with whatever may be going on in society. In fact, to find a time when cabaret adopted a clear standpoint on political or social issues, we have to go back far into the past.

In 1971 the imminent visit to the Netherlands by the Japanese Emperor Hirohito prompted Wim Kan to launch a campaign – ultimately to no avail – to prevent the visit. In a song full of bitterness Kan, who in 1943 had been forced to work on the Burma railway, voiced his protest against the Emperor and against the state visit. Another legendary campaign was organised in 1978 by Freek de Jonge together with his partner at the time Bram Vermeulen, under the title *Blood on the Post* (Bloed aan de paal). When the Dutch national football team qualified for the World Cup in Argentina, Dutch leftists protested against the team travelling to a country where the dictatorial regime of General Videla was suspected of murder and abduction on a huge scale. De Jonge and Vermeulen's campaign – which, like Kan's earlier campaign, failed – gave a voice to this protest.

The latest generation of cabaret performers openly distance themselves from such concerns, and in fact it is unthinkable that any of them should commit themselves in this way to any current political or social topic. In the cabaret of the last two decades, when it has become a genre entirely without pretension, even the most highly charged topics merely serve as a vehicle for non-committed provocation, and rarely lead to an openly voiced protest. The present champion of this 'nihilistic' school is Hans Teeuwen (1967-), an artist who was initially part of a duo with Ronald Smeenk, until the latter was killed in a car crash in 1992. Teeuwen leaves no taboo untouched – not that his predecessors were shy of tackling taboo subjects – and appears to regard entire sections of the population more as enemies than friends. It is as if he does his utmost to be as politically and socially incorrect as possible: he does not take up arms for society's losers and outcasts, but rather hammers home their deplorable situation even more harshly. And even the most avid fan sometimes feels uncomfortable in the unbridled flood of sick jokes and insults which Teeuwen spews out over the auditorium. And his colleagues are not spared, either: in his fourth full-evening show *No, But That...Well... Yes* (Dat dan weer wel, 2001) the 'outdated' cabaret of De Jonge and Van 't Hek is rubbished in a series of vicious side-swipes. And all this takes place in a direct, unreasoned manner which lacks any hint of stylisation or nuance; the audience allows itself to be made a fool of, not on the basis of a mutually understood irony, but personally, by an 'angry' Hans Teeuwen. Teeuwen can permit himself this *Publikumsbeschimpfung*: his talent is unquestionable, and he is especially loved by the young.

Stand-up comedy

Before he was able to make the great leap to the theatre, Hans Teeuwen spent a short period working in stand-up comedy – the form of 'cabaret' which has largely dominated theatre entertainment in the Netherlands in the last ten years, and whose roots lie in legendary figures from the past such as Lenny Bruce and Richard Pryor. Following the massive rise in popularity of this genre, especially in the 1980s, in both the United States and the United Kingdom, Raoul Heertje (1966-) introduced stand-up comedy in the Netherlands in 1990. Together with a group of colleagues he created the Comedytrain, a company whose members mainly performed in bars – a setting where the artist has to prove himself, has to conquer an audience which

Hans Teeuwen (1967-).
Photo by Sanne Peper /
courtesy of Hummelinck
Stuurman Theaterbureau,
Amsterdam.

has not come into the bar primarily to hear comedy. In the words of Hans Teeuwen: '*The advantage of performing in a bar is that you learn to fight for attention. It's no feather bed; you really have to try hard to strike the right note.*' (*TheaterMaker*, December 2000). A characteristic of the stand-up comedian is the humorous dialogue – usually rather strident in tone – in which the artist tries to engage with those around him; a dialogue in which he has to keep the thread going throughout. As soon as he notices that the audience is becoming indifferent or resistant, he has to find new avenues to 'make' his act a success.

This harsh apprenticeship to which the stand-up comedians subject themselves has proved to be one which time and again produces major artists. Hans Sibbel (1958-), Dolf Jansen (1963-) – together the duo Lebbis and Jansen – Lenette van Dongen (1958-), Theo Maassen (1966-): these are just a few of the celebrated cabaret performers who made their names in the Comedytrain. These bar-room performances usually lead to an appearance at one of the four main national cabaret festivals. If an artist manages to win a prize at one of these festivals, it is essential for his or her future success that the electronic media are then brought into the picture as soon as possible in order to give the young artist a helping hand. To put it bluntly, if his or her face does not appear on the nation's television screens within a reasonable time, he or she can forget a career in cabaret.

Television as the platform

The broadcasting organisation VARA, which has traditionally represented the socialist wing in the public broadcasting system, has always supported Dutch cabaret. But now that cabaret is enjoying something of a boom, the other broadcasting associations are only too keen to share in the benefits. Which is why not a week seems to go by without some form of cabaret on the TV: Paul de Leeuw (1962-), Marc-Marie Huibregts (1967-), Dolf Jansen and Jörgen Raymann (1966-) have all been given their own talk shows; cabaret artists are used as front men or cameos in various entertainment programmes; and many full-length theatre shows are broadcast in their entirety in one or two transmissions.

Then there are the Cabarestafettes. This is a constantly changing group of three new artists, usually winners of one of the national festivals, which tours the nation's theatres accompanied by an experienced presenter. Later, compilations of these shows are broadcast on TV, and their importance cannot be underestimated: whereas in the past an emerging new talent had to embark on a lengthy and laborious tour of community and youth centres, fifteen minutes on television is now enough to generate a loyal following for the artist in question.

Finally, there is cabaret which can only be enjoyed via radio and television. Between 1974 and 1998 Kees van Kooten (1941-) and his childhood friend Wim de Bie (1939-) were probably the most talked-about act on Dutch television, having first demonstrated their enormous talent on radio. The duo commented on the spirit of the times in the best tradition of 'classical' cabaret, in an extremely incisive way and with an extraordinary feel for the possibilities of language. After De Bie had continued as a solo act

Wim de Bie (1939-) as Driek the Gadget Freak.

on television for a while, he expanded his activities to the Internet. Referring to his website, entitled Bieslog (bieslog.vpro.nl) he says: '*It's opened up lots of new options for me in terms of content. I can combine everything I've ever done, radio, TV, writing. And the advantage over television is that people are able to react immediately.*' (*Vrij Nederland*, August 2002). This has made De Bie the first artist in the Netherlands to demonstrate that the digital era makes possible new, interactive forms of cabaret. Another, more current example of television cabaret is the programme *Jiskefet*, which has achieved unprecedented popularity in the last ten years. While it is true that the three makers of the programme – who also made their debut on radio – seek their inspiration more in the absurdism of programmes such as *Monty Python's Flying Circus* than in the world of cabaret, the sketches in which they appear – particularly those recorded in front of a live audience – bear an unmistakable relationship to the unconventional and contrary work of someone like Hans Teeuwen.

The cabaret artist as actor

The notion of cabaret has broadened and now includes general entertainment for which the audience does not even have to leave home. It was not entirely without justification that a TV reviewer commented that '*It seems as if every evening one half of the population is watching the other half being funny on stage*'. (*NRC Handelsblad*, 7 January 2002). Outside the media, another entertainment genre, the musical, has developed strongly in recent years thanks to hefty investment by a number of large commercial producers. Musicals with well-known figures from radio and TV playing the main parts are proving to be an ideal form of diversion for those Dutch citizens who can afford it, as well as an appropriate staff outing for larger companies.

In the wake of these two developments, the conventional stage is in danger of becoming the poor relation, a genre where the string-pulling surrounding the four-yearly government subsidies has become almost a caricature and where the ageing of the audience continues at a worrying pace. It is also noticeable here that it is precisely those companies with cabaret-like elements in their performances which are holding their own best. A good example is Carver, a successful three-strong group which has its roots in mime and for more than twelve years has teetered on the boundary between theatre and cabaret. The performances are always the result of improvisations; there is little in the way of narrative; rather, what they do is more of a 'theatrical documentary', like a cabaret programme, composed of individual scenes with limited relationship to each other. The actors are extremely well versed in creating character types, have a tremendous sense of timing and are adept at laying bare the absurdity of the everyday with unerring accuracy. Carver's audiences consist mainly of young people who – just like a cabaret audience – really want only one thing: to be entertained from start to finish. A reviewer of Carver's production *Pi, Po, Pu, Pa & Pé* (2001-2002 season) even refers in this connection to a chronic problem: *'The group's reputation – "Carver, that'll be a laugh" – means that visitors are already chuckling when they come in and their belly laughs drive every nuance out of the narrative.'* (*NRC Handelsblad*, 22 December 2001).

In addition to Carver there are several other groups – Orkater, Alex d'Electrique, Echte Mannen, Mug met de Gouden Tand – who put on performances in which the spirit of cabaret is present to a greater or lesser extent. Humour, visuality and playing direct to the audience are characteristic features of the theatre produced by these companies.

This fruitful interaction between cabaret and theatre is also evident from the ever more frequent appearance of cabaret performers as actors in more or less classical plays. As long ago as the 1993-1994 season Freek de Jonge played the role of the Fool in Shakespeare's *King Lear* for the Nationale Toneel theatre in The Hague; in the 2000-2001 season Peter Heerschop (1960-) and Viggo Waas (1962-) from the cabaret group Niet Uit Het Raam (NUHR) played in a performance of Beckett's *Waiting for Godot* at the Groningen-based Noord Nederlands Toneel theatre; in the 2001-2002 season, cabaret artist Eric van Sauers (1964-) played the title role in a hilarious version of Shakespeare's *Othello*, again for the Noord Nederlands Toneel. And later in that season the same company performed *Lenny Bruce*, written by director Koos Terpstra and with stand-up comedian Raoul Heertje and cabaret artist Hans Sibbel taking turns in the lead role. Finally, the cabaret artist Theo Maassen, who already has experience as a film actor, has been named for the lead role in a Dutch version of *The Elephant Man* by Bernard Pomerance, being produced by Opus One Productions. And it is not only on stage that the acting talent of cabaret performers is in demand: they are increasingly appearing in television series and in films, and by no means solely in comic roles.

Jeu sans frontières

The fact that cabaret artists are increasingly developing into all-round performing artists – on television, in the theatre, on the cinema screen – does not by definition mean that all of them are multi-talented. It does however say something about the marketability of the 'product' cabaret in the

Netherlands. That marketability is so strong that cabaret now accounts for a substantial part of the nation's cultural life, with the names of its top starts cropping up not only in the electronic media, but also in the written media. In later life Toon Hermans began publishing collections of poems and reflections; Freek de Jonge has published the scripts of his first shows, as well as a few autobiographical narratives and novels; Youp van 't Hek has for many years written columns in a national newspaper, and when collected in book form his efforts achieve sales which are every publisher's dream. Other cabaret artists occasionally opt to exchange the ephemerality of their trade for the durability of the printed word.

Putting on cabaret, performing as an actor on stage or in film, writing stories and columns, drawing cartoons: these are all artistic expressions which are increasingly developing as corollaries of each other, and sometimes the process works both ways as some artists, albeit temporarily, move in the opposite direction, for example from writer to cabaret performer. Thus, for example, the writer Boudewijn Büch (1948-2002) saw his name recognition increase as a result of his regular appearances as a travel reporter, following which in the 1996-1997 season he made a first – and, it has to be said, not terribly successful – leap to the cabaret stage. And to take just one further example, in the 2000-2001 season the cartoonist Gummbah (pseudonym of Gert-Jan van Leeuwen (1966-) performed together with Hans Teeuwen and director-cabaret artist Pieter Bouwman (1958-) in *Poelmo, Slave of the South* (Poelmo, slaaf van het zuiden), a series of theatre shows which was broadcast on Dutch television in eight instalments starting in January 2002.

Cabaret in the Netherlands has become a game without boundaries, *a jeu sans frontières*. It is a game in which – fortunately – more and more artists with a non-Dutch background are taking part, including Jörgen Raymann, who was raised in Surinam, the originally Turkish Nilgün Yerli (1969-), and the Morocco-born Najib Amhali (1970-). All three exploit their non-indigenous background, but their satire is aimed at all the cultures that enrich their new homeland, and in addition to their undoubted talents, this is one of the reasons that they have found favour with a wide, multicultural audience.

There is some reason to wonder whether the unbridled expansion of cabaret does not bring with it the danger of a degree of overexposure – all the more so since the increase in quantity is by no means always accompanied by an increase in quality. Juries at national festivals increasingly complain of declining standards, and anyone looking at the latest generation of cabaret performers on stage or on television cannot fail to notice the occasional embarrassing mediocrity. On top of this, a form of entertainment which illuminates society only from a safe, satirical perspective, will ultimately become boring.

It would be a good thing for the standard of cabaret in the Netherlands, therefore, if other forms of public entertainment – forms which do take seriously trends in politics and society – were able to strengthen their competitive position. In other words, the ball is now in the court of the makers of mainstream repertory theatre, of the groups which have become alienated from the general public in recent years as a result of an over-developed desire to experiment. It is up to them to find the path back to basics and to begin restoring a certain balance to the performing arts. It is a restoration for which the time is more than ripe.

JOS NIJHOF
Translated by Julian Ross.

Extracts

Freek de Jonge
An extract from 'You can't sing'

You can't sing about god
For god doesn't exist
And what doesn't exist
you don't sing about
Except love
For love leaves you lost for words
Love is priceless

Yes god is love they say
And in that way try
to sneak him in through the back door
But they can't fool me
You can't sing about god

Well some priests can
I can hear people say
But priests can't sing
Priests mustn't even try to sing
They must pray in silence
As if it isn't bad enough
That god doesn't exist
They insist with their caterwauling
On rubbing a bit more salt into the wound

For I happen to believe that god once existed
But that when the priests started singing
He scarpered – in other words
He took a rocket and escaped
to another galaxy or something similar
I don't know enough about that
God is the only one who can escape
He's gone and doesn't exist any more

You can't sing about the devil
Although the devil actually exists
He lives in France
He lives there as god
With his drunk cup of red wine
He makes the South Pacific unsafe
With his nuclear tests
And he is anti-drugs
Because they are divine
You could sing a song about that
The devil's dead keen on that
On songs about himself
It can't be out of tune enough for him
The devil's mad about Jeff Beck
But even madder about Mick Jagger

You can't sing
About the misery in the world
For that's been done too often already
And Bob Dylan is only born
Once in a thousand years
Thank god I'm tempted to say
But god doesn't exist
Though Bob Dylan would like to convince us other-
wise
Let him go on writing protest songs
Lots of material

From *Owt Rhymes with Nowt – Collected Songs 1967-1996* (lets rijmt op niets – Verzamelde liedjes 1967-1996). Amsterdam, 1997.
Translated by John Irons.

Youp van 't Hek

'What am I to do, then?' the psychiatrist said. 'Am I to start taking all you national health rejects seriously? My waiting room's bursting at the seams with twits like you. Everyone comes every week and squirts this sort of crap at me. About his mother complex. About his father who's never understood him. His completely misunderstood youth. His penetration-oriented lover and god knows what else. Sod off. Not just you – the whole lot of you.'

He threw open the door of the waiting room and began to verbally beat the bejesus out of all the wrecks sitting there. He shook the anorexia skeleton till it rattled and said: 'Get going, stuff yourself, you bitch. Clear off. Bugger off.'

He grabbed the breasts of the maybe-lesbian and said: 'Nag and you'll get a shag. Piss off.'

To the man who had been trying for seven years to get his Nazi grandpa out of his head he said: 'Heil Hitler. Bugger off.'

At the man with chronic hosophobia he shouted: 'Hey, come closer...' and he spat right in his face.

'Doctor Van Tilburg's practice is closed as of now. I don't want to take part in this ghastly social welfare circus, this stupid carnival any more. If you feel you've anything to complain about, go to central Africa, to Burundi, and explain that we in this country don't find things all that easy. But piss off. Rent some turf hut or other in Drenthe and spend a weekend doing bisexual cooking under the guidance of some sandal-wearing softie or other. Go gay-golfing in Zeewolde. Do a Gestalt weekend in an old villa in Hattem. Have your cock head pierced and say you have discovered yourself at last with a ring through your dick. But bugger off. Beat it.'

I said: 'You need help, doctor. You are in urgent need of professional help.'

From Playing with Your Life (Spelen met je leven). Amsterdam, 1996.
Translated by John Irons.

Hans Teeuwen & Ronald Smeenk
Extract from *Heist*

'I mean, of course they must decide for themselves to be black or not. But if they're then discriminated against, they shouldn't come over all surprised. I didn't ask them to be black, did I? Did you?'

'No.'

'Well, then.'

'But, er... I've got this friend, OK, and he's from Indonesia – but he's more brown-like...'

'Well, yes, I mean: a touch of brown, that's no big deal, is it, but I mean: if against your better judgment you're black as pitch, then you're asking for it!'

'Yeah... then you're really provoking people!'

'Exactly, provoking people. I mean: have you ever been given a hundred guilders by a black man?'

'No...no, never as yet. Well, once, but that was under threat.'

'Oooh yes, under threat, well! Get hold of them and bring out a soldering iron, and they play Santa in no time, don't they! But I mean, normal like, out of the goodness of their heart?'

'No, never as yet.'

'Well, then, there you are. And I haven't even said anything about those knives, have I?'

'What knives?'

'Those knives! The one's they're always planting in your back!'

'Oh, right.'

'I mean, the fact it happens once, I don't find that so bad – I've probably done it myself on occasion, but they're always at it, get it, and that's the difference. They can't keep things in proportion.'

'No, no... But they've got this sense of rhythm, haven't they!'

'Well, you know who I really admire? Adolf Hitler. Heard of him?'

'Adolf Hitler.. the one from the Second World War?'

'That's him.'

'Oh yeah, heard of him, right.'

'They're always on about the bad stuff with Hitler, aren't they, always the bad stuff. But the good stuff – the motorways, Volkswagens, concentration camps – they never mention them. You've got to get an all-round picture. You can't blame the Jews for everything everywhere. If two people quarrel, there's two to blame, that's my opinion. I mean, the Germans weren't all as nice as pie, you know...'

'Weren't they?'

'Oh no, oh no. For when you sometimes hear those stories...'

'Oh yes, those stories. Yes, yes.'

'Then I sometimes also think to myself: Oh ho, oh ho!'

'...what stories was that, then?'

'I mean, you don't know of course how much of it's true. A lot gets exaggerated, naturally, but sometimes you hear that the Germans, that at night they sometimes did some house searches and that they bashed away with the butts of their rifles on doors in the middle of the night... so you got woken up! While they didn't even know for sure if there were people in hiding there.'

'Get away!'

'Well, I mean, you just can't do things like that, right. If you bash away against a door with your rifle butt in the middle of the night, you bloody well have to be sure that there are people there who're in hiding, in my opinion. But, then again, of course they're a load of trumped-up stories.'

'Exactly.'

From *I Am a Rough Stone = Conférences* (Ik ben een ruwe pit = conférences). Amsterdam, 1996.
Translated by John Irons.

Wim de Bie
Driek the Gadget Freak

NOTICE AND WARNING!!!!

This is a WARNING and also an ALERT MESSAGE to all UFO observers in Central Holland.

Dear All,

If dozens of UFO sightings should take place this afternoon, don't raise any major alarm.
The thing is, there is a very large chance (99%) that you are dealing here with a UFO that's come from me, Driek the Gadget Freak.

This afternoon, at 13.17 hours, I launched a UFO that I had ordered via the Internet.
It is (was) a masterpiece, consisting of a radio-controlled cupola, to which a choice of two balloons could be attached – a UFO or an airship.

If you want to fly it, you need to clamp one of the balloons onto the vehicle, after which you go to a flower shop or a party shop to get the balloon filled with helium.
Yesterday, I went to the Ome Gijs party shop to have my UFO filled. This morning it was still fully inflated and this afternoon I launched it from the empty parking lot of the C1000 Supermarket.
The sun shone and my silver UFO ascended at breakneck speed into the atmosphere. It was a breathtaking spectacle. And then it happened...

Because I was standing gaping looking upwards, I forgot the radio control!
When I had recovered my wits, my UFO was already out of range and had soon disappeared over the horizon.
(In the manual it admittedly states that it is for indoor fun, but what's the point of a UFO indoors? That's no fun at all.)

Help!
I'm counting on all Internet users. If you see it fly past, just send Bieslog a mail. Thank you very much!

With best regards
Driek, in sackcloth and ashes

From bieslog.vpro.nl
Translated by John Irons.

Paint

as Mercurochrome

On Vincent Geyskens

The painter is a zombie. Vincent Geyskens, himself a zombie, says so.

Geyskens is a well-educated young painter (1971-): Academy and Higher Institute in Antwerp, cultural studies in Leuven, visiting student at the Rijksacademie in Amsterdam. In 1997 he went on to become one of the prize-winners – and one of the few painters – of *Jeune Peinture*, a major competition for young visual artists. His first one-man show followed that same year. The first work I ever saw of his was in the now celebrated *Trouble Spot* exhibition, mounted at the Museum of Contemporary Art (MUHKA) in Antwerp in 1999.

It was a pleasurable introduction, not least thanks to *Sylvia,* a charming portrait of a beautiful blonde. A fairly small canvas, 60 by 55 cm, but a powerful painting. I was immediately drawn to this picture because it expressed something it does not express. The fact is that, despite her explicit pose and purposeful presence, it was as if Sylvia was not real in the painting. There was something about her expression that troubled me too: she looks, but she doesn't see.

Later on I learnt that Sylvia is, *was*, a photograph, from one of the millions of magazines available from news-stands today. So she didn't really exist for the painter. She posed for someone else, for something else, another medium - a camera. She came to the painter as a picture, a gorgeous yet mundane snapshot. A close-up, the sort of picture produced so often that we scarcely see it any more. It almost cancels itself out. There are lots of this sort of pictures around and they are growing in number all the time.

And in the meantime the painter is left wondering: what shall I paint next? Because there are an awful lot of paintings around too.

Whether Sylvia does in fact *really* exist or not, is not altogether clear. What is 'real' nowadays? There are more images produced than there are eyes to look at them. And that image mountain looks increasingly real. The concept of authenticity is going through a long-drawn-out identity crisis. In his turn, many an artist is at odds with his, by definition, artificial and phoney occupation.

Sylvia is beautifully and subtly painted. It is just that it is 'not quite real', and the painting concentrates on that *not quite*. The colour of the skin, the

Vincent Geyskens, *Sylvia*.
1998. Canvas, 60 x 55 cm.
Photo courtesy Galerie
Annette de Keyser,
Antwerp.

lips, the hair – it is all just a little too much. Moreover, the eyes are looking in slightly different directions, so that together they are not looking anywhere. We are talking here of minute differences, which set it apart from the original. We are talking of a slight deviation, which is not intended as a comment – Geyskens does not want to go in for cultural criticism here – but, rather, subtly shows what the art of painting is capable of, for it is in those slight exaggerations and anomalies that the paint manifests itself. It is the paint that creates Sylvia's strange state of painted image of a photographed image.

In the case of photographs, the question of likeness rarely arises as it does in paintings. *Sylvia* is, of course, not deconstructed à la Picasso into an unrecognisable jumble of forms – she looks solid enough. But who does she look like? Or what? The paint has stripped her, more than the photo, of references to a real person. Yet I am pretty sure that this picture is more alive than the photograph on which it is based.

Vincent Geyskens is painting at a time when that is not the obvious thing to do – contemporaries who paint are rare, for most artists now use more

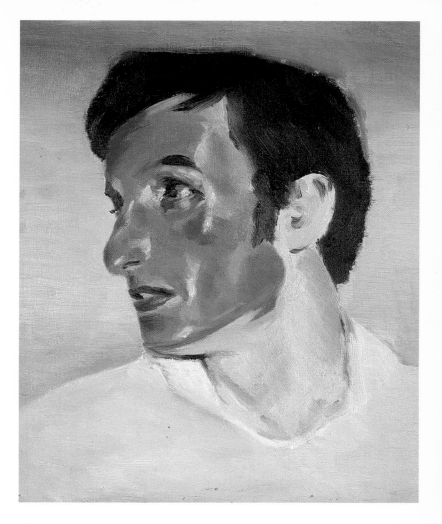

Vincent Geyskens, *Self-Portrait*. 1999. Canvas, 50 x 40 cm. Photo courtesy Galerie Annette de Keyser, Antwerp.

modern means to express themselves. He is aware of this, gives lectures about it and the subject is implicit in his every painting. Each is an exercise in *survival* and in denial. In other words, nowadays the art of painting is an act of denial, and therefore an act of affirmation.

After all, no painter can ignore the science that not so long ago proclaimed the end of his profession – often with much pseudo-intellectual aplomb. Anyone putting a brush to canvas today automatically refutes that obituary notice. Or is, as Geyskens claims, one of the living dead. The painter sets to work post-mortem, lives and works *after* the conclusion of a matter. As Geyskens writes in his essay 'Bildungsidealen' in the magazine *A-Prior,* the art of painting '*wanders round restlessly, unable to justify its existence*'.

That is as problematic as you want to make it. '*The problem of painting*', Geyskens relativised in a lecture for students of art history, '*is one that concerns the theory of art, and is rarely a problem for the painter who paints*'. That is not to say that Geyskens paints away merrily with a free hand; the reality is that he thinks quite a lot about matters of art theory while he is

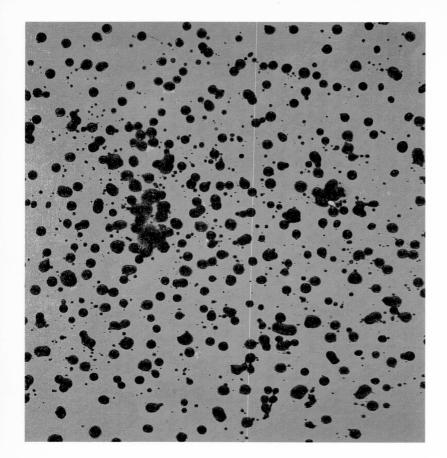

Vincent Geyskens,
Taches de beauté. 2000.
Canvas, 55 x 50 cm.
Photo courtesy Galerie
Annette de Keyser,
Antwerp.

working. That thinking does not prevent the pleasure he takes in painting radiating from many canvases, nor does it deter his drive to master all the tricks of this age-old and cunning medium. Geyskens paints figurative, paints abstract, paints the two together, paints portraits, but also a loaf of bread, boxing gloves, skulls, flowers, a baker's oven, bodies, parrots, confetti, pornographic images, horses, and – just once – himself.

That one self-portrait is again taken from a photograph, but this time from one the painter took of himself. He made himself up for the pose, or rather, he smeared his face with a browny cream. His face is shown in profile, thereby drawing attention to the fact that throat, neck and ears are free of makeup. He has made his lips red and also applied a smudge of red to his cheekbone. The whole mask makes an oily or at least a fresh impression – it glistens with paint.

The painter has made himself up ostentatiously and he wants us to see this. The masquerade is quite obvious, the pose is unmistakable. Moreover, this is a mirror image – anyone who has seen the painter in person will immediately look for a likeness. So here a man has expressly made himself up, in the mirror of course, and then taken a photograph of that unnatural, back-to-front image. On top of all that, he is not even looking at us. So what is he trying to tell us?

That we are all wearing masks and that we should perhaps acknowledge

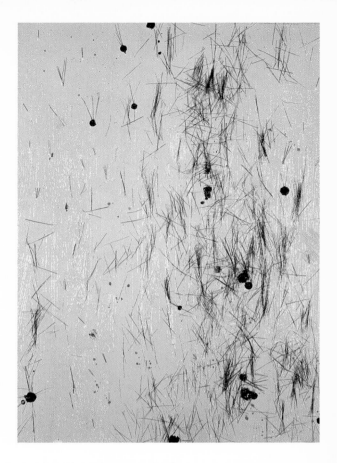

Vincent Geyskens,
Calvinist Skin. 2000.
Canvas, 50 x 35 cm.
Photo courtesy Galerie
Annette de Keyser,
Antwerp.

the fact? That authenticity is only a thin layer of make-up? Perhaps he is wondering if something like the true face exists, for he first painted out his 'real' face with make-up and then painted it back in. Or is what we now see his 'true' face? Is he pointing out to us the impossibility of depicting man, by so distinctly and self-consciously painting the double obstacle he puts in our way – the make-up and the mirror image?

This is a painting I cannot immediately get to grips with. It is an ambiguous self-portrait of the self-portrait. It is extremely self-conscious – pose, mirror image, make-up – but, at the same time, it is empty, it lacks identity. Here something terribly absent is made to exist, and heightened with paint. Vincent Geyskens is fascinated by our modern-day attitude to the body and the image. In its craving for perfection and flawlessness, the image wants to rid the body of its imperfections and the ravages of time. There is also a work, for instance, which looks abstract, yet is anything but. It is, in fact, uncomfortably real. Entitled *Taches de beauté*, what it indeed shows is beauty spots. But how! The orangey-pink background of the canvas, which reminds us of skin, is dotted with thick, shrivelled, deep black blotches – with many paint flakes diluted with linseed oil and pressed onto the canvas with a thin brush.

It is not a pretty sight. A beauty spot exists by the grace of its unicity, its sublime monopoly on an unblemished face. But Geyskens contests that

Vincent Geyskens,
Encore une fois. 2000.
Canvas, 55 x 40 cm.
Photo courtesy Galerie
Annette de Keyser,
Antwerp.

myth by letting loose a whole hoard of those ideals of beauty on us and on
his canvas with thick and creamy, messy paint. The result is a rather repulsive disorder. An ugly skin disease, but then one that has a certain beauty,
albeit as a painting.

A counterpart to *Taches de beauté* is *Calvinist Skin* (globalisation has also
spread to the titles of works of art), if possible an even more unpleasant
sight. On a comparable skin-like background, apart from a few 'beauty
spots', the painter has applied mainly hairs, perhaps brush hairs. This, too,
is an allusion to nosophobia in the way our body is portrayed: everyone is as
smooth as glass – chest hair, underarm hair, pubic hair, it has all been shaved
off for the photograph. Geyskens takes a sardonic pleasure in having it grow
profusely on his canvas. And this painting, too, shows that abstract work can
be very real. It does not contain a single image, and yet it is more tangible,
more tactile than many a figurative work.

Geyskens' most unsavoury painting to date is figurative. *Encore une fois* shows the head of a woman immediately after a face-lift operation, an unpleasant, zombie-like image, brushed in almost pastel shades, rough, fast and seemingly unfinished. The painting combines various antitheses: the charm of the light-blue and rosy tints versus the repulsive subject, the unfinished canvas versus the clear rendering of the battered face, the portrait that is more an anti-portrait.

Vincent Geyskens likes to work with antitheses. For his graduation piece he took one of the most hackneyed symbols in art – the skull –, not to present it yet again in a deathly quiet still life, but to paint it out gradually in an oppressive series of canvases. But something has to be there before it can be made to disappear. The skull is never done away with altogether, a vague suggestive streak of paint always remains – a trace of the living hand that brought the dead subject to life by painting it out.

The series is of course an artistic comment – what can a contemporary painter do with the overexposed icons of his own visual culture? However, it also deals with the human condition: skulls as well as ships perish. All is vanity.

Yet we would prefer not to have known that blatant piece of wisdom, with all its grotesque consequences. Man who flaunts himself while decaying in his own presence. That grotesqueness recurs frequently in Geyskens' heterogeneous work. He doesn't denounce it, he shows it. But not just like that – there is always something ambiguous involved. And often there is that sardonic pleasure, which is bound up with the joy of painting. Geyskens' paint is generally refined, controlled, even captivating, but the undertone varies from mildly ironic to bitter.

Undertone and undercoat are just as important as overtone and topcoat in this work. Even the background is important, in a different way from many recent Flemish paintings – often by followers of guru Luc Tuymans, which all too easily have a uniform, neutral surface. Even in those canvases of Geyskens that are relatively empty, nothing is left untouched. The flatness of the canvas is never absolute, open space must offer relief, suggest depth, reveal paint. The art of painting has rules and this artist plays with them. He doesn't necessarily need to call them into question, that has been done time and time again. Thanks to the lull after the storm, life after death, he can now deal with them in a relatively uninhibited way and as he sees fit.

That leads, as I have said, to a fairly divergent body of work and to an usually large canvas – at least by Geyskens' standards – which, unlike much of his other work, is mostly jet-black. On closer inspection that black consists of many layers – dark piled on dark. Left and right of the canvas, two lines run from the top almost to the bottom, a few centimetres from the edge. They are narrow, luminous bands of paint, meticulously made up of numerous colours: white, yellow, red, purple, orange and light blue. At the bottom of the canvas some mauve filters through and we see that red (among other colours) is concealed under the black. A dark, thrilling painting executed using a whole palette of colours.

It is called *Barbados*, undoubtedly one of those half-ironic titles. What is it referring to; what is the canvas about? Distance yourself a metre or two from a painting and that distance can be bridged. Then the bands of light remind you of neon lighting of the sort that illuminates the carnal sin in red-

Vincent Geyskens,
Barbados. 2000. Canvas,
150 x 90 cm. Photo
courtesy Galerie Annette
de Keyser, Antwerp.

light districts. In this light, *Barbados* could simply have been taken from the naturalistic yet artificial reality of a red-light district. Between the two bands of light we stand, dark flesh and blood, unlit body, pitch-black desire.

In some of his drawings, too, Geyskens uses the ambiguous – both seductive and misleading – lighting typical of a red-light district to make beautiful, mysterious work. As in the oeuvre of many a painter, in this work too the preoccupation with light is a constant. Geyskens does not think much of the romanticism of painting by the only true light, the north light. His own studio is lit by strip lighting, as if it were a kitchen or an abattoir. A painting is an artificial thing, so it is lit by artificial light. But that light can differ from one canvas to another. And this painter works hard at that – I often find the light in his work unreal and intermediate – does it come from inside or outside the canvas? And, above all, do the numerous eyes in these paintings actually notice it?

Is there anyone who *sees* in this work? They do look – more or less -, but often with a fixed, lifeless expression. What, for instance, animates the many women Geyskens has portrayed: Virgina, Lydia, Vera, Sandrine, Elisa, Caroline, Gina, Miranda and Emmy? Something has been taken away from them, and that is animation. Sometimes their expression is hollow, sometimes they stare, in one case she seems almost to have reached a state of ecstasy. Or is it the flash that precedes extinction? The painter has deliberately *forgotten* them, nullified them for the sake of his painting.

The destructive streak in Geyskens – and in many contemporary painters – is understandable. Despite all manner of rebirths, the painter is a threatened species, and the main threat is the increasing production of instant images. Every day the world acquires dozens more, very temporary icons. What can the deliberation of paint provide in exchange? A young painter living in incomprehensible Flanders, Geyskens is only too aware of the much discussed right-handed punch – the unstoppable rise of the extreme right, the Vlaams Blok. That Blok has taken a pair of red boxing gloves as its symbol, a thoroughly demagogic image that really does work.

What can be done with nothing but paint and brush? *Negate.*

On a fairly large canvas, most of which is left blank, Geyskens painted a pair of red boxing gloves at the bottom, technically superb, pictorially perfect. It is, as far as I am concerned, an amazing yet naïve attempt to cleanse this dirty symbol, with paint and mercurochrome.

The painter is a cleanser. In *Envoi* (1997) Geyskens rids a communistic propaganda picture of any possible ideological attribute and presents a rather insubstantial man's head, decapitated and set against a – nevertheless again ambiguous – bright-red background.

And so in this work there are more examples to be found of the desire for cleansing, for purity. But it is ambiguous. How does this *artistic* desire for purity differ from the endlessly depicted and trivialised ideal of beauty the painter so comprehensively demolishes? Perhaps it simply has to do with the paint. Perhaps as a zombie, the painter, in the hereafter of his profession, really can justify the illusion that he, that *his paint* can begin again on an immaculate world on a blank canvas.

Perhaps.

The fact is that this young painter handles an apparently tired medium in a dapper and varied way – so much so that I cannot help wondering if the medium really is so tired. Can a painter achieve anything more beautiful nowadays? To me, at any rate, it was very agreeable to have seen such a lively zombie once again.

BERNARD DEWULF
Translated by Alison Mouthaan-Gwillim.

This article originally appeared in Bernard Dewulfs' *Enlightenments: Looking at Painters* (Bijlichtingen: kijken naar schilders. Amsterdam: Atlas, 2001; pp. 138-146).

irports

and the Environmental Burden of a National Status Symbol

Just about everywhere in Europe the way is being cleared, often with a great deal of political effort, for decisions to expand what is still somewhat endearingly described as 'the national airport'. London Heathrow is full and looking for space to expand; in Paris, even the combination of Roissy Charles de Gaulle, Orly and Le Bourget no longer offers enough capacity and eyes are turning hopefully to a new airport situated (well) to the north of the capital. Zurich is looking for more space; Amsterdam Airport Schiphol is hoping finally to get its fifth runway – and, if it has its way, a sixth shortly thereafter – and Frankfurt also has ambitions for further expansion, though it is also counting on cooperation with the airport in Hahn to accommodate the growth in air travel.

This latter development immediately illustrates a second trend, in which over-full 'national' airports lead to regional airports handling more and more flights: after Stansted, the airports in Luton, Cambridge and other localities are taking over London's excess traffic; Hahn, Hanover and Saarbrücken are doing the same for Frankfurt, as is Rotterdam for Schiphol, Charleroi and Bierset for Brussels, and so on. This dispersal of air traffic is intended partly to relieve pressure on the central airports, but also as a means of escaping from them. Low-cost tourist flights and night-time freight traffic, in particular, are eager to move out to the regions, partly to avoid high landing fees and delays, but partly also to circumvent the nuisance of environmental regulations and restrictions. At the same time, local authorities in the regions around Florence, Seville and other places are hoping that expansion of their regional airports will attract more travellers to their area. Consequently, the political battle about the expansion of the 'national' airports is now being duplicated around many of Europe's 'regional' airports. These political battles focus on noise nuisance versus air travel, on risks versus economic growth, and on the question of how these pros and cons can and should be weighed against each other.

SABENA poster from the 1930s to promote the connection Belgium-Congo: a time when people clearly did not mind planes flying over.

(Inter)continental hubs and regional spokes

There was a time when airports were a focus of national pride. The biggest airport in Belgium is still called 'Brussels-National', and no book on the history of the Netherlands fails to mention the building of Schiphol Airport on the reclaimed bed of the former Haarlemmermeer lake. Governments regarded a national airport as a public utility, comparable with the energy supply and road construction. In times of political upheaval in the (former) colonies, the airport also took on the role, both physically and symbolically, of national refuge. In addition, together with the often massive government support to both the national airline and the national aircraft industry, the airport also had to help ensure that every nation-state was able to play its part in this new economic and technological sector. The close geographic and economic ties between Schiphol Airport, Royal Dutch Airlines KLM and the aircraft manufacturer Fokker symbolised the tripartite and interwoven national and colonial importance of airport, airline and aircraft industry.

Internationalisation, increased prosperity and privatisation have since led to radical changes in the aviation sector. The term 'internationalisation' refers in the first place to the growth in international collaboration and ties between companies and markets. This has led to a rapid growth in international travel, not least by air. Not only has it become very common to fly to the United States, Asia or South America 'on business', but employees also fly daily from Brussels-National and Schiphol to London, Frankfurt, Paris, Milan or Copenhagen, returning home each evening. While it is true that within France and between Brussels and Paris there has been some substitution of air travel by train travel using the high-speed TGV, apart from these specific connections, high-speed trains have not (yet?) had much impact on the amount of air traffic.

In non-business air travel, the trend towards internationalisation has been reinforced by the growth in prosperity and the resultant 'democratisation' of air travel. Holidays by air, until the 1970s the privilege of the happy few, have become available to almost everyone. The popularity of a week spent in the Balearics or the Canaries in spring has pushed Palma de Mallorca into the top 15, and Gran Canaria and Tenerife into the top 30 European airport destinations with more than 15 million and around 10 million passengers per year, respectively. By way of comparison, the top European airports, in London and Frankfurt, each handle 50-60 million passengers a year, while the three airports serving Paris handle around 70 million. Schiphol handles more than 30 million passengers, Brussels around 15 million. More and more of these passengers, too, as well as those using the airports at Rome, Vienna, Milan and Prague – the latter gaining rapidly in popularity recently – are embarking on 'long weekend city trips' as tourists. This area of air travel did fall after 11 September 2001, as non-business passengers in particular were understandably deeply affected by those momentous events. Until that time air travel had been the fastest growing transport sector virtually everywhere in Europe, and unless more unforeseen events occur the upward trend is predicted to resume rapidly. It also has to be borne in mind that freight travel by air was barely affected at all by the terrorist assaults in the US.

Internationalisation and the democratisation of air travel have in any event resulted in the large 'national' European airports, in particular, increasingly developing into continental and especially intercontinental centres. In fact, Europe's top airports – London Heathrow, Frankfurt, Paris Charles de Gaulle, Amsterdam Schiphol, followed closely by Paris Orly and London Gatwick, which in turn are followed at some distance by Rome, Madrid en Zurich – are in competition with each other to serve as nodes in an intercontinental network. This by no means implies that these airports are not of crucial importance for the national economies of France, Germany, the UK, the Netherlands, and so on; what it does mean is that their importance, both as a starting point for passengers and above all as a magnet for yet other economic activities, increasingly depends on competition with other airports which are very close even though located in another country. For example, tourists can now easily begin their journey by travelling first to Paris, Schiphol or Frankfurt if they can arrange their intercontinental travel from there more cheaply, more quickly or more easily; the 'national' airport is no longer always the obvious choice. Moreover, companies that operate internationally sometimes relocate parts of their operation from one airport to another at short notice. This is especially easy because, as the crow – or in this case the aeroplane – flies, the top five airports in Europe are each situated less than 500 kilometres from one or two competing airports. Despite the rapid internationalisation and despite European integration, battle between 'national' interests continues unabated when it comes to air travel. And that battle by no means produces only winners.

The internationalisation process means that the adjective 'national' when applied to airports is at the very least paradoxical. And as regards the political control over those airports, it is a label that is becoming less and less applicable. In parallel with the gradual corporatisation and privatisation of the formerly state-owned national aircraft industries and national airlines, the operation of airports has also increasingly been placed in the hands of the private sector. In fact that privatisation, and the need it has created for increases of scale, has created far more problems for the aviation sector than the disastrous events of 11 September 2001. The aircraft industry has had to stand on its own feet since the 1970s and 1980s, and this has led to increases of scale, international cooperation and, as a corollary, painful business closures all over Europe. The demise of the Dutch aircraft-builder Fokker, to take just one example, made clear how important the aircraft industry was as a symbol of national pride. As a result of that symbolism, economic calculations relating to survival chances, employment and profitability were often overruled by political considerations. Those considerations were and are also decisive factors in ensuring continued government support for airlines. Through all the years of government support for Swissair and Sabena, right up to their failure in 2001, this mix of economic calculation and symbolic considerations was clearly visible.

But back to the airports. Virtually everywhere, their operation has now been placed in the hands of the private sector, albeit sometimes with some government support. The wave of privatisation which washed over once publicly-owned utilities such as energy and communications has thus also reached the airports. The arguments for and effects of that privatisation are also comparable. In listening to the arguments, we hear time and time again that the provision of such utilities no longer forms part of the 'core business' of the government, and that the private sector can moreover do it 'better' and 'more cheaply'. Furthermore, the argument goes, outsourcing puts an end to the odd duality of the government's position in weighing up economic and environmental interests. The effects of privatisation also reflect what has happened in other sectors: airports now operate as businesses just as in other sectors, compete (even) more fiercely, enter into mergers or far-reaching strategic alliances, look to float their shares on the stock market, in turn contract out some tasks themselves, etc. And that inevitably influences the (power) relations with government. When a single company, such as the British BAA for example, owns no fewer than seven airports throughout the UK, that company not only enjoys a whole range of advantages of scale, it also has a remarkably strong position in the national and regional political debate on aviation, on its distribution between the various airports, etc. And this once again throws the spotlight on the importance of regional airports: if the 'national airport' is the 'hub', then regional airports are the 'spokes' of a network, from where passengers can be carried to and from the 'hub' by smaller subsidiaries and smaller aircraft.. In the larger European countries in particular, the 'national' airport is increasingly playing the role of an international hub, with the regional airports as satellites.

Schiphol airport as departure point for Friesian cattle to Canada (1949).

Environmental burden

The growth in air travel has also led to a sharp increase in the nuisance it causes. Moreover, increasing environmental awareness has raised the level of sensitivity to this nuisance. The result of all this is that more or less heated political debates are taking place all over Europe regarding the future of this or that specific airport and, sadly to a much lesser extent, regarding the future of air travel itself. The regionalisation of air travel to all manner of what until now have been relatively small airports means that the environmental debate is now no longer restricted to the large airports, but has been literally and figuratively regionalised.

In substance, the debate naturally focuses in the first place on noise nuisance and, to a lesser extent, on the risks posed by air travel. Accidents such as that involving the El Al Boeing in Amsterdam, Concorde in Paris and the accident in Zurich in 2002 play an important role in this latter debate. If aviation no longer occupies a proud and exclusive national position, but is simply a business sector like any other, then it should be treated and assessed on its risks in the same way as the chemical industry, the nuclear industry, etc. It is in fact remarkable – and symptomatic of that exclusive position – how late this now virtually self-evident idea penetrated aviation and came to play a part, albeit extremely gradually, in the decision-making process. The terrorist assaults of 11 September 2001 will undoubtedly contribute to the carving out of a bigger role for safety and risk prevention around airports, though mainly from the perspective of combating terrorism.

The key element in all discussions about airports, however, is the issue of noise nuisance, followed at some distance by environmental issues such as odour nuisance, land use and the greenhouse effect. As regards noise nuisance, very similar discussion patterns are found around virtually all airports. In the first place, it often takes years before there is a consensus on the precise magnitude of the problem. This is partly because noise nuisance around airports is traditionally – at least around the major airports – not measured, but calculated. Put simply, noise contours are defined on the basis of the number of aircraft movements, and within these contours a certain percentage of the population is regarded as suffering nuisance from noise. But the noise nuisance estimated in this way in no way corresponds with the noise nuisance experienced by those concerned. That is dependent on a host of objective and subjective factors, ranging from the actual noise levels produced by aircraft, the time of day and the wind direction, to all manner of collective and personal characteristics and sensitivities. The result is that the first phase of the environmental battle around airports almost always focuses on setting up a measurement campaign which seeks first and foremost to establish the actual level of noise nuisance and that perceived by local residents. In the Tijdelijk Overlegplatform Schiphol (Temporary Schiphol Consultative Platform) set up by the Dutch government in an attempt to break through the years of stalemate regarding the expansion of the airport, it was precisely the way in which noise nuisance ought to the measured that ultimately proved to be the breaking point.

Another traditional point for debate concerns the expectations regarding the future reduction of noise nuisance by technical means. One of these is changing flight paths so that aircraft spend less time flying over built-up areas and do so at higher altitudes. Another involves the phasing out of noisy types of aircraft. In fact, measures even came into force at European level recently concerning a number of Russian-made aircraft. Optimists believe that these measures will lead to a reduction in noise nuisance in the near future. Sceptics, by contrast, believe that the increase in the number of aircraft movements will more than cancel out any reduction in the noise nuisance produced by each individual aircraft. As is so often the case in environmental issues, the environmental impact per unit may well be reduced, but the overall growth leads to a net increase in that impact.

Another continually recurring item in the debate is 'the length of the night'. The increasing volume of air traffic and the privatisation of airports has pumped up the pressure to turn airports as far as possible into enterprises which operate round the clock. However, the noise nuisance this creates is irreconcilable with people's right to a quiet night's sleep. As a result, political debates are taking place all over Europe on what length of time should be defined as 'night-time', and the courts issue rulings in which they determine the length of the night. In practice, the night-time period around several European airports is set at between 6 and 7.5 hours. Freight traffic and cheap charters are only too keen to make use of the hours 'on the margins' of the night. After local residents have sometimes had to spend years convincing politicians and courts to restrict night-time air traffic at 'national' airports, we are now seeing a clear trend towards simply transferring the noise nuisance to the regions. The economic growth which increased air traffic is expected to bring to the region means that regional authorities are often quite ready to accept more noise nuisance. Moreover, they are often (even) less troubled by active environmental groups. There are virtually no systematic noise measurement campaigns at regional airports. The noise nuisance thus relocates – as is so often the case with environmental misery – to areas less able to defend themselves.

A 'participative mediation approach'

And yet the larger airports in particular – almost all of which, following the wave of privatisations, have become private-sector companies – have evidently gradually become aware of the importance of the environmental debate to their own development opportunities. The websites of all the major European airports devote considerable attention to environmental issues, particularly noise nuisance. Protecting the environment is not only explicitly referred to as an aim, but almost all airports also provide extensive information on their environmental performance. BIAC, which operates Brussels airport, proudly announces that its environmental report was voted the best in 2001 by the Belgian Institute of Auditors (IBR).

However, there is sometimes a considerable gulf between theory and reality; that gulf is often called 'credibility', and on this point the airports and political authorities carry particularly awkward historical baggage. Precisely because of their exclusive position as the locus and focus of national pride, airports and air traffic have to date been subjected to less rigorous environmental constraints than other economic activities, from agriculture to chemicals. This is reflected among other things in the frequent lack of specific environmental targets and the fact that airports often do not have to acquire an environmental licence, or need only a partial licence. It is only very recently that they have been regarded as enterprises like any other when it comes to the environment; enterprises which, again like any other, must render public account for their environmental performance.

It is precisely on this latter point that a sea change appears to be taking place. Experiments involving a much more 'participative approach' have been carried out around a number of major European airports, including Frankfurt, Zurich and Schiphol. The central plank of this approach is not to heighten the potential conflicts between the airport and its surroundings, but rather to mediate, to arbitrate between the various interests. Simply allowing the conflict between the (mainly) local burden imposed by an airport and the (mainly) national benefits it brings to escalate only leads to complete political stalemates. Several airports therefore resort to 'mediation techniques', in which all those involved are in the first instance invited to sit around the table and look at whether particular opposing interests can be reconciled or even traded off against each other. As a means of conflict management, this approach is not new; similar approaches have been and are used, with more or less success, in other politically tricky issues such as the choice of location for storing nuclear waste, or in difficult discussions at regional level between the interests of agriculture and the natural environment.

The Temporary Schiphol Consultative Platform referred to earlier was an attempt to break the years of impasse regarding the expansion of Schiphol by facilitating dialogue between all concerned: the airport, public authorities, the business community, local residents and environmental groups. As also stated, the Platform failed to achieve its aim; after initially hesitating about whether or not they should take part at all, the environmental movement and local residents ultimately stormed out of the consultations. Noise nuisance, and especially the way in which it should be measured and monitored, proved the breaking point, though it was by no means the only area of dispute. It remains to be seen whether the mediation approach in Frankfurt, Zurich and elsewhere proves more successful.

This is by no means self-evident. Historically, the aviation sector has been able to rely on political support because of its close ties with national economic and technology policies; and today, aviation still plays a key role in national economies and can therefore count on solid political support. It is therefore no surprise that the Dutch government to this day insists that in expanding Schiphol, economic goals can go hand in hand with environmental targets. At the same time, figures and scenarios irrefutably demonstrate the unfeasibility of this 'dual mission'; if the environmental targets are to be achieved, particularly with regard to noise, there is ultimately no choice but to restrict the volume of air traffic. It may be that the government will ultimately decide to drop its environmental targets. After the failure of the mediation approach, the recently submitted bill for a new Aviation Act in fact reinforces the exclusive position of airports rather than treating them as ordinary businesses, since safeguarding the ability of Schiphol to compete with other European airports is a key aim. And so we see that airports are still a source of national pride, for which a degree of environmental impact is evidently acceptable.

PIETER LEROY
Translated by Julian Ross.

scapist

Survivalism

From AVL to AVL-Ville and Back Again

Few artists make the news as often as Joep van Lieshout (1963-). The products of his company, Atelier van Lieshout (AVL), sometimes elicit violent reactions. It is not that he sets out to shock, in fact he most likes to give pleasure, but his unadulterated lust for freedom simply means he deals with subjects that approach the moral boundaries of those whose thinking is more orthodox. He trained as a sculptor and has expanded the notion of sculpture both towards pure design and to a conceptual approach to our society. His style manifests itself in no-nonsense, sober and functional designs in light wood or brightly-coloured polyester, and he also uses existing shipping containers which he arranges as functional units.

Most of the works produced by the studio with its twenty-strong team are manifestos that come out against the bigoted mechanisms that prevail in contemporary society. To give two examples, Joep van Lieshout designed a multi-woman bed for men who like to make love to more than one woman, and a sculpture which, despite its stylised curves, leaves one in no doubt that this is a male member of gigantic proportions (*Bioprick*, 1992, coll. Boijmans van Beuningen Museum). A photo of the artist lugging a *Bioprick*, an allusion to the saying that a man 'is guided by his prick' or derives a huge ego from his manhood, was for some time used in an advertising campaign (by Anthon Beeke) for the art loan centres in the Netherlands. If it were not that he showed so much humour, Van Lieshout's machismo would be irritating. But he is at one and the same time dominant yet charming, mischievous yet helpful, aggressive yet soft, a star and yet a community man.

On mortars, free-range chickens and much, much more

In May 2002 the newspapers reported a police raid on AVL-Ville, the anarchic free state in an unfrequented corner of the port of Rotterdam. They were looking for illegally-held weapons. Whether this was a consequence of the recent fear of terrorism or of excessive zeal on the part of the police is not certain. But the confiscation of an 80 mm mortar under the Law on Weapons and Munitions was quite odd. This home-made work of art was indistinguishable from the real weapon and the missing firing pin could easily have been inserted, according to the police. Their interest in a Mercedes converted into a pickup truck with a 40 mm cannon mounted in the back resulted in its immediate purchase by Museum Boijmans van Beuningen, the museum which had previously displayed it. The raid occurred after the ideologically self-sufficient AVL-Ville saw its local authority support crumbling away when a permit for a restaurant was denied them in late 2001. The studio village was already closed to the public on 28 November 2001, six months after its opening. The fact that the codes of local authority regulations clash with those of art is nothing unusual. Art takes the lead in those fields where the power of imagination is the norm and where codes may consequently expand in total freedom while conversely, the law is based on safeguards against the *abuse* of freedom.

AVL uses the art label as a brand name for designs that festively emphasise that which in our regulated society is hypocritically kept out of view. In a country that is home to fewer people than pigs for consumption, people react in shock to the traditional slaughter of a pig and are horrified by the pots in which the meat is kept. Today's supermarket consumers consider customs that were normal for centuries cruel and inappropriate. For the Atelier van Lieshout working community, slaughter, hunting, fishing and growing vegetables are, just like weapons and medical care, essential elements in their independent style of life. A farm is a self-evident part of it all. Long before a place was found for AVL-Ville where all the parts could be brought together, some of them functioned in the art world. And they regularly led to controversy. Even an innocent thing like a chicken run was the object of protest. *Alfa Alfa* (1999) was a contribution to the Munich Festspiele in summer 1999, and was set up immediately in front of the opera house. Despite having sufficient straw, water and feed, these free-range chickens aroused the ire of animal rights activists. The chickens were liberated by the police because they were said to have been too hot in a run that was mounted on

AVL-Ville, Rotterdam, 2002. Photo courtesy of AVL / © SABAM Belgium 2003.

The *Autarka Belt*, indispensable for escapist survivalists. Photo courtesy of AVL / © SABAM Belgium 2003.

a converted car. By handing his own old Alfa Romeo over to the chickens, Joep van Lieshout was not only showing how one could keep chickens in proper conditions with few resources, but was also recollecting his native province of Brabant, where animals are often kept in inventive ways.

A nice side-effect of this sort of commotion is that journalists like to record the artist's comments. As a result, Van Lieshout's opinion on the absurdity of the public criticising his alternative pursuits while uncritically accepting horrific battery farms was heard by a large audience. In cases like this, the artist (by chance following in the footsteps of Beuys) functions as the outsider who confronts society with an ecological paradigm.

In 2001 a conflict again arose between the codes of art and those of society, this time from an unexpected source. This occurred when a team of women gynaecologists and nurses sailed in an 'abortion ship' organised by Women on Waves to various places, including Ireland (though outside territorial waters), to help girls who had become pregnant against their will. The initiative met with a storm of criticism, even more so because they had not yet been given a licence. Part of the reason for the negative reporting was the fact that the design of the operating area had been *subsidised* from the national art budget (through the Mondrian Foundation), which was at odds with the alleged illegal nature of the enterprise. By creating this design for what was called the *A-Portable*, AVL once again demonstrated that it did not shrink from special requests and sensitive matters.

Joep van Lieshout showed the same sensitivity when designing a monument for the grave of Peter Giele. This artist died in Amsterdam on 17 June 1999. He too had made the fusion of art and life into his life's work, but in an entirely different way. His greatest creation was Club RoXy, a discotheque where nightlife and art in the nineties had become interwoven in an unparalleled way. Giele had always been enthusiastic about Van Lieshout's *Skulls* and one of these capsules formed the basis of the monument. From the outside it has a modest appearance and looks a little like a flat vehicle with an opal glass window; inside it contains a meditation space for two people who can lie or sit and share their memories. However, it is four years on and the monument has still not been installed. Although Zorgvlied has a name as a progressive cemetery, its administrators are nervous about the idea that visitors to the grave can withdraw into seclusion to remember the deceased. It is not the work of art itself that is criticised or causes the problem, but its positioning in the context of another code.

A mobile brothel

The most notorious collision with convention took place in the French village of Rabastens, near Toulouse, in the summer of 1998. In this case the mayor closed down the AVL exhibition one day after a festive opening that displayed all the affectation of political self-satisfaction. Criticism by the inhabitants had alarmed the mayor. The exhibition was entitled *The Good, the Bad and the Ugly*, after the film by Sergio Leone, and comprised several parts. There was an Atelier des Armes et des Bombes, an Atelier de l'Alcool et des Médicaments and, as well as several camper vans, the Mercedes with the cannon mentioned above. All in all the exhibition contained quite a bit of provocative bombast, by which Van Lieshout did great credit to his reputation as an 'Easy Rider'. However, this workshop for terrorist activity contained no materials that were not on sale in the local shops and it was very doubtful whether the medical lab really was a pharmaceutical or alcoholic enterprise. All the fuss started when a film crew arrived to make a documentary. AVL drove around in the Mercedes and acted out a combat situation with broad smiles on their faces. It all looks innocent in the photos. But what is allowed on film is not permitted in art. The objects had to stay where they were in the exhibition. The population grumbled that it was like the occupation all over again. But the straw that broke the camel's back was a vis-

Interior of the *A-Portable*, the operating area on an 'abortion ship'. Photo courtesy of AVL / © SABAM Belgium 2003.

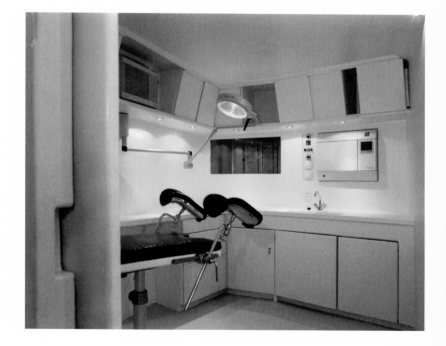

The *Bais-ô-Drôme* (1995), a camper van in the form of a phallus, intended as a mobile brothel. FRAC Rhône-Alpes collection. Photo courtesy of AVL / © SABAM Belgium 2003.

it by a female inhabitant to one of the camper vans. One early morning she found a couple in bed who had been allowed to stay there after the opening because all the hotels were full. The active use of something that is presented as art naturally goes against all accepted ideas and this made the mayor suspicious of the whole exhibition. His argument was that, considering the lack of information and the symbols used (behaviour, violence, weapons, alcohol, drugs and sex), it was not a product of art but a deliberate provocation. The poor man met with a storm of protest from his very own socialist supporters. In the countless reactions that appeared in the press, two issues struggled for priority: the question of where the limits of tolerance lie and the call for freedom of speech.

Unfortunately one particular object went unnoticed in the tumult, perhaps because it is in the FRAC Rhône-Alpes collection, and this is the *Bais-ô-Drôme* (1995). It is a camper van in the form of a phallus and is intended as a mobile brothel. The interior is covered with soft fabric, there is a minibar and a radio. It can be parked at the side of the road to provide a comfortable place for the young girls who wait on the routes running in and out of Europe's cities. The phenomenon of street prostitution is age-old, but the contemporary variant, involving women who, deprived of any form of safety or hygiene, offer their services to anonymous drivers along the motorway is a problem for which there are few effective political solutions. Thanks in part to its humorous association with a *vélodrome*, Van Lieshout was able, charmingly, to introduce the problem of these young prostitutes into our empathic consciousness. And it lodges there, in the domain of socially-critical art, as a symbol with latent practical applicability.

Solid and sexy

The *Autocrat*, part of the AVL prefab pioneer set. Photo courtesy of AVL / © SABAM Belgium 2003.

It was several years ago that the notion of a safe haven arose, a creative community that possesses the fundamental conditions for survival. It was Van Lieshout's response to a request by the new local authority of Almere. This town, in the most recently reclaimed polder in the Netherlands, was the ideal location for a utopian project like this. A prefab pioneer set was developed for the purpose, including a farm, fisherman's cabins and an *Autocrat* (for hunting and skinning). The plan assumed such concrete form that when Almere gave up on its construction, AVL tried to get its own local authority in Rotterdam interested in the project. Agreement on a large polluted site near Zestienhoven Airport promised a stable future for AVL, until recently, when a change in policy brought a cut in the art budget. The question remains whether the wish to withdraw from social conventions can be reconciled with a regulatory authority. When, during a well-attended symposium at the present AVL-Ville in early 2002, Joep van Lieshout showed that he was discouraged by the somewhat uncooperative attitude of Rotterdam, he demonstrated how dependent Utopia is on the real world. Anyway, in summer 2002 the pioneer set was put up in the Middelheim Park in Antwerp, as part of an *AVL Franchise Unit*. A journalist in *The Bulletin* wrote, '*It contains everything necessary for survival. If only people would just cut loose and move in.*' But there was also – yet again – vehement protest about what AVL had done to the site, which had been laid out by the French landscape architect Michel Desvigne. In an article in a Flemish newspaper (under the headline 'The Scandal of Middelheim'), AVL was accused of lack of respect for the park, even of complete contempt for its original intention. The tyre tracks in the mud, wrecked cars and facilities for pigs and chickens found no

favour at all: '*Not only are no accents added, the text itself is utterly and unashamedly ignored and even erased.*' But Middelheim Park acquired the *Unit* as a permanent feature. A definite settlement for AVL-Ville is under discussion with Lille (European capital of culture in 2004) and Essen, both of which cities are determined to transform old industrial sites into cultural areas. And in 2002 in Sao Paolo AVL came up with an indisputable public favourite: the *Sportopia*, an all-round fitness device which attracted many onlookers but was also, and more importantly, intensively used.

Much of the work of AVL is on commission. The team displays an infectious inventiveness. Everything fits in with the unpolished straightforward beauty that Joep van Lieshout has been developing since the early nineties, especially in the sparkling colours of the polyester, a material that gives a solid but sexy look to toilet bowls, bathrooms, offices, meeting rooms and caravans. Since 1994 the Grand Palais in Lille has been home to 60 sanitary spaces that Van Lieshout designed on commission to Rem Koolhaas. He has also made the toilets for several museums, including the Central Museum in Utrecht, while numerous private individuals are delighted with their AVL kitchen, studio or bookcase. For Fons Welters, his gallery in Amsterdam, he designed a bulging facade with a window that looks like a swollen blister. The cafeteria trolleys at MoMa in New York are another example of apparently mass-produced items from a handicraft factory. Little wonder, given the whole range of basic design, the book published in 1997 to accompany the retrospective exhibition at the Kölnischer Kunstverein in Cologne and the Boijmans van Beuningen Museum in Rotterdam is called *A Manual* and is intended to be a guide for DIY enthusiasts who want to provide themselves with an AVL interior. It was because of the great flood of commissions that in 1995 Van Lieshout decided to carry on with AVL.

Their most important creations are indisputably the camper vans. A house on wheels is everyone's symbol of the flight from the land of rules. It is the simplest form of seclusion combined with freedom and with his striking designs in orange, mint green and egg yellow Van Lieshout makes escape fun. He also invented the *Skulls*, small capsules on legs with a big flap so that one person can hide themselves away in it. These cells are based on the American psychiatrist Wilhelm Reich's 'orgone accumulator'. Inside a capsule like this, a human encounters his own body heat and this then increases by one degree, as a result of which he is charged up with orgones and therefore with new energy. When shown in a museum room, these skulls break with the convention that sculptures are not to be touched.

The real camper vans, a marvellously proportioned specimen of which is owned by the Kröller-Müller Museum in Otterlo, are kept outside. Their shape and colour mean they contrast with any surroundings and are thereby irresistibly attractive. One could just step in and drive off, and everything inside works. But in fact nothing is finer than an aroused yearning. According to the codes of art, a metaphor has the greatest impact. AVL has made the boundaries between art and life permeable. As a playground for ideas and imagination, the domain of a museum definitely has its advantages too.

TINEKE REIJNDERS
Translated by Gregory Ball.

www.ateliervanlieshout.com
or www.avl-ville.com

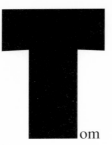om

Lanoye, Literary Multinational

Story-writer, novelist, playwright, translator, columnist, pamphleteer and performer, Tom Lanoye (1958-) is a versatile and much talked-about author. During the course of his twenty-year career, he has become an authority in various literary disciplines, but he has also shown himself to be a shrewd commentator on social matters that extend far beyond the realms of literature.

In the mid-eighties Tom Lanoye was one of the first Flemish writers to show he was not content merely to question the insistence on doctrinaire political commitment in literature, which had completely paralysed the novel as epic narrative; he had the courage to sweep it brusquely aside. Furthermore, he rubbished the obligatory earnestness in literature, which took itself so seriously that any attempt to keep a sense of proportion seemed sacrilegious.

A man with a plan

It began officially (i.e. after a few works which he published himself) with a collection of '*scathing reviews*' entitled *Moonlight and Roses* (Rozegeur en maneschijn, 1983), in which he wiped the floor with writers of seemingly sacrosanct reputation, satirised their style and brutally obliterated the mild criticism of their work that appeared in the leading newspapers. In *Mud* (Bagger, 1984) he collected a number of poems debunking the genre, which were a complete departure from the norm both in tone and subject-matter. He regarded the writing of his critical reviews, especially, as training in the art of writing: his direct, appealing style and cutting, satirical tone, with the necessary effects where appropriate, were designed to hold the reader spellbound. Reading between the lines of the literary rubble left in Lanoye's wake, the reader could see what Lanoye was driving at without it being expressed as a coherent vision, never mind a programme: formulating an accusation against the calcification of literature and the soullessness of society as a whole, which had allowed inertia and hypocrisy to proliferate and made the uncritical middle-class state the highest virtue. A sort of political correctness before the term was invented, though one weighed down by defeatism. On the back flap of *Moonlight and Roses* Lanoye writes: '*The only purpose of this little book is to leave the world as I found it: cunning, vicious, blasphemous and as ugly as sin.*'

He has not written much more poetry, but has on occasion found it a fitting medium for his undeniable sensitivity and circumspection. In *Cock's Tail* (Hanestaart, 1990) he blends irony and verbal pyrotechnics with melancholy at the so-great imperfection of life, something he rebels against again and again in various areas of his work. It was recognition of this sense of moral defence against a powerful, destructive and unreasoning fate that mankind sometimes brings upon itself which spurred him to translate the poems by British War Poets which appeared in *No Man's Land. Poems from the Great War* (Niemands Land. Gedichten uit de Groote Oorlog, 2002).

Initially the career Tom Lanoye mapped out for himself was restricted to literature. He wanted to have written a book of poetry, a book of stories, a book of polemics, a play and a novel by the time he was thirty. The novel, which appeared one month before his thirtieth birthday, *Everything Must Go* (Alles moet weg (1988), filmed by Jan Verheyen in 1996) was an ode to the mercantile spirit of industrious Flanders, seen through the eyes of an unassuming, self-employed travelling salesman. But Lanoye's lyrical descriptions of the achievements of the entrepreneurial spirit appear to cloak an ambivalent love-hate relationship with his country, initially with ambiguous, later with unadulterated irony. The country's material wealth conceals spiritual poverty, emotional narrow-mindedness and petty short-sightedness. In his vision of the world, Lanoye is overcome by the banality of life. All higher things are merely semblance, the rather unedifying reality sets the tone. In 'Sold! Apology of a Travelling Salesman' ('Vendu! Apologie van een handelsreiziger') in the collection *I Used to Be Better* (Vroeger was ik beter, 1989) he claims '*that everything is by definition banal. (…) All you can do is sing a lament about the inevitability of the banal, and call that lament art, and hope that it brings solace. And otherwise sit back and wait for death.*' This view was probably influenced, as various references in his work suggest, by the death of his brother in a car crash.

Tom Lanoye sought to re-establish a link with epic literature, declared redundant by the political commitment that typified writers in the 1970s, and referred with a shamelessly ironic attitude to the previously unexploited potential of the narrative form. In so doing he opened the floodgates for a new generation of writers, unhindered by convention or slogans, by discretion or modesty. In his autobiographical novel *Cardboard Boxes* (Kartonnen dozen, 1991), with its originality of form, he gave a sensitive account of his youth and of his awareness as a boy of his homosexuality.

Epic of a nation which loves to fiddle

Meanwhile he had made quite a name for himself in Flanders and the Netherlands as a performer and columnist. But he also let it be known that he still had aspirations as a novelist. Between 1997 and 2002 his three-part novel epic appeared, starting with *The Divine Monster* (Het goddelijke monster) which, concentrated into a powerful family history set in the nineties, put the spotlight on the width and breadth of *la Flandre profonde*. What is going on in a country where (in 1996) one man – Marc Dutroux – with a few accomplices can abduct and murder a number of children? What prompts three hundred thousand people to take to the streets of Brussels, one Sunday in October 1996, in a long march that was not inspired by any political or ideological motive? Mass hysteria or heartfelt indignation? Or an attempt to exorcise the evil in society, which had manifested itself in a very real way and which was even suddenly embodied in one man? The epic is full of references to important figures, to recognisable facts and situations, and the second part *Black Tears* (Zwarte tranen, 1999) ends with a 'White March'. But in *Malicious Tongues* (Boze tongen, 2002) he transcends recognisable reality and concentrates a whole generation's view of life in the tragic mental breakdown of his female protagonist, the weak link in her family unit. The ruin of the family, culminating in a masterful apotheosis of destruction, stands as a symbol of the moral decay of an entire society at the end of the millennium, a turning point which will hopefully also bring about a new mentality.

In this epic work Lanoye brings together a number of recognisable evils in one story, not for their own sake, but to bed them in a society, in a mentality that sows the seeds of such situations and to provide a picture of the sort of poisoned ground they thrive in. A tangle of power and interests, hypocrisy and excesses, laxness and lack of responsibility. In that society, in which things are never what they seem, people feel uncomfortable and cannot be themselves. Against this background, the banality that dominates this society takes on alarming traits.

The greatest achievement of this epic is its impressive scope, the many independent visions, analyses, opinions and suggestions expressed throughout by different characters, designed to provide a balanced overall picture of a Belgium riven by wangling and cheating and scheming, and yet where so much goodwill is nevertheless alive. Where three hundred thousand people did indeed take to the streets in the name of innocence. But did so '*with that subservient, polite awkwardness typical of the inarticulate Belgian, who is the epitome of backwardness and hypocrisy and disguised skulduggery*'.

The writer as managing director

Behind Lanoye's harsh views and merciless sarcasm lie, albeit well-concealed, great rage, a sense of impotence and disappointment, which he subjugates with tremendous liveliness and ironic elusiveness. Some conflicts or paradoxes he refutes with the tactic of '*If you can't beat them, join them*'. By its reluctance to keep company with commerce traditional literature lost touch with society. From the outset, when Tom Lanoye took to the stage it was to deliver his texts with great bravura. In so doing he reached a wider public, and he quickly attracted the attention of the media. His reputation stimulated sales of his books. Though no advocate of the commercialisation of literature, he nevertheless believed that since it could not be avoided, authors would be well advised to use it to their advantage: '*The point I am making is that commercialisation is an inevitable phenomenon and one that conditions our age and our society*'. In total accordance with this, and again not without an ironic undertone, in 1992 Tom Lanoye formed the public limited company L.A.N.O.Y.E., whose social objectives as formulated in the articles of the company are: to supply (his own) texts, organise (his own) appearances, produce and distribute video and film recordings and to publicise all this. He appointed himself managing director. As early as 1986 he had said in an interview: '*I would most like to become a literary multinational*.'

As a playwright, he made his international breakthrough with *To War* (Ten oorlog, 1997), his adaptation of Shakespeare's history plays – actually, he rewrote them and updated the language –, an eight-hour theatre marathon presented in three parts. With particularly powerful dramatic expression and using a current idiom, he translated the perennial themes of these plays into a contemporary attitude to life, which he tried to record like a seismologist. Though there are no references to recognisable persons or events in this work, it does reflect on wider associations of power and the abuse of power, on dubious motives and political responsibility. Thus the public, who cannot remain indifferent to the overwhelming physical and visual power of the spectacle, is presented with a penetrating metaphorical view of the contemporary world. At the same time it casts doubt on the position of the author in a world which makes it impossible for him to be indifferent to politics, and on the power of language as his medium. *To War* received considerable press coverage, both in the Low Countries and in Germany. It was a milestone in the often controversial recent development of the theatre in Flanders and the Netherlands, and in the history of the adaptation of the works of Shakespeare. Similarly, in 2001 Lanoye turned Euripides' *Medea* and Apollonius of Rhodes' *Argonauts* into *Mamma Medea*, a drama about the discordant relationship between man and woman as a metaphor for contemporary cultural differences.

As a columnist, a formidable observer and commentator, in fact the first of his kind in Flanders, Tom Lanoye speaks for the conscience of progressive Flanders. Shrewd and incisive, with hilarious irony or merciless sarcasm, he keeps close track of political and social developments. His columns, appearing mainly in the popular weekly *Humo* and later anthologised in *Do it!* (Doén!, 1992) and *Weights and Measures* (Maten en gewichten, 1994), have quite a large circulation and an avid readership. His critical voice reverberates in all sections of society and is even heard in parliament. In 1989 the Christian Democrat Member of Parliament Eric van Rompuy – ten years later (oh, irony!) Minister of the Government of Flanders for Economic Affairs, SME, Agriculture and Media – published an appeal in two Flemish newspapers for a *Kulturkampf* against the prevailing '*nihilism*' and '*permissiveness*' that are poisoning the cultural climate in Flanders and '*undermining the link with traditional Flemish culture*'. Moreover, he refers by name and exclusively to Tom Lanoye's novel *Everything Must Go*. Perhaps he has read and understood too little of Lanoye to grasp the true concern that underlies his crushing sarcasm, or to comprehend the means available to the artist to offer resistance. But above all the word *Kulturkampf* was an extremely unfortunate choice in a country where the extreme right made steady headway in the successive elections of the eighties and nineties.

From iconoclast to authority

In his columns Lanoye broaches the most diverse subjects, but most frequently he focuses on alarming political developments, particularly in the city of Antwerp, where he lives and where the extreme right-wing political party, the Vlaams Blok, has made the most headway. With undiminished drive and fearless satire, he analyses the party's success and invalidates its arguments and dubious principles and objectives. In his writing, through his appearances, stands and strategies, he has caused shifts in the democratic camp and provoked about-turns, crystallised the progressive ideology and helped along a number of developments. For instance, he persuaded two well-known politicians from different parties, Mieke Vogels and Patsy Sörensen, to join forces. And it was bound to happen: anyone who makes political comment his cause, is sooner or later confronted with the question of whether his views would not be better served with a political mandate. In 1999, Tom Lanoye was unexpectedly elected to Antwerp district council as a member of the ecological party AGALEV.

Tom Lanoye (1958-). Photo by David Samyn.

Many in his circle of acquaintances, writers and politicians feared that this was a step too far. His influence as a man of letters and performer is much more important and more forceful; it is also more in his blood than the job of political representative. Moreover, columnists with so much charisma are all too rare. Lanoye decided to renounce his seat.

After twenty years in the literary business, Tom Lanoye is now a feared but also respected analyst and critic of modern-day society, in Flanders and abroad – because in the meantime he has fallen in love with South Africa and, for all its paradoxes, that country too occupies an important place in his columns. In his work he combines social insight with style, he couples profound earnestness and merciless humour, honesty and integrity, personal motivation and social commitment. The sheer range of his talent has generated a widely recognised authority. The boyish iconoclast has become a veritable institution.

JOS BORRÉ
Translated by Alison Mouthaan-Gwillim.

www.lanoye.be

In the meantime trucks were speeding past Tony, loudly honking their horns, flashing their headlights and throwing up a curtain of water, which the Transit had to drive through as if it were a waterfall.

Just let my windscreen wiper keep working, thought Tony anxiously. The other one had given up half an hour ago, with the first heavy rainfall.

Please don't let it die on me, thought Tony. That would be a disaster. Then I'd have to wait on the side of the road for God knows how long. It can rain for days around here. And I haven't got the money to have it fixed. I've got to get to Antwerp. Then my problems are solved. There I can sell this monster, with its broken windscreen wiper, worn-out motor, a sieve instead of a roof and who knows what else. Whoever wants it can have it. I'll be lucky to get five thousand francs for it.

But the wiper kept going. It waved bravely on, struggling against the water. And so it came to pass that Tony was able to reach Antwerp, the biggest city in the country, without any unscheduled stops or accidents.

Antwerp sits on a bend of the once mighty river Scheldt like a yoke on a hunchback. Centre of diamonds, of gastronomy and folk traditions, among them gluttony, hard drinking and showing off. City which had gone through nearly all the riches that had been dragged in from the colonies and squandered, fruits of cruelty, of torture, of slavery. Like a broody hen on a wind-egg she sits on her port, which was at one time the biggest in the world but was now, despite all the dredging operations and political plotting, steadily declining in importance. Faded glory, lost dominion.

City where fifty years ago the last architect was sewn into a leather sack, which was weighted down with lead balls and dumped into a bottomless dock, and where since then new buildings have been designed by the politically-appointed brother of the sister of the cleaning lady of the man who can copy the old style so perfectly. A place under the dictatorship of oak beams in every ceiling, of the rusticity of the brick wall with an antique wagon wheel against it, of pompous facades with curlicues meant to look baroque, of greyness, drabness, hatred of colour and imagination.

City where boasting passes for conviviality, just as cattle pass for women in the paintings of Rubens.

Where the cathedral has only a tower and a half instead of two, because once upon a time stinginess won out over devotion and a sense of aesthetics, and where since then people think that tower and a half is the most beautiful in the world, because good sense is no match for chauvinism.

Breeding ground for painters and writers, shunned in life, forgotten in death. Or worse, interred in a musty museum and worshipped, not their work, but for their ties to this village among metropolises.

City of the empty church and the full pub, and the boredom is greater in the latter.

Centre of everything that is old and worn-out and reeks of decay.

City of past jazz triumphs, of bygone hippiedom and days of yore. Fat city, flabby city, heart attack and liver disease. Sore which will dry up rather than burst, due to its laziness. Acidification, salinisation, waterways clogged with silt. The Bruges of the twentieth century.

This Antwerp, once a symbol of trade and commerce, was the city where Tony's salesman's dreams would run aground for good. What was past was past. And even so he would let himself get carried away one more time; for one more day he would have hope and believe in those dreams himself. After that he would disappear.

The freeway merged into an imposing network of highways. Roads coming from and leading to every corner of the country came together here and formed a complicated pattern of cloverleaves, overpasses and on-ramps.

Tony drove past high-rise apartment buildings, the indoor stadium and the two gigantic spheres of the water purification plant. In the distance he could see the start of the harbour.

Cranes, antennas, smokestacks and seagulls, in the diffuse grey of the falling rain. Ships from every corner of the world were piloted here along the Scheldt; they tied up and were then unloaded and re-loaded. Containers lay stacked up; freight cars were shunted to the right docks. Tankers were hooked up to pipelines, which were connected to terminals and silos. Warehouses dominated the picture. And above the refineries burned the eternal flame, high atop a special chimney. Here a jubilant industry flickered away its abundance of energy, like a breast discharging excess milk.

From *Everything Must Go* (Alles moet weg). Amsterdam: Bert Bakker, 1988, pp. 232-234.
Translated by S.J. Leinbach.

Extract from *Weights and Measures*

Passport to Nowhere

'Have you already come up with a title for that show you're never going to write?' I ask. Marianne and I are on our way to D.F. Malan Airport. I am flying back to Belgium; she is going to Malawi.

'Yeah, no. I have a few new ones, but I'm not sure about them. *The Unbearable Dykeness of Being*. Then only the intellectual dykes are going to come. There are only five in the whole country. And I've had all five, and I'm on bad terms with all of them. I'd rather call it *Schindler's Lifts*. About a serial victim who picks up female hitchhikers in miniskirts and gets raped by them every time...'

'Did you have a nice time here these last few weeks?' she asks later, as she lifts my suitcase out of her car.

'Do you want an honest answer or a mean one?' I ask, taking her backpack out of the car.

'A mean one,' she grins, my asthma-diva *sans* moustache, 'you know me, right?'

'OK,' I say, looking into her eyes, 'mean it will be. There is nowhere else in the world I'd rather have spent these last three weeks than here, in this country, more specifically by your side.'

She immediately puts on her most sultry Gina Lollobrigida kissy-face: 'You little devil, you breakka ma heart. Oh, I beg you, bear my children! They'll all be boys, and I'll jerk them off before you get anywhere near them.'

In the departure hall we have half an hour to kill. 'You've got to keep something for me,' she says. 'During apartheid it was one of the most valuable possessions a white person had.' She shows me a little notebook with a stiff cover.

'What is it?'

'A British passport. Almost everyone I know had one. It could get you get out of the country quickly, in times of rebellion or persecution. It was a last resort, above all in a psychological sense. I used it once. I didn't think I could live here anymore. I fled to Canada, to Europe...But I found it even more stifling there than here.' She presses the passport into my hands. 'I don't need it anymore. I'm not British. I'm South African.'

'I can't very well give you my passport in return, I...'

'Got it stolen on the Parade, you asshole! Our pickpockets are the best in the world. I told you not to bring anything with you!'

'I know, I'm sorry.'

'Yeah, yeah...It's actually nicer this way. You're leaving behind a Belgian passport which is no use to anybody, and you're taking one back to Belgium which is no use to you. *De la poésie pure.*'

'Why are you going to Malawi?' I ask, with fifteen minutes to go.

'The elections are coming up,' she replies, 'I've got addicted to them. And you, why are you going to Antwerp?'

'Elections are coming up,' I laugh.

'No kidding!' she says, ' When?'

'The European one on June 12 and the important ones on October 9: for the city councils. On that day the Vlaams Blok might break through in Antwerp.'

'June and October! Two elections in four months! Jeez...Shall I come and give you a hand? I know all about them. Ballot boxes with grass inside, computer pirates, hand counting...You can learn a lot from a South African!'

'As a matter of fact, we already are. What's happening here is unique. One nation, many cultures, that's the philosophy of the new South Africa, right? That's the complete opposite of what's happening in the rest of the world. The ethnic troubles in Yugoslavia and Rwanda, the break-up of the Soviet Union and Czechoslovakia, fundamentalism in the East, the extreme right in the West... Maybe your election marks a turning point; maybe it's a positive signal!'

'I wouldn't count on it, babycakes. Most of the time we send out the wrong signals. In '45 you guys drove fascism out of Western Europe; three years later it landed on our doorstep. So now that we've kicked out apartheid, it may just happen that in Western Europe, at some time in the future...Know what I mean?'

Five minutes to go. We are both standing with our boarding passes in one hand and our baggage in the other. 'Why don't you come along?' I say.

'Ag, *kàk*. You should stay in Africa, man.'

'Jeezus,' I laugh. ' This is like the end of *E.T.*!'

'Eugène Terreblanche?'

'No, dummy, the Spielberg film. About that space monster and that little kid. At the end they act out the same love scene: *You come. You stay.* You can pick which one you want to be, the little boy or the extra-terrestrial.'

She puts her hands on her hips one last time and looks at me, her eyes narrowed to slits. 'Consider yourself lucky, mate,' she grins. ' The end of *E.T.* is still better than the middle of *Jurassic Park*. Because there you don't get a choice. If only one of us gets to play the Tyrannosaurus Rex, you don't stand a chance!'

'I know,' I say. While I stand on tiptoes to kiss her goodbye.

From *Weights and Measures* (Maten en gewichten). Amsterdam: Prometheus, 1994, pp. 196-198. Translated by S.J. Leinbach.

An

On-Off Affair

Three Hundred and Fifty Years of Dutch-South African Relations

Jan van Riebeeck's first encounter with the Khoikhoi in 1652, painted by Charles Bell in 1850. SA Library, Cape Town.

On 6 April 1652 Jan van Riebeeck sailed into Table Bay. Since the founding of the Dutch East India Company (VOC) on 20 March 1602, almost exactly half a century earlier, VOC ships had anchored there on a regular basis to take on water, purchase livestock from the local Khoikhoi people, and 'freshen up' crew and ship en route to or from the East. But now the directors of the VOC were looking for a more secure and permanent outpost and ordered that a regular station be set up. This was also intended to prevent the British from settling there (the first in a series of Anglo-Dutch naval wars broke out later that year). Alternatives such as Saint Helena and Mauritius had proved to be unsatisfactory. Jansen and Proot, who spent almost a year at the Cape after being shipwrecked, sent back positive reports. Van Riebeeck's supply post – initially nothing more than a ramshackle fortress, a vegetable garden and some stables for livestock – soon developed into

a settlement. Free burghers settled there from 1657 onwards. These people were mainly arable and livestock farmers, which is why their descendants are still known as Boers (the Dutch word for farmers). Over time they expanded further inland, some of them settling hundreds of kilometres from Cape Town. When the English conquered the Cape in 1795 the population numbered more than 20,000 Afrikaner Boers, at least as many male and female slaves (mostly from South and South-East Asia) and an unknown number of Khoisan natives.

The hazards of the Great Trek: in October 1836 some 40 Boers and their families defeated 6,000 Ndebele warriors during the Battle of Vegkop.

In the course of the nineteenth century, during what came to be known as the Great Trek (1834-1854), thousands of Boers left the Cape Colony and settled in Natal, across the Orange River, and even further north, in the Transvaal. Here they fought off the native Bantu-speaking peoples and founded a number of free republics, but they could not withstand the might of the British Empire. Natal was British from 1842, the Anglo-Boer War (1899-1902) brought the whole of southern Africa under British rule, and in 1910 the former Boer republics became part of the Union of South Africa, along with Cape Colony and Natal. The Union of South Africa acquired dominion status in 1926, became a republic in 1961, and between 1990 and 1994 was transformed into South Africa as we now know it. The man who, 350 years ago, had stood on the shore of Table Bay, pointing to the site for the first VOC buildings, had unwittingly laid the foundation stone for today's South Africa.

The fall of the founding fathers

On 6 April 2002, the South African government did not lay a wreath at the statue of the man who founded South Africa at Cape Town. On 20 March, there were no South African representatives at the official commemoration of the founding of the VOC in The Hague. Clearly the new South Africa does not feel the need to celebrate either the 6th of April or four hundred years of the VOC – which was, after all, an instrument of European expansion and a symbol of western supremacy. Jan van Riebeeck is no longer a founding father, but the man who, on 6 April 1652, brought colonial oppression, exploitation, dependency and apartheid to South Africa. He dispossessed native South Africans of their land and freedom, and imported slaves from all corners of Asia and Africa. In 2002, the new South Africa prefers to celebrate the repatriation of the remains of Saartjie Baartman, a Khoi woman who emigrated to England, where she became a circus attraction known as 'the Hottentot Venus'. When she died, her body was preserved and exhibited as a curiosity at the Musée de l'Homme in Paris.

Jan van Riebeeck still stands at the top of Adderley Street in Cape Town, together with his wife, Maria de la Queillerie. The statues were a present from the Netherlands. The dwindling respect for his achievements is not confined to politically correct politicians. Today, Cape Coloureds united in Khoi organisations, demonstrate at the foot of his statue and demand recognition and compensation. For white South Africans too Van Riebeeck has fallen from grace. Surely this ubiquitous figure, ever-present in schoolbooks and commemorative speeches, was only a political creation? What can we believe about him, if even his portrait depicts someone else? Earlier this year a sharp polemic developed in the South African media on the *real* Jan van Riebeeck. Surely he was just a common thief who was so greedy in his private dealings in Tonkin that he was sent home in disgrace? An ambitious and callous man who trampled on others to reach the top? An orthodox Calvinist who imposed his religion in order to maintain his authority, but loved money and drink? A racist who washed his hands after shaking hands with a Hottentot? The founder of South Africa, who had only one ideal: to leave his own settlement as soon as he could?

Today, discussions about Jan van Riebeeck in South Africa are not discussions about a man, but about a symbol; about perceptions and ideology, as the theologian Russel Botman wrote in the weekly newspaper *Rapport* on the eve of 6 April. History is still very much a hot potato for politicians and the government in South Africa, so there were no official celebrations to mark 350 years of Cape Town and the VOC. Unofficial celebrations did not amount to much, and began with protests by Khoisan organisations. In the Great Church at Cape Town the Dutch Reformed Church held a service to commemorate 350 years of Reformed theology and church life in South Africa. An international conference was held at the University of Stellenbosch and emphasised the comparative historical perspective, but no particular attention was paid to Van Riebeeck. There was room to discuss controversial aspects of the past, even at the Great Church, but a church service is not the right place to hold such a debate. The same applied to the Afrikaans *Die Burger*, a Cape daily which dedicated its Saturday supplement to the VOC on 6 April. The articles were critical, even to an account of the '*the*

blackest page in the Company's history'. This – surprisingly enough – was the Ambon massacre of 1623, an incident rooted in Anglo-Dutch colonial rivalry.

Liberating historiography

During the years of apartheid, Afrikaans literature was an important vehicle for discussion, protest and resistance. That literary *engagement* continues in the new South Africa, and the best contributions to the debate surrounding South Africa's past date from recent years. That debate is essential. South Africa has a historiographical backlog, the Afrikaner historian F.A. van Jaarsveld wrote some twenty years ago. It is imprisoned by its past – or, at least, its perceptions of the past. And this has been the case since 1994. Why has this happened in South Africa? Where did its history take a wrong turning? Is South Africa doomed by its past? History still plays a role in South Africa: it is used to confirm or deny the present on the basis of today's beliefs and emotions.

If there is one man of letters who has discovered and fought against this, that man is Karel Schoeman. *'It is a fairly fruitless exercise to imprison the past in a dilemma of shame and pride'* writes Schoeman, echoing the words of the Dutch historian A.Th. van Deursen in *Armosyn of the Cape, the World of a Slave, 1652-1733* (Armosyn van die Kaap, die wêreld van 'n slavin, 1652-1733). The new South Africa does not need a new history - it needs an untrammelled historiography.

Schoeman's *Armosyn* is an example of liberating historiography. It is a massive work in two parts (published in 1999 and 2001), amounting to more than a thousand pages. It is a history soundly based on historical fact, but written by the experienced hand of a novelist. Schoeman's book is rich in detail and focuses on daily life – *la condition humaine* – at a time when '*all life events were in much sharper relief than they are today*' (Huizinga) and '*there was less comfort in the face of tragedy and want*'. Schoeman offers convincing proof that the Cape under the VOC was far from the idealised aristocratic society depicted under the influence of the Groot Constantia syndrome (a popular image that represents life at the Cape during the eighteenth century as of matchless elegance and grace), but neither was it a world of proto-apartheid. Consider his heroine: a black woman, a freed slave and a successful businesswoman, a slave owner and a progenitor of many families. Her biography takes up only a few dozen pages, but her life is reflected in the descriptions of the era and the world in which she lived. Schoeman describes a society in transition; a society moving away from its European and Dutch heritage towards a new Africa. It is a society full of confrontation, gradual adaptation and acceptance, but also an open society that is full of opportunity. It is an expansive society in terms of time and space – the cradle of today's South Africa – in which the migrating Boers (black as well as white) and slaves are the most important actors. Schoeman's description is completely different to the perception of the last century.

Dalene Matthee also chose a woman for the title of his book *Pieternella of the Cape* (Pieternella van die Kaap, 2000), a historical novel about a contemporary of Armosyn. Pieternella was the daughter of the VOC sergeant Pieter van Meerhoff, a Dane who explored southern Africa and brought slaves from Madagascar. But Matthee's book says just as much about Pieternella's mother, the Goringhaicona woman Krotoa, an interpreter who lived in the Van Riebeeck household and was baptised Eva. Both women lived in two completely different worlds, and both experienced the confrontation between Europe, Africa and multicultural South Africa – a conflict which was the downfall of one of them (Eva), while the other (Pieternella) eventually learned to understand and accept both cultures. With the help of a number of Europeans who, in Schoeman's words, had '*made the transition from Europe to Africa*' – while Van Riebeeck, the official symbol of that world and culture, according to Matthee underwent no such metamorphosis.

Pieternella van Meerhoff also has a prominent role in the novel *Islands* (*Eilande*, 2002) by the historian Dan Sleigh, who claims, however, that his book (which Sleigh prefers to describe as an anthology of novellas) is about men in the seventeenth century: seven men, all of whom '*carried her in their heart from before her birth to after her death*'. The seven were very different. Pieternella's uncle, the Goringhaicona Autshumao, led the group of *Strandlopers* (beachcombers) who lived at the foot of Table Mountain. The Europeans called him Herry (Harry) but in many respects he was Van Riebeeck's opposite number. Under Sleigh's pen he acquires a personality and his honour is restored. Then we have Pieternella's father, who was killed by natives in Madagascar when she was still a child; her stepfather, a Dutch fisherman who brought her up as his daughter; Jan Vos, her mother's East Indian slave; Johannes Gulielmus de Grevenbroeck, the very learned Police

Drawl's caricature of Paul Kruger (1825-1904), President of the Transvaal, in *Vanity Fair* (March 1900).

Council secretary; and a couple more. In Sleigh's engaging novel, written through the eyes of these very diverse characters, we experience almost every aspect of Cape life during the fifty years following Van Riebeeck's arrival. Sleigh the historian is familiar with every scrap of paper in the Cape archive of the voc, and Sleigh the novelist certainly knows how to bring them to life. *Islands* unveils much of the Cape's early history. It was a very unappealing, rough place. It was poor and inaccessible, the work was hard, and its people were a motley bunch from very different backgrounds who were indifferent and harsh towards each other. Jan van Riebeeck could only maintain order by ruling with a rod of iron. The voc was only interested in power and money. The Khoikhoi were rendered dependent on alcohol and tobacco, so that they could more easily be dispossessed of their land and livestock. Slaves were cruelly exploited. The voc showed no mercy to those who broke its laws, and punishments were as barbarous as the age itself. However, Sleigh adds an important – and topical – footnote to this perception of the Cape during the voc era: the challenge of building a new world and a new society is too much for ordinary people and cannot be achieved without struggle and victims. So the Khoikhoi, the slaves, and the ordinary men and women were not the only victims. All the people of South Africa were the victims of circumstance and social structure; and Jan van Riebeeck was no exception.

The Cape: out of sight, out of mind

In Afrikaans, when something has been put to rights they say: '*die Kaap is weer Hollands*' ('the Cape is Dutch again'). A curious idiom, given that it was a time that no-one looks back on with pleasure. Why would one want to return to it? For most South Africans, the Netherlands is a vague and distant country and as the homeland of Van Riebeeck and Verwoerd can have little to recommend it. Even people who claim it as their mother country usually have very little contact with it. South Africans regard the Dutch as they would a jaunty, know-it-all schoolmaster. Older people remember a much stronger expression: *Hollanderhaat* (Hollander Hate). So how were relations between the Netherlands and South Africa over the past 350 years?

The Netherlands shed no tears when the Cape came under British sovereignty in 1814. There were other problems and challenges to be faced, and in any case they had paid very little attention to South Africa. For the voc, the Cape was an essential but costly possession. Occasionally news filtered through of tensions and conflicts between the colonists and local voc officials, for example the dispute at the beginning of the eighteenth century involving Governor Willem Adriaan van der Stel, and in the 1780s when the Cape Patriot movement sought the support of its counterpart in the Netherlands. Apart from the stereotypical descriptions of the Cape by voc officials who spent a few weeks there, a few interesting works were also published. The earliest include books by Kolbe (1727) and Valentijn (1729), and later works by Sparrman (1783), Thunberg (1788) and Lichtenstein (1812). The reports of the Netherlands Missionary Society (founded in 1797) found a wider readership. The Hottentots and Bushmen, the natives of the Cape, had always fired the imagination. In the early nineteenth century they were not seen in a very positive light: a very primitive people, which had not climbed more than a few rungs on the ladder of civilisation. They were nomads, hunter-gatherers and herdsmen who had neither houses nor temples – and obviously no religion or science. Hardly suited to physical work, they were lazy and addicted to the demon drink.

After 1814 the Dutch lost sight of the Cape completely. There was little contact, the Cape church moved closer to the Churches of England and Scotland, and the handful of South Africans studying at Leiden University did not count. Those who wanted to emigrate went to America or the East Indies, where there was space enough for the Dutch to indulge their colonial ambitions. The Dutch did not yet have a 'Greater Netherlands' sense of patriotism. Very little was written about the Cape in the Netherlands. Nothing was known of events in southern Africa: the tensions between the Griquas, Boers and Xhosa, the border wars and even the Mfecane, the massive black migrations caused by the Zulu warrior-king Shaka. Reports of the Great Trek took five or six years to reach the Netherlands.

Gradually, information became available about the fate of *The Cape Migrants or our Dutch Kinsmen in South Africa* (De Kaapsche Landverhuizers of Neerlands afstammelingen in Zuid-Afrika, the title of a book by U.G. Lauts published in 1849). Contacts developed, and a committee in Amsterdam even sent improving literature to the Boer Republics. In this way the Dutch came to learn about the Voortrekkers, Blood River, the Battle of Vegkop, Winburg, the republics of Natalia and the Orange Free State, and the South African Republic. Lauts emphasised the piety of the Boers and their kinship with the Dutch while at the same time painting a contrasting picture of black Africans as predatory, bloodthirsty, inhuman and cruel savages. But the general perception of the Boers was less positive. A typical example is an article from the *Hollandsch Penning-Magazijn voor de jeugd* in 1841. This publication for young people praised the uplifting efforts of their kinsmen in Africa's dark interior who, constantly fighting off wild beasts and *'those thieving Kaffirs'*, were struggling to preserve the morals and language of the Dutch. At the same time, however, it had to admit that its Afrikaner cousins were also harsh, particularly in their treatment of *'the Hottentots and other Africans who were their slaves'*. According to the renowned Christian politician Groen van Prinsterer, the Boers appeared to be more interested in *'subjection and mastery than in converting the natives to Christianity'*. Various missionaries confirmed this view. The Boers did not wish to be seen in the same light as their coloured compatriots, wrote D.P.D. Huet in 1869 in his book *The Fate of the Blacks in Transvaal* (Het lot der zwarten in de Transvaal). Huet and other Dutchmen who had visited South Africa also talked of the *'stiff-necked'* Boers who had little in common with the *'jaunty'* Dutch. In his book *Memories of Transvaal* (Herinneringen uit Transvaal), published in 1879, Theodoor Tromp described the people of Transvaal as cowardly, malicious, hypocritical, perjurious, immoral, inhospitable, lazy, dirty and ungrateful.

Jannie Smuts (1870-1950) during the second Boer War.

Long-lost brothers

In December 1880, the Transvaal Afrikaners put an end to the British an-

'Typical' Boers, as portrayed in *Graphic* (May 1881). Their civilian clothes accentuate the British view of Boers as renegades.

Hendrik Verwoerd (1901-1966) and British Prime Minister Harold Macmillan (l.) during the latter's visit to South Africa in 1960.

nexation of their territory and proved their strength in the Battle of Majuba. Suddenly the Dutch became wholehearted supporters of the victorious Boers; no longer were they referred to as a strange, backward people, who fought among themselves and mistreated the poor Kaffirs. The Boers were now compared to the Beggars who had liberated the Netherlands from Spain: kinsmen, sons of the motherland, scions of the Dutch family. The Netherlands embraced the Afrikaners as long-lost brothers. All manner of cultural and economic relations were born. The President of the Transvaal, Paul Kruger, welcomed this support. The Dutch became actively involved in the development of the South African Republic, particularly in the fields of education and public service.

It is clear that the strong Dutch support for the Afrikaners at the end of the nineteenth century was an expression of nationalism and cultural imperialism. A New Netherlands was being born in South Africa; part of the great Dutch cultural empire based on a common history, kinship, language, culture and religion. The fact that the Dutch and the Afrikaners – although related – were very different peoples became apparent, however, whenever the Dutch and the Boers had to cooperate. That led to misunderstandings, irritation and even *Hollanderhaat*. The Anglo-Boer War virtually put an end to direct Dutch influence in South Africa although, after 1902, important contacts remained between academics and clergy. And there was a regular but small influx of Dutch immigrants, who settled among their Dutch-speaking kin. One of these was Hendrik Verwoerd, Amsterdam-born but raised and educated in South Africa. In the 1960s, when he was Mr Apartheid, this background posed a problem both for the Dutch and for many South Africans.

Thanks to memories of the Boer War and the myth of kinship, the Dutch continued to regard the Afrikaners with affection during the first half of the twentieth century and followed their struggle for self-government with sympathy. The Dutch admired Jannie Smuts – Boer general, politician, philosopher, member of the London War Cabinet during World War I – who worked for reconciliation and cooperation between Afrikaner and British South Africans. From the beginning the Dutch have watched the develop-

Queen Beatrix of the Netherlands and Nelson Mandela in Leiden. On 12 March 1999 Mandela received an honorary doctorate at the University of Leiden. Photo courtesy of NZAV Fotoarchief, Amsterdam / M. de Haan.

ment of Afrikaner culture with interest. Literary histories and anthologies always include Afrikaans literature. In the Netherlands, the name of Jan van Riebeeck became increasingly familiar. He was mentioned in every history textbook and streets were named after him in new neighbourhoods dedicated to naval heroes, explorers and colonials. His fame reached a peak in 1952, when his achievements were celebrated all over the Netherlands – no doubt to compensate for the regrettable decolonisation of Indonesia.

The Second World War and the German occupation of the Netherlands did not really change Dutch sympathies for South Africa after 1945. South Africa had been one of the Allies and liberators of the Netherlands. Field Marshal Smuts, a declared enemy of Nazism and by now a senior world leader, founding father of the United Nations, was revered as the godfather of the airborne food drops early in 1945 which saved the hungry Dutch. The defeat of Smuts and his more liberal race policy in the South African elections of 1948 was a disappointment to many in the Netherlands, but the Dutch were willing to give the Nationalists – kin of their kin, many of them students of its own universities – a chance. Moreover, during the 1930s, 40s and 50s many thousands of Dutch settled in South Africa, and these newcomers described apartheid as a benign colonialism.

Following the Sharpeville demonstrations in 1960, the sympathy of the Dutch for their Afrikaner kinsmen turned to aversion. With the policy of apartheid, South African society was developing in a completely different direction to the Netherlands, which, during the 1960s and 1970s was undergoing a social revolution driven by decolonisation, memories of anti-Semitism, depillarisation, democratisation and the human rights movement. A broad spectrum of anti-apartheid organisations grew up, and the Netherlands felt increasing sympathy for the victims of apartheid. When Nelson Mandela visited the Netherlands he received a hero's welcome, the like of which had not been seen since the visit of another South African president, Paul Kruger. There is no other country in the world with which the Dutch have such close ties as the country that is the legacy of Van Riebeeck.

G.J. SCHUTTE
Translated by Yvette Mead.

rom

Dreams to Deeds

Greens in the Belgian Government: the First Four Years

The Belgian parliamentary elections of June 1999 were historic in more senses than one. Not only were the Christian Democrats, from 1884 to 1999 incontrovertibly the most important party in Belgium, forced into opposition for the first time in more than four decades, but the Green parties Agalev (Dutch-speaking) and Ecolo (French-speaking) joined the coalition government for the first time. The Belgian political system was traditionally characterised by a high degree of stability, with the same three large political groups (Socialists, Liberals and Christian Democrats) dominating the political scene for more than a century. It is therefore quite extraordinary that a new political party should enter the highest decision-making levels in this way.

Yet Agalev and Ecolo (they are not in competition, but stand only in their own language areas) are not doing much more than following an international trend. Since 1995 Greens had also joined coalition governments in Finland, France, Italy and Germany, though with varying success. However, the Greens' role in government in Belgium has several special features. To start with there is the fact that in no other country have the Greens been so successful: from 1978 to 2000 they won an average of 7 % of the votes, significantly more than the *Grünen* in Germany. In addition, the 1999 elections gave them a resounding victory: the combined votes for Agalev and Ecolo took them from 8.4 % in 1995 to no less than 14.4% in 1999. The result of this victory was that the Greens' position in Belgium was better than anywhere else. The Belgian political landscape is singularly fragmented, with even the largest party in government, the Liberals headed by Prime Minister Guy Verhofstadt, gaining no more than 24% of votes. So the Greens, with their 14 %, had more than a fair chance of making their mark on the policies of the new coalition of Liberals, Socialists and Greens. In this respect, the Belgian Greens start from a much more favourable position than their German counterparts, who, with their 9 %, are little more than a 'junior partner' in the coalition with the much larger SPD, which has almost 40 %. The Greens' participation in the Belgian government is interesting for another reason too. Although there is a tendency to label the Greens as single-issue parties, concerned solely with environmental matters, there is of course a broader Green ideology. This body of left-libertarian thought focuses on such elements as personal independence, equality and anti-institutionalism, and the same views are to be found in all Europe's Green parties. On the other hand, the traditional Belgian political culture is characterised by compromise, discussion behind closed doors and the powerful influence of particular interests. In other words there is a clear contrast between Green thinking and the prevailing way of doing business in Belgian politics. The question is, therefore, what are the consequences of this clash between Green ideology and traditional political culture.

Realpolitik

However, it is not very easy to draw up an unambiguous balance-sheet of almost four years of Green participation in government. The picture is clouded by Belgium's complicated federal structure: in 1999 the Greens joined not only the national government, but also the governments of the Flemish, Walloon and Brussels regions, as well as that of the French cultural community. All these administrative levels function independently of each other, and we must consider the Greens' contribution in each one of them.

It was in fact on the government of the Flemish Region that the Greens had most influence, and this is partly because they control two key elements at this level of authority: welfare and the environment. They have several striking achievements in both areas (a new employment agreement in the welfare sector, reforestation initiatives, a policy to counter surplus slurry, etc.) and despite a few lively incidents between the parties in government, it must be said that so far this Flemish government has not made any serious blunders. Nevertheless, the Green movement had to swallow a number of compromises at this level too. Agalev was born twenty-five years ago out of several environmental and other groups which, among other things, opposed the expansion of the port of Antwerp over an ever greater area. The Green ministers now joined their coalition colleagues in passing a scheme whereby an entire polder village (Doel, near Antwerp) would disappear to make way for a new dock. Despite some murmuring by its original grass-roots supporters, the party has emerged from this compromise more or less in one piece. The party's strong man, Jos Geysels, who is clearly in favour of pursuing a realistic policy, succeeded in keeping the dissident voices in his party more or less in line.

Ecolo's participation in the French-speaking and Walloon governments is rather less striking. This is partly due to the different political culture in French-speaking Belgium: whereas in Flanders even the traditional political parties say they are in favour of a 'culture of open debate', which comes closer to the more libertarian thinking of the Greens, political mores in French-speaking Belgium are in this respect a good deal more cliquish. The big Liberal and Socialist parties do not much hesitate to use their position of power, so that the smaller Ecolo hardly gets a look in. There are also problems in Ecolo itself: whereas the Agalev supporters are relatively disciplined in their acceptance of participation in government, this was clearly not the case among members of Ecolo. Louis Michel, the Liberal Minister of Foreign Affairs, was frequently irritated by what he saw as the lack of loyalty on the part of his Ecolo coalition partners, whom he once described as '*the opposition within the government*'.

Doel: a nuclear plant in a polder village which has to disappear to make way for an extension to the port of Antwerp.

Achievements and failures

Although more and more powers in Belgium are being wielded by the Flemish, Walloon and Brussels governments, it is political debate at the national level that still receives most attention. It is here after all, that ideological contrasts are at their sharpest: while a more pragmatic culture of consultation is often found at the regional level, the country's Chamber of Representatives still provides the ideal stage for truly fierce political debates.

Here, too, the green parties can boast of several obvious achievements. For example, Belgium has decided that nuclear power stations will gradually have to close, and it also plays a pioneering role in international environmental negotiations. Control of food quality (one of the main topics in the 1999 election campaign, which was plagued by health scandals) was improved immensely due to the efforts of Magda Aelvoet, the Green Minister of Public Health. There was a markedly liberal law on euthanasia, a regulation for the toleration of soft drugs, and at the request of the Greens the position of several tens of thousands of illegal immigrants was regularised. These are substantial achievements, but there have also been a number of failures. Despite the fact that a Green minister has responsibility for transport, it has not been possible to revitalise the railways. The Greens were equally unsuccessful in granting local election voting rights to immigrants, even though this was symbolically an extremely important issue for their supporters. In the end the Liberal party in government sabotaged this proposal because it feared that even more voters would be pushed towards the far-right Vlaams Blok party. The controversial arms sales to Nepal also went through in the end, in spite of the resignation of Magda Aelvoet (the Green Minister of Public Health and Vice-Premier), whose view it was that no arms should be supplied to undemocratic regimes.

The Green party, and the Green movement in general, grew out of concern about several fundamental issues such as care for the environment, equal opportunities, transport problems and world peace. As far as the environment is concerned there are now some clear achievements, but in other areas Green voters have had to accept some tough compromises. This is of course inevitable in a coalition government, but for a passionate and idealistic party like the Greens, it was a hard lesson. The members of Ecolo, in particular, expressed their displeasure in no uncertain terms at several party conferences.

Too much softball?

Why did the Green parties not manage to get more done, despite representing at least 14 % of the electorate? Firstly there is the fundamental problem that they have extremely ambitious objectives, so that translating their ideals into concrete government decisions will always involve an element of disappointment. However, another problem for the Green ministers turned out to be their lack of experience in the sheer game of power played out between the coalition partners. In Belgium, policy decisions are usually made in the 'inner cabinet', the weekly meeting of the Prime Minister and the six most important ministers in his government (one from each party). All the sensitive issues that will later be discussed in the full cabinet are prepared here first, and if there is disagreement between the coalition partners, it is first sorted out in the inner cabinet. Insiders often describe the decision-making in this inner cabinet as a game of political hard-ball, with the various government parties each stubbornly seeking to defend and push through its own party's policy. In fact each of these top seven ministers has a special staff of private advisors whose sole task is to prepare for the discussions at this meeting. One gets the impression that the two Green vice-premiers (one from each party) were initially not equal to the power games played by the more traditional parties in this core cabinet. For example, the politically sensitive issue of arms sales was dealt with at one of these inner cabinet meetings, but the two Green vice-premiers were unable to make much of an impression.

This lack of political success was not only because the Greens have less experience in this sort of negotiation, but also because they are relatively isolated within the coalition. On the one hand there is the substantial ideological difference with the Liberal party headed by the Prime Minister, Guy Verhofstadt. For example, on an issue like voting rights for non-EU subjects, it turned out that the two parties have completely different concepts of the multicultural society. The fact that the Greens wanted to legalise soft drugs did not always go down well with the conservative-liberal grass-roots either.

Ideologically, the kinship between the Greens and the Socialists is much closer, but in practice this does not necessarily lead to a more cordial relationship. Quite the reverse, in fact. The fundamental problem here is that Socialists and Greens are competitors: election research has shown very clearly that there is a large group of progressive voters who are not really committed to any one party: they might vote for the Socialists on one occasion and for the Greens on another. The Socialist parties are thoroughly aware of this and so for strategic electoral reasons they do not want the Greens' participation in government to be too successful. Ideologically they may agree on a number of issues, but the Socialist ministers very definitely want to prevent the Green ministers getting their own way too often, because then even more voters would be likely to shift from the Socialists to the Greens.

Revolution serving tradition?

Together, all these factors mean that the balance-sheet of almost four years of Green participation in government shows rather mixed results: a number of important decisions have been taken, but the Greens have had to back down on a number of issues dear to their hearts. This is largely due to their lack of government experience: while almost the entire press (even the non-socialist papers) is full of praise for the effectiveness of the Socialist ministers, there is much more criticism of the inexperience of certain Green ministers. It is true that this sometimes leads to tactical errors, resulting in the Greens being bullied into things. A typical example of this is the action of the Socialist politician Steve Stevaert, who forcefully presents himself as a supporter of what are traditionally 'green' arguments, such as road safety and public transport. In addition, he is able to surround himself with a small army of experienced private advisors and thus succeeds better than anyone else in arousing media interest in his environmental initiatives.

In this way the Greens' participation in government creates a particularly strange situation. On the one hand the fact that, only twenty years after its birth, this party is already part of government is a clear sign of political innovation. On the other hand the Green ministers are now accused of being 'inexperienced', and the long-standing parties sometimes manage to grab a number of traditionally 'green' issues for themselves. The Socialists in particular, looking for a second wind after their historic election defeat in 1999, are only too ready to concern themselves with the electoral wishes of the young and well-educated Green supporters. Their longer experience of administration naturally puts them in a better position to achieve something concrete. It may well turn out, with the irony of history, that the great revolution of 1999 will, after all, ultimately reinforce the power position of the big traditional parties. We shall have to wait and see the results of the elections on 18 May 2003.

MARC HOOGHE
Translated by Gregory Ball.
1 March 2003

Gain

versus Godliness

The Dutch Slave Trade

On 1 July 2002, in the presence of Queen Beatrix, the National Slavery Monument was unveiled in Amsterdam's Oosterpark. Not only to honour the slaves and their descendants, but also to symbolise the close ties that exist both between the countries that were once involved in the slave trade and between the different racial groups now living in the Netherlands.

The origins, rise and fall of the Dutch slave trade

The Netherlanders did not start transporting slaves from Africa to the New World on impulse. They followed the example of the Spanish and the Portuguese who, on their voyages to the New World, had first taken African slaves back home and then shipped them to their new colonies in South Ameri-

The National Slavery Monument (by Erwin de Vries) in Amsterdam. Photo by Klaas Koppe.

A drawing by Frans Post of a sugar mill in Dutch Brazil (1624-1654). Stichting Atlas van Stolk, Rotterdam.

ca. Around the year 1500, about three per cent of the population of the Iberian Peninsula were slaves. To outsiders this Iberian trade in human beings initially seemed rather secretive and repellent. However, Dutch objections to the slave trade did not last for very long. After capturing part of Brazil from the Portuguese in 1630, it quickly became apparent that the demand for sugar by Dutch dealers could only be met by a regular supply of slaves. These dealers were members of the West India Company (WIC), which enjoyed a monopoly of trade and colonisation in the Atlantic area. When a number of traders first expressed a desire to engage in the slave trade, the WIC's board of directors, in good Dutch tradition, set up a committee to consider the moral implications of such activity. Unfortunately the minutes of this committee have been lost; but although its recommendations will remain unknown, the outcome speaks volumes. The WIC became involved in the slave trade. Even an enlightened thinker like Hugo Grotius was not averse to the concept of slavery or to the slave trade so long as the slaves were prisoners of war.

Originally the Dutch slave trade was almost entirely focused on Brazil, and between 1635 and 1645 about 25,000 slaves were transported there. But when the Portuguese retook the territory, the WIC had to find new customers. It found them in the Caribbean, where Spanish, French and English planters were desperate for cheap labour once they realised that sugar plantations could turn the region into a 'second Brazil'. Precisely how and when the knowledge and the materials required for growing and processing sugar

199

cane passed from Brazil to the Caribbean remains unclear, but there is ample evidence to suggest that Dutch slave traders played an enthusiastic part in the process. Between 1645 and 1670 they sold about 10,000 slaves. Furthermore, Dutch slave traders also did occasional business in North America. Even before the foundation of the WIC, in 1619, a Dutch 'Man of Warre' had arrived in Jamestown, Virginia with 20 slaves on board, the first to be introduced into North America.

Eventually, however, the Dutch were also denied access to the English and French islands since these could be supplied by slavers from their respective mother countries. The ban gave rise to a new crisis in the Dutch slave trade. Again it looked as if this untypical branch of Dutch commerce was destined to wither away, just as it had seemed after the loss of Brazil. But now it was Curaçao that offered relief. At first sight this might seem strange, since little could be cultivated on a rocky little island where the rainfall was both inadequate and irregular. It was difficult enough to grow enough food, let alone sugar. The Dutch colonists, however, made a virtue out of necessity by turning the island into one of the most important transit ports in the region. From 1658, the transport of slaves to Curaçao got under way. Later on the Dutch island of St Eustatius also attempted to pick up a few crumbs from this transit trade in slaves, but without success. It lay too far from the South American coast to attract buyers from Venezuela, and although it was well placed for planters in Puerto Rico, Cuba, Guadeloupe and Martinique, that area of the Caribbean was dominated by English and French slave traders. But eventually the transit trade in slaves via Curaçao also came to an end. From Jamaica the English were able virtually to monopolise the supply of slaves to mainland South America. In total, Dutch slave ships transported about 200,000 slaves to the Caribbean islands, and most of them ended up in the Spanish colonies.

Nevertheless, the Dutch slave trade continued to expand because, apart from Curaçao, a second market had opened up in the Dutch colonies on the 'Wild Coast'. These became the principal destination for the majority of slaves: 200,000 to Surinam, 16,000 to Essequebo, 15,000 to Berbice and 11,000 to Demerara. Indeed, the demand for slaves in these plantation colonies was so great that the WIC was unable to meet it and from 1734 the Company lost its monopoly and the slave trade was decontrolled. On payment of a fee, any Dutch shipping company could obtain a licence to engage in the slave trade. The result was a rapid proliferation: more than 30 companies, including a number of quite small firms – particularly in Middleburg and Flushing – began trading in slaves. That growth came to an abrupt end after 1775 when it became clear that the planters in Surinam were heavily over-mortgaged and no longer able to meet their financial obligations. Most of them went bankrupt and the shipping firms, who usually supplied the slaves on credit, lost a great deal of money. That was why at the end of the eighteenth century the government in The Hague seriously considered subsidising the slave trade. In the end the government did not go that far, but it did abolish all taxes on the transportation of slaves. The definitive death-blow was the French invasion of 1795. Only during the peace year of 1802-1803 were there one or two more slaving voyages.

The slave trade in practice

Preparing a slave ship for sea differed somewhat from the preparations required by an ordinary trading ship. The difference lay not so much in signing on the crew or the stocking of provisions, but in the purchase of wares for barter. If their goods were not of a high quality, the ships' captains found it almost impossible to obtain slaves. African slave dealers were extremely fussy since at any one time there were usually so many European slave ships lying off the coast that they could choose from an overwhelming range of European goods. More than half the value of most of the cargos consisted of various kinds of textiles. Guns and gunpowder followed in second place. Wines and spirits accounted for about 10% of the value. Besides that there were also 'mixed goods', which included such things as glass beads, mirrors, wine glasses, cream jugs, cutlery, Delft sugar bowls and other crockery, aniseed, bells for horse-drawn sleighs (!), lead, and iron bars.

Over the years, the manner in which African slaves were bought underwent a number of changes. Initially, Dutch slave ships bought their human wares at the forts that the WIC had built along the coast. The garrisons first bought the slaves from African dealers. The slaves were then locked up in the fort's cellars until such time as they were resold to the captain of a Dutch slave ship in exchange for goods that he had on board. This was undoubted-

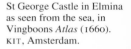

St George Castle in Elmina as seen from the sea, in Vingboons *Atlas* (1660). KIT, Amsterdam.

ALDUS VERTHOONT HET CASTEEL DE MINA VYT DER ZEE.

ly the most efficient method of purchase. The central fort for the Dutch slave trade was Fort Elmina on the Gold Coast (now Ghana), which the Dutch had taken from the Portuguese in 1637. When the Dutch Prince Willem-Alexander and Princess Máxima visited this former slave fort in April 2002, they expressed regret for this black page in the history of the Netherlands.

Eventually, as the slave trade expanded in the course of the seventeenth century, stretches of the coast without European forts started to get involved and the purchase of slaves took place increasingly on board the slave ship itself. Most slavers would spend several months sailing up and down the West African coast in order to give as many African slave dealers as possible the opportunity to offer their wares. When a canoe came alongside, a rope ladder was let down and the dealer climbed on board with his slaves. The captain or his first mate and the ship's doctor would stand ready to inspect the slaves. If it came to a sale, a selection of wares was displayed on deck. The African dealer then made a choice from a number of rolls of fabric, a gun, a bar of iron, and some bottles of liquor. Naturally there was some haggling, but usually the two sides reached an agreement. The dealer put the goods in his canoe, pushed off, and paddled back to the coast. The ship's doctor took the slaves down to the hold where they were given something to eat and drink and then chained up. This method meant that it generally took more than six months before a slave ship had a reasonable number of slaves in its hold. The third method of buying slaves consisted of building a wooden shed on the beach where the goods for barter were stored. The dealers brought along their slaves who, if a deal was struck, would have to spend

Female slave being sold at a Surinam slave market, from P.J. Benoit's *Voyage à Surinam* (1839). KIT, Amsterdam.

one or more nights on the beach before being transported by boat to the slave ship.

An allegory of gain: an African maiden with the horn of plenty, in Johannes Blaeu's *Atlas Maior* (Amsterdam, 1662).

Profit or loss?

Why did Dutch ship owners become involved in the transport of slaves? Why did officers and sailors take part in the slave trade with all its attendant risks, even though they may have regarded the transport and sale of slaves as morally repugnant? Was it because so much money could be made from the slave trade? In fact, the Dutch slave trade was not particularly profitable and there were even periods when many owners of slave ships made a loss. The WIC alone lost 4.5 million guilders in the slave trade to Dutch Brazil because the Portuguese planters in the colony did not pay their debts, in the expectation that their compatriots would soon free them from the Dutch yoke. And the Company did not do much better in the eighteenth century. In spite of all kinds of government subsidies, when the WIC was finally liquidated its debt amounted to as much as four million guilders. Individual shipping firms did somewhat better because they did not have the same level of overheads as the WIC. Unfortunately, the records of only one such shipping firm have survived: those of the Middleburg Commercial Company. Its profits were between two and three per cent. Nowadays we would consider that much too low, but in the eighteenth century such returns were quite normal. In any case, interest rates were no higher.

Abolition: the British clergyman and the Dutch merchant

By the end of the eighteenth century the slave trade was facing increasing opposition. Criticism was also being expressed in a number of publications on slavery in Surinam such as Voltaire's *Candide* and John Gabriel Stedman's book on the cruelty of the planters. In the Netherlands, however, little concern was shown. Perhaps this was to be expected since, in contrast to England, France and Portugal, this particular branch of commerce was in decline from 1780. The question is whether it would still have been the case if the Dutch slave trade had been flourishing. Around 1800, the leading lights of Dutch society were far from being in the vanguard of the enlightened thinkers who dominated European political debate at the time. The new ideas about liberty, equality and fraternity met with a lukewarm response in the Netherlands. The Dutch had to concede that the slave trade and slavery were not exactly philanthropic institutions. Nevertheless, one had somehow to earn a crust – or preferably sugar and coffee – and that would be impossible without slavery and the slave trade. One of the more remarkable defences of the trade in human beings came from the hand of Jacobus Elisa Johannes Capitein, a Ghanaian who came to the Netherlands as a slave and returned to Africa a free man with a doctorate in theology. In 1742 '*the Moor from Africa*' graduated from Leiden University with a dissertation that was to become a best seller. In it, the black preacher with a white heart defended the proposition that slavery was compatible with the Christian faith. It has recently been translated from the Latin into English by the American historian Grant Parker (*The Agony of Asar: A Thesis on Slavery by the Former Slave Jacobus Elisa Johannes Capitein, 1717-47*. Princeton (NJ), 2000).

In the Netherlands, ideals are tried out only after their financial implications have been carefully calculated. It is true that towards the end of the eighteenth century the Dutch slave trade was no longer particularly profitable, but was that a good enough reason to forbid it? On the other hand, the English slave trade yielded far greater profits and it is a remarkable paradox that England was the first to abolish the slave trade. There were two main reasons for this difference between the Netherlands and Great Britain. In the first place, the eighteenth century saw several important religious changes

Portrait of Jacobus Elisa Johannes Capitein. The first line of the poem by Brandyn Ryser reads: '*See this Moor ! His skin is black, but white is his soul*'. Engraving by François van Bleiswijk.

in England. Numerous new radical groups such as the Methodists, Quakers and Baptists were urging their members to strive for reform in their religious and social life, and to do so immediately. The Netherlands had no such groups.

Furthermore, at the end of the eighteenth century England had a fast-growing economy and a new middle class that sought to distinguish itself in all kinds of ways from the ruling elite. The abolition of slavery and of the slave trade was one way of doing this, and the House of Commons had never been bombarded with so many petitions as it was on these subjects. Moreover, the new science of economics, with Adam Smith as its leading light, regarded slavery as old-fashioned. Forced labour could never be profitable, whatever the planters might say. In December 1806 the House of Commons passed a law forbidding all British subjects to engage in the slave trade with effect from 1 March 1808. Radical Protestantism and the new ideology of liberalism had won the day in England.

Holland's neighbour across the North Sea paid dearly for this ideological U-turn. Innumerable successful British slaving companies were compelled, from one day to the next, to develop totally new markets. And the abolition of the slave trade was followed in 1833 by the abolition of slavery, which cost the British taxpayer a further £20 million. Again England was out in front but on its own, for the abolition of slavery in the British colonies meant that a mere 4% of the world's slaves gained their freedom.

In the Netherlands it was the other way around. In contrast to Great Britain, when it came to abolishing the slave trade and slavery the interests of the trader came first. There was no political lobby campaigning for abolition, and the pressure group that did exist remained insignificant. In 1814 King William I, under pressure from England, issued a ban on the Dutch slave trade, ten years after it had already ended. In this way the Netherlands could make a philanthropic gesture without it costing anything. It was not until 1 July 1863 that the Dutch parliament abolished slavery, long after England (1833), France (1848) and Denmark (1848). The long delay in abolition was due not just to lack of pressure from the public but also to the refusal of Dutch politicians to use taxpayers' money to buy freedom for the slaves. However, the situation changed after the introduction of the forced farming system in Java. The sugar and coffee that the Javanese village communities were compelled to cultivate eventually generated so much profit that a single year's production could have bought freedom for the entire slave population of the Dutch West Indies. Forced labour in the East enabled The Hague to abolish forced labour in the West. It opened the way to providing compensation for the slave owners, though not for the slaves themselves. In ending the slave trade and in buying freedom for the slaves, the Dutch merchant had proved more than a match for the Dutch clergy. In the contest between Gain and Godliness, Gain won comfortably.

P.C. EMMER
Translated by Chris Emery.

FURTHER READING

EMMER, P.C., *De Nederlandse slavenhandel, 1500-1850*. Amsterdam, 2000. (English translation in preparation)

EMMER, P.C., 'The Dutch in the Atlantic Economy, 1580-1880'. In: *Trade, Slavery and Emancipation*. Aldershot, 1998.

MENNE POSTMA, JOHANNES, *The Dutch in the Atlantic Slave Trade, 1600-1815*. Cambridge, 1990.

OOSTINDIE, GERT (ed.), *Fifty Years Later. Anti-Slavery, Capitalism and Modernity in the Dutch Orbit*. Leiden, 1995.

Perpetual Masquerade

The Work of Gerrit Komrij

On 26 January 2000 Gerrit Komrij (1944-) was chosen Poet Laureate of the Netherlands for a period of five years by a poll taken among Dutch poetry readers. Appropriate indeed for a man who knew ever since he was a child that he would become a poet: '*I wanted to be a poet as far back as I can remember. It suited me to a T, and I wanted to prove it to the world.*' Following the British example, however, the Poet Laureate would henceforth be required to write a poem to honour every national celebration as well as every national disaster. Was that task really suited to Komrij? Wasn't he in fact the poet who claimed that poetry was affectation, who never wrote what he really meant, whose readers were 'sent off with a verse to sink into the slough of their own self-conceit'? '*Poetry is a whore,*' he wrote in an essay, '*a real poem means nothing. The emptier the verse, the more perfect it is. Poetry, dear reader, is the very height of deceit*'. Or was this, too, deceit?

Upon accepting his appointment Komrij stated that, with respect to his new duties, he saw himself chiefly as an ambassador of poetry, acting '*in the interest of poetry and poets, but especially in the interest of the public. I want to reach people who would never otherwise come into contact with poetry*'. Indeed, Komrij seems cut out for this role. His omnivorous interests, his missionary zeal, and his infectious but ruthless style have all contributed to his formidable reputation in the land of letters. This reputation was doubtless of decisive importance in his selection as Poet Laureate, as it had been when he was awarded the P.C. Hooft Prize in 1993. Komrij received that prize as an essayist. In an interview he reacted with a typical mixture of defensiveness and indignation: '*I'm receiving the prize for my essays. What an awful word. I've never written an essay in my life. Exercises in prose is what they are. If something doesn't rhyme and if it's not a story about two people who break up and get together again, it's called an essay. The word originally meant "an attempt to arrive at something", but now it stands for everything that is academic and unreadable. My work stems from poetry, the mother and source of all things. My contemplative writings probably won a prize because they're more in the public eye. Poetry is a low-profile labour of love. Nobody reads the stuff.*'

Unconventional

Komrij's work may stem from poetry, but he has certainly not confined himself to that genre. In addition to more than ten volumes of poetry, he has published many essays, novellas, short stories, plays and pastiches, several novels, numerous translations and various controversial anthologies.

Komrij began as a poet in the late 1960s, but was catapulted to fame by the reviews he wrote in the early 1970s for the newspaper *NRC Handelsblad*. Later on, collections of his vitriolic reviews and essays were published under such revealing titles as *The Door Is That Way* (Daar is het gat van de deur, 1974), *The Evil Eye* (Het boze oog, 1983) and *With the Blood Called Printers' Ink* (Met het bloed dat drukinkt heet, 1991). Sparing no one, Komrij dragged established reputations through the mud, and the names he blackened included Mulisch, Claus, Wolkers and Bernlef. He even targeted the now nearly canonical 'Vijftigers' (the young, 'experimental' poets whose noisy word-slinging set the tone for Dutch poetry in the 1950s): '*If a company of "Vijftigers" were to step into a lift together, no one would have to push the button. The combination of inflated egos and hot air would make them rise of their own accord, and they would shoot straight up through the roof into oblivion.*' Komrij delights in the rough-and-tumble approach to literary criticism, as witnessed by his portrait of two 'Vijftigers': '*Vinkenoog is beginning to look more and more like a cross between a socially inept grasshopper and a squeaking mussel. And as for Schierbeek, his tragic case is well known. The first two volumes of his collected works – whose weight has already exceeded that of his brain by an astronomical amount, though their content has no weight whatsoever – are the preferred projectiles hurled by quarrelling couples and families with rebellious adolescents. Are these our modern poets?*' The catchword in those days was 'anything goes', and the 1970s – an extremely boring period in Dutch literature – were in need of some pepping up. Moreover, and even more importantly: a quarter of a century later Komrij's caustic style still makes us laugh.

Komrij did not confine himself to heaping insults on the literary world, however. Architecture, and television too, were weighed in the balance and found wanting: '*The infantile and intellectually comatose state of Dutch television proved to be the status quo.*' Komrij also concerned himself with social questions. The corruption of language by politicians, feminism's blind spots, the appeal of Scientology, as well as such delicate subjects as sexual abuse, pornography and refugees – these were all subjects on which Komrij not infrequently voiced an unconventional opinion.

Komrij has occasionally linked his unconventionality with his homosexuality. Homosexuals are outsiders and non-conformists in many respects, though in this regard he refuses to be pigeon-holed: '*I don't like minorities who stick together to the exclusion of everyone else. I only want to be considered part of the smallest possible minority: myself.*' In another respect Komrij does see a direct link between his sexual proclivities and the way he experiences art: '*A homosexual is not just an ordinary person who happens to have a 'different' sexual orientation. Rather, it is by virtue of his sexual orientation that domains are opened up to him which are closed to the middling masses. It is not only his sexual preference that is different, but also his way of thinking, his attitude to life, the sensations he experiences. While mediocre man interacts with his surroundings in an unimaginative and pro-saic way, the homosexual experiences a kind of heightened sensitivity to ev-erything around him. The beauty of art reveals itself in full only to the ho-mosexual artist.'*

Heightened sensitivity

This heightened sensitivity is, according to Komrij, a prerequisite of poetry. Komrij's debut volume, *Magdeburg Hemispheres and Other Poems* (Maag-denburgse halve bollen en andere gedichten), appeared in 1968, followed a year later by *All Flesh is Grass or The Charnel-House on God's Acre* (Alle vlees is als gras of Het knekelhuis op de dodenakker). The titles alone point to Komrij's place in the tradition of dark romanticism. Surrealist influences were also unmistakably present. At that time Komrij was translating work by Salvador Dali, Alfred Jarry and Oscar Wilde. Gradually, over the course of many volumes and anthologies, Komrij developed more in the direction of neo-classical poetry, in which the form – well-thought-out and clear – was of prime importance. His most recent volume of poetry, *Mirages* (Luchtspiegelingen, 2001), even bears the subtitle '*mainly elegiac*'. During this later period Komrij translated works by Goethe and Schiller, as well as various plays by Shakespeare.

Komrij finds the tension he seeks primarily in the act of writing itself. '*Writing involves suffering, physical suffering: you lift the lid of the kettle ever so slightly and let off a bit of steam.*' A regularly recurring image is that of the writer struggling mightily to get the door of a crammed cupboard to open just a crack so that he can let out minuscule amounts of anger, wonder, passion: '*While writing you live in mortal fear of triggering a volcanic erup-tion, a spewing-forth of monsters and prodigies, an unstoppable lava-flow of brilliant constructs and deranged fantasies. In short, you're terrified of causing the whole damn thing to explode. Writing is a frantic process of repression.*'

'*But,*' the poet continues, '*the bits that escape must have the right composition. They must shock, bite, stink. And a little laughing gas can be thrown in for good measure*'. Poetry is supposed to shock. These words are echoed in Komrij's autobiographical novel *Arcadia Ravaged* (Verwoest Arcadië, 1980): '*Whether it was stupid or clever, poetry had to shock. It was a linguistic earthquake.... Poetry was a question of seismography. Poetry was measured on the Richter scale, not on the scales of morality or seri-ousness.*'

Poetry readers with a fine appreciation of morality and gravity therefore find Komrij's poetry hard to take at times. Gravity and laughing gas mingle effortlessly, loftiness and coarseness go hand in hand. Often this results in bitter irony, which Komrij finds indispensable: '*I think the great things in life – death, sickness, loneliness – should be dismissed with a jeer and lard-ed with irony.*' In his poetry it is often the last line that gives an ironical twist to all that has gone before: '*I prefer to think of a poem as a kind of suicide mission. The form kills the content. The last line is the fatal stab.... I could never resist the urge to wring a poem's neck.*' Such notions, alongside pro-nouncements like '*a real poem means nothing*' have often caused critics to emphasise the form, to draw attention to Komrij's virtuoso versifying. On this subject, too, Komrij speaks in antitheses. '*Rhyme is the essence of poetry. Only those who in the process of writing have experienced the wondrous contrasts, loop-the-loops, escapes, catapults and leap-frogs that rhyme can lead to … know how absurd it is to be contemptuous of rhyme.*' And: '*Naturally people tend to misjudge my poems because they adhere to a strict form, as though rhyme has any value in a poem. For years I've been shouting at the top of my voice that you can read right over the rhyme.... It is really very annoying when only the outward characteristics are emphasised, and all the things you've managed to fit in so nicely are completely overlooked.*'

In essence Komrij is constantly playing the devil's advocate: when asked about the rhyme he will point almost indignantly to the content; when asked about the content he takes refuge in irony and virtuosity. The key to understanding this continual changing of hats is perhaps to be found in *Arcadia Ravaged*: '*Ever since childhood Jacob had felt, at first only as a sneaking suspicion, but gradually more distinctly and self-consciously, that his life was literature, nothing but literature. It was not in his nature "to be who he was". He had no aptitude for everyday ennui. He had to stop the flow of* real *tears. Only the* formula *brought a man to life, only a* story *breathed any spirit into events that would otherwise pass unnoticed, vanishing wordlessly. Only by* pretending *could he adopt a pose. Only through literature could he escape.*'

Ambassador

His life was literature. Despite all his unconventionality and irony Komrij is constantly grappling with the question of how literature and life are connected. Many of his essays deal with the question of how one should approach literature, what literature can possibly mean to people. During a lecture given in 1999 Komrij argued: '*You read poetry with your whole being, body and soul. You're not reading poetry properly until you realise with absolute certainty that it is an experience which, all by itself, makes it worthwhile to have lived. Nothing more, nothing less.*' In 1998 a series of essays appeared in which Komrij attempted – in relatively short, easy pieces – to make one hundred classic Dutch poems accessible to a broad public. In addition, he compiled a monumental anthology of Dutch poetry in three volumes: *Dutch Poetry from the Twelfth to the Twentieth Century in 3000 and Some Poems* (De Nederlandse poëzie van de twaalfde tot en met de twintigste eeuw in 3000 en enige gedichten), in which he resurrected completely forgotten poets of centuries past and placed them alongside incontestable greats. The anthology for the twentieth century has even become a yardstick of appreciation for readers and poets alike. Each reprinting has many poets quaking at the thought of how many of their poems will make it into 'Komrij' this time. He recently added an equally monumental anthology of Afrikaans poetry, *Afrikaans Poetry in 1000 and Some Poems* (De Afrikaanse poëzie in 1000 en enige gedichten).

All these publications naturally fit in with Komrij's idea of his role as ambassador. Although the Poet Laureate is doing his utmost to make poetry accessible to a broad public, in his opinion poetry must also make itself more accessible by improving its image. Poetry is not just for a small group of insiders or learned exegetes. Accordingly, Komrij regularly defends young poets; even rappers have been able to count on his support. A bit of entertainment along the way can certainly do no harm: '*It has only been a couple of centuries since poets have persuaded themselves that they don't belong at fairs or circuses, though these were in fact their traditional venues. Any poet worth his salt must be able to go into a café, put one leg up on a chair, strum a guitar if need be, recite to his heart's content and then pass the hat. That's poetry's only hope, and if that doesn't happen, poetry is dead.*' Fairs, circuses: in the end the serious ambassador also finds himself taking part in a perpetual masquerade.

KOEN VERGEER
Translated by Diane L. Webb.

Gerrit Komrij, *Forgotten City & Other Poems* (Tr. John Irons). Plumpstead / Cape Town, 2001.

Four Poems and an Extract
by Gerrit Komrij

The Language-Forger

Language's consonants and vowels portray
The corset and the flaccid belly's spread.
A poet's one who's able to display
An ease when boning them that seems inbred.

Obese or slim, his words without delay
Unite, in fluid couplets sweetly wed.
His secret's effortlessness, not to lay
A smoke screen. He takes language off to bed.

His flask of wine is language – A to Z.
And when half-drunk – albeit just in play –
He spawns a child, an epic or quartet,

Or something in-between – a sonnet, say.
His fight with blubber, though, and whalebone stay
The reader never knows is left unsaid.

From *All Poems up to Yesterday* (Alle gedichten tot gisteren). Amsterdam:
De Arbeiderspers, 1994.
Translated by John Irons.

De taalsmid

De klinker en de medeklinker zijn
De weke onderbuik en het korset.
Dichter is hij die, schijnbaar zonder pijn,
Het vormeloze in de steigers zet.

Zijn woorden, corpulent of slank van lijn,
Verenigen zich vloeiend tot couplet.
De moeiteloosheid, niet het rookgordijn,
Is zijn geheim. Met taal gaat hij naar bed.

De taal, van A tot Z, is zijn fles wijn.
Halfdronken wordt er, zomaar voor de pret,
Een kind verwekt, een epos of kwatrijn,

Of iets daartussenin, zeg een sonnet,
Terwijl de lezer onbekend blijft met
Zijn worsteling met spekvet en balein.

Love

They lie atop each other, scab on rash.
Flakes are heard crackling. Dandruff makes them gag.
Their skulls both glitter with tiara-flash
She fondly strokes his swollen gizzard-bag.

His pinky's gone – a bloody abcess snares.
She squirms. Slime from her mouth forms a balloon
That bursts. His crop grows bluer. Now he dares.
He rolls her on her back. He calls the tune.

His worn-out limbs begin to wave and thrash.
Much grinding now ensues. A pus-filled smell
Of slobber seems to well up from a gash.
She pukes. God's wonder in a nutshell.

From *The Ox on the Bell-Tower* (De os op de klokketoren). Amsterdam:
De Arbeiderspers, 1981.
Translated by John Irons.

Liefde

Ze liggen op elkaar, schurft op eczeem.
Je hoort de schilfers knappen. Roos stuift op.
Hun schedels glimmen als een diadeem.
Ze liefkoost teder zijn gezwollen krop.

Zijn pink verdwijnt in een abces van bloed.
Ze kronkelt. Uit haar mond springt slijm. Een blaas
ontploft. Zijn krop wordt blauwer. Hij vat moed.
Hij rolt haar op haar rug. Hij is de baas.

Dan gaan zijn sleetse lendenen tekeer.
Het is een machtig knarsen. Het gesop
van kwijl in etter kent geen einde meer.
Zij kotst. Gods wonder in een notedop.

A Poem

Line one is simply there to get things going.
Line two is line eleven when up-ended.
Line three's to gain a bit more ground for hoeing.
Line four rhymes with line two - that's what's intended.

Line five gives you a sudden spiteful zap.
Line six's a dozen that's been split in two.
Line seven's such an awful load of crap,
Line eight's dead serious – vice versa, too.

Line nine repeats a now familiar ditty.
Line ten could turn out quite a disillusion
Line eleven's eleventh – more's the pity.
Line twelve's a nothing's ultimate conclusion

From *Magdeburg Hemispheres and Other Poems* (Maagdenburgse halve
bollen en andere gedichten). Amsterdam: De Arbeiderspers, 1968.
Translated by John Irons.

Een gedicht

De eerste regel is om te beginnen.
De tweede is de elfde van beneden.
De derde is om wat terrein te winnen.
De vierde moet weer rijmen op de tweede.

De vijfde draait u plotseling een loer.
De zesde heeft het twaalftal gehalveerd.
De zevende schijnt zwaar geouwehoer,
De achtste bloedserieus. Of omgekeerd.

De negende vertelt nog eens hetzelfde.
De tiende is misschien een desillusie.
De elfde is niets anders dan de elfde.
De twaalfde is van niets de eindconclusie.

The Forthcoming Marriage

My son's about to be married.
My heart dances. There is no lovelier day
for a mother.
A day of rocks that melt,
a day of sparks and light,
the day of my son's wedding.

He has a regal smile. The wind
plays wildly through his hair.
All is well between him and the world.
He will be happy,
he *must* be happy,
I am after all his mother.

Look, how folk acclaim him.
The streets are swarming with people.
His neck rises majestically from his collar,
the collar of his snow-white jacket.
He will disappear among the crowd
and this time I cry with joy.

I am his proud mother.
My name is Elisa Del Carmen,
from the house with the dark scorch mark.
His name was Héctor Alejandro.
He has been gone now twenty years,
just like Pablo and Ramón, his friends.

They call me mad Elisa.
Who can prevent a mother from dreaming?
Look, the wind tossing his black locks.
At his side a wonderful young woman.
Celebrate, Elisa! I deserve such a wedding day.
I cannot get used to his death.

From *NRC Handelsblad*, 26 October 2001; written on the occasion of
the engagement of the Dutch Prince Willem-Alexander and Argentinian
Máxima Zorreguieta, who married in February 2002.
Translated by John Irons.

Het aanstaande huwelijk

Straks trouwt mijn zoon.
Mijn hart danst. Er is geen mooier dag
voor een moeder.
Een dag van rotsen die smelten,
een dag van vonken en licht,
de trouwdag van mijn zoon.

Hij heeft een koninklijke lach. Wild
speelt de wind door zijn haar.
Het gaat goed tussen hem en de wereld.
Hij zal gelukkig worden,
hij *moet* gelukkig worden,
ik ben immers zijn moeder.

Kijk, hoe hij wordt toegejuicht.
De straten zien zwart van volk.
Zijn nek staat fier in zijn kraag,
de kraag van zijn sneeuwwitte jas.
Hij zal verdwijnen tussen de mensen
en dit keer huil ik van vreugde.

Ik ben zijn trotse moeder.
Mijn naam is Elisa Del Carmen,
uit het huis met de donkere schroeiplek.
Zijn naam was Héctor Alejandro.
Twintig jaar is hij nu verdwenen,
net als Pablo en Ramón, zijn vrienden.

Ze noemen me gekke Elisa.
Wie verbiedt een moeder te dromen?
Kijk, de storm in zijn zwarte lokken.
Aan zijn zijde een prachtige meid.
Feest, Elisa! Zo'n trouwdag verdien ik.
Ik kan niet wennen aan zijn dood.

Is happiness worth longing for?

Parsons, psychiatrists and chaplains are all experts in happiness. They can talk about it with piety and conviction.

One can hardly expect a writer to say anything sensible about happiness because it's not his subject.

Yet, my beloved brethren, I would like to ponder on happiness for a moment. Without irony.

Now and then discussions do arise as to whether it would be advisable to have irony marks in Dutch. As well as the exclamation mark and the question mark, there should be some sort of mark to indicate that the writer means 'something else' or 'just the opposite'.

Preferably a pair of marks, indicating that the irony begins here and ends there. In the same way as one opens and closes the parentheses of a quotation. If such a pair of marks did exist they would render illegible the pages of many a writer who deals with happiness, love, loneliness and other Lofty Feelings: kilos of opening irony marks and kilos of closing irony marks would make an eyesore of each page.

The irony mark would contribute exuberantly to ugliness in the world.

This mark wouldn't only be ugly, it would also be undesirable. During the discussions on irony someone rightly suggested that irony that announced itself as such would cease to be irony.

The mark wouldn't only be ugly and undesirable, it would also be superfluous. When one writes of happiness, love or solitude, of sorrow, hate or trust there already are irony marks, an opening one and a closing one: the first is the cradle, the second the grave.

On happiness, then, briefly, without irony and without marks.

Happiness is no theme for a writer, because happiness is stultifying.

From the very moment happiness *exists*, everything turns to stagnation, contentment, milk and honey. Looking at an idyllic painting would send anyone to sleep. When reading utopias about some earthly paradise you feel confronted by the new order. An order of harmony, health and purity.

Perfect happiness is fascist.

It is not for nothing that people jokingly say that they hope they will never get to heaven, where they would be obliged to spend the rest of their eternal existence smirking beatifically and plucking harp strings, and that they would much rather continue their sinful lives in hell, despite the hardships.

Happiness doesn't mean the existence of happiness, happiness means striving for happiness, striving for an ideal that seems to us to be happiness. When you know that this striving will never be achieved – and this you do know – our only happiness then consists of dissatisfaction. Of being unhappy.

The thought of happiness makes you unhappy. Seeing the happiness of others makes you even more unhappy. And anyone who thinks he has obtained a measure of happiness considers it as a punishment, for he knows it is undeserved.

Most people would not even be able to cope with happiness, drastic as it is. On the other hand, when I look around I see many who can handle unhappiness, who can drag themselves through unhappiness quite well. And the better they are at it the less unhappy they feel.

The only form of happiness that is granted us, the only form of happiness there really is, is to live in such a way as to avoid as much unhappiness as possible. That means steering clear of obstacles, looking for loopholes, compromising, sticking your head in the sand, collaborating.

This means reassessing as positive all those characteristics that till now had been labelled cowardly, half-hearted and spineless.

Once again, a notion of happiness that a writer is hardly capable of dealing with.

From *Intimacies* (Intimiteiten). Amsterdam: De Arbeiderspers, 1993, pp. 81-83.
Translated by Peter Flynn.

Gerrit Komrij (1944-).
Photo by Klaas Koppe.

R ichard

Minne, Poetry's Freedom Fighter

In his influential anthology *Dutch Poetry of the Nineteenth and Twentieth Centuries in a Thousand and Some Poems* (De Nederlandse poëzie van de negentiende en twintigste eeuw in duizend en enige gedichten, 1979), Gerrit Komrij indicates his preferences by the number of poems he selects from any given poet. Judging by this, Komrij clearly regards the Fleming Richard Minne (1891-1965) as one of the most important of Dutch-language poets. He accorded him maximum representation: ten poems.

Other poets and critics, too, rate Minne among the greatest Flemish poets of the twentieth century. But his work is no longer in print, and today he has become something of a cult poet. Sometimes his lines surface as protective incantations in select gatherings. Among the public at large he is little known. His poems are 'contrary', with an un- or even anti-poetic quality to them, a tough shell for the surprised reader to bite into. On top of this, Minne's work is too 'Flemish' for many Dutch people, even though it is in no way regionalist.

Revolutionary and poet

Richard Minne was born and raised in Ghent, city of poets, scoffers and other independent spirits. He grew up in a liberal petit-bourgeois family, but became caught up in Ghent's motley band of revolutionaries. Before and during the Great War he was one of a group of lapsed pacifists in the socialist party. After a lengthy rebellion against the party leadership and its war policy the trail-blazers were expelled en masse. Embittered, Minne turned his back on politics; the scars of this affair stayed with him for the rest of his life. But now, free of political slogans, the poet in him could come to maturity. From 1921 until 1924 Minne co-edited the mini-periodical *'t Fonteintje* together with Raymond Herreman, Maurice Roelants and Karel Leroux. Some of the poetry that appeared in it he later published, supplemented with other poems, in his one and only volume: *Open House* (In den zoeten inval, 1927).

Minne's approach to poetry was quite different to that of the great names of the time. Karel van de Woestijne's classical tone was alien to him and he disliked Paul van Ostaijen's modernist techniques. Like Van Ostaijen, Minne was musical and outspoken – he wrote poems on a vast range of subjects, some of them uncommon ones for poetry – but he worked with traditional forms such as rhyme and the quatrain. Yet Minne too was an innovator, especially as a propagandist for language. He introduced the *parlando* style, humour and irony into Flemish poetry, using an unusual and, when one looks closely, a rich vocabulary. Richard Minne never rejected a subject or a word, not even 'unpoetic' concepts or dialect words. They are in his poems, because they *existed*.

With totally unrestricted content and an open-minded approach to language, Minne updated traditional ideas of poetry *from within*. It takes a pure poet, with an absolute mastery of technique and language, to do that.

The demolition man rebuilds

Minne was a master both of the ultra-short and the longer poem. At first sight his longer poems appear to be of epic proportions, not least because of their biblical subjects. The Good Book fascinated him, perhaps surprisingly in someone who at one time doubted whether it should really have a place on his bookshelf. '*Don't read the Bible, it's a load of claptrap, two good lines for every five hundred silly ones*', he advised his friend Raymond Herreman. But some of those 'good lines' inspired him to create three long poems.

On closer inspection, the supposed epic qualities of these three turn out to be far more a matter of caricature and demystification. 'The Wasps and the Apple-Tree' ('De wespen en de appelaar'), for instance, is a free version of the Creation story in which God's exalted work is reduced to routine craftsman's work: '*God grew tired and tetchy. / He'd been creating for hours: / tigers, dandelions, / rheumatics and cauliflowers.*'

The punishment meted out to the reckless Adam and Eve after the business with the apple also undergoes a remarkable transformation at Minne's hands. It is as if we are in a schoolroom rather than the Garden of Eden: '*But there God rose to His feet / and looked over the wall. / – "Pack your bags, you!" and showed / them the door once for all.*'

Another disconcerting, demythologising poem is 'Noah' ('Noë'), set against the backdrop of the Flood. Here Noah is a Ghent boatman who survives '*the great purge*', as do a motley bunch of saints from every corner of the world. Once the waters have retreated these take up their lives again as before, heedless and arrogant. But not their polar opposite: '*Just there, by his heart, Noah felt a wound. / – Come on, St Nobody, he said, and headed out.*' Noah rejects all dogma and turns his back on the world. And that is exactly the nature of Minne's poetry too: relativising and self-willed.

This is not only a constant in the *content* of Minne's work. It is also his *poetics*: upsetting the established order, the aforementioned contrariness as driving force. Minne himself later described his poetry as 'a demolition business'. It was as though he was beginning poetry afresh, attacking not the old forms, as Paul van Ostaijen did, but the old tones and values.

The quest for purity

Minne was a sensitive wielder of sarcasm, who spoke his mind in a colour-ful style and sometimes compelling witty phrases. What interested him most in the Bible was the life of Jesus – and still more the literary reworkings of it. His third 'biblical' poem, 'Prayer before the gallows' ('Gebed voor de galg', 1926) was a quasi-autobiography of Jesus, whose life story, in Min-ne's opinion, almost cried out for an irreverent revamping. Papini's *Storia di Christo* was a failure, he wrote to Herreman; Papini wrote abusive prose '*like a fishwife [...]. What a masterpiece Renan's "Vie de Jesus" is compared to this! Just imagine: the Jesus motif in the hands of a Stendhal! (or a Poe)*'.

Or, for that matter, in his own hands… In late 1929 he volunteered: '*I'm still dreaming of writing a scandalous, debauched life of Jesus. Perhaps the fellow will never before have been so close to us. He's been made a monkey of long enough. I'm going to drag him off his donkey and stroll arm in arm with him over the heather and do the round of the pubs. Dominus vobiscum.*' Eventually he did produce a variant on this idea in his longest prose work, *Heineke Vos and his Biographer* (Heineke Vos en zijn biograaf, 1933).

It is the history – fragmentary, kaleidoscopic, like a collage of no fixed style – of Heineke Vos: misfit, outcast and poet. Heineke is also a kind of ancestor of Monty Python's Brian: a para-Jesus. He is born on Christmas Day, and his delighted father exclaims '*You were sent from God!*'. Father's brother-in-law, who turns up immediately after the birth, is called Melchior. Heineke also has unusual qualities: he can even talk already. Like his bibli-cal predecessor, throughout his life he has to face disbelief, scepticism and indifference. He is driven out of his community and after various doomed relationships and unsuccessful jobs finds human warmth among a few unpretentious, sympathetic souls in a café. Violent fevers put an end to his life, whose surrealistic final scene coincides with the Apocalypse. On '*33 January 1*' Heineke speaks his last words: '*All the saints together don't add up to heaven.*'

The rejection of holiness is a leitmotiv in Minne's work. In many respects Heineke is that Jesus '*dragged off his donkey*' with whom Minne '*did the round of the pubs*'. As he did with God, Adam, Eve and Noah in his bibli-cal poems, so in *Heineke Vos* Minne humanises the Jesus figure. And here too the tone is not blasphemous, but relativising and cleansing. The under-lying idea is the same as in his most famous and least ironic poem, 'Ode to the Solitary One' ('Ode aan den eenzame'): the '*clearness*' of a solitary man, of the independent being is without parallel, '*no shepherd*' even can come close to it.

Richard Minne (1891-1965). AMVC, Antwerp.

A solitary gardener

No different in essence, but more introverted, are Minne's shorter poems. Among the classics here are the ten 'Horticulturist's Poems', the first of which has become the emblem of Minne's personality:

I was besotted with far
seas.
Now I seek happiness
with my peas.

A small fenced plot is all
I need,
and has the value
of a deed.

Minne's melancholy verging on bitterness stems from an unfulfilled yearning which was also a feature of such contemporaries as Jan van Nijlen and J.C. Bloem. At the time he wrote this, between 1924 and 1928, he was working as a farmer in a remote hamlet. For Minne this existence was synonymous with disappointments: a mental illness, for which rural life had been prescribed as therapy; the isolation which robbed him of the 'far seas' of his dreams; and the heavy physical work which undermined his frail physique. But at the same time there is a note of aloofness, of pride in this enforced isolation; and then again, self-mockery at that. This is even subtly worked into the title. The term 'horticulturist' ('*hovenier*') is a euphemism; what he means is a gardener ('*tuinman*'). In reality he was a small farmer ('*boer*'). But no way was Minne going to call this autobiographical cycle 'Farmer's Poems'; with a measure of self-mockery he labels himself a gardener. Add in the simultaneous elevation to horticulturist, and you have self-mockery squared.

The multi-layered quality of Richard Minne's poetry resided *in* the mockery and irony which became his principal trademark. As a writer Minne was a kinsman of the much-admired Voltaire, Heine, Sterne and Smollett, but with a shorter wind. '*Do you really believe that irony is not part of the supreme essence of lyric?*' he asked Herreman rhetorically in 1928. His use of that figure of speech was often self-chastening, as in the 'Horticulturist's Poems'.

This ironic technique did nothing to enhance appreciation of Minne's work. No Flemish poet had ever done anything like it before. Moreover, most of the critics knew nothing of his background. Consequently they found this kind of poetry obscure; one even described it as '*weak, insipid doggerel*'.

On top of this, the poems were far too plain-spoken for the Flanders of the 1920s and '30s. '*Repulsive*' was the label applied by the Flemish Catholic daily *De Standaard* to one poem in the first issue of *Fonteintje*. Probably this reputation was only reinforced by verses with 'Prayer' in the title (such as 'Prayer to the Month of May', 'Prayer to Prayer' or 'Quick Prayer') or constructed in prayer form. However, these were in no way intended to give offence. For Minne 'God' was the ultimate concept against which to measure his existential doubts and his longing for freedom; as his poem 'Triptych' ('*Drieluik*') clearly shows.

'... a flash, a blow...'

The lack of response and Minne's shattered pride came on top of his earlier disappointments, in politics, in his career and in his health. They set in train a slow end to his poethood. After the publication of his one volume he was left with no work, no self-discipline and eventually no money. Salvation came – the irony of it! – from the movement which had cast him out years before. In 1931 Minne got a job on *Vooruit*, the daily newspaper of socialist Ghent.

For the rest of his life the 'red republic' would be his (uneasy) biotope. Minne even went on to become one of the most important Flemish journalists of the twentieth century. His 'Letter from Peterkin' ('Brief van Pierken'), a serial in a sort of Ghent dialect, became extremely popular. After the Second World War he became the paper's arts editor and devoted innumerable articles to his beloved French literature, notably to Jules Renard, Jules Vallès, Diderot, Alain and Léautaud.

At this time he became known above all for his daily column 'In 20 lines'. This really did embody Minne's second youth as a writer. '*I like things short and sweet*', he wrote once, and that literary motto certainly applies to his '20 lines', two collections of which were published. They lean heavily on literature that packs a great deal into a small compass, such as Montaigne's *Essais* and the *Fables* of De la Fontaine – respectively in Minne's striving for a highly concentrated philosophy and in the hints of moralism that flicker through them. The raw materials were exactly the same as in his poems: love of nature, a melancholy shrinking from progress and praise of the individual. The irony and terseness of the old days also returned. His daily column became the natural substitute for his silted-up poetic vein.

After 1927 Minne wrote only a handful of poems, among them 'Resisting Winter' ('Verweer tegen de winter'). These were published in the volume *Snares and Pitfalls* (Wolfijzers en schietgeweren, 1942), together with excerpts from his letters. The latter provided the much-needed biographical background, and understanding and appreciation then followed. But for Minne the poet they came far too late.

Richard Minne had the weaknesses of a tragic Keatsian figure: a sickly, impractical, easily defeated loner who blossomed briefly, dazzlingly, as a poet. In the case of the Dutch poets Jacques Perk and Hans Lodeizen, for instance, that is accepted without a murmur, but Minne is often reproached for producing such a limited oeuvre. After all, unlike Perk and Lodeizen, he didn't die young. Essentially he was no different to them: an introverted, self-contained natural talent, fused with his poetry; with all the vulnerability that brought.

MARCO DAANE
Translated by Tanis Guest.

Eight Poems
by Richard Minne

XII

Oh they talk about me.
But what's there they can say?
Shall I dab on some scent
And twist my hair into ringlets, pray?

Translated by Tanis Guest

XII

O ze spreken van mij.
Wat mogen ze toch zeggen?
Zal ik reukwerk nemen
en mijn haar in krullekes leggen?

The Poet's Vademecum

Act more stupid than you are,
but watch for snares that trip you;
both time and space ignore
but bustle just like hens do.

Work without plan or measure,
But peep through every curtain;
Despise the solid burgher,
But drink deep of his flagon.

Translated by Tanis Guest

Vademecum voor den dichter

Doe dommer dan ge zijt,
maar mijd u voor de klippen;
leef buiten ruimte en tijd
doch spoed u lijk de kippen.

Werk zonder mate of plan,
maar spied door alle luiken;
veracht den burgerman,
doch ledig zijne kruiken.

The new republic

The new republic is strong.
Men write it on blank walls.
Schoolboys stare at it long
and sing an Anacreontic song.

The sun shoots up and falls
to pieces across the eaves.
Everyone, wonder of wonders,
is somehow involved in the deed.

When night falls on the square,
round a brasero, silly and warm,
a fashion seamstress dances
with a democratic gendarme.

Translated by James S. Holmes.

De jonge republiek

De jonge republiek is schoon.
Men schrijft het op de blinde muren.
De schooljeugd staat er op te turen
en zingt een liedje van Anakreoon.

De zon rukt op en tuimelt
uiteen over de daken.
Wonder boven wonder: elkeen
heeft er iets mee te maken.

Des avonds op het plein,
rond een brasero, dwaas en warm,
danst het kleine modistje met
een demokratischen gendarm.

Antidote

Fame attained
by singing a song
is only a flower
that fades before long;

is only a feather,
a golden scale
you can press between
finger and nail.

Is only a flash,
is only a blow.
It's already being
covered with snow.

Translated by James S. Holmes.

Anti-dotum

Gewonnen roem
bij 't zingen van een lied
is maar een bloem
die ge even ziet;

is maar een pluim,
een gouden schub
die ge zo tussen duim
en vinger drukt.

Is maar een flits,
is maar een knal.
Daar is de sneeuw
en dekt het al.

Day of Beauty

The bursting bud; the bee a-buzzing;
the wind that whispers foolishness:
what men know simply as the spring
whose coming drives the earth quite senseless;
now my brain's fizzing with all that -
I'd stick a feather in my hat
if I weren't so respectable,
so stiff in my black frock-coat.
Oh, if I only could unbutton
In one big bunch I'd take you all on,
you lasses from the byre, the town,
you knowing one, you yokel-dumb,
you from the big house, from the slum,
and you, oh tree, and grass, and down,
you too, white slowly-pacing father,
you horse, you sun, you cloud, you water,
and I'd dance in amongst you all,
if I weren't so respectable,
so stiff in my black frock-coat.

Translated by Tanis Guest

Dag van schoonheid

De bot, die berst; de bij, die zoemt;
de wind, die zotheid gaat vertellen:
wat men kortweg de lente noemt
en de aarde komt op stelten stellen;
dat klotst nu alles door mijn kop,
en 'k stak er wel een pluimken op,
als ik maar niet zo deftig was,
zo stijf in mijn geklede jas.
Als ik den band maar los kon knopen,
nam ik u allen dubbelthope:
gij meiskens uit de stad, den stal,
gij wijs als 't boek, gij dom als oordje,
gij uit 't kasteel en gij uit 't poortje,
en gij, o boom, en gras, en wal,
gij witte, wandelende pater,
gij paard, gij zon, gij wolk, gij water,
en 'k danste midden in uw tas,
als ik maar niet zo deftig was,
zo stijf in mijn geklede jas.

Melancholy

A fool or a genius I wanted to be.
Now I'm something in between.
Hence the eternal hopeful waiting
and the outcome: melancholy.

Translated by Tanis Guest

Gogol

I'm reading Gogol. He's the best.
He talks of love and death,
and says people are small
and poison each to all
and still, despite all that,
this life's not to be sneezed at.

Translated by Tanis Guest.

Ode to the Solitary One

You are like a bourn
in the sun of the morn
on the highland of Pamir.

No shepherd on land
in the palm of his hand
ever held your clearness.

From the distant far
only one star
shoots by – and submits.

Translated by Franz de Backer.

All poems from *Open House and Other Poems* (In den
zoeten inval en andere gedichten). Amsterdam: Van
Oorschot, 1955.

Melancholie

Ik wenste snul te zijn of genie.
Nu hang ik tussen beiden.
Vandaar het eeuwig verbeiden,
en de uitkomst: melancholie.

Gogol

Ik lees Gogol. Hij is groot.
Hij spreekt van liefde en dood,
en dat de mensen klein zijn
en voor elkaar venijn zijn
en dat, trots alles, dit leven
nog hoog staat aangeschreven.

Ode aan den eenzame

Gelijk een bron
zijt ge in de zon
op de hoogvlakte van Pamir.

Geen herder zelfs
die in 't gewelf
van zijne hand uw klaarheid schept.

Van heinde en ver
alleen een ster
schiet toe en geeft zich gewonnen.

Trilingualism

in the Low Countries

*Latin for the clergy and the academics, French for the upper
classes and the Huguenots, and Dutch for everyone else*

This article is an abstract of a book about the interaction of the three languages which an educated Dutchman in the period 1400-1800 was expected to read and write: Latin, French and Dutch. These three languages were taught in schools: in Primary schools, in French schools and in Latin schools. There were no English or German schools, and I don't know of any Dutchman of that period who was able to write fluently in English – except Mandeville, of course.

In order to assess the importance of the literature (in a broad sense – everything that is printed) in these languages, I made a list of famous writers who worked in the area that is now the Netherlands and Belgium. I applied three criteria in making my selection: international conferences are devoted to them; foreign scholars write monographs on them; and even if the authors were not native to the Low Countries they settled and put down roots there. Erasmus and Grotius are my absolute stars, with Janus Secundus a good third. All three owe their fame to their works in Latin.

A further condition is that they should all have worked within the framework of Dutch culture. So although the Rotterdammer Bernard Mandeville, whose satire *The Fable of the Bees*, subtitled 'Private Vice, Public Benefit' (1705), stimulated Adam Smith's free market ideas, would seem to satisfy the criteria, he has been omitted from the list because he lived in England and had no influence on Dutch intellectual life. Mme de Charrière (Belle van Zuylen) is left out for the same reason: she belongs to French literature. On the other hand, the immigrants on the list did make a substantial contribution to Dutch culture. The debate about Descartes and Spinoza began in Holland. Amsterdam was not only the capital of the book market but also the international centre of the Republic of Letters, which is to say of the uncensored exchange of opinions between learned men throughout Europe.

The list comprises 33 names, of which 10 wrote in Dutch; 6 wrote Dutch poetry; 2 are famous for their Latin poetry. My book will give more details on all thirty-three of them; here I will list those who are known, at least by name, to the educated public; the mystics Ruusbroec and Thomas à Kempis, the humanists Erasmus and Coornhert, the philologist, philosopher of natural law, theologian, poet in Dutch and Latin and much more, Grotius, the poet Vondel who wrote almost exclusively in Dutch and the poet Constan-

tine Huygens who wrote in Latin, Dutch and French, the poet and professor Daniel Heinsius who wrote in Latin and Dutch and Janus Secundus who wrote exclusively in Latin, the philosophers Descartes, Spinoza and Hemsterhuis, the scientists Christian Huygens (son of Constantine), Boerhaave and Van Leeuwenhoek, the gifted women Anna Maria van Schuurman and Maria Sibylle Merian.

Antoine Wiertz, *La Liseuse de Romans*. 1853. Canvas, 125 x 157 cm. Koninklijk Museum voor Schone Kunsten, Brussels.

French in the South, Dutch in the North

In the Netherlands, as in Italy and France, the humanists promoted the literary use of the vernacular. Chambers of Rhetoric were established after French models, and when the French Pléiade poets in 1550 rejected the artificiality of the *rhétoriqueurs*, the Dutch followed suit by imitating the Pléiade, the Calvinist Du Bartas being unfortunately the most admired poet in the early seventeenth century.

Bible translations in Dutch were at first translations of the Lutheran Bible, but the Calvinists replaced the Lutherans. Dutch psalms and hymns were translated from the French. Mysticism on the other hand, always had strong ties with the German borderland; but it was of a kind that easily connected with Dutch liberal Protestantism and Catholicism.

French influence was most apparent in court culture, but also of course in the bourgeois educated classes. It worked its way north from Southern Belgium towards Holland in the sixteenth and seventeenth centuries, while on the other hand in the Calvinist principalities and Lutheran states of the Baltic region people read moralistic or polemical works in Dutch and Dutch theatre companies went there on tour. Dutch (*Nederduits*) was of course akin to Low-German (*Laagduits*), but it was also understood in Sweden: Queen Christina was able to speak Dutch. Seventeenth-century architecture in the Baltic was clearly influenced by the Dutch; Göteborg was a Dutch city. The language of commerce in Northern Europe was Dutch.

Babel in Mechelen

Johan Huizinga, in his *The Waning of the Middle Ages* (Herfsttij der middeleeuwen, 1919), gives a vivid impression of Burgundian culture in the Netherlands (and in Paris) during the fourteenth and fifteenth centuries. The only Dutch-speaking writer he names is Ruusbroec. The Burgundian court was French, and it remained French after medieval winter gave way to Renaissance springtime in the sixteenth century. In 1507 Margaret of Austria became Regent of the Netherlands for her young nephew Charles v. She had been raised in France and had been married to the Duke of Savoy. She chose Mechelen as her residence.

Her court poet was a French *rhétoriqueur*, in her palace Van Eyck's pictures hung among famous Brussels carpets, and all her public appearances, and those of her nephew the Emperor, were accompanied by Burgundian music. Painting, tapestry, music, all were art forms for which the Italians then envied the Low Countries. The songs that were sung at court are preserved in her Poetry Album; they are in French with the exception of one in Latin and one in Dutch.

The Great Council, the supreme judicial organ, was also based in Mechelen. Consisting of humanist lawyers, it was a centre of Latin culture which maintained close contacts with the Collegium Trilingue in the neighbouring university town of Leuven. This College was inspired, and promoted, by Erasmus for the humanist-scholarly study of the three sacred languages, Hebrew, Greek and Latin, and was set up in 1518. Janus Secundus, son of the President of the Great Council, penned his first love poems in Mechelen in Latin, as he did his intimate correspondence with his brothers and friends.

And then, of course, there were the clergy, the numerous religious festivals as well as the flourishing Netherlandish chambers of rhetoric. So Mechelen was host to four different cultures based on four different languages, since humanist Latin was quite different from the scholastic Latin of the Church, and all in a small town of perhaps 10,000 inhabitants!

French gains the upper hand

Philip Marnix of St Aldegonde was the son of a nobleman who had accompanied Margaret of Austria when she left Savoy on the death of her husband the Duke. He became a Calvinist and worked closely with William the Silent during the Revolt. Dutch was his second language. He is believed to have written the Wilhelmus, the Dutch national anthem. In 1569 he published a vicious satire in Dutch on Catholic belief, in the form of a defence of it, entitled *The Beehive of the Holy Roman Church* (Den Byencorf der H. Roomsche Kerke). A year later a German translation appeared, perhaps by his own hand, and after that yet another German and an English version. At the end of his life, following the same pattern, he published the *Tableau of Religious Controversies* (Tableau des Différends de la Religion), a French-language book that is twice as thick and is remarkable for its exuberant vocabulary, reminiscent of Rabelais. Unfortunately, because academic disciplines are divided according to language, Dutch specialists study his Dutch writings, but St Aldegonde's French work is ignored by Romance scholars.

From the sixteenth century, French was standardised in the interests of an upper class of administrators and aristocrats. But sixteenth-century French was still too verbose, too impure, and its syntax still too chaotic. True classical French, the French of Racine and Bossuet, emerged in the seventeenth century. Frenchmen became increasingly attached to it and declared it to be a universal language, a worthy successor to Latin. The humanists had asserted that anything that could not be said in good Latin must be nonsense. Now the French were proclaiming '*la clarté Française*' as the touchstone for clear thinking.

But it had to be the language of the native French, and their standard was the French of the Court, which looked down on everybody else's manners, in speech or gesture. In gestures the uncouth Netherlanders certainly fell short of the mark. They had no idea how to proffer a pinch of snuff elegantly, and they didn't care. Conversely, the Dutch found the French too frivolous. Even in the nineteenth century, warnings were still sounded about French frivolity and the immorality of French novels.

Only Belle van Zuylen passed the acid test of the French purists. Attempts by Justus van Effen to publish French-language journals similar to the Spectator had little success in France. And indeed much of what he published in French was actually directed at readers in the Netherlands. Anglomania was a French import... But when Van Effen finally began to write his witty character sketches in Dutch, he realised that this would cost him his fashionable lady readers.

The court of the House of Orange was French. William the Silent had been raised in the Burgundian court and his last words were: '*Mon Dieu, ayiez pitié de moi et de mon pauvre peuple*' ('My God, have pity on me and my poor people'). Frederick Henry, the second son of William the Silent, was brought up entirely in French. The presence of his court turned The Hague into a French city with its own *Gazette de la Haye*. Military commands were given in French and there were so many French officers in the army that the garrison town of Maastricht had a French opera company, as did The Hague.

The Hague was a French city, but that tells us little about Dutch culture in general since the Stadholder and his court contributed little to it. The cultural centre was Amsterdam. However, like the rest of Europe after 1650, the Netherlands was swept along by French Classicism and Louis XIV's 'golden age'. The Nil Volentibus Arduum society ('Nothing is too difficult if you really want it') aimed to purify and polish Dutch language and morality by promoting plays modelled on French tragedies and comedies. The Stadholder William III, who became King of England in 1688, built his hunting lodge Het Loo in the French style with French decoration and French gardens even though his political sympathies were anti-French.

The upper classes were educated by tutors, or more usually by governesses, recruited from Protestant families in France or Switzerland. We should not over-estimate their active knowledge of French. Their French was conversational; they could not really write it.

For those who could not afford a private tutor for their children, there were the French schools. These schools began to appear at the start of the sixteenth century; Amsterdam had its first in 1503. Every little town in the Republic (and there were many) had one Latin school and one or more French schools. The Latin schools were municipal; the French schools were private institutions. The aim of the Latin schools was to teach piety and Latin. Any possibility that their teaching might be relevant to future merchants and traders was avoided; if geography ever got a mention it was the geography of the ancient world. So where did these boys, these future merchants, learn to read, write and do arithmetic?

Protestant enlightenment

When the Northern Netherlands became a Protestant nation and the Revolt looked likely to succeed, the North became a safe haven for Calvinists from the South regardless of whether they spoke Dutch or French. This 'refuge' function was underlined after the Revocation of the Edict of Nantes in 1685, when the Huguenots were united with their Walloon brethren who had fled persecution in Southern Belgium a century before. Among them were many intellectuals, who played an important role in the diffusion of new ideas.

From 1684 on, Pierre Bayle published his periodical, *Nouvelles de la République des Lettres* and worked on his *Dictionnaire philosophique*, which became the model for the French encyclopedists. How could Bayle, a Calvinist, influence the French *philosophes*? Simply by the fact that Protestantism is itself an Enlightenment, just as Italian Humanism had been in the fifteenth century and Erasmian Humanism around 1500. Such Enlightenment consists in the free investigation of sources and historical criticism based on philology, even when it is applied to traditional articles of faith. Enlightenment is opposed to belief in authority. In the fifteenth century Lorenzo Valla had exposed as a forgery the Donation of Constantine, the purported grant of political authority by the Emperor Constantine to the Bishops of Rome which had long been an important element in justifying papal claims to political authority over the whole of Western Europe. The Protestants rejected most of the Catholic tradition on the same grounds.

Christian orthodoxy could also be criticised on rational grounds, and the prestige that Descartes gave to Reason encouraged the spread of freethinking. Reason suggests that it is unlikely that the women who were burned for witchcraft really were witches. Balthasar Bekker demonstrated this in *The World Bewitched* (De Betoverde Weereld, 1691-1693): witches do not even exist, any more than demons, and the Devil is powerless, he wrote. This is good rationalism but poor theology.

Spinoza tried to keep these two types of scriptural criticism separate. In his *Tractatus Theologico-Politicus* (1670) he argued that the Old Testament was virtually unreadable through its lack of historical context, and in his *Ethica* (1677) that one does not need revelation to be inspired by an awareness of and love for the true God. When these two ideas combined in the minds of his readers, the mixture was explosive. The Church authorities realised that if the Bible were not divinely inspired, and if Reason could lead to an awareness of God without the help of Revelation, the Church would be superfluous.

Another French intellectual is Jean Leclerc, a liberal Protestant. One can regard him as a journalist because he published a periodical in which he reviewed, like Bayle, every possible kind of work. But he was also the publisher of the only complete *Opera Omnia* of Erasmus, so he was primarily a philologist. He was a professor of Church History too. Leclerc's periodical, *Bibliothèque Universelle* (1686-1693), could be bought openly in Holland but had to be smuggled into France. A comparable Dutch-language periodical was *De Boekzaal van Europa*, aimed at those who could read neither Latin nor French. It was a periodical of high quality, however, and reflected the thirst for knowledge.

We now seem justified in asking: if one is writing a book that conflicts with revealed religion, when does one write it in Latin, when in French and when in Dutch? Latin was used to address the large group of ex-pupils of the Latin schools. Their extensive study of classical authors made them less likely to be shocked than those who were uneducated or illiterate, and their conservative bent made them less dangerous; they formed an exclusive gentlemen's club in the Republic of Letters.

However, Balthasar Bekker wrote *The World Bewitched* in Dutch precisely because he wanted his attack on superstition to have the widest possible exposure '*so as to win the approval of educated minds and to instruct the uneducated*', as he wrote in his foreword. And whoever wrote in French, or published French periodicals, did so because he had always spoken French, could be sure of having a readership in the Netherlands and wanted to provide liberal spirits abroad with learned but forbidden information. Books in Latin or French could be published with little risk of censorship.

The original cultural contributions of the Low Countries are mysticism (Ruusbroec), leading to the *Devotia Moderna* (Thomas à Kempis), which links up with the continuation of Italian Humanism (Erasmus), the historico-critical examination of texts in liberal Protestantism, and the free examination of conscience. This was then fed by scepticism (Bayle) and resulted in relativism and tolerance, which finally culminated in the loss of faith and the indifference characteristic of modern Dutch society. Exactly as the orthodox had predicted, up to and including moral degeneracy. Only it happened much later, and quite differently.

J.P. GUÉPIN
Translated by Chris Emery.

BIBLIOGRAPHY

BRUNOT, J., *Histoire de la Langue Française des origines à 1900, VIII, 1, V, Le Français en Hollande.* Paris, 1904.
BOTS, H., G.H.M. POSTHUMUS MEYJES and F. WIERINGA, *Vlucht naar de Vrijheid.* Amsterdam, 1985.
GOBBERS, W., *Jean-Jacques Rousseau in Holland, een onderzoek naar de invloed van de mens en het werk (ca 1760-ca 1810).* Ghent, 1963.
GUÉPIN, J.P., *Drietaligheid.* Forthcoming (Uitg. Voltaire).
RIEMENS, K.J., *Esquisse historique de l'Enseignement du Français en Hollande du XVIe au XIXe Siècle.* Leiden, 1919.

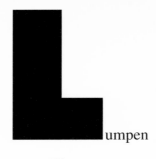umpen

Elegance

The Sculptural Mathemathics of Neutelings Riedijk Architects

'*A building should be lumpen, surly and sullen. It should stand there, in all its ham-fisted glory, anchored in the earth ...*' Architects do not often use the terms 'lumpen', 'surly', 'sullen' and 'ham-fisted', and certainly not when they are describing their own work. Yet these adjectives capture the essence of the work of Willem Jan Neutelings (1959-), who runs the architectural firm Neutelings Riedijk Architects with Michiel Riedijk (1964-).

The sex appeal of gravity

For Neutelings and Riedijk, architecture does not have to be beautiful or graceful. Quite the opposite; they see architecture as a brave submission to the forces of gravity, while many of their fellow architects see it in terms of weightlessness and buoyancy, evading the gravitational pull of the earth. A building is, after all, '*a mountain of heaped-up matter*'. That is why, for Neutelings and Riedijk, depicting gravity is '*in our case, depicting weight, not the slenderness of its resolved vectors. Elegant structures call upon an idealised image rather than on reality, much like photographers' models in a glossy magazine*', as Neutelings wrote in the article 'The Sex Appeal of Gravity' in the architectural journal *Archis*, an ode to the '*gravity, density and inertia*' of buildings, appropriately summarised under the name '*immovable property*'. According to Neutelings en Riedijk, the '*glorious ham-fistedness*' of immovable property is best expressed in architecture by using the '*most tangible representation*' of gravity.

More than a century ago, in *The Tall Office Building Artistically Considered* (1896), the American architect Louis Sullivan defined the skyscraper: '*it must be tall, every inch of it tall.*' By analogy, Neutelings and Riedijk have determined that a building, whether large or small, must be *heavy*; every kilo of it must be heavy.

For Neutelings Riedijk, the best tangible representation of gravity is the cantilever, which, in Neutelings own words, is threatening and poetic at the same time. The cantilever is '*the precarious condition of a foreshadowed fall. An imminent threat, an unsettling balancing act. It refers to ominous cracks, deafening roars and muffled cries*'.

The sense of imminent threat predominates in the work of Neutelings, the clearest example being the fire station in Breda. This building is a bastion in brick, crowned by the commandant's office on the top floor, which protrudes dangerously from the rest of the building. The following are based on a similar concept: the residential tower block in Amsterdam, where a large 'bite' appears to have been taken out of the base; the Netherlands Audiovisual Archive in Hilversum, where a vast open internal space is overshadowed by the bulk of the upper storeys; the competition design for the concert hall in Bruges, which has the cumbrous lithesomeness of a circus elephant balancing on two legs.

If a cantilever needs support, Neutelings Riedijk refuse to use columns that look like '*oversized toothpicks*' and deny the force of gravity. Instead they prefer to use those columns that look least capable of bearing a load, thereby maintaining the visual illusion of the cantilever. Neutelings and Riedijk search for supporting elements based on the classical example of the caryatids, the beautifully carved female figures that are used as supporting columns for an entablature. One such solution is the steel letters used as a supporting element for the Minnaert Building, the main building of the *De Uithof* campus of the University of Utrecht. The structural steel letters spell the name of the scholar after whom the building was named: Professor M.G.J. Minnaert, who was a biologist, astronomer and physicist.

The weight of the Minnaert Building is accentuated not only by anchoring it firmly into the earth, but also by using materials that evoke the appearance of a monolith. For elevations, Neutelings Riedijk prefer to use ma-

Neutelings Riedijk Architects, residential tower block, Amsterdam, 1993-1998.

Neutelings Riedijk Architects, fire station, Breda, 1996-1998.

Neutelings Riedijk
Architects, Minnaert
building, Utrecht,
1994-1998.

Neutelings Riedijk
Architects, Housing project,
Ghent, 1998. Photo by
Christian Richters.

terials such as concrete and brick in dark colours in order to emphasise the
forces of gravity. The fire station in Breda is built entirely of brick, and the
fire station in Maastricht is dark green concrete. The elevations of the
Minnaert Building are clad with sprayed concrete containing an iron aggre-
gate that gives it the colour of rust. The sprayed concrete cladding is 'wrin-
kled', as if the skin of the building is loose, but this can be interpreted as
a reference to Minnaert's research into wave patterns.

Hidden elegance and glorious ham-fistedness

Neutelings en Riedijk's focus on gravity has earned them a unique place in contemporary architecture both in the Netherlands and in Flanders, where they are the most frequently commissioned Dutch architects. The work of Flemish architects, and occasionally Walloon architects, is increasingly seen in the Netherlands. The reverse is seldom true, however, and Neutelings Riedijk Architecten is the exception. Even before his association with Michiel Riedijk, Willem Jan Neutelings designed two small apartment blocks in Antwerp. More recently, the firm has worked on a housing project in Ghent and a post office in Scherpenheuvel. Neutelings and Riedijk also designed the new STUC cultural centre in Leuven and will complete Antwerp's Museum aan de Stroom in 2006.

The Museum aan de Stroom (Museum by the River) has the appearance of asymmetrically stacked boxes and expresses another important distinguishing feature of Neutelings Riedijk's work: the radical way in which they analyse programmes of requirements as if they were mathematical equations that can be reduced to their most basic form. Therein lies the elegance of their work; an elegance that is not perceptible on the surface, but is often concealed within a coarse tangible form. Their approach to architecture is perfectly captured in the title of a small exhibition on their work, held in 2001 in Hilversum: *Sculptural Mathematics*.

The elegance with which they interpret a brief can be seen in the Minnaert Building. They have overturned the conventional layout of an educational building containing lecture halls, laboratories and offices connected by a maze of corridors. The circulation area is above rather than next to the rooms and halls. In the words of Neutelings and Riedijk, every building, in addition to a 'nett programme' also has a 'tare programme' of circulation, facilities and architecture. In the Minnaert Building, the original programme of spaces has been concentrated as far as possible into a single area: the vast central hall on the first floor, which reveals virtually the full nett programme. The hall contains a large *impluvium* into which rainwater cascades.

Neutelings Riedijk Architects, model for Museum aan de Stroom, Antwerp. Photo courtesy of Projectbureau Museum aan de Stroom, Antwerp.

The water is used to cool the building by means of a technique that is simpler and more cost-effective than conventional air conditioning. The water clatters noisily into the building through large funnels, demanding more attention from the senses than usual. The roof of the hall is constructed of pre-cast concrete slabs suspended below pre-cast beams. In road building, these prefabricated elements are used in reverse (slabs above, beams below) to construct overpasses. The supporting frame on the ground floor is also a new structural invention. Instead of a row of thick supporting columns placed at regular intervals, the architects chose a series of slender columns that are also window mullions and bear their load just as unobtrusively as the letter columns.

For Neutelings Riedijk, the first step in the design process is to reduce an architectonic commission to a simple 'mathematical' equation. They maintain that *'buildings are born naked'*. The idea comes first, then the visual manifestation. If these designers are to be taken at their word, exteriors are not important. Laconically they point out that, once they have determined the rational basis for a design, the ultimate result is often random and intuitive. But it would be wrong to conclude that they are indifferent to form; Neutelings and Riedijk devote a great deal of attention to it. This is borne out by the many scale models that are produced before they reach a final decision on wall cladding. These numerous models show that a single idea can take on any number of appearances. They also imply that the visual manifestation of a building is not random, but the considered expression of Willem Jan Neutelings and Michiel Riedijk's personal preference for glorious ham-fistedness.

HANS IBELINGS
Translated by Yvette Mead.

Behind
the Icon Curtain

Dutch and Flemish Art in Central and Eastern Europe

One of several Russian postage stamp series featuring work of Rembrandt.

When in 1998 the Pushkin Museum in Moscow celebrated its hundredth birthday, it did so in an unexpected way. The museum undertook a complete cataloguing and exhibition project of its paintings and drawings from Flanders and the Netherlands. Under difficult financial circumstances, the museum managed in the course of four years to publish and display these precious holdings in three monumental, fully illustrated volumes, accompanying three large exhibitions. The series began with the late Xenia Egorova's catalogue of 66 fifteenth- and sixteenth-century paintings from the Northern and Southern Netherlands, 194 Flemish paintings of the seventeenth and eighteenth centuries and 40 Belgian paintings of the nineteenth and twentieth centuries. In addition to works by the well-known masters, these included such obscure masterpieces, to take a striking example, as an *Allegory of Patience* – one sees only after a long look that this evening landscape is an allegory at all – by the extremely rare artist Engelbert Ergo.

400 Dutch paintings of the seventeenth to nineteenth centuries followed in the year 2000, catalogued by Marina Senenko. (One of the images looks more Russian than Dutch: Vincent van Gogh's *Prison Courtyard* matches to perfection the popular conception of the Lubyanka, the infamous KGB prison not a mile from the Pushkin museum. Actually, the painting is a copy of a Doré engraving of Newgate Prison in London.) Finally, in 2002 came the exhibition of Low Countries drawings of the sixteenth-eighteenth centuries and Belgian and Dutch drawings of the nineteenth and twentieth centuries. The curator who compiled the catalogue of the 627 sheets from the

Vincent van Gogh (1853-1890), *Prison Courtyard*. Canvas, 80 x 64 cm. State Pushkin Museum of Fine Arts, Moscow.

Low Countries is Vadim Sadkov, former head of the department of prints and drawings and now head of the department of European and American paintings. The catalogue is full of discoveries. Such as the coincidental juxtaposition of two unrelated drawings of young ladies, next to each in the catalogue: *La Mère des Satyrions* by Félicien Rops and the nearly identically posed *Girl Knitting* by Hobbe Smith.

With this campaign successfully completed, the Pushkin Museum has become the only major museum to have brought out complete new scholarly catalogues of all its paintings and drawings from the Low Countries.

West winds from Holland

How did 1,327 Dutch and Flemish paintings and drawings end up in the Pushkin Museum, and why should the museum have given them pride of place in its own celebrations? The story begins in the seventeenth century, at the very beginning of the Europeanisation of Russia. This phrase is not to be taken lightly. Until the late seventeenth century, at a time when Dutch and Flemish art was thoroughly international, Russian artists worked very much from their own books. They were trained in the Armory School in Moscow and worked in a closed, Byzantine-inspired iconographic and stylistic system that was controlled by the church and the court. When a two-wave Westernisation occurred, first in the later part of the seventeenth and then in the early eighteenth centuries, both sources came from Holland. As Igor Grabar discovered in the 1920s, the new narrative formulas of the 1670s in icon and mural painting were based on a single source: the illustrated *Theatrum Biblicum* of Claes Jansz. Visscher, also known as Nicolaus Johannes Piscator. This album of prints with captions was first published in Amsterdam in 1639 and was reprinted several times in the course of the seventeenth century. The engravings are based on compositions by sixteenth-century masters such as Maarten de Vos and Maarten van Heemskerck. A typical adaptation of one of these prints for Russian monumental art is a painting of the Prophet Elisha and the son of the Shunamite woman (2 Kings 4:8-37) in the Church of the Prophet Elijah in Yaroslavl. All the main

The juxtapostion of Rops and Smith in the Low Countries catalogue of the Pushkin Museum.

с 1948 в ГМИИ.
Инв. 10319

Выставки: 1925 Москва, кат. № 6.

593
МАТЕРИНСТВО,
ИЛИ МАТЬ САТИРОВ
(LA MÈRE DE SATYRIONS)
Черный мел, кисть, гуашь, белила
на желтоватой бумаге
310 x 211
Справа внизу подпись: *Félicien Rops*

СМИТ, Хоббе
SMITH, Hobbe
1862 Витмарсум – 1942 Амстердам

594
ЗЕЛАНДКА, СИДЯЩАЯ
У СТОЛА
Акварель. 585 x 380
Слева внизу подпись: *Hobbe Smith*

Происхожден   в ГМИИ
из Дома ветер;   Москва.

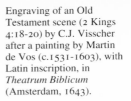

Engraving of an Old Testament scene (2 Kings 4:18-20) by C.J. Visscher after a painting by Martin de Vos (c.1531-1603), with Latin inscription, in *Theatrum Biblicum* (Amsterdam, 1643).

Fragment of a mural depicting the same scene, with Slavonic inscription. Church of the Prophet Elisha, Yaroslavl.

elements of the composition are taken over, but flattened and stylised in native modes. For the artists who painted this work, a 40-year-old Dutch engraving after a 120-year-old Dutch model was the marker of the Russian future.

Even if this is not what we mean in the first place when we speak of Dutch art in Russia, it does indicate that Dutch art meant more to the Russians than just an interesting novelty. It was the first European school that penetrated the artistic awareness of Russian artists, at a time when they were still training in the Moscow Armory. It also shows that Dutch art did not necessarily have the connotations that it later acquired: an art of the everyday, distinguished for its secularism and realism. The first use to which it was put in Russia, as we see, was not secular at all.

Nor was the second, more famous wave of Dutch art in Russia primarily secular. In the revolution of Russian imagery engineered quite deliberately by Tsar Peter the Great (who reigned from 1682 on) after his Grand Embassy to North-Western Europe in 1697-98, religious paintings were just as important as portraits and genre scenes. The first known reference in a Russian source to a European painter mentioned by name occurs in the journal of Peter's ambassador to the Netherlands, A.A. Matveev. Visiting the Jesuit church in Antwerp in 1705 – as late as that! – he wrote that it was hung with works '*by the most glorious painters of the past century, especially the worthy Robens and Vandeik*'. In undermining the authority of the Armory School, Peter's intention was not to do away with religious art for Russia but to reform it in a western mode.

The earliest direct purchase of art in Europe for the Russian court – 121 not very distinguished paintings, including Rembrandt's presently disputed *David and Jonathan* – was also carried out in the Low Countries, by Peter's emissary Boris Kurakin in 1716 in Brussels and Antwerp. However, it would be a mistake to think that Peter's Occidentalisation toward the Low Countries represented an artistic, let alone aesthetic choice for Netherlandish art as such. It was part of a grand importation of Western science, scholarship, education and technique via the Netherlands, not unlike the way the Japanese acquired their knowledge of the West through the Dutch connection. For Peter, who imported into Russia not only art but artists, the documentary and instructive value of his collections was paramount. Maria Sibylla Merian was collected as a naturalist, and Adam Silo as a maritime expert. This specialist artist, who is now known only to specialist art historians, was Peter's favourite Dutch painter. His canvases occupied pride of place in Peter's palace Monplaisir – '*the ancestor of all other art galleries in Russia*' – even above his one Rembrandt. (Which goes to show that the standard canon should not be taken as a guide in judging the choices of collectors with priorities of their own.)

Warfare by other means

In terms of sheer collection-building nothing in Russian history can compare to the campaign of Peter's most dynamic successor, the German princess Sophie August Friederike von Anhalt-Zerbst who in 1762 became Empress Catherine the Great. In fact, the qualification is misplaced. There is nothing in *world* history that can compare to Catherine's art buying. Art collecting for Catherine was not only a matter of acquisition; it was an extension of warfare by other means. Catherine derived immense satisfaction from taking out of France and England collections that were considered national treasures. The consternation left behind in Paris and London by her legal marauding of the art market must have given her at least as much pleasure as unpacking the crates when they arrived. The sheer mass and sheer overwhelmingness of the display has made the Hermitage in St Petersburg one of the great world symbols of artistic possession. The collections she assembled have never been properly catalogued, from her day to ours. The present-day Hermitage, even after several major depletions to which we will return in a moment, requires the services of hundreds of specialist curators to keep track of its treasures. They work with hand-written inventories that are passed on from one generation of functionaries to the next.

At the scale at which Catherine built and filled the Hermitage, there could be no question of fine distinctions between European schools. Masterpieces of Dutch and Flemish art came with the territory that she conquered. While the paintings and drawings are reasonably well known to foreign specialists, they nonetheless do not figure in Western art history at the level they deserve. The value in nineteenth-century terms of Catherine's Rembrandt paintings, bought not individually but as part of her package purchases, exceeds that of any other royal or imperial collection of its kind. To single out a work or two is foolish in historical terms, but it allows us to indulge in the superior pleasure that is our inheritance from Catherine's phenomenal extravagance. Two of the rarest paintings in the Hermitage are group portraits by Dirck Jacobsz. of Amsterdam musketeers, which Catherine acquired in Dresden in 1769 as part of the Heinrich Brühl collection from Berlin. How he acquired them the Lord knows. All the other known 57 surviving Amsterdam civic guard portraits are still in that city, where they belong.

Following Catherine's death only one pre-Revolutionary addition of Dutch and Flemish art to the Russian state collections can be called more than marginal. However, this exception is worthy of notice. The only Russian who can be mentioned in one breath with Catherine the Great as a collector of art from the Netherlands was (I quote from the indispensable *Dutch Paintings in Soviet Museums* of 1982 by Yuri Kuznetsov and his wife Irina Linnik) the '*famous Russian scholar and explorer, Piotr Semionov-Tien-Shansky, [who] began collecting pictures by Dutch masters in 1861. Aided by his extensive knowledge of painting, he set out with an amazing perseverance to gather works by minor Dutch and Flemish masters largely or totally unrepresented in the Hermitage. By 1910 he had acquired 719 works by 340 artists of whom 190 had not formerly been exhibited there*'. His collections entered the Imperial Hermitage in 1915. In the 1981 catalogue of paintings of the Hermitage I counted 1773 pieces by Dutch and Flemish Masters.

Antidotes and new icons

The nationalisations and forced donations that took place from 1918 on added significantly to the state holdings. Collections of aristocratic families dating from the eighteenth century on, as well as the nineteenth- and twentieth-century collections assembled by merchants and bankers, found their way into public museums. The Communist regime also depleted the nation's holdings in the 1930s by selling off large parts of the Hermitage to raise cash. Some world treasures – think only of Jan van Eyck's *Madonna in a Church* now in the National Gallery of Art in Washington – were de-accessioned in connection with oil deals with Western capitalists.

Rembrandt H. van Rijn
(1606-1669), *The Return of
the Prodigal Son*. Canvas,
262 x 206 cm. Hermitage,
St Petersburg.

However, the greatest impact of the Revolution on Russian collections of
Dutch and Flemish art was to spread them out over the country. In January
1918 the Third Congress of Soviets adopted wide-ranging resolutions to improve education and preserve the national heritage. As part of this programme, museums were set up all over the vast territories of the country.
Some of the new institutions were stocked with works from local public or
nationalised private collections, but much art was also transferred from the
main repository in the country, the Hermitage. Good samples of seventeenth-century art from the Netherlands found their way to public museums
in provincial capitals deep into the immense Soviet Union. Of course this
great migration was not limited to art from the Netherlands, but Dutch art
had a particular place in the project. Kuznetsov and Linnik report that a special fund was set up to facilitate the study of Dutch art, a fund that was used
to train Soviet art historians.

'*The same period,*' they wrote, '*saw the inauguration of museums in*

Jan van Scorel (1495-1562),
Madonna and Child.
Canvas, 66 x 44 cm.
Regional Picture Gallery,
Tambov.

Ulyanovsk, Gorky, Tambov, and Perm. The Soviet government's prime achievement in the museum field, though, was the organisation of art galleries in the outlying areas of the former Russian Empire – the cities of Central Asia and Transcaucasia, Siberia and the Far East'. The rediscovery of these dispersed works, which does not seem to have been accounted for with published lists of the transferred objects, is still in progress. It was an exciting moment when one of the most famous of them, a *Madonna and Child* by Jan van Scorel from the Tambov museum, was displayed in the Centraal Museum in Utrecht in 2000 in the company of other, better-known paintings by the Utrecht master. It was during this period that the Pushkin

Museum acquired many of the objects that went into those three catalogues in 1998-2001.

The Leninist project resembles a continuation in an easterly direction of Peter the Great's didactic import into St Petersburg of paintings from the Low Countries. It too can be seen as a secularising *mission civilisatrice*, a challenge to the powerful tradition of sacred imagery of the Russian Orthodox Church, which occasionally borders on the idolatrous. The Communist propagation of Dutch art in particular had a stronger ideological component than that of Peter the Great. The themes of Dutch art were seen to be closer to the people, to workers and peasants, than those of other schools. In manner of production as well it was interpreted as a revolutionary breakaway from a culture dominated by the church and the aristocracy. The 'realism' of Dutch art was claimed by Soviet art history as a benign bourgeois foreshadowing of socialist realism.

Insofar as they brought Dutch art into play as an antidote to idolatry, the projects of Peter and Lenin fell short of their full aim. In a forthcoming essay on Rembrandt in Russia, Irina Sokolova, chief curator of Dutch painting at the Hermitage, shows that the reception of the artist in her country betrays a strong tendency toward iconicisation. His old men and women are seen as mirrors of the Russian soul, serving for semi-lapsed believers the role that the faces of Christ and the Madonna and the saints might do for the Orthodox. The painting of his that has made the greatest impact in Russia, *The Return of the Prodigal Son*, has functioned in ways that defied Tsarist and later Stalinist authority, offering a promise of reconciliation with a heavenly father placed above the lords of the land. Sokolova: '*In the eternal duality of Russian artistic culture, of which Dostoevsky wrote "We have two native lands. One is Russia, the other Europe," [Rembrandt] occupies a unique and perhaps even now not fully comprehended role.*'

From Transylvania to Bucharest

Russia was not the only country where collections of Netherlandish art were brought in by the government to push back Orthodoxy. Similar motives lay behind the import of Western art in Romania. An effort of this kind that deserves more attention than it has received was the establishment in the 1780s in the German-speaking capital of Transylvania of a full-fledged gallery of Western painting. The owner of the collection was the newly appointed governor of the Habsburg province of Transylvania, Samuel von Brukenthal. Appointed in 1777 by the Habsburg empress Maria Theresa to usher Transylvania into the modern world, Brukenthal brought to Hermannstadt (today the Romanian-speaking city of Sibiu) his acclaimed collection of no fewer than 1300 Western European paintings, including some 450 from the Northern and Southern Netherlands. In the years 1778-1786 he built a palatial residence and gallery on the main square of the city. In 1817 it became a public museum, making it one of the oldest continuously functioning institutions of this kind in Europe. Because Transylvania is no longer a focus of general interest, the Brukenthal Museum has escaped the attention not only of tourists but even of specialists. The first visit of a major delegation of museum curators to the museum took place as late as March 2000, when

25 members of CODART, a worldwide network of curators of Dutch and Flemish art, came to the city and were amazed at what they found there. A checklist of the Dutch and Flemish paintings in the museum, with images of 77 of them, can be seen on the CODART website, www.codart.nl. One painting that stands out for its idiosyncratic characterisations is a small panel by Jan van der Venne of the story of the satyr and the peasant (see p. 249).

One reason that Sibiu is so little known to the art world is that 19 of the most important paintings in the collection were removed after the Second World War. In a reverse impulse to that which led the Russian Communists to disperse art treasures throughout the country, the Romanian Communists brought the most important objects from the hinterland to the capital, Bucharest. Among them is the portrait of a man in a hat by Jan van Eyck that adorned the cover of the catalogue of the exhibition in Bruges in 2002, *Jan van Eyck, Early Netherlandish Painting and the South*. The group also includes pendant portraits by Hans Memling. The Brukenthal Museum is awaiting the right opportunity to lay claim once more to these works.

The National Museum of Art of Romania in Bucharest is the repository of a second major group of Dutch and Flemish paintings as well, from the former royal collection. Like the Brukenthal holdings, these works too entered Romania through a Germanic imperial connection, in this case not the Habsburgs but the Hohenzollerns. In 1866 the government of the United Romanian Principalities, in an act of nation-forming, invited Karl Eitel Friedrich von Hohenzollern-Sigmaringen to become prince and in 1881 king of Romania as Carol I. Carol, who had studied art history in Berlin under Anton Springer, brought to his task a belief in the value of artistic culture in getting his new subjects up to European speed. In 1875-83 he built a legendary German Renaissance Revival palace in the resort village of Sinaia, Peleş Castle. Many of the rooms in this vast pile are furnished with objects from and recreations of a different period or centre of world art. It goes without saying that among the treasures put into place in this still-impressive ensemble were paintings and *objets d'art* from Holland and Flanders. In the same post-World War Two centralisation campaign that saw the removal to Bucharest of Sibiu's 19 top paintings, the royal collections too were moved to the new National Museum of Art of Romania, in the former royal palace of Bucharest. The building and its collections were so badly damaged in the revolution of 1989 that put an end to the reign of Nicolae Ceauşescu that the Foreign Art Galleries remained closed until May 2000, when they were reopened with the partial help of the Prins Bernhard Cultuurfonds and other Dutch and Flemish institutions, among others.

Ur-Netherlandish art in Prague

Russia and Romania are exceptional cases in our perspective. They are both countries in which the tension between Eastern Orthodoxy and the Western churches finds significant expression – conscious, programmatic expression – in art collections and their implementation. The other culturally developed countries of Eastern Europe, the nations of the Caucasus, Greece and Bulgaria, never even began to import Western European art. With all due reservation, one can hypothesise that the icon tradition and the easel-painting tra-

Jan van Eyck (1390-1441), *Portrait of a Man with Blue Hat*. Muzeul National de Arta al României, Bucharest.

dition, exemplified par excellence in Dutch and Flemish art, are mutually antagonistic. Another fascinating shared characteristic of the Russian and Romanian collections is that once they were in place, they remained. Many fewer of the paintings imported by the Romanovs, Hapsburgs and Hohenzollerns into Russia and Romania were later lost than in the Catholic countries to be discussed below. That this too might reflect a form of iconicisation is a more speculative suggestion, but it is worth keeping in mind.

Seen in this light, Dutch and Flemish art in the Catholic territories of Central and Eastern Europe – the Baltic lands, Poland, the Czech Republic and Hungary – have long been more closely integrated into local society and culture than in Russia and Romania. The import of art and artists from the Netherlands into these territories required no special ideological justification, nor did it obtain one. The integration of Netherlandish art into the local culture could not go much further than it did in the Prague of Emperor Rudolf II (emperor from 1576 to 1661). During the formative period of

Golden Age art Prague was in fact one of the great centres of Dutch and Flemish art. Alongside the Italian and French masters that Rudolf brought to his court, he also became a major patron of such influential Dutch and Flemish artists as Joris Hoefnagel, Pieter Isaacsz., Dirck de Quade van Ravesteyn, Hans and Paul Vredeman de Vries and Adriaen de Vries.

The art of these masters is usually seen in a certain light. They are thought of as Mannerists, over-refined creatures of the court, creators of an un-Netherlandish art of exaggeration and decadence. The *Allegory of the Court of Rudolf II* by the Hague artist Dirck de Quade van Ravesteyn in Prague goes quite a way to support that thesis. That is however not the whole story. According to one of the leading experts in Rudolfine art, Thomas DaCosta Kaufmann, the court in Prague was also the crucible in which the ur-Netherlandish specialties of landscape, still life and genre matured or were invented. The interests of the emperor and his court were not exclusively sophisticated. The court also cultivated a sense of wonder before simple plants, animals and people, a taste that was shared and cultivated by his artists. When their terms at court came to an end, and they returned to Western Europe (not all of them did), they brought with them new specialties that later came to be identified with their home countries. Roelant Savery's flower still lifes, a genre that originated in Prague though all the world thinks of it as Dutch, is a case in point.

One reason this demonstrable truth is no longer apparent to the world is that so little work from the Rudolfine period has remained in Prague. Had it done so, the castle, museums, churches and palaces of Prague would have formed an ensemble of great international art of about 1600 on a par with Rome for the art of 1500. Of the 422 items in DaCosta Kaufmann's catalogue of all surviving paintings by Rudolfine court artists done during their period of imperial service, only 45 are still in Prague today. The dispersal began in Rudolf's time, as art was taken away by artists or sent abroad by patrons, spreading the reputation and impact of his artistic policies. However, it is after Rudolf's death that Prague was emptied. The largest single group of Rudolfine art is in the Kunsthistorisches Museum in Vienna, where it was taken by Rudolf's imperial Habsburg successors. The rest is spread over more than 130 collections in Europe and America. The big bang that initiated this dispersal took place in 1648, when Swedish troops looted Prague and took its treasures home. From there they were sold off over the course of time.

The poignancy of this diaspora came across to me two years ago, on a study trip to Spain with CODART. One of the participants was Eliška Fučíková, curator of the present-day collections of the former imperial castle in Prague, the great Hrad. At the Cloister of the Descalzas Reales she recognised some sixteenth-century paintings as having come from the collection of Rudolf. They were probably brought to Madrid, she surmised, by Habsburg patrons of the cloister, which was founded by Joanna of Austria, the daughter of Charles V. Wherever Fučíková travels, she encounters and notes the dispersed remnants of the fabled Habsburg holdings in Prague, which in its time was probably the greatest single collection of Dutch and Flemish art in existence. The Netherlandish paintings in Czech museums today come more often from private collections than from the court.

Dirk de Quade van Ravesteyn (1589-1619), *Allegory of the Court of Rudolf II*. Canvas, 213 x 142 cm. Strahov, Prague.

Lost art

Like the Czech story, that of Dutch and Flemish art in Poland is largely a tale of past glory. In the mid-sixteenth century the Jagellonians ruled over a kingdom that stretched from Western Prussia to the Black Sea, and maintained a capital in Kraków and a power base at Wawel Castle that was far more sophisticated than any court further east. The Flemish tapestries in Wawel form to this day one of the greatest ensembles of its kind in the world. Concerning the collecting of paintings by the Jagellonians there is a contradiction in the secondary sources. Jan Białostocki and Michal Walicki remark with regret in their 1957 overview of the history of painting collecting in Poland that the powerful late Jagellonians, who spent fortunes on palaces and jewellery and tapestries, showed no detectable interest in painting. A different tone was struck in 1988, in the exhibition catalogue *Europäische Malerei des Barock*, which travelled to Braunschweig, Utrecht, Munich and Cologne. In her introduction, Janina Michalkowa reports that the sixteenth-century palace was adorned with paintings, mainly Italian paintings, which however were destroyed in the fires of 1595 and 1702. Be that as it may, not a single painting can today be traced to that legendary house.

That the succeeding dynasty of the Wasas did collect on a lavish scale is no cause for lasting joy in Poland. The holdings they accumulated were lost in even more annoying ways than fires. In 1655 Swedish armies occupied Poland, dragging off, as Michalkowa puts it, anything that was draggable: furniture, sculptures, paintings, marble. When the last Wasa abdicated in 1672, he took his collection with him to France, where 150 paintings were sold for a song and dispersed. The collections of the Sobieski kings ended up in Rome, those of the Saxons in Dresden, and of the Poniatowskis, including 2000 paintings, in miscellaneous sales.

It took patricians and patriots rather than potentates to help Poland build national art collections. Michalkowa described the quite manic collecting behaviour of wealthy Polish burgers and aristocrats. The Czartoryskis and Ossolinskis, in the nineteenth century, founded museums based on nationalistic premises. The art historian and diplomat Atanazy Raczynski built a splendid collection during his missions as legate of the King of Prussia. The palace in Berlin where it was preserved was demolished in 1884 to make way for the Reichstag. The paintings were then moved to five rooms of their own in the Nationalgalerie, but in 1903 the citizens of Posen held a campaign to build a museum at their own expense and succeeded in luring the collection back to Poland, in a rare reversal of a long and sad trend.

The founding in 1862 of the immense National Museum in Warsaw (until 1916 the Museum of Fine Arts) was a direct expression of Polish nationalism on the eve of the 1863 insurrection against Russia. The late date of founding did not prevent the museum from acquiring an important collection of Dutch and Flemish painting. Nearly symbolic of this is the oil sketch by the Fleming Jacob Jordaens (1593-1678) for *The Apotheosis of Frederick Henry*, the painting itself still in the Oranjezaal in Huis ten Bosch, for which it was painted in 1652. The Jordaens was purchased by the Warsaw museum in 1871.

The final great collection of art from the Low Countries in Central and Eastern Europe is in Hungary. The Museum of Fine Arts in Budapest boasts a gallery of 755 Dutch and Flemish paintings. Most of them are from the remnants of the Esterházy collection, purchased by the Hungarian state in 1871. The Esterházys were an ancient family of Hungarian aristocrats who, in the words of the *Dictionary of Art*, '*rose to prominence during the Turkish wars of the sixteenth and seventeenth centuries to become one of the leading, most influential and richest families of eastern Europe. Their absolute loyalty to the Habsburgs secured for them great power and wealth*'. Although they had lost much of their wealth and belongings by the latter nineteenth century, what was left by the time of the purchase was enough to assure Budapest of a perpetual major role in the international circuit of mu-

seums of fine arts. Jan Miense Molenaer's jolly *Tavern of the Crescent Moon* from the Esterházy collection is a vivid evocation of the European family having the kind of fun that even an Esterházy could share with their peasant dependents.

Jan van der Venne (1616-1650), *Satyr and Peasant in a Tavern*.
Panel, 38 x 54 cm.
Bruckenthal Museum, Sibiu.

A corrective conclusion

This quick look at Dutch and Flemish art in Central and Eastern Europe is fragmentary and arbitrary in any number of ways. For one thing, it is limited mainly to paintings. The collections of drawings and prints would multiply the numbers of objects and collections considerably. An augmentation of another order altogether would be obtained were we to look at the arts of sculpture, architecture and tapestry. For much of the sixteenth and seventeenth centuries, ateliers in or from the Low Countries were the leading purveyors of these monumental arts to courts and cities to the north and east of their mother country. One reason this has not penetrated the consciousness of the Western art world is that Dutch and Flemish sculptors, masons and architects did not work in recognisably Netherlandish styles but in the current international idioms, especially classicism. For entire provinces not only of Eastern Europe but also Scandinavia and the British Isles, nearly all art was Dutch and Flemish art.

In another sense as well, this bird's-eye view is insufficient. In keeping with present-day usage, it is restricted to the countries behind the late, unlamented Iron Curtain. Before the 1940s no European would have understood a discussion of Central Europe that dealt with Prague and Budapest and not Vienna. Or for that matter with Berlin and Dresden, Leipzig and Munich as well. With that corrective in mind, we can only end by concluding that Central and Eastern Europe are inseparable not only from our continent but most emphatically from the part of European cultural heritage that we call Dutch and Flemish art.

GARY SCHWARTZ

BIBLIOGRAPHY

Catalogues of the museums discussed in the article

CRACRAFT, JAMES, *The Petrine Revolution in Russian Imagery*. Chicago / London, 1997.

FOLGA-JANUSZEWSKA, DOROTA and KATARZYNA MURAWSKA-MUTHESIUS, *National Museum in Warsaw: Guide*. Warsaw, 2001.

KAUFFMANN, THOMAS DACOSTA, *The School of Prague: Painting at the Court of Rudolf II*. Chicago / London, 1988.

KUZNETSOV, YURY AND IRENE LINNIK, *Dutch Painting in Soviet Museums*. Amsterdam and Leningrad, 1982.

hilippe

Herrewege, a Versatile Musical Shrink

Musicians from Flanders with great international careers to their credit can be counted on the fingers of one hand; but with his activities as a conductor and his extensive discography Philippe Herreweghe (1947-) has become one of the stars of the international music industry. As with so many of his generation, Herreweghe's road to fame started with early music. With his choir, Collegium Vocale, he was the first to apply the principles of authentic performance technique to vocal music, and especially to that of Johann Sebastian Bach. Since then the Collegium Vocale has become the foremost reference point for performing the cantatas and passions of the Thomascantor. He also established other ensembles, such as the Chapelle Royale and the Orchestre des Champs-Elysées, and became musical director of the Royal Philharmonic Orchestra of Flanders.

Made to measure In such a strange environment as an orchestra, with its collection of often highly talented but always self-willed musicians, a knowledge of people and an understanding of group dynamics is far from being an unnecessary luxury. This being so, Herreweghe's medical and psychiatric studies may have been a somewhat unusual starting-point for a musical career; but with hindsight they certainly made sense. It was while studying at university that he set up the Collegium Vocale in 1970. Originally the choir consisted of friends and music-loving amateurs, but gradually it took on a more professional character. Herreweghe needed trained singers to achieve his ambitious aim: to create a vocal counterpart to the great instrumental baroque ensembles established from the late 1960s at the instigation of such great names as Gustav Leonhardt, Nikolaus Harnoncourt and the Kuijken brothers. And through study of vocal performance technique, a good deal of experimentation and a perfect feeling for the essence of baroque music, he managed it. The Collegium Vocale became a flexible chamber choir that did away with the romantic, monumental performance tradition with its uniform legato, exaggerated vibrato and inflated dynamics. In their place came concern for clear rendering of the text, impeccable musical phrasing and articulation, greater transparency and a strongly rhetorical performance. Rhetoric and doctrine of affects are key concepts in baroque music, and who better to preach passion than a psychiatrist (who, incidentally, never practised this profession) turned conductor?

The results Herreweghe achieved with his choir in interpreting baroque music did not go unnoticed. Harnoncourt and Leonhardt called on the Collegium Vocale for their recording of the complete Bach Cantatas; and thus Herreweghe's international reputation was established at a stroke. In France, especially, people were fascinated by his approach. As a result of this interest, in 1977 he was able to set up the ensemble La Chapelle Royale, the main object of which was to perform the rich but sorely neglected French baroque repertoire. Herreweghe then created the Ensemble Vocal Européen to interpret the music of the Renaissance, and the Orchestre des Champs-Elysées for nineteenth-century symphonic works. The principle is childishly simple, but takes a great deal of musical and organisational talent: to set up a separate specialised ensemble for each repertoire, and have that ensemble play on (copies of) period instruments in accordance with the playing technique of the time.

Self-willed and versatile

As Herreweghe began to develop an interest in a number of repertoires, so the range of instruments he had to deal with expanded rapidly and exponentially. If he was to perform music from the period 1870-1950 adequately, Herreweghe could no longer walk around the symphony orchestra in a great arc. After engagements as guest conductor with top European orchestras like the Vienna and Berlin Philharmonics and the Concertgebouw, in 1998 he became musical director of the Royal Philharmonic Orchestra of Flanders. After brief consideration he recently extended this contract to 2008. One project with this orchestra which has attracted attention is to perform the complete symphonies of Bruckner. The music of late-romantic composers such as Mahler, Brahms, Bruckner and Fauré holds no secrets for Herreweghe, and twentieth-century greats like Stravinsky, Schönberg and Weill do not escape his notice. Sometimes the Collegium Vocale is called on for these performances. Although at present this Collegium cannot really compete with the best specialist choirs from abroad in performing contemporary music by Feldman or Gubaidulina, some exploration of other musical worlds is vital to a choir whose thirty-year hegemony of Bach interpretation is still unbroken. Be that as it may, the versatility and extent of Herreweghe's musical activities compels great respect. Over a period of 15 years he has produced nearly 50 CDs, and on top of that he is also artistic director of the Académies musicales in the small French town of Saintes.

Herreweghe seems to have coped well with this lightning-swift growth and diversification. Of course it is a very different thing to conduct a 100-strong symphony orchestra in romantic and modern work rather than a chamber choir that has been hanging on his baton for 30 years already. Orchestral musicians have been known to complain of his idiosyncratic conducting technique, but on the other hand they have great respect for his musical insight and enthusiasm-kindling performance. Inevitably, his proliferating activities leave him with less and less time to go back and study the sources. For his Bruckner project, for instance, Herreweghe cannot allow himself nearly as much preparatory study as he once put into his Bach in-

Philippe Herreweghe (1947-). Photo by Eric Larrayadieu.

terpretations. Nonetheless, Bruckner's symphonies with their countless *Fassungen* cry out for authentic performance practice. Pressure from a large record company like Harmonia Mundi, which wants to market as much as possible of an artist's work while he or she is in demand, can place a severe burden on an artistic career. Then there is Herreweghe's music festival, a showcase for his own and kindred ensembles: some 25 concerts in the space of 10 days, which together with the hours of rehearsal makes for a very heavy workload. The remarkable thing is that as a visitor you notice little of this. The quality of the ensembles, the imaginative programming and the unique concert venue of the Abbaye des Dames combine to make the Saintes Music Festival a memorable experience.

Apart from its sheer size, his CD output is notable for some features of its content. It goes without saying that the great masterpieces from *a capella* choral literature and the vocal-instrumental repertoire are well represented. Along with works by – of course – Bach there are also many recordings of music by Mendelssohn and Schumann. The most striking thing about Herreweghe's discography, though, is the astonishing number of compositions relating to death. Should we put this down to a hidden streak of hypochondria in Herreweghe, or – more plausibly – to a record company's awareness that even in an exalted genre like classical music tears sell better? As examples we can cite, together with Bach's *Passions*, the *Requiems* of Gilles, Campra, Mozart, Brahms, Fauré and Weill; but also such works as Josquin Desprez' *Stabat Mater*, Lassus' *Lamentations* and *Lagrime di San Pietro*, Gesualdo's *Tenebrae*, Purcell's *Funeral Sentences* and Schütz' *Musikalische Exequien*. In this respect, too, Philippe Herreweghe shows himself to be a versatile musical shrink.

MARK DELAERE
Translated by Tanis Guest

SELECTIVE DISCOGRAPHY

Anthology of works by various Renaissance composers (Pathways of Renaissance Music, 1480-1600): HMX 2908016.20 (1998)
Anthologies of works from the Renaissance to the 20th century by, among others, Lassus, Schütz, Schein, Bach, Beethoven, Mendelssohn, Berlioz, Brahms, Schönberg and Weill: HMX 2901636 (1997) and HMX 2908123 (2002)
Bach, *St Matthew Passion*: HMC 951676.78 (1999), *St John Passion*: HMC 901748.49 (2002), *Mass in B minor*: HMC 2908110.12 (2001) and a selection from the *Cantatas*: HMC 2908116.118 (2001)
Beethoven, *Symphony no. 9*: HMX 2981687 (2001) and *Missa Solemnis*: HMX 2981557 (2002)
Mendelssohn, *Elijah*: HMC 901463.64 (1993), *St Paul*: HMC 901584.85 (1996) and *A Midsummer Night's Dream*: HMX 2981502 (2001)
Schumann, *Symphony no. 4* and *Cello Concerto*: HMC 901598 (1997), scenes from *Faust*: HMC 901661.62 and *Cello and Piano Concertos*: HMA 1951365 (2001)
Brahms, *Motets*: HMC 901122 (1987) and *A German Requiem*: HMX 2981608 (2002)
Fauré, *Requiem*: HMX 2981292 (2001) and HMC 901771 (2002)
Schönberg, *Pierrot lunaire*: HMC 901390 (1992)
Weill, *Berlin Requiem*: HMX 2981422 (2002)

bout

Flute Stops, Reeds, and Much More

Organs in the Low Countries

Along with the visual arts and polyphony, organs and organ music in the Low Countries were from an early date of high quality and much in demand. As early as the fourteenth century Flemings are recorded as organists to the French royal courts. From the twelfth century onwards archive texts indicate the presence of organs and organists in the Low Countries. The first organist whose name we know was Petrus de Dam, i.e. from Damme, who played the *orgel in capitolio* in the halls of Bruges in 1301.

The oldest organs in image and sound

The Flemish primitives provide the earliest representations of organs. The best-known positiv (organ) is in Jan van Eyck's *The Adoration of the Lamb* (1432) on the panel depicting angels playing musical instruments. And in another work by Van Eyck in the National Gallery in London the Bruges organist Jacob Couterman, a notorious bigamist, is portrayed as Tymotheos. In about 1485 Hans Memling painted an angel with a small portative (portable) organ, with a double rank of chromatically arranged pipes, on the original wings of the organ in the church of Santa Maria la Real in Nagera, Castille. A portative organ served to accompany and/or play the music both in church and during processions. A painting from 1636 by Pieter Saenredam in the Rijksmuseum in Amsterdam portrays an early pedal tower with bass pipes (the so-called '*Bordoenen*') from an earlier organ of 1471 in the old St Bavo's Church in Haarlem.

The organ case (1493) in the St Germanus' Church in Tienen is the oldest surviving example of late gothic organ culture in Flanders. The Englishman A.G. Hill recorded this unique organ facade in a drawing made in 1883 during a tour of the Low Countries and published it in *Organ-Cases and Organs of the Middle Ages and Renaissance*. Alkmaar in North Holland possesses the oldest playable organ in the Netherlands in the sixteenth-century organ loft in St Laurens' Church. It is a rare piece of work by the organ builder Jan van Covelen (1511) who made an important contribution to the transition from the gothic to the renaissance organ. Next to the earlier

The organ (1493) in St Germanus' Church, Tienen. It was built by Daniël van Distelen (1493). The case is the oldest surviving example of late gothic organ culture in Flanders. Photo by Oswald Pauwels / Courtesy of M & L, Brussels.

Blockwerk on the *Hauptwerk* he added new kinds of stops on separate chests. The Dutch *Oberwerk* grew out of this. Although already renowned as very special in the eighteenth century, the old Alkmaar small organ was for a long time overshadowed by the large grand organ.

The oldest playable organ in the Netherlands, St Laurens' Church, Alkmaar. It was built by Jan van Covelen (1511). Rijksdienst voor Monumentenzorg, Zeist.

Organ builders of Brabant and Holland

After the religious upheavals the northern provinces of the Low Countries (now the Netherlands) became Protestant, and the southern provinces (now Flanders) remained Roman Catholic. During the Reformation all organ music was initially barred. Thus Jan Pieterszoon Sweelinck played the Niehoff organs in Amsterdam's Oude Kerk only on market days for traders, bystanders and passers-by. These were social and cultural events, and as such the direct precursor of *Abendmusiken* and festivals. Because of this public function the organs and their maintenance were taken over by the city councils. What had once been an ecclesiastical musical instrument now became a municipal organ. In his treatise *Ghebruyck of onghebruyck van 't orgel in de kerken der vereenighde Nederlanden* (1641; new edition 1974) the Dutch poet Constantine Huygens argued for the use of the organ to accompany community singing. In that sphere the organist could accompany, support and even lead the community singing. Within the Reformation the organ thus gradually regained an important role supporting hymns of praise and the preaching of the Word.

After a period of study with Jan van Covelen, around 1520 Hendrik Niehoff began using the springchest. With this the registers could be used separately and in a different way. New groups of pipes and sound tones were introduced. With three keyboards and independent pedalchests, with diapason as well as flute stops and reeds, the new organ took on the form which to a great extent it still has today.

Through Niehoff and others 's Hertogenbosch became an organ-building centre of great international influence. The achievements of this Brabant renaissance style in the organ builder's art spread to Northern Holland, the Rhineland, Westphalia, Northern Germany and Liège.

Some of Holland's greatest organists, like Peter Swybertsz, the father of Jan Pieterszoon Sweelinck, Cornelius Boskoop, J.P. Sweelinck and his son Dirck Sweelinck performed in Amsterdam's Oude Kerk on organs made by Niehoff and his contemporaries. They embodied the transition from the choral music of the renaissance style to early baroque keyboard music. The organ music of J.P. Sweelinck was circulated in manuscript to Uppsala, Lüneburg, Krakow, Liège, London, Oxford, Vienna and elsewhere. Known as the *Deutschen Organistenmacher*, he was the founder of a school of organ music which via his pupils led to J.S. Bach.

In Hasselt, Nicolaes and Jacob Niehoff (Hendrik's son and grandson respectively) built an organ for St Quintens Church (now the cathedral) in 1592/93. This was a great three-keyboard organ, progressive both in concept and impact.

A unique organ by Galtus and Germer van Hagerbeer (1643) stands in St Peter's Church in Leiden. This is a municipal organ that during its long existence has twice fallen prey to modernisation. It still contains a number of pipes from the original organ, dating from 1446, which makes this pipework some of the oldest in the world which can still be heard. In a recent restoration it was returned to the original 1643 condition with the authentic pitch, meantone temperament and specification. The sound is exceptionally impressive and as a result the music of Sweelinck and his contemporaries really comes into its own here.

Organ brilliance in the Southern Netherlands

Organ construction in the Southern Netherlands in the seventeenth century expanded with great élan. These Flemish organs are, partly because of their different liturgical function, generally smaller. They were solo instruments upon which preludes, fantasias and *versetten* were played alternating with the Gregorian chant. But they were of very high quality with a style all their

own, colourful stops, numerous combination possibilities, a clear deeply penetrating *plein jeu*, a proud scintillating *grand jeu*, flamboyant trumpets and beautiful *tierce* stops, amongst which is a strong cornet.

The dynamism of the Counter-Reformation is further visible in the brilliant craftsmanship of the sculptured organ-cases with their harmonious design and extreme elegance, executed in durable materials.

Ypres was a centre of organ-building from about 1480 till 1720. The Langhedul family, mainly based in Ypres, was a distinguished line of organ builders between about 1480 and 1636, in great demand in the old County of Flanders and in France, comparable with the impact of the Niehoffs in the North. Jan Langhedul, who lived for a while in Paris, introduced the Flemish-type organ there with a number of mutation stops with which he laid the foundations for the French baroque organ. Many experts believe that he and his followers did the groundwork for typical French stops like the *cornet*

A unique organ by Galtus and Germer van Hagerbeer in St Peter's Church in Leiden. This municipal organ was recently returned to its original 1643 condition. Photo by Koos Schippers.

257

à Boucquin, also called the *Cornet de Flandres*. Flemish organists and organ-builders in Paris likewise introduced all kinds of combinations of stops. In 1589 Jan returned to Flanders. His epitaph in the Dominican church in Ghent reads: '*organ-builder and organist to the King of France*'. His son Matthijs maintained the four organs made by G. Brebos (from Antwerp) in the Escorial in Madrid, and built one himself for Saint-Gervais in Paris. This latter was a great instrument which the Couperin family played, and some of its original pipes are still preserved in the present day organ. In Brussels in 1613 he became '*organ builder to their Highnesses*' the Archdukes. His design for a new organ at 's Hertogenbosch was praised and recommended by no less a person than John Bull.

An organ by Van Belle, an organ builder of the Ypres school, features in the list of the 300 most notable organs in the world. Initially built for a church in St.Omaars, it was added to by another Ypres organ builder, Jacobus van Eynde. This magnificent baroque organ is now in Nielles-Les-Ardres in Northern France. In 1717-19 the same Jacobus Van Eynde, the last important representative of the Ypres school of organ-builders, built his grandest organ in St Salvator's Church, now Bruges Cathedral. It was situated in a choir loft, with the great organ facing towards the nave and the chair organ front toward the choir stalls. The main organ case stood like a musical crown above Quellinus the Ancient's monumental statue of God the Father. In 1935 the whole thing was moved to the back of the church, against the west wall. Recently plans have been drawn up to restore the entire organ to its original construction.

The oldest Flemish organ to be preserved in its entirety in the beguinage at St Truiden. It was built by Christian Ancion (1644-46). Photo by Oswald Pauwels / Courtesy of M & L, Brussels.

The Andries Severin organ (1652) in the Basilica of Our Lady at Maastricht. Photo by Koos Schippers.

The Liège School

The oldest Flemish organ to be preserved in its entirety originates from the early baroque Liège organ school and stands in the beguinage at St Truiden. Christian Ancion made this relatively small four-feet instrument in 1644-46. It has a simple organ-case with modest woodcarving and a melodious, forthright, lively sound. Two noteworthy instruments by Andries Séverin, the most important organ-builder of the Liège school, can still be heard today: the vocal singing organ (1652) in the Basilica of Our Lady at Maastricht, centre of the European organ festival *l' Europe et l' Orgue*, and the still more authentic one in the North Brabant town of Cuijck (circa 1650), where even the original chests of the great organ and the chair organ have been preserved. In the eighteenth century this Liège school was continued by the organ-building families of Le Picard, Robustelly and still later Graindorge.

Organ doors

In his *Spiegel der Orgelmacher und Organisten* (1511) Arnolt Schlick pointed out that organ doors were essential, not only for protection against dust and dirt, but also to keep out birds, bats, rats and mice. Many old organs of the period had painted doors or wings along both sides of the organ case. These were usually painted both inside and outside, on the one side in festive colours and the other in greyish tints. Their use was determined by the liturgical ceremonies. On high feast days the painted doors were opened to display the colourful panels, while during Lent and at other austere times the doors were closed so that only the grisaille could be seen. The sound was also considerably more muffled then.

A representation of an organ with organ wings can be seen in Hendrik van Steenwijck II's painting of the interior of St Peter's Church in Leuven. Here the great organ is portrayed with painted doors opened and the small organ with doors closed.

In the Netherlands there are no fewer than 23 historic organs with their painted doors intact, like those in the Church of Our Lady in Breda (painted by an artist of the Antwerp School) and Alkmaar's Great or St Laurence Church (painted by Cesar van Everdingen). In Flanders too there are neo-Gothic organ painted doors, for instance in Vivenkapelle (painted by August Friedrich Martin). A modern version can be seen in the chapel of Male Abbey.

Jean Baptiste Forceville and the Van Peteghem dynasty

Jean Baptiste Forceville originated from St-Omaars, the Artesian town on the border of the County of Flanders. He is one of the founders of eighteenth-century organ culture in the Southern Netherlands. Until about 1705 his organs were fairly traditional, in the baroque style. Later he designed organs with daring constructions in a newer style, the forerunner of the elegant Rococo. Northern French, Flemish, Southern German and Austrian stylistic concepts influenced him in the design of different types of organ. Two projects (1706) for Brussels Cathedral were typical of his daring and stylistic diversity.

In St Jacob's Church in Antwerp one can admire the structural width of Forceville's choir organ (1727-28). Two parts of the great organ, climbing up towards both side pillars, are linked together by a chair organ set lower down. A similar construction can be seen in the St Carolus Borromeus Church (1720-22). Forceville's *silver organ* (circa 1720), formerly in St Paul's Church in Antwerp, is now in Broechem. It has been beautifully restored and sounds delightful.

After working as a foreman for Forceville, Pieter van Peteghem started to work for himself. He is the patriarch of an organ-building dynasty that would create, over four generations, their own organ landscape in Flanders.

The best-preserved larger instrument made by Pieter and Lambert-Benoit van Peteghem (1778) in St Martinus' Church, Haringe.

Pieter van Peteghem's oldest completely preserved organ (1750-1751) is at Verrebroek. It is a single-keyboard balustrade organ with the keyboard at the back.

In the West Flemish village of Haringe one finds the most famous and best-preserved larger instrument (1778) made by Pieter and Lambert-Benoit van Peteghem. The organ furniture is in Louis XV style. It comprises one unit with the entire substructure from the entry door and also has elegant carving on the rood loft balustrade. This organ has 17 stops on the great organ, 10 stops on the chair organ, 2 half stops on the echo, coupled pedal, drums, nightingale and a tremulant. It is a remarkable instrument with distinguished diapasons, inspiring flutes, clear solo registers, a rich *plein jeu* and a sonorous *grand jeu*. After lengthy restoration work on the church and exposure to open air temperatures for a considerable period, the instrument remained relatively intact – indubitable proof of the technical mastery of its makers.

Until after 1860 the Van Peteghems remained loyal to the traditional courtly Rococo style, aimed at a style of music-making that had developed from the harpsichord. This is apparent from the keyboard extension to the organ that Pierre Charles junior made for the Church of Our Lady and St Peter in Ghent (1847). This instrument is impressive and has remained fairly intact.

Foreign experts

During his two tours of the Low Countries Wolfgang Amadeus Mozart played various important organs, the high point being the famous Müller organ (1735-38) in Haarlem. At 9 years of age he was in Ghent. On 19th September 1765 Leopold Mozart wrote to L. Hagenauer in Salzburg about a visit to the new Van Peteghem organ in the Bernardine Abbey of Baudelo in Ghent (since 1822 in Vlaardingen) and about the organ in Antwerp Cathedral: '*Man findet in Flandern und Brabant durchaus gute Orgelwerke.*'

The English musicologist Charles Burney wrote in *The Present State of Music in Germany, the Netherlands and United Provinces* (1773) about the Van Peteghem in St Martin's Church at Aalst. '*Here I found, in the church of St. Martin, a noble organ, built by Van Petigham, and son, of Ghent, but five years since, which fills the whole west end of the church; its form is elegant, and the ornaments are in a good taste. It has fifty-three stops, three sets of keys, great organ, choir organ, and echo, down to F, on the fourth line in the base. [The pedals went down two octaves lower.] The touch is not so heavy as might be expected from the great resistance of such a column of air as is necessary for so considerable a number of stops. The reed stops are well tuned, the diapasons well voiced, and the effect of the whole chorus rich and noble: I was the more particular in my observations upon this instrument in order to enable myself to compare its contents with those of the large organs which I expected to see hereafter in Holland and Germany.*' About his visit to Antwerp he was less complimentary: '*I did not meet with one single organ in the whole town that was in tune.*'

François Joseph Fétis and Jaak Nikolaas Lemmens

François Joseph Fétis, grandson of an organ-builder, the first director of the Royal Conservatory in Brussels, dominated musical life in Belgium during the first half of the nineteenth century. As a founder of modern musicology he still has great authority in the international music world. Fétis put together a collection of historical musical instruments (later the Instrument Museum) where various valuable old reed and cabinet organs bear witness to the popularity of domestic and social music-making.

The rediscovery and revival of historical interpretations in the Low Countries is not something that happened only after the Second World War; it was Fétis who set that ball rolling. He began by organising historical concerts in Brussels in 1837 and 1839. Renaissance music was rediscovered, scored and performed on instruments of the period.

In an effort to breathe new life into organ music, and also to outdo the Paris Conservatory, Fétis sent his pupil Jaak Nikolaas Lemmens to Germany to study with Hesse. Lemmens subsequently gained great international renown and influence as the founder of the Belgian-French school of organists, which included such masters as Clément Loret, Charles-Marie Widor and Alexandre Guilmant. Lemmens was also the first performer to acquaint the Low Countries, France and England with the works of Bach.

The Lemmens tradition also reached the Netherlands via his pupil A. Mailly. The Belgian organist Jean Baptiste de Pauw, who graduated in

Brussels in 1873, became professor of organ and piano at the Amsterdam Conservatory. As such he played a key role in the development of Dutch organ playing during the late nineteenth and early twentieth century; his pupils included, among others, Evert Cornelis and Hendrik Andriessen.

Pierre Schyven and Aristide Cavaillé-Coll

In the Royal Church at Laken stands the most beautiful organ (1872-74) of the Brussels master organ-builder Pierre Schyven. Its inaugural recital was given by the French master Alexandre Guilmant, who composed his *Organ Sonata in D Minor*, dedicated to King Leopold II, for the occasion. Schyven built many great symphonic organs in several European countries and also worked in South America.

A great organ (1880) by Cavaillé-Coll, the most brilliant organ-builder of the nineteenth century, stands in the Conservatory in Brussels; thus Brussels shares with Moscow the distinction of being the only music school in the world to possess such a renowned instrument. One of Cavaillé-Coll's masterpieces is in St Niklaas Church (1856) in Ghent. There are plans to restore this unique instrument, so that it can once again be played and will attract interest all over the world.

During the fifties there was still a steadfast conviction in Flanders that all organ compositions could be played on big organs with electro-pneumatic action The cathedral organ at Mechelen is one of the last of this type. Today these instruments are labelled *compromise* organs.

The Netherlands - land of organs

The Netherlands is a country with an extraordinarily rich organ heritage that includes no fewer than two thousand instruments from many periods. The international Mecca of the organ can be found in St Bavo's Church in Haarlem with its unique Müller organ and its celebrated improvisation competition. Alkmaar, Amsterdam, Leiden, Groningen, Maastricht, Utrecht and numerous other centres are known throughout the world as *Organ city, Organ region, Organ country*. And a fine illustration of Holland's organ wealth is the concentration of unique historical organs in the Eems-Dollart region of East Friesland, where nearly every village can boast a high-quality instrument.

In the twentieth century Dutch organ-builders once again gained a worldwide reputation for their construction of mechanical organs, following on from the great tradition of the seventeenth and eighteenth centuries. The three-keyboard, completely mechanical Flentrop organ built at Driebergen in 1948 signalled the conversion to a renewed professional approach to organ-building. Meanwhile people were looking for closer links with the instrument's history. Archival and scientific researches led to the manufacture of a number of historical organ types, sometimes copying instruments of a variety of styles. In building new organs they copied or reconstructed historical instruments and (re)discovered sounds and colours from the past that had an invigorating effect both on instrumentalists and listeners.

The Marcussen organ (1956) in Nicolai Church, Utrecht. Photo by Koos Schippers.

Choir organ made by Joris Potvlieghe (1999) in St Servaas' Basilica, Grimbergen. Its design, the wood carving and some technical aspects indicate a shift to greater historical authenticity. Photo by Bert Vanderlinden.

So it was that in 1999, at the suggestion of the curator of the Drente museum in Assen, a brand new medieval organ was constructed for the first time. The design was based on various sources from the tenth to the thirteenth centuries. Similar research led to the building of a Couperin organ for Amsterdam Free University, whilst in Katwijk a new French, romantic symphonic organ was created .

The vast heritage of historic organs was also studied further, catalogued and documented by organists, organologists, scientific centres and organ journals. The National Institute of Organ Art crowned this work with their impressive twelve-volume organ encyclopaedia *The Historical Organ in the Netherlands*.

Organ Dynamics in Flanders

Over the last 35 years, with the support of the Department of Monuments and Environments, Flemish craftspeople have been able to reduce a large backlog in organ building and restoration. The Flemish organ heritage is now being protected, maintained, conserved and where necessary restored. But there are still many years of work outstanding.

In Male Abbey in 1971 a craftsman-built organ was installed, the first to reflect earlier craftsmanship in every respect. In St Gillis Church in Bruges, in accordance with a plan by Antoon Fauconnier, a municipal organ (the only one in Flanders) was constructed to enable Bach's works to be performed – an example followed by Xavier Darasse in Toulouse.

In Flemish Brabant two organs inspired by the Sweelinck type were constructed: one in Grimbergen in 1981 by Ghislain Potvlieghe (now in Erpe-Mere), the other in Herfelingen-Herne in 1995 by Stan Arnauts, based on a preliminary study by Koos van de Linde.

In 1993 Antwerp Cathedral acquired a great new organ built by Metzler of Switzerland in a traditional baroque organ style, striving for a synthesis between a French and a Central German organ type. In 2000 Joris Potvlieghe made a choir organ for Grimbergen Basilica in late-seventeenth century Southern Netherlands style.

All these developments were based on data in the Flemish organ journals *De Schalmei* (1946-1951), *De Prestant* (1951-1972) and *Orgelkunst* (1978-) and in Flemish organ inventories. This trend has continued in J.P. Felix's Mélanges d'Organologie and the Walloon organ catalogues.

The organ and society

The secularisation of society has brought with it an estrangement from the organ. With changes in the liturgy people look for new forms of expression using other instruments and a different musical repertoire. Churches, monasteries and convents are closed and new uses sought for them. The question is, what to do with their – sometimes very valuable – organs.

In spite of these social developments there is in the Netherlands and Flanders a lively interest in the organ that translates into a generous provision of organ concerts (in the Netherlands more than 1000 a year), organ happenings, organ excursions, study days, courses, festivals and competitions. Organ museums and exhibitions display period instruments. Music colleges, conservatories and universities, municipal and local institutions are training large numbers of organ students. In the Low Countries the organ is still very far from drawing its last breath.

KAMIEL D'HOOGHE
Translated by Derek Denné.

BIBLIOGRAPHY

EECKELOO, J., *Orgelluiken, liturgie en uitvoeringspraktijk*. Rotterdam, 2001.

FAUCONNIER, A., G. POTVLIEGHE and P. ROOSE, *Het Historisch Orgel in Vlaanderen* (catalogue, 5 vols.). Brussels, 1994-1986.

FAUCONNIER, A. and P. ROOSE, *Orgels van Vlaanderen*. Brussels, 1991.

FAUCONNIER, A. and G. POTVLIEGHE, *Vlaanderen* (periodical), no. 129, vol. 21, Nov. 1972.

Het historische orgel in Nederland (encyclopedia, 12 vols). Amsterdam, 1997.

Het Orgel (periodical). Koninklijke Nederlandse Organistenvereniging, The Hague.

LEMMENS, M., *Het Limburgse orgellandschap*. Hasselt, 1996.

Orgelkunst (periodical). Vlaamse Vereniging ter Bevordering van de Orgelkunst, Grimbergen.

PEETERS, F. and M. VENTE, *De Orgelkunst in de Nederlanden*. Antwerp, 1971.

POTVLIEGHE, J., *Programme* (inauguration of choral organ). Grimbergen, 2000

VENTE, M., *Die Brabanter Orgel*. Amsterdam, 1963.

hronicle

Pork Chops from the sky High-Rise Pig Farming from the Architects of MVRDV

'What if?' That is the crowbar with which the Rotterdam architectural bureau MVRDV, prises open the real world; that, together with detailed calculation and measurement. Winy Maas, Jacob van Rijs en Natalie de Vries, the founders of the bureau whose name combines the initials of their surnames, use it to show Dutch society the possible consequences of current land use. In their view, the acute shortage of space being experienced by the small and heavily populated Netherlands can only be solved by radically intensifying the use of land in some areas in order to relieve the pressure on, or even free up, other areas.

Their remedy is to build vertically – to 'stack'. What that can lead to was graphically illustrated in the Dutch Pavilion at Expo 2000 in Hanover. It was a tower of stacked landscapes that included a concrete dunescape, a greenhouse landscape, a forest, a 'rain room' where water was collected for the trees and greenhouse plants, topped by a roof area with windmills.

The same principle, though in a much more radical form, is at the heart of Pig City, a project developed in 2001 to illustrate an alternative method of organising the Dutch pig industry. In a country where there are nearly as many pigs as people it is an issue of some importance.

In designing Pig City, MVRDV worked out how the stacking principle might be applied to the entire Dutch pig sector and what architectural form it should have. The outcome was 76 towers, each 622 metres high, with a pig farm measuring 87 metres square on every floor. At the bottom of each of these skyscrapers is an abattoir, while at the top there rises a hundred-metre high dome where slurry is converted into biogas. Each tower is not only self-sufficient in electricity but can also generate enough surplus to heat 2,250 homes.

Pig City's skyscraper farms are the result of research into the implications of growing public concern about animal welfare in the light of the recent epidemics of animal disease, and so also about the health of human consumers. 'If we want to give pigs better living conditions than current factory farming provides, what then?' was the question the architects asked. We could, of course, all become vegetarians. This would halve the area required by agriculture, as MVRDV had already demonstrated in a previous project. At the other end of the spectrum, switching to organic pork would require

The Pig City project, as
visualised by MVRDV.
Photo courtesy of MVRDV.

much more space for the pigs themselves and even more for the production of organic pig feed. At present, MVRDV calculates that if one includes the land required for producing feed, each one of the 15 million or more pigs requires 664 square metres. Half of what they are fed consists of grain products, while the other half is made up of what is rather ominously called 'industrial by-products'. But if their diet consisted entirely of organically grown grain, each animal would need 1726 square metres. That means that if the pig industry alone became fully organic, it would take up three quarters of the surface area of the Netherlands.

But suppose that meat consumption and meat exports remain the same, and that the Dutch want to improve conditions for the pigs while reserving some free space for uses other than pig farming. A compromise solution is to send the pigs skywards, giving each animal enough room to root around on a plot of land and on 'truffle balconies' planted with oak trees sticking out of the tower at every level. The truffles, however, are not for the pigs. Their menu consists of the industrial by-products that they already eat, mixed with vegetable waste and fish instead of grain. The fish is produced in-house, in enormous reservoirs in the towers. The system is so designed that the pigs eat the fish products, and the pig manure in turn produces food for the fish, for which the architects have in mind the tilapia, '*the most productive and concentrated protein producer in existence*'. The 200,000 tonnes of pig manure produced in each tower can feed 16,000 tonnes of fish, which will provide 20% of the feed requirements. The water that the pigs need (1.2 billion litres per year) is collected on a $1\frac{1}{2}$ kilometre-wide belt of reeds around the tower, and then purified and stored in large tanks. If the diameter of each tower's reed field were increased to 7,5 kilometres, there would also be enough straw for the whole year. MVRDV envisages the straw as mega-rolls of toilet paper hanging up on every floor. They have thought of everything. They have even calculated the amount of air that must be circulated to avoid emissions of ammonia, the quantity of fertiliser that the ammonia will produce, and what acreage of arable land it will fertilise.

In this way, each tower of pig flats becomes a virtually self-sufficient meat machine whose scope is only limited by the capacity of the abattoir below, which can process 247,000 pigs per year. By placing the abattoirs in the towers, the pigs are spared the suffering inflicted by road transport, and by building towers where the ham and pork chops will be eaten transport costs are also kept to a minimum. In the interests of efficiency, MVRDV recommends that meat for the export market should be produced in 44 towers built around a major distribution point such as the port of Rotterdam. There the real Pig City could be built, surrounded by a massive expanse of reeds.

It is heart-warming that MVRDV should have put so much effort into designing improved living conditions for pigs, but this should not just be seen as an idealistic plan for a better world. At most, it is a scheme for improving the organisation of the world that in broad lines already exists. The meat industry will see it as proof that fully organic agriculture on a large scale is impossible in this small country. And it might also pick up on the idea that intensive meat production can be made even more intensive. Pig City combines creative thinking with an accountant's precision. The project de-monstrates the extreme architectural consequences of a widely held feeling that livestock in this overpopulated country should enjoy a rather better life before being converted into meat.

HANS IBELINGS
Translated by Chris Emery.

MVRDV: P.O. Box 63136 / 3002 JC / Rotterdam / The Netherlands / tel. +31 10 4772860 / fax +31 10 4773627 / www.mvrdv.archined.nl

The Right Distance The Architecture of M. José van Hee

One of the very first designs by the architect Marie-José van Hee (1950-) to be built was an electricity substation for the City of Ghent. That dates from 1982. In 2002, crowning a career that now spans more than 20 years, the ModeNatie in Antwerp (see p. 301) stands like a beacon. Both these buildings were official commissions for public amenities; but Van Hee is best known as an architect of private houses. In her approach to architecture she has followed her own course with great constancy and has had little truck with the neo-modern tendencies of much contemporary Flemish architecture. Her highly individual approach was already visible in the electricity substation in Ghent; unceasing work on form has given it masterful shape in several private houses, and it clearly permeates the ModeNatie too.

Nationalestraat in Antwerp was constructed in the late nineteenth century in the Parisian style, as a straight, modern connection between the city centre and the new district round the docks at the southern end of the city. In 1894 the monumental Hotel Central was built on one of the corner sites on this would-be boulevard. Taking nineteenth-century metropolitan architecture as its model, it had a rounded gable to its frontage, an abundance of mouldings and frontons and a sturdy dome. In short, it displayed an urban coquetry to match the vanity of Antwerp.

Work on adapting the building to house the ModeNatie began with the removal of all later roofs, intermediate floors and outbuildings. Van Hee returned the building to its original state in order to reinstate the clear basic structure. Her changes to the outside of the building have been kept extremely discreet. The new rooftop storey, for example, is hardly visible from the street, since the attention is led to a massive cornice that combines the edge of the roof and the parapet in a quasi-traditional crowning of the facade. She has avoided showy additions in order to keep the external appearance of this nineteenth-century building as intact as possible.

267

M. José van Hee, the
Antwerp Modenatie's staircase (2002). Photo by
Kristien Daem.

In addition to restrained changes, Van Hee has also made one grand gesture. Not a pointless flourish, but a worthy addition to the public space of the city. Broad new doorways have been pierced into each of the street-fronts, giving access to the former courtyard which has been covered with a glass roof and now forms an intermediate space between interior and exterior. This means that from now on there is a public passageway running right through the block containing the ModeNatie. All the activities of the ModeNatie are accessed from this single central space by means of an utterly overwhelming staircase, a real mountain of steps, passages and landings. The mountain of stairs can undoubtedly be traced back to Van Hee's mountain journeys and the ascending routes she admires there. It illustrates the thoroughly three-dimensional and dynamic experience Van Hee's architecture requires. Interior views and well-considered spaces ensure that the atrium is visible from everywhere in the building. In this way it truly forms the heart of the ModeNatie.

The enclosed inner space is a constant feature in Van Hee's work. Atrium, courtyard, patio, terrace, outdoor room, small garden, cortile or carport: in numerous designs they provide the structuring principle of the plan. Van Hee's penchant for outdoor rooms has Latin roots. This is certainly obvious in the elegant nonchalance with which herbs, potted plants and cats occupy space under the outdoor arcades of her own house in Ghent. As the way her house is used makes abundantly clear, the courtyard is very definitely its focal point. Not only do almost all the rooms open onto it, so that it can be used as an alternative route from one to another, but in addition this creates diagonal views from one room to another across the outdoor courtyard area.

Van Hee has created a courtyard at the ModeNatie too. The former open courtyard of the main building has been roofed with glass and is now what is called an atrium. In many office buildings, shopping centres and hotels the atrium serves as a substitute for the outside world, where the real city is. It is a safe but selective cocoon containing shops, cafés and other activities that normally belong in the public space of the city. On the ground floor of the ModeNatie are a bookshop and a brasserie, but they bear no relation to those trappings of today's inclusive museum complexes: the art shop and the themed café. They are not intended primarily for visitors to the museum and are not even accessible from the atrium. In other words, the ModeNatie atrium was not designed, like North American examples, as an anti-urban device that interiorises public life and

M. José van Hee, the
courtyard of her own home
in Ghent (1996). Photo by
Francis Strauven.

brings about the loss of urban public space. The normal way of things, with shops and cafés opening onto the street, has been maintained. With an effect comparable to Victor Horta's Palace of Fine Arts in Brussels, the ModeNatie building is edged with a plinth of independent commercial enterprises. Van Hee has not made a monotonous monolith of the ModeNatie, but has actually enhanced the liveliness of the street.

Visitors to the top floor of the ModeNatie have a delightful view of the centre of Antwerp. Virtually the entire facade is composed of windows, but the opposite wall of each room is completely closed. From the top of the stairs there is nothing to indicate the roof terrace behind this blank wall, with the South Quays still blocked from view and the panorama over the Scheldt not yet revealed. Van Hee never reveals everything at once, in fact she finds that a bit obscene. The phantasm of the 360° view, of the transparent box, the absent facade, is alien to her. In her architecture the view is not total but measured, masked and mediated.

In her own home Van Hee has expanded the facade into a cupboard as long as the room, which together with the deep window recesses keeps the life of the streets at a distance. At the ModeNatie too the sections of wall between the windows on the street front of the exhibition rooms are deeply encased so that the windows are set in deep recesses. If one stands by the window one has a clear view of the city, but the view in from the street is limited. It is easier to look out than in. This effect, which safeguards the privacy of the interior without closing it off from the outside world, is another of the constants in Van Hee's work. It works by doubling the enclosure of the building by means of successive screens that are opened up in different ways. It is here that the distinction between mask and face stands out. The face of the building, the nature of the life that the building accommodates, only becomes visible once one is past the mask of the outer facade. The mask is more closed, immobile and distant, but it is not hermetic.

It would be possible, but wrong, to see the relationship between city and building in Van Hee's architecture as a turning away from the outside world of the public domain, the building of a rampart against danger, ugliness and curiosity. The house as a small fortress. However, this is actually a mediating and protective architecture. It shows that there is life inside without showing the people who live there. It does not reveal everything, and so it does not have to be truly closed off. On the street-front of Van Hee's own house the window is above eye-level and no curtains are ever drawn, so in the evening you see the lights burning from outside. This architecture is absolutely urban because it seeks a measured contact with the life of the streets. It keeps the right distance.

KRISTIAAN BORRET
Translated by Gregory Ball.

M. José van Hee: Kortrijksesteenweg 553 / 9000 Ghent / Belgium
tel. +32 9 222 01 16 / fax. +32 9 222 62 76

A Dutch Collection in Dublin The Fagel Library at Trinity College

In the centre of Dublin stands splendid Trinity College. The college library contains the world's largest collection of Irish medieval manuscripts, with the illuminated manuscript of the gospels known as *The Book of Kells* (from around 800) as its greatest treasure and tourist attraction par excellence. Trinity College consists of a collection of classicist buildings, among them the Old Library (1713-1773) by the architect Burgh. In 1857 another architect, Woodward, renovated the building and turned the upper floor with its barrel vaulting into one of Ireland's most breathtaking interiors, with books from floor to ceiling and marble busts of Irish writers such as Jonathan Swift.

A less well-known fact is that housed within the Old Library is a large, originally Dutch collection of books: the Fagel Library from The Hague. This collection, put together by François and Hendrik Fagel, was auctioned by Hendrik's grandson Hendrik Fagel Jr in London in 1802 and purchased *en bloc* by Trinity College as '*one of the best private collections in Europe*', according to Lord Thomas Pelham, the then Chief Secretary of Ireland.

For more than three centuries the Fagel family occupied a unique position among the ruling aristocratic families in the Netherlands. Between 1670 to 1795 the family furnished an uninterrupted sequence of six *griffiers* for the States General of the Republic of the United Netherlands. The *griffier* held a high official position in the Republic; he was the politically independent secretary of the parliament and an important advisor to the stadholder. The post was always held by lawyers.

Almost all the young Fagels studied law in Leiden and spent their free time immersed in religion and political science. They maintained good contacts with the Orange family of stadholders. To the outside world they behaved as though they were a noble family, whereas in fact the Fagels were influential commoners. Their children married the children of aristocratic families from The Hague, by which the Fagels acquired a great deal of power, prestige and money. In 1680 the family acquired a large mansion at number 140 Noordeinde in The Hague. In the garden a summer house was built by the famous architect Daniel Marot. Wall and ceiling paintings were executed by the artist Terwesten. The house contained a large collection of family portraits as well as a collection of drawings, prints, coins and medals. But most important was the collection of books, which had been put together by the *griffiers* François Fagel the Elder (1690-1744) and his nephew Hendrik Fagel the Elder (1706-1790).

Hendrik Fagel was a stiff, somewhat colourless official who discharged his duties conscientiously. According to family tradition he was also a faithful

269

supporter of the Oranges and pro-English. His firm intractability caused a great deal of irritation among the other aristocrats. Stadholder Willem V spoke of him in less than flattering terms. In the forty-six years that he held the post of *griffier*, though, he was able to get on quite well with the various Grand Pensionaries.

This Fagel may have been dull as an official and equally uninteresting as a traveller – unlike his Uncle François, who made a Grand Tour of Italy as early as 1712 – but his vast knowledge of unusual books, pamphlets and topographical maps earned him important status in The Hague's political and cultural circles. He left his collection to his grandson, Hendrik Fagel Jr (1765-1838), who succeeded him in the post of *griffier* of the States General. His son François had died in 1773.

After the political upheaval in the Republic and the flight of Willem V and his family to England in 1795, Hendrik Fagel Jr decided to follow the stadholder into exile. Fearing that his property in the Republic would be confiscated, he had all his possessions – 160 chests of books, paintings and prints – shipped from Amsterdam to England by way of Germany (where he stayed with Countess Bentinck in Varèl). In 1802, finding himself in financial straits, he auctioned off his entire book collection at Christie's in London. The entire collection was purchased by Trinity College, Dublin, for 8,000 pounds – equivalent in purchasing power to almost £362,000 today.

The auction catalogue of 1802 provides a summary of 9,844 books. In addition, 10,000 political pamphlets (lot number 7593) were offered for sale. Almost the entire book collection can still be found in the Fagel Room at Trinity College. Books with the prefix 'Fag' are clearly part of the collection. According to the auction catalogue, the collection of *griffier* Fagel of The Hague contains '*a choice collection of Books, in various Languages, in Theology and Ecclesiastical History; in Classical and Philosophical Learning and in most Branches of Political Literature; in Philosophy, Physics and Natural History, in Painting, Architecture, Engraving, and the whole Body of Arts and Sciences: in Chronology, Egyptian, Greek and Roman Antiquities, in Ancient and Modern History and Topography, including many choice Books of Prints: in Genealogy and Jurisprudence and in Geography, Voyages and Travels (...)*'. The catalogue was compiled by Samuel Paterson. Because of his poor command of the Dutch language, the collection of Dutch books was split between several different categories. Further research is needed to determine the value of the Dutch works within the Fagel collection.

It is quite clear, however, that the bulk of the collection consists of eighteenth-century publications. The later generations of Fagels in particular made a significant contribution to the growth of the library. It gives the impression of being a 'universal library', a survey of the general state of affairs in the realm of *humaniora* at the time. Paterson arranged the collection systematically so that the classifications provide a good overview of the different collection areas.

Italian, French, German and Dutch history and classical antiquity are especially well represented. There are also many topographical works, atlases, maps and street plans, plus theological books from the time of François Fagel Sr and works of 'enlightened philosophers' such as Voltaire, Rousseau and Hemsterhuis. All the classical authors are there. The collection also includes books about coins and medals, and about natural history. Within this last group the botanical and zoological books with their many illustrations (work by Maria S. Merian, among others) are especially worth a look. Books of this kind were an essential part of a 'universal library'. We find a similar range in two other major book collections in The Hague: the library of Stadholder Willem V and that of Johan Meerman, a contemporary of Hendrik Fagel Jr.

Although it is regrettable that this important collection has disappeared from the Netherlands, it is to the credit of the Trinity College board of governors that the collection has for two centuries now remained intact as the 'Fagel collection' and has been managed with so much care. Dutch scholars will find it worth their while to take a closer look at the collection and, someday, to present it to the Dutch public in the form of an exhibition.

MARIE CHRISTINE VAN DER SMAN
Translated by Nancy Forest-Flier.

The Long Room at the   designed by Thomas Burgh
Trinity College Library,   and completed 1732.

Trinity College Library: College Street / Dublin 2 / Ireland /
tel. +353 1 677 2941 / fax. +353 1 671 9003 / www.tcd.ie/library

Braches, E., *Rapport Fagel-bibliotheek*. Unpublished typed report from 1962, now in Trinity College Library.

Brummel, L., 'The Fagel Library in Trinity College, Dublin'. In: *Miscellanea Libraria*. The Hague, 1957, pp. 204-234.

Gabriëls, A.J.C.M., *De heren als dienaren en de dienaar als heer. Het stadhouderlijk stelsel in de tweede helft van de achttiende eeuw*. The Hague, 1990.

Japikse, N.M., *Fagel, een Nederlands regentengeslacht, 1585-1929*. Amsterdam / The Hague, 1962.

The Irish College in Leuven

The old centre of Leuven is really quite small. Over time, anyone who has been connected with the university for nearly thirty years gets to know a bit about the buildings and their history. But now and then a surprise comes along. You would never have thought that Janseniusstraat (the former Broekstraat), right by Damiaanplein, not the most obviously prepossessing of streets, would hold such a surprise. The Irish College has a fairly inconspicuous facade in a fairly inconspicuous street. A couple of flags by the front door are more or less all that is unusual about it. Inside you find an area much larger than you would have suspected. A delightful garden is flanked by buildings that are partly guest accommodation, partly conference space.

Newcomers learn that they are not actually in the Irish College here. For that you have to go to the neighbours, the Irish Franciscans, the successors of the historic Irish College, who have their entrance on the Damiaanplein. Here we are in the Irish Institute for European Affairs. Everyone always thinks of both buildings as 'the Irish College', but strictly speaking that is not correct, or not any more.

To discover the origin of the Irish College in Leuven we need to go back a couple of centuries. In the late sixteenth and early seventeenth centuries England was giving the Irish Catholics an extremely hard time. Catholic education was forbidden. The most essential instruction was provided by hedge schools, but the need for higher education could not be met on home ground. Thus so-called 'Irish Colleges' were established all over Europe, from Prague to Lisbon, where young people with potential, or the intelligentsia, could go for (further) education. These were mostly Catholic clergy. Indeed, no fewer than three such colleges were established in Leuven, of which the building in Janseniusstraat is the only one to survive. But nearby is still to be found Ierse Predikherenstraat (Irish Preachers' Street), which points to that period.

The Irish were very well received in Leuven, both by the university and by the Spanish authorities. The site for the college was a personal gift from Philip III, and Albert and Isabella gave positive support to its establishment. The Irish College in Leuven usually housed some 50 to 60 friars. Leuven developed into *the* bastion of the Irish Counter-Reformation; one cannot write Irish religious, intellectual and political history without taking into account the influence of Leuven. This huge importance can be illustrated in various ways. For instance, there was the very first text to be published in Irish, which used a font designed in Leuven. In the seventeenth century Leuven became something of a power-house of, and for, Irish publications. The first Irish dictionary was produced here, and so was the first Irish grammar. In addition Leuven ensured the survival of the Irish heritage. At the end of his studies Brother O'Cleary went back to Ireland, and for twelve years worked there with three colleagues on the collection and copying of a large number of manuscripts. After that he came back to Leuven, where he wrote a history of Ireland based on those manuscripts. Every Irishman with a little bit of education knows this work as *The Annals of the Four Masters*.

At the beginning of the seventeenth century a number of leaders from eminent Irish families were looking for support in their fight against the English. Originally they wanted to go to Spain, but that was not possible, so they came to Leuven. From here they (the O'Neills and the O'Donnells, for instance) travelled all over Europe, but alas, to little avail. Their wives and children, who stayed behind in Leuven, lie buried in the university town. The tale of *The Flight of the Earls* is to be found in every Irish history book.

Many of the Irish intelligentsia not only studied at the University of Leuven but also taught there, and very successfully. Among the Leuven Vice-Chancellors of this period there are no fewer than *ten* Irishmen! The Irish College was the centre of the Irish presence in Leuven, and Leuven and its university have played a key role in the religious and cultural history of Ireland.

The bond between Leuven and Ireland held firm well into the twentieth century. When the Irish Republic was established, Rome encouraged greater attention to education within the new country's own borders. As a result, the need for contact with universities abroad gradually diminished. The increasing Dutch influence on the University of Leuven also made contact more difficult, while the decrease in the number of people in religious orders naturally took its toll too. Towards the end of the 1970s all this almost culminated in the end of the Irish College.

Meanwhile, however, Ireland had become a member of the European Community, and that proved to be just the thing to save the Irish College. Understandably, the Franciscan Order did not wish to let its building simply fall into decay. When the Irish Institute for European Affairs was established in 1984, that provided the dreamed-of formula to turn the building once more into a centre for good relations between Ireland and the continent. The Irish College became the Irish Institute, and since then it has developed a whole array of activities. Important in all this is the fact that it maintains equally good relations with Dublin and with Belfast. Indeed, a considerable part of its work is aimed at serving as a bridgehead between the two.

A great deal of thought goes into the organisation of

The Irish College in Leuven. Photo by Rob Stevens.

the annual seminars, when some 700 Irish students, mostly of MBA and Business Studies, come to Leuven for one or two weeks. The main aim of these seminars is to strengthen European thinking. In addition there are annual meetings for civil servants, with separate meetings for the different levels. For years Leuven was the *only* place where top civil servants from the Irish Republic and from Northern Ireland could meet each other. In this way the Irish College/Irish Institute creates an important basis of trust between the civil servants of the whole island, which can go a long way towards ensuring that the political noses all point in the same direction. There are also programmes for regional and local authorities which complement each other in one way or another, but are divided by the border. An example: the port authorities for Galway on the Republic's west coast, and those for Belfast, sit round the same table in the Irish College. Finally. the Irish College also organises business seminars to familiarise Irish business leaders with the European market.

The traffic is not all one way. The College has good contacts with various national and European authorities, who in their turn are made familiar with certain Irish affairs or experiences. The work of the College is never directed at individuals but at organisations, and it is these which can invite their members to participate in one programme or another.

The activities are only occasionally carried out by the Irish College's own staff, which is actually very small. Almost always specialists from outside are called upon, very often from the University of Leuven. Yet there is still a lot of room for growth in the relationship with the university. For instance, it is far too little known that the Irish College has outstanding conference facilities, meeting rooms, rooms for around 100 people, and so on. The university and the Irish College have lived next to each other for years, but in the last few years a renewed interest has clearly been developing. Without doubt this will lead to splendid opportunities, by means of which the historic link between Ireland and the university town can be continued and built on.

LUDO MEYVIS (© *Campuskrant*)
Translated by Sheila M. Dale.

The Irish Institute for European Affairs: Janseniusstraat 1 / 3000 Leuven / Belgium / tel. +32 16 310430 / fax +32 16 310431

Showcase on the Rapenburg
Leiden's Bibliotheca Thysiana

As someone living in the twenty-first century you can hardly imagine it: a man in his early thirties with a collection of 2,500 books. Equally difficult to conceive of: a six-year old who gets a cake from his uncle as a birthday present and writes in his thank-you letter: '*Dear Uncle, thank you for the cake, but next year can I have a book please?*' Whether this ever really happened is not entirely sure, but what is certain is that the Leiden literature and law student, Johannes Thys (1622-1653) – Thysius in Latin – already had a sizeable library at an early age.

Now, it was not unusual in the seventeenth century for rich students to build up a library – and from the age of fourteen Thysius studied Latin, Greek and Hebrew, among other subjects. What is unique about the Bibliotheca Thysiana is that it is the only one in the Republic that was founded with its own building. Both the collection and the building, on the Rapenburg in Leiden, have been restored over the last few years, and on 27 October 2001 the Bibliotheca Thysiana was reopened and the public were allowed in. And so the Rapenburg gained another gem, in building and collection alike.

Of a somewhat irreverent nature, Thysius collected a bit of everything that was available, although the emphasis is on history and all that went with it, from astronomy to travel. Both the ancient works and the contemporary literature of the seventeenth century are well represented. The numerous prints and pamphlets – with 15,000 examples only the Royal Library's collection is larger – are housed in the print gallery and the University Library. Thysius, who often bought his books in batches of ten or so at a time in auctions, had a weakness for 'beautiful' books: those with plates. Floras, astronomy books with movable illustrations of heavenly bodies, carpenters' handbooks, books of architecture, books of prints of seventeenth century celebrities, but also copies of works that were already antiquarian at the time – all these are to be found in the library, which currently comprises some six thousand volumes.

Thysius himself, a descendant of a rich Flemish merchant family that moved to the North after the fall of Antwerp, did not live to see his beautiful, austere library: he died in 1653 at the age of 31. In the will that he had drawn up a few days before his death, he decreed '*that my library shall be deployed for the public service of study by my nephew, the Young Gentleman Marcus de Tour*'. Thysius bequeathed enormous sums of money for the building of a library and a yearly sum for adding to the collection.

Thysius' last wish was quickly carried out. In 1655 the Bibliotheca Thysiana was built on the corner of Groenhazengracht. It was designed by the city architect Arent van 's-Gravensande, who also designed the Lakenhal (now the municipal museum). On the ground floor, among other things, was the accommodation for the library's Keeper, and on the first floor the book room, in a large open area of seven metres by fourteen. It was furnished according to the latest library fashion: in the centre stood a reading table where people could look at the books, and along the walls, behind balus-

trades, the presses from which the assistant could fetch the books for the borrowers. In 1653 the University Library had also been arranged in this way.

'*Setting up a private library seems somewhat exceptional in the Netherlands, but probably it should be regarded in the same way as the innumerable almshouses in cities*', says Pieter Oberma, former Keeper of Leiden University Library. '*This is how the rich immortalised themselves.*' In the reception room there hangs a modest portrait of the young founder, the family crest is displayed and his name is on the gable.

According to Oberma, the fact that Thysius did not leave his collection to the University Library (where a member of his family wielded the sceptre) may well have something to do with his fear that the University Library, which did not have very much space to spare, might refuse part of his collection and so it would be broken up.

Up to about 1700 the library continued to expand, acquiring among other items the expensive fourteen-volume Blaeu Atlas, which at that time cost five hundred guilders, including the case that went with it. After that time the collection fell into decline. Many books, such as the innumerable legal handbooks, lost their significance. Nowadays the collection is only augmented by gifts that are appropriate to it. Surprising discoveries are still being made in the collection. In October 2002 researchers stumbled upon an extremely rare United East India Company receipt from the early seventeenth century.

The involvement of Van 's-Gravensande, and the beautiful example of Dutch Classicism that he built, were sufficient reason for the Hendrik de Keyser Association, which had already saved many buildings of historic interest, to assume ownership of the build-

The interior of the restored Bibliotheca Thysiana. Photo by H. Snaterse / courtesy of Vereniging Hendrick de Keyser.

ing in 1996 and to pay for its restoration. The building was repainted in the original colours throughout and the numerous windows in the library room (people only had daylight in those days) were fitted with a UV filter so that leather and parchment can no longer be damaged by the light. The trustees' room, complete with fireplace with overmantel and built-in bed, has been made suitable for receptions and now serves as a meeting room. And so one of the showcase Dutch historic monuments is accessible once more.

FRIEDERIKE DE RAAT (© *NRC Handelsblad, 25 October 2001*)
Translated by Sheila M. Dale.

Bibliotheca Thysiana: Rapenburg 25 / 2311 GG Leiden / The Netherlands / tel. +31 71 52 72 810

What's on an Old Man's Mind?
Luc Perceval's *King Lear*

In 1997-1998 the Flemish director Luk Perceval staged *To War* (Ten Oorlog), the stunning and fascinating version of Shakespeare's two tetralogies of history plays written by Tom Lanoye (see p. 176) in collaboration with the director himself. It was a major event in the recent theatre history of the Low Countries. Soon after its run in Flanders and The Netherlands, the production also achieved international renown: a German version entitled *Schlachten!* was produced at the Salzburg Festival and subsequently played in Hamburg. *To War* was the culmination and at the same time the end of an adventure on which Luk Perceval had set out in 1984 when, together with Guy Joosten, he founded the Blauwe Maandag Company. For a decade and a half this company, by combining a thorough exploration of dramatic texts with a strongly visual style, represented the best of what was to be seen in Flemish theatre. In 1998 it amalgamated with the Royal Dutch Theatre (KNS) in Antwerp to form Het Toneelhuis with Perceval as artistic director, a post he will be holding until 2005. In many productions with both Blauwe Maandag and Het Toneelhuis Perceval has shown himself a highly idiosyncratic director, tirelessly searching for hidden levels of meaning in the dramatic material and with a particular preoccupation with the forces of family relationships.

It should therefore come as no surprise that he recently turned to Shakespeare's *King Lear*. It seems that the success of *Schlachten!* stimulated cooperation between Flemish and German theatre artists. For indeed, *L. King of Pain*, a radical rewriting of Shakespeare's tragedy, was jointly produced by the Antwerp-based Het Toneelhuis, Brugge 2002 (Bruges, European Cultural Capital 2002), Schauspielhannover and the Schauspielhaus Zürich, with a mixed cast of Flemish and German actors. The multilingual text was written by Peter Perceval, Klaus Reichert and Luk Perceval, the music by Bart Maris.

The set (designed by Katrin Brack) was dominated by a huge, gnarled, and significantly also uprooted tree placed centre stage. This impressive image obviously had symbolic overtones: the spectator associated it with Lear himself, but it also represented the force of Nature and evoked the tree of life. In the opening scene the family members gather around the tree. Gradually it becomes clear that the action is situated in an institution – a mental hospital or a home for the elderly – where L.'s family come to visit on him.

The adaptation focuses entirely on the main character, and its plot meticulously follows Shakespeare's to the extent that it traces Lear's madness. In *L. King of Pain*, however, L. is already demented from the beginning. Whereas in Shakespeare madness is part of a process of regeneration, Perceval shows a poignant picture of a man imprisoned in his own hallucinations, with no hope of redemption whatsoever.

The whole of Shakespeare's drama seems to take place in the mind of L., an old man who imagines himself to be King Lear. Around him two groups of characters can be distinguished. On the one hand there are L.'s daughters and their husbands, and on the other a group of inmates who go along completely with Lear's acting out of his imaginings. His family do this only to a certain extent. The daughters are Caroline, Stefanie and Yvon who respectively play the roles of Goneril, Regan and Cordelia. Except for Kent, who in Perceval's version is married to Cordelia, their husbands are given only a minor role. As in Shakespeare, here too Kent supports L. and struggles with him in an attempt to free him of his delusion. The other characters from *King Lear* reappear as the inmates in the home. One of them is Gloster, a friend of L. whose dark glasses remind the spectator of his blindness in the original play. His two sons, Mong the Bastard and Edgar, are presented as rather grotesque figures.

In Shakespeare's *King Lear* the theme of madness is penetratingly explored, not only through the poignant depiction of the different phases of Lear's collapse but also because Lear is accompanied by characters who themselves represent different forms of madness. Thus the Fool playfully confronts his master with the reality of his own foolishness and Edgar who pretends to be Poor Tom holds up a mirror of man as a '*poor, bare, forked animal*'.

In *L. King of Pain*, in which everything centres around L. and the other characters could even merely be voices in his head, the Fool and Edgar are an all but symbolic presence. The Fool is called '*der Stumme*' and does not speak a single word. Perhaps silent acquiescence is the lesson he is teaching Lear. Also Edgar as Poor Tom fulfils the function he has in *King Lear* in a largely visual manner. While L. is raging in his madness Edgar, naked but for a loincloth, shins up the tree clinging to it like a '*forked animal*'. As in Shakespeare's play, this 'king' also undresses to regain his awareness of being but a humble human creature.

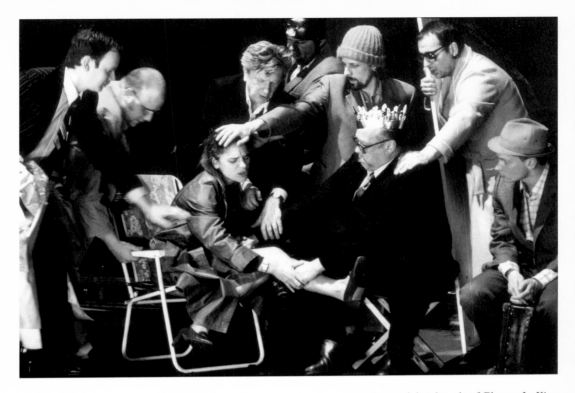

Luc Perceval, *L. King of Pain*. Photo by Phile Deprez / courtesy of Het Toneelhuis.

Particularly moving is the scene in which the Fool helps L. to put on a patient's long shirt. To the characters accompanying L. Perceval also added a 'Singer', who almost seems to represent a split-off aspect of the Fool. In contrast to the latter's total silence, the Singer represents the sublimation of suffering in art.

Critics have sometimes objected to the improbability of the opening scene in Shakespeare's play, in which Lear divides his kingdom and sets up the love test for his daughters. By situating the action in L.'s imagination this difficulty is removed. But the adaptors have also provided a strong motivation by having L. refer to the recent death of his wife. In the course of the play he desperately calls on her several times. Perhaps Perceval was inspired by *The True Chronicle History of King Leir* (1605), the play which Shakespeare also used as a source for his tragedy. The loss of the mother/wife also accounts for L.'s ambiguous and even sexually coloured relationship with his daughters. At times L. seems to identify Yvon with her dead mother. This is particularly clear in the profoundly moving final scene where L., lying stretched out on the floor, presses Yvon's body to himself. Whereas in Shakespeare's play Cordelia is dead and Lear draws hope from the delusion that she still breathes, Perceval's L. imagines Yvon, who is alive, to be dead because of his identification of her with his wife.

This emphasis on L.'s longing for the mother/wife

to some extent also explains the role of Gloster. In *King Lear* Gloster is the character who most explicitly voices a belief in the natural order of the universe. 'Unnatural' phenomena such as eclipses of the sun and moon are related to the unnatural behaviour of human beings. Taking his cue from this aspect of the figure of Gloster, Perceval tries to make him into a representative of the forces of Nature. Under his dressing-gown this Gloster is wearing women's clothes. In *To War* too Perceval introduced a drag queen, La Falstaff, who united the roles of mother, Madonna and lover in one character. Like La Falstaff, Gloster, who in Shakespeare's play takes a role mirroring Lear's, is clearly meant to represent the female values, which L. may have repressed in the past.

The inmates of the institution where he lives reflect the role of the knights in *King Lear*. In the second act of the play he and his friends put a long plank on their knees so that they are sitting close together at a table. They are given an orange and try to cheer up the melancholy L. This is the beginning of a lengthy bout of horseplay which eventually gets out of hand and leads to the inmates' revolt against L.'s daughters. Turned out of the house, L. is now entirely at the mercy of the elements. In this desperate situation he calls on his '*moederke*' ('mummy'). As in Shakespeare's play, the core of the drama unfolds on the heath, in Nature, where L. becomes aware of his human nature and his mortality. Towards the end he asks to be visited by an angel, '*der mir sagt, dat ik träume / Denn wir sind doch nur träume / In den Köpfen der Götter*'. The insight which L. has gained here reminds us of Prospero's wisdom: 'We are such stuff as dreams are made on / And our little life is rounded by a sleep.'

As the short quotation from the play demonstrates, its language is a curious mix of Dutch and German. L's daughters at times also speak French, which indicates their alienation from their environment. Again, the mix of languages in some parts of *To War* may have provided the model for this. But practical circumstances – the international context and the mixed cast of Flemish and German actors – are likely to have led to this choice. Yet both writers and actors seem to have achieved a natural fluency, while the alienating effect which necessarily results from the use of different languages is in keeping with the strange introverted world of the main character.

A considerable part of the credit for the production's impact must go to the German actor Thomas Thieme's stunning performance as L. He is a helpless, depressed man, pathetically angling for some affection from his daughters. But in his stubbornness and aggression he achieves an impressive grandeur. His fits of anger are overwhelming outbursts of madness which are in strong contrast with the long silences and the often all but muttered passages. Thieme's performance is fascinating throughout the show, but his depiction of the storm must be singled out here. While imitating the sound of the wind by whistling, he keeps banging the long wooden board on the floor until it splits into pieces. Nature unleashed coincides completely with the desperate L. himself.

Clearly *L. King of Pain* is a radical adaptation of Shakespeare's play, which starts from a specific view of the character of Lear. Shakespeare's most comprehensive tragedy seems to be reduced to the case of an old man who is becoming demented. For all that, it is remarkable that the play's psychological development is largely followed and that most characters also find their place in the adaptation. The cosmic scale and the effect of the double plot in *King Lear* may have disappeared in the adaptation, but the depiction of the demented old man surrounded by children who have grown alienated from him speaks to the contemporary spectator. Moreover, *L. King of Pain* derives its impact from the persistent echoes of Shakespeare's play. *King Lear* is always present in the background and to a certain extent shapes the play. The role of Edgar for instance is a very limited one, but the sight of the naked figure in the tree immediately brings to mind '*poor Tom*' from *King Lear*. The bunches of flowers which the daughters give their father but which get scattered in the ensuing chaos reflect the image of the mad king '*fantastically dressed with wild flowers*'. I have already mentioned the dark glasses of Gloster. By means of these details the original play constantly resonates in the action and gives depth to it. With the additional strength of the symbolic setting, the case of L. thus develops into a poignant rendering of the 'condition humaine'. And so the performance which takes place entirely around or in front of the uprooted tree of life

gradually unfolds with the force of a compelling ritual.

JOZEF DE VOS

Het Toneelhuis: Komedieplaats 18 / 2000 Antwerp / Belgium www.toneelhuis.be

Drama and Pure Dance
The Choreographic Quest of Ed Wubbe

Dutch choreographer Ed Wubbe (1957-) once named *Rameau* and *Kathleen* as his essential ballets, because of their extreme, dramatic nature. As such they mark the musical and theatrical lines along which his work unfolds. *Rameau* represents the dancing-to-music line which he initiated in ballets set to Handel (*Messiah*) and Vivaldi (*Nisi Dominus*), both of which were sparkling choreographic works that accentuated the energy and dynamics of the music, and continued in *Parts* and *Perfect Skin*, set to Bach. However, something of the drama of *Kathleen*, which turned out to be the overture to a theatrical line, also lay dormant in *Rameau*. He combined his fascination for the cool, formal harpsichord music of the baroque composer Rameau with the last days of courtly music and thus with the disenchantment of the French nobility waiting resignedly for the guillotine. In a contemporary setting some of the dancers, slightly bored, watch the wilful duets and solos performed by dancers in leather jackets and sturdy boots.

In *Rameau*, Wubbe made a deep scratch in the gloss of the ballet aesthetics he had been given in his classical training and as a dancer and choreographer at the Nederlands Dans Theater and Introdans. Initially, he was still very much influenced by Jiří Kylián. *White Streams*, set to Arvo Pärt, was a successful example of a music ballet in which the continuous flow of movements in an organic dance idiom yielded a fine lyrical image. By contrast, his idiom became angular and sharp when he worked with the classical dancers of the Scapino Ballet and learned to make use of their dancing in ballet slippers, as in *Nisi Dominus*, *Rameau*, *Parts* and *Perfect Skin*.

Kathleen was a real turning-point, as an intense dance ritual set to music by Godflesh, with vivacious trios, aggressive group dances and a gripping male solo. This was a powerful work that displayed a pessimistic nihilism on which it made implicit comment. This contemporary *West Side Story* was also a statement by a choreographer who had been able to free himself entirely from the tradition that had characterised the Scapino youth ballet company since its founding in 1946. None of his subsequent ballets was as furious as *Kathleen*. Even his *Le Sacre du Printemps* was a refined combination of dance, music, light and set, for which he deliberately chose not Stravinsky's violent orchestral work but Maarten Bon's subtle adaptation for pianos.

His theatrical work was cerebral rather than compelling, and was impressionist in tone as a result of its

Ed Wubbe & Scapino Ballet, *Tsjaikovski, p.i.* (2002). Photo by Hans Gerritsen.

light dance idiom and associative storyline. For example, he set *Romeo & Julia* to an amalgam of non-western music – love songs – and concentrated the story into twelve scenes. Writings by Shakespeare, Yourcenar, Da Vinci and Marinetti touched upon the original love tragedy. The love duet – the balcony scene – was a particular scorcher, after which the vengeful Tybalt made sure the burning love charred into a pile of smouldering ash. *The Schliemann Pieces* focussed on the passion with which the amateur archaeologist Schliemann once sought for Troy. Excerpts from his diary and from the *Iliad* were quoted. Apart from Schliemann, the Greek beauty Sophia was also identifiable as a character.

The leading character's feverish quest seemed to represent the equally single-minded way Wubbe sought a formula for making theatrical work that was not predictable. He was more successful at this in *Nico*, about the life and music of the legendary singer. Its great asset was the music specially composed by John Cale, a member of The Velvet Underground at the time and a former lover of Nico. Cale's music was alternated with songs by Nico on tape. One could follow the course of Nico's life in the danced scenes, without resort to anecdote: the Chelsea Girl in New York who created a furore with her organ and seasoned singing in the seventies, until her sojourn and death on Ibiza. This piece, where music, dance and drama were all of a piece, was made especially gripping by the performance of Beth Bartholomew.

Rosary was a successful example of the new style of music ballet. It was a sparkling group work that playfully and organically translated the emotions from Schubert's *String Quartet in C*. With thanks to the dancers, who creamed off the articulated movements of the legs and fitful turns of the torso and in their stockinged feet made them appear feather-light. An utterly lyrical ballet that nevertheless did not come across as overly sweet, in which he proved his mature

ability as a creator of pure dance constructions and duets.

As a modern choreographer and leader of the leading Scapino company, now brought up to date, Wubbe wants to establish links with other disciplines and art institutions in Rotterdam. He has for example collaborated with Winy Maas of the MVRDV firm of architects (see p. 266). Using computer graphics, designers translated her stratified concept of 'the stacked city' into a virtual stage set, a kaleidoscopic panorama of abstract images in which dancers performed like symbols of the human dimension. *Manyfacts, Life in the 3D City* was about the interaction between anonymous and personal, abstraction and emotion. Wubbe wants to express this personal aspect in his dances. His classically-based modern dance is nevertheless highly stylised, but this does not stop the dancers from making their own mark on it: in the past there were Charlotte Baines and Keith-Derrick Randolph, and now Mischa van Leeuwen, Bonnie Doets, Hanna Lee, Sherida Lie, Annabelle Lopez Ochoa, Massimo Molinari and other high-quality expressive dancers.

In *Tsjaikovski, p.i.* Wubbe continues his music ballets, though again he has introduced a slight narrative line. Tsjaikovski's *Violin Concerto in D* lures him into a highly musical choreography for sixteen dancers. The dancing is light and elegant, sparkling, and the structure delicate, like woven damask. A subtle game of seduction between men and women is sketched with a light touch. Duets and trios allow space for the deeper layers of feeling. Unease, melancholy and loneliness – clearly to be heard in the inspired violin solo – are reflected in a magisterial solo danced by Kevin O'Halloran, in which he seems to be Tsjaikovski's alter ego. 'Part 2' is danced to an electronic Tsjaikovski adaptation by DJ Tim Simenon and is in every respect the reverse of what had gone before: from white, light and lyrical to black, heavy and dramatic. Enjoyment gives way to doom and gloom, and in dramatic terms the contrast works well. What *Tsjaikovski, p.i.* shows most clearly, though, is how much Wubbe's strength lies in pure dance and lyricism rather than in passionate dance-drama. Even so, he manages to keep his dance free of predictable sentiment and excessive sweetness.

ISABELLA LANZ
Translated by Gregory Ball and Tanis Guest.

Scapino Ballet Rotterdam: Eendrachtstraat 8 / 3012 XL Rotterdam The Netherlands / Tel. : +31 10 414 24 14 / fax.: + 31 10 413 22 50 www.scapinoballet.nl

Choosing is Losing Dominique Deruddere: Twixt Turnhout and LA

2001 saw the Flemish film-maker Dominique Deruddere (born in Turnhout in 1957) achieve big-time international recognition when his most recent film, *Everybody Famous!* (Iedereen beroemd!), which had been released the year before and enjoyed a more or less uneventful run on the Flemish cinema circuit, found itself one of four contenders for the 2001 Academy Award for Best Foreign Language Film. And if some may argue that an Oscar doesn't exactly represent the acme of artistic achievement, it still remains the industry's most celebrated accolade, and not something for which a nomination is likely to come a director's way too often. So, well done.

But did the film really deserve all this acclaim? Sure, *Everybody Famous!* is an engaging enough little film with a strong feel-good factor and an appealing social message. But one of the five outstanding foreign (non-English) language films of the year? Surely not. This aside, however, the nomination itself certainly showed a nice sense of irony in raising to instant celebrity a film dealing with the pathological craving for celebrity endemic to our media-obsessed society. The story charts how ugly duckling Marva (Eva van der Gucht), thanks to the single-minded determination of her father (played by Deruddere regular Josse de Pauw), makes her way to stardom in the world of Flemish showbiz. The plot offers trials and tribulations galore, including kidnapping, a mega-media stunt, blackmail, and lots more besides, in the course of an outrageous scheme which – as is only right and proper in a comedy – succeeds precisely because it is outrageous. Thus Marva gets to be a star, *Everybody Famous!* becomes famous a while later and Flemish film, world cinema's ugly duckling, just for an instant basks in the global limelight. In the end, of course, the Oscar went to *Crouching Tiger, Hidden Dragon* by Taiwanese-American director Ang Lee – and let it be said that no one, even in Flanders, saw this as a slight on Deruddere or Flemish cinema.

This was not the first time Dominique Deruddere's international credibility took his homeland by surprise. Back in 1989 he was picked by Francis Ford Coppola's Zoetrope Corporation to direct *Wait Until Spring, Bandini*, based on John Fante's novel and starring Faye Dunaway, Joe Mantegna, Ornella Muti and, from his own stable of Flemish regulars, Josse de Pauw. This was a production on a scale unheard-of in Flemish cinema. At most, because of their roots in the Belgian dual language culture, some of our cineasts, the recently deceased André Delvaux for one, have gone in for co-productions within the Romance sphere. A Flemish synergy with the US, though, was a completely new departure. The Netherlands by then had its trailblazer in Paul Verhoeven, who had gone off to America to make box-office action films, a trail followed by the Fleming Jan Verheyen in 1995 with *The Little Death*. But Deruddere's American debut was a pioneering venture in that it concerned a production of some art house appeal.

The spontaneous affinity with an Anglo-Saxon mindset which informs *Wait Until Spring, Bandini* may have astonished Flanders, but this affinity was nevertheless already implicit in the very first Deruddere film, *Crazy Love*, of 1986, in which the main character, Harry Voss (Josse de Pauw) is taken from a short story by Charles Bukowski, *The Copulating Mermaid of Venice*. This film received a good many positive reactions, not least from Bukowski himself, who lauded his young Belgian disciple enthusiastically.

The third Deruddere film (the next after *Wait Until Spring, Bandini*) was the 'erotic thriller' *Suite Sixteen*, in which Deruddere approaches Anglo-Saxon themes from a European vantage point. This turned out to be an infelicitous concept. To begin with the production set-up proved insufficient to carry the film. In subsequent interviews the director has made no secret of the fact that he counts his experiences with Corsan producer Paul Breuls among the darkest of his career. And though the final product was visually very polished, in substance *Suite Sixteen* nonetheless represented a creative step backwards. The story follows the progress of a young gigolo trawling the French Riviera for elderly women to seduce and rob, until he falls into the clutches of a mysterious invalid played by British actor Pete Postlethwaite. The film failed to be taken seriously either by critics or the public, not least because the majority of actors in what was supposed to be an English-language film were native Dutch speakers, which only served to accentuate its already over-contrived plot and atmosphere.

Considering that Deruddere is one of Flanders' most internationally-minded and internationally most highly-regarded film-makers, it is disconcerting to realise on how tenuous a basis he has always had to work. Following the *Suite Sixteen* trauma, Deruddere determined always to be his own producer in future, and also to go for uncomplicated projects with a firm footing in Flemish soil. *Hombres Complicados* saw the debut of this new, all-Flemish, Deruddere. This, ironically enough, at just the time that more and more Flemish directors were starting to opt for working in English: Robbe de Hert (*Gaston's War*), Erik van Looy (*Shades*), and more recently Hans Herbots (*Falling*) and Frank van Passel (*Villa des Roses*). *Hombres Complicados* was made on a rock-bottom budget with logisti-

Dominique Deruddere,
Everybody Famous!
(Iedereen beroemd!, 2000).

cal support from the Hogeschool Sint-Lucas, where Deruddere teaches film; the script was co-written with Marc Didden, a Sint-Lucas colleague. The main characters are two brothers, Bruno and Roger Declerq, played by Josse de Pauw and Dirk Roofthooft. Bruno is a straight-and-narrow civil servant, Roger an adventurer in every way, especially in business. When one of his gambles goes wrong he appeals to Bruno, who cooks up an ingenious scheme to haul him out of trouble. As always with Deruddere, the rawer aspects of existence are juxtaposed with the more tender side of life, while the whole is awash with black humour. For this film Deruddere has drawn directly on Flemish and Belgian reality. As with *Everybody Famous!* later, the results are mixed; in places it comes off, in others it doesn't. The atmosphere is light and easy, but the characters, and also the script, sometimes lack bite and originality. Patience is and always has been a valuable asset in the world of film-making – and nowhere more so, perhaps, than in Flanders, where film virtually has to reinvent itself with every new production. In this respect the career of Dominique Deruddere is an object lesson in itself. His trajectory exemplifies the many practical and fundamental questions facing anyone out to be a film-maker in Flanders, for which no simple, elegant solutions have yet been found.

For Deruddere, his Oscar nomination at first seemed to have put paid to all his worries. Miramax bought the US rights and offered a first-look deal whereby they would have first option on all Deruddere's future projects. Even more exciting, Miramax was going to put out an American remake of *Everybody Famous!*. In return, Deruddere would direct a remake of *The Heartbreak Kid* (1972). But here we are, two years on, with not one of these projects having cleared its pre-financing hurdles. Dominique Deruddere's actual output is matched – probably exceeded – by a substantial and constantly growing volume of unrealised work. That is, films into which tons of energy have been put, but

which then, for any number of reasons, get scrapped at the last moment. There was *Dipenda* for instance, in which Deruddere invested years of work after completing *Bandini*. *Dipenda* was set in the Congo in the run-up to independence, and is about a young white man having to choose between two women and two continents. And then – wham! – the whole thing collapsed when Provoost, the producer, out of the blue chose to drop the project in favour of the Dutch film *Oeroeg*, which had a similar theme but an Indonesian setting. Similarly, an Italian project with the working title *La bicicletta*, for which Giancarlo Giannini had been secured as star, foundered on production differences at Corsan. *The Grotto* (De grot), based on a Tim Krabbé novel, got the thumbs down from the Flemish Film Commission. This is just the tip of the iceberg, a random sample from Deruddere's – and not just his – shelf of 'almost-work'. Awaiting attention a shelf down are lined up yet more projects and part-projects almost certainly destined to go no farther. Right now, Deruddere is mulling over a Brel-project, and has also for a while had in mind *Berlin Palace*, whose theme is Brussels during the Second World War, when the city was the swing jazz capital of the world. The story is that of a young jazz player who (like Deruddere himself) is faced with either going for instant, sure success (play what the occupying Germans want to hear) or opting for the harder path of staying true to his own truth. Meanwhile, a new Provoost project under the working title *Lune De Guerre*, has come into the pipeline.

A further complication for Deruddere is that, while going his own way, he doesn't seem entirely clear what that way is. Does it indeed lie in small-scale Flemish productions, as he proclaimed at the première of *Everybody Famous!*? Or could it perhaps be that he prefers to have his name associated with major Dutch-language projects – such as *The Mysterious Diamond* (*De Duistere Diamant*), a film version of one of the

Bob & Bobette (Suske & Wiske) comic strip series (from which he has in the interim already pulled out for budgetary reasons) – with guaranteed audience appeal? These are options it's never easy for a film-maker to choose between; on top of which there is yet another decision to be made, which you could call the *Dipenda*-dilemma: to make Flemish films in Flanders, or to make English-language films in the States (viz. *The Heartbreak Kid*). Choosing is never easy and, as Deruddere's celluloid heroes go to show, people often can't resist trying out the jackass route for starters.

ERIK MARTENS
Translated by Sonja Prescod.

History

A Night of Disaster in the South-West Netherlands 1 February 1953

People lived differently fifty years ago. Almost no one had television or a telephone. They listened to the radio, they read the newspaper, some wrote letters and many regularly exchanged bits of news in the shops, in cafés, on a bench in the park or at the village pump. The means of communication were far more limited than they are nowadays. And that could have important consequences. As on the night of 31 January 1953 when, in the well-organised Netherlands, thousands of people and tens of thousands of animals (horses, cows, sheep, pigs, dogs, cats, chickens, rabbits) were caught without warning by a spring tide accompanied by a severe and prolonged storm – a fatal combination. Such things only happen once in every three hundred years. 1853 people lost their lives in the icy waters, and hundreds spent many dreadful hours in attics, on the roofs of houses and barns, in trees or floating on driftwood. 72,000 people were evacuated and the damage to houses and buildings was enormous. On Schouwen-Duiveland an entire village, Capelle, disappeared under the waves; only two houses were spared. Of over one hundred inhabitants, forty-two lost their lives. Worst hit were the islands of Zeeland and South Holland. But the high winds and destructive waters also wreaked havoc in northwest Brabant, Texel and parts of Zeeland-Flanders. There too the dikes gave way. And across the North Sea the same storm also caused quite a number of casualties in southeast England.

On 31 January, the fifteenth birthday of Princess Beatrix, the radio had broadcast warnings of gales and high water, but there was no great sense of alarm. On Saturday evening, a few hours before the fatal event, a voice on the radio announced: '*A severe north-westerly storm is raging in the northern and western sectors of the North Sea. The depression is deepening and the storm is expected to continue throughout the night.*'

As a matter of fact, the sea- and river-dikes were too low and had not been properly maintained; but the people did not know that. They thought they were safe behind them. But the layers of clay and the grass cover were in poor condition. Muskrats had dug innumerable holes in the dikes, making them less stable. After the Second World War dike, maintenance was not a priority; financial attention was concentrated almost entirely on defence and reconstruction. Furthermore, the inhabitants of the stricken areas were quite used to boiling seas and raging storms rattling their shutters and roof tiles during the winter months. In the evenings they would sit by their coal-fired stoves doing embroidery, reading, playing games or listening to the radio. After that it was bedtime.

But then came the flood.

The floods of 1953 gave rise to the ambitious Delta Plan: all dikes in the devastated areas were to be raised and strengthened, an enormous storm surge barrier was built in the Eastern Scheldt estuary and all inlets and sea gates were closed off. The only exception was the Western Scheldt. As the only access to the international port of Antwerp, it was allowed to remain open. It took over thirty years to complete the impressive Delta Works.

In 1953 I was sixteen years old and lived with my parents in Lamswaarde, a village in East Zeeland-Flanders. Hulst, 'the most Flemish town in the Netherlands', is nearby. Lamswaarde lies a stone's throw from the great Western Scheldt estuary, in the middle of a vast polder landscape and an endless expanse of sky. The skies are usually friendly, but sometimes they can be menacing. The salt marshes of Saeftinghe, retaken by the sea in the seventeenth century, are only a few kilometres away. In that beautiful and mysterious nature reserve, once-prosperous villages have lain for centuries beneath metres of thick mud. Lamswaarde is situated just behind a dike. It was built in the late Middle Ages by the Cistercian monks of Boudeloo when they were draining and reclaiming the area. Mainly elms and pollard willows grew on the Boudeloo Dike and one looked out over the Kruis Polder, which was the property of a few gentlemen farmers. Behind the sea dike – we referred to the Scheldt as '*the sea*' – flows the Western Scheldt, which was in many respects a paradise for the young. There we learned the dog paddle, caught vicious crabs in the salt marshes, and hunted for mussels and winkles on the basalt slabs and breakwaters. We lazed in the sun watching the great ships that passed frequently on their way to and from Antwerp. After the night of the storm I was intensely aware of the enormous contrast between that vast peaceful landscape and the violence of nature manifested in the primitive forces of wind and water. The waters of the Scheldt did not reach the village of Lamswaarde, but stopped at the dike which had been reinforced with sandbags. We had helped carry them there. On the afternoon of Sunday 1 February, driven by curiosity, I cycled over the wet mud still covering the Boudeloo Dike and the Kleine Dike to the points along '*the sea*' which had been worst hit. Terrifying stories had been circulating in the village. In the Kruis Polder I saw farms and houses still under water, and

Tens of thousands of animals were killed in the 1953 flood.

dozens of swollen animal carcases floating in the filthy grey water. I saw household effects bobbing up and down or stuck in the mud: tables, chairs, cupboards. I remember seeing bicycles, carts and even joints of meat washed out of the brine-barrels in which they were stored – there were no fridges in those days.

With some difficulty, for the wind had remained high since the disaster, I reached the Scheldt Dike. The sloping sides, the black wooden posts and the concrete walls of the dike had proved unable to withstand the abnormal ferocity and height of the waves. In the immediate neighbourhood of Baalhoek I saw drifting fishing boats that had broken loose from their moorings. But by far the worst hit was the hamlet of Duivenhoek, which didn't even lie on the banks of the Scheldt. Everywhere there was water, muddy sludge, a howling wind and dozens of helpful, agitated people. In Duivenhoek the water had broken through the inner dike. Three houses built into the embankment had been swept away. In one of them four family members lost their lives, in another three: a young woman of thirty-three and her two young children of six and eight. I can still see the father walking around in a daze; his clothes were greyish brown and he was wearing muddy boots and a cap. The tidal surge had hit without warning while he and his neighbours were attempting to close the gaps in the dike. *'Hurry up and get dressed. I'll be back for you in a minute'*, he had called to his wife and children. In the little hamlet of Duivenhoek alone the survivors were left to mourn eight deaths. Duivenhoek or 'Doves Corner', it sounds so peaceful … But in my East-Flemish dialect Duivenhoek is called Duvelsoek, 'Devil's Corner'. On 1 February 1953 that was a more appropriate name.

ANTON CLAESSENS
Translated by Chris Emery.

Tyndale's Testament

Who is the father of the English language? Chaucer, as is usually claimed? William Shakespeare? Or was it William Tyndale, who translated the Bible into English? No other English writer has reached so many people as Tyndale. His work has had ten thousand times more readers than Chaucer, and the British Library describes his translation of the New Testament as '*the most important printed book in the English language*'. Which is why it was willing to spend over £1,000,000 on one of the two surviving complete copies. Most of the rest had either been burned or literally read to pieces.

Tyndale was born in about 1494, probably in Gloucestershire. He studied in Oxford and Cambridge and entered Holy Orders. At some point he resolved to translate the Bible into English and tried to obtain the support of the Bishop of London, but in vain. So he crossed to the continent and completed his translation of the New Testament in 1525. After a failed attempt to get it printed in Cologne, it was eventually published in 1526 in Worms. Later that year he left for Antwerp, which was relatively safe and where he hoped it would be easier to have his translations published. The city authorities there were comparatively tolerant, and so long as he enjoyed the protection of the English merchant community Antwerp would be less dangerous than elsewhere in Catholic Europe. Furthermore, translation of the Bible into the vernacular had given rise to feverish printing activity by about half a dozen Antwerp presses, most of which were concentrated in the same neighbourhood. When Tyndale arrived they had already published three different translations of the New Testament, based on versions by Erasmus and Luther and on the Vulgate. The first Dutch Bible had just been printed and the first French Bible was nearing completion.

The only extant title page of a printed version of William Tyndale's translation of the New Testament (1526). Württembergische Landesblibliothek, Stuttgart.

A small group of English Bible translators gathered around Tyndale in Antwerp, among whom were George Joye, Miles Coverdale and John Rogers. Tyndale worked on his polemical writings, corrected his translation of the New Testament and translated parts of the Old Testament. In all this, the proximity of Leuven was important. Not only was it the only university town in the Low Countries and a bulwark of Roman Catholic belief, but from 1517 to 1521 it had also been the home base of Erasmus who with like-minded colleagues had driven the university in a more progressive direction. Indeed, there are echoes of Erasmus in Tyndale's famous statement '... *I wille cause a boy that driveth the plough shall know more of the scripture than thou dost*'.

But Leuven played yet another part in Tyndale's life. It was a student of this university, the Englishman Henry Phillips, who in May 1535 tricked Tyndale into leaving his safe haven in Antwerp and betrayed him to the soldiers of Emperor Charles v. He was taken to the castle of Vilvoorde, near Brussels. From his cell Tyndale wrote a letter asking for some warm clothes and also for a Hebrew Bible, grammar and dictionary. This letter is the only surviving manuscript that is quite certainly written in Tyndale's own hand. In September 1536, Tyndale was strangled and burned.

A year earlier, in 1535, Miles Coverdale, a collaborator and assistant of Tyndale's, produced the first complete English Bible (which is usually thought to have been published in Cologne, but it is argued in *Tyndale's Testament* that it was actually printed in Antwerp, possibly by Merten de Keyser, where Coverdale also worked as a corrector). Since Coverdale could not understand Greek or Hebrew, he drew heavily on Tyndale's work and translated the rest from existing German and Latin versions. But about half of the Old Testament and the whole of the New were essentially the work of Tyndale. Nevertheless, by omitting Tyndale's more controversial passages and annotations the Coverdale Bible met with some degree of official acceptance in England and paved the way for John Rogers' Matthew Bible which was published a few months after Tyndale's death. The Matthew Bible was the first complete English version of the Bible to receive Henry viii's official approval, but again, apart from a few small changes, it was based solidly on Tyndale's published and unpublished work. According to the Fleming Guido Latré its printer was probably Matthias Crom of Antwerp. Then in 1539 Thomas Cromwell issued an injunction that every parish church should acquire a copy of the 'Great Bible', Miles Coverdale's revised version of the Matthew Bible. This in turn heavily influenced the King James version of 1611. It has been calculated that about eighty per cent of Tyndale's Old Testament and ninety per cent of his New Testament appears in the Authorised Version.

The biblical and polemical work of Tyndale not only furthered the growth of standard English, both written and spoken, it also influenced political thinking. The ordinary man and woman in England now had direct access to the Bible, the book that in Tyndale's age was seen as the ultimate justification of all earthly power.

In 1913, the Trinitarian Bible Society financed the erection of a monument to William Tyndale in Vilvoorde. (The liberal, free-thinking mayor of Vilvoorde seized on the event as an opportunity to show the Catholic Church in a bad light rather than to honour Protestantism.) In 1986, a small Tyndale Museum was opened. In 2002, from 3 September until 1 December, the Plantin-Moretus Museum in Antwerp devoted an exhibition to Tyndale. The museum is an ideal venue for such an exhibition since it also houses the oldest printing presses in the world and provides a picture of the role played by Antwerp in the sixteenth-century world of typography and printing. To accompany the exhibition it published a book, the above-mentioned *Tyndale's Testament*, which includes not only the exhibition catalogue but also a range of contributions on Tyndale and the Antwerp printers, Tyndale's importance for language and culture, the Bible and the early Reformation, the smuggling of forbidden books from Antwerp to England and finally the Antwerp roots of the Coverdale Bible, still a controversial subject. There are Dutch and English versions of the work. It is a small tribute to a relatively little-known man who made an important contribution to the formation of the English language and culture.

DIRK VAN ASSCHE
Translated by Chris Emery.

Paul Arblaster, Gergely Juhàsz, Guido Latré (eds.), *Tyndale's Testament*. Turnhout: Brepols, 2002; 195 pp. ISBN 2-503-51411-1.

Dutch Jewry

In 1997, two years after the publication of the Dutch edition of *The History of the Jews in the Netherlands*, a conference was held at University College London. There leading experts in the field of Dutch Jewry reassessed and investigated further the issues discussed in that volume, which was received with much acclaim and enthusiasm. This new volume consists of seventeen studies on the history and literary culture of the Jews in the Netherlands and Antwerp, divided into two parts: nine contributions deal with a range of subjects in the early modern era, eight are included under 'modern Dutch Jewry'. The division itself is arbitrary and serves no clear purpose with regard to the themes of the contributions.

In the first article of *Dutch Jewry. Its History and Secular Culture* Arend H. Huussen deals with the legal position of the Jews in the Dutch Republic during the period 1590-1796, the year that the old federal Republic of the United Provinces collapsed and was subsequently transformed into a new state in 1813 through the impact of the French Revolution and Napoleon, events which greatly affected the organisation of the Jewish community. Hubert P.H. Nusteling presents some figures on the number and dispersion of Jews living in the Republic, showing that Jews have always preferred to live in the cities and particularly in Amsterdam. Tirtsah Levie Bernfeld has investigated the financing of poor relief in the Spanish-Portuguese Jewish community in Amsterdam in the seventeenth and eighteenth centuries. Yosef Kaplan discusses the moral panic in the eighteenth-century Sephardi community of Amsterdam. Cases of adultery, clandestine marriages, and premarital sexual relations rocked the community leadership, who tried to avert this '*threat from Eros*' by ordinances and punishments like excommunication, mostly to no avail. Jonathan Israel deals with the question of Spinoza's immersion in philosophy alongside his life within the community and in commerce. Spinoza's expulsion from the Amsterdam Portuguese-Jewish community in 1656 had relatively little to do with the recent changes in his intellectual outlook, a view endorsed by Odette Vlessing's re-evaluation of archive materials. She adduces convincing arguments for the financial and secular reasons that led to Spinoza resigning his community membership, an embarrassment 'solved' by a formal excommunication. Alan Cohen grapples with the relationship between Rembrandt and the Jews in his interpretation of various biblical scenes which suggest a Jewish connotation, exemplified in a more detailed manner by the Hebrew script in some of his paintings. Hetty Berg turns to the eighteenth-century Yiddish theatrical tradition of Amsterdam as a preparation for the leading role Jews were to play in the development of the entertainment industry in the Netherlands. Marion Aptroot discusses the role of Yiddish within the Amsterdam Jewish community in the so-called *Diskursn*, pamphlets published in 1797 and 1798 shortly after the Dutch Jews were granted emancipation. Very recently these *Diskursn* have been published in a separate volume.

Part Two opens with J.C.H. Blom's article on Dutch Jewry, which is entirely based on two previous articles on the persecution of the Jews in the Netherlands published in *The History of the Jews* and in *European History Quarterly*. Selma Leydesdorff reconsiders the integration of Dutch Jews, using much argumentation from her important book *We lived with Dignity, The Jewish Proletariat of Amsterdam 1900-1940*, published in Detroit in 1994. Piet H. Schrijvers offers a far from complete picture of the life of David Cohen, Professor of Ancient History at Amsterdam University and a notorious president of the Jewish Council in the Netherlands during the Second World War. This article too largely derives from Schrijver's biography of David Cohen, published in Groningen in 2000. Peter Romijn deals with the inability of Dutch society to respond adequately and promptly to the restrictive measures and terror of the Nazi persecutors. He creates a well-balanced picture of this catastrophic period, which led to a large-scale destruction of Jewish life. One great merit of this book is the presentation of the post-war Jewish history of the Netherlands, discussed in a comprehensive and partly updated study by Chaya Brasz. Despite the many problems, external as well as internal, Jewish institutions were re-established in line with pre-war patterns, but by the end of the twentieth century the number of Jews in the organised community must be considerably lower than their total number. Ludo Abicht presents a short survey of historical facts and events concerning the Jews of Antwerp. He concludes that today's community in Antwerp is remarkably varied: it consists of two religious denominations, ranging from Orthodox and Hassidic to elements of Liberal or Reform Judaism, surrounded by a secular fringe. Thus, Antwerp is a fascinating example of a pluralist diaspora community, in which Jews can successfully survive and even thrive in a multicultural city.

The volume concludes with two literary essays on the diaries of Anne Frank and the novels of Marga Minco. Together with the second publication, the English version of *The History of the Jews in the Netherlands*, the book adds momentum to the increasingly widespread and intense interest in the history and culture of Dutch Jewry. Like *Dutch Jewry*, the second book too is a set of varied contributions in a chronology of successive periods involving the collaboration of various leading authorities and showing a consistency of thematic approach. Nowhere do these books aim to

Emanuel de Witte, *Interior of the Portugese Synagogue, Amsterdam*. 1680. Canvas, 110 x 99 cm. Rijksmuseum, Amsterdam.

be especially radical, original or comprehensive; rather, they seek to present a survey of facts and developments for those who wish to gain a clearer idea of this history or to pursue aspects of this fascinating topic in greater depth. It is therefore somewhat disappointing that the English edition of *The History* has not been supplemented by an up-to-date bibliography of publications that appeared between 1995 and 2002.

Nonetheless, both the historical and the contemporary observations add to the large amount of information offered in these two volumes, and together with their numerous references these works will prove mandatory reading for the future investigation and re-examination of Jewish history and culture in the Netherlands.

W.J. VAN BEKKUM

Jonathan Israel and Reinier Salverda (eds.), *Dutch Jewry, Its History and Secular Culture (1500-2000)*. Leiden / Boston / Cologne: Brill, 2002; 335 pp. ISBN 90-04-12436-5.

J.C.H. Blom, R.G. Fuks-Mansfeld and I. Schöffer (eds.), *The History of the Jews in the Netherlands*, Oxford / Portland, OR: The Littman Library of Jewish Civilization, 2002. 508 pp. ISBN 1-874774-51-X.

Language

The Future of Dutch as a Language of Science

'Science supplements' are a popular feature in Dutch newspapers. Each weekend readers receive a supplement full of articles highlighting all manner of recent scientific developments, from language neurology to gene technology. In addition, the Friday 'culture supplements' often contain information on the latest publications in the fields of history, history of art and literature, and sometimes also include publications in the social sciences and scholarly theses.

These science supplements are all printed in Dutch, and that is how things will remain for a long time to come. They are after all aimed at a Dutch-language readership, and that readership is still more than large enough to justify the existence of commercial publications (such as newspapers) in the Dutch language. In addition, interest in new scientific developments is if anything growing rather than diminishing among this target group.

Consequently, when some scientists now claim that Dutch is rapidly losing ground as a language of scholarship, perhaps with the odd exception such as the study of Dutch literature or the national historiography, they are evidently not talking about the language in which scientific developments are revealed to interested readers – often academics from other disciplines. Rather, they are talking about their own communication with other scientists within their own individual disciplines, communication between peers who read each others' work, appraise it and derive inspiration from it. The fact that something serious is going on here is evident from the fact that the venerable Royal Netherlands Academy of Arts and Sciences, KNAW, this year devoted a memorandum to the question of whether Dutch is under threat as a language of science and scholarship.

Concern about this issue has developed only gradually in the Netherlands. After specialists in Dutch language and culture raised the alarm as long ago as 1995, other scholars in the arts gradually awoke to the danger, followed by their colleagues from the social sciences. In the wake of all manner of changes in the organisation of university research, output funding has come to play an ever bigger part in the financing of that research and in the allocation of research time to individual scientists and scholars. Traditionally, the work of researchers at Dutch universities has consisted of two closely interrelated core tasks: teaching and research. In the last ten years, however, the importance of research has increasingly come to be judged in isolation from the teaching elements, and tangible production measurement has become a 'stand-alone' criterion of quality. In measuring that 'output', increasing use has been made of international – for which read 'Anglo-Saxon'– indicators. Citation scores, publications in 'refereed' journals: the adding up and weighing of research output led to scientific production in the Dutch language disappearing almost completely. At first this happened only in international rankings, but later it also crept into national review procedures. In many cases things eventually went so far that in assessments of scientific output, research publications were actually marked down if they were written in Dutch.

Since then a fierce debate has got under way: does research today still have any relevance if it is not published worldwide – and thus in English? Influenced by the practice in the exact and medical sciences, many people were initially inclined to answer this question with a straight 'no'. Gradually, however, more subtle reactions are emerging, such as:

- it depends on the nature of the research;
- it depends on the target group;
- research publications can be published in both Dutch and English;
- there is no direct relationship between scientific quality and language of publication.

And these more subtle responses are also giving rise to counter-arguments. To cite just a couple:

- It is important that science should retain its links with the community, and that community still speaks Dutch. This applies to those sectors which are the frequent focus of research, but it also applies to the press, to politics, to the policy which determines how much public money is made available for fundamental research. People must be able to learn about scientific research in their own language; Dutch must be equipped with the appropriate terminology and language register to enable people to write and talk about it.
- There are some relevant research domains which are so closely bound up with the specific Dutch situation that their importance for the Netherlands is matched only by their irrelevance for other countries, and whose importance means that that research must continue. The understanding is beginning to dawn that Anglo-Saxon/American choices of research domains and methods do not necessarily match the research needs of other language areas. Sociology, for example, is often closely related to the specific social context of a particular language community. And historical research is often embedded in local history and historiography.

And then there is education. In a recent discussion at the University of Amsterdam, all the professors present felt that it was best for students in the early years of their studies to be able to master academic argumentation and thought processes in their mother tongue. Generally speaking, it is only then that they are able to achieve sufficient depth and awareness of subtleties. Academic education in another language – usually English – ought therefore not to begin at least until the second phase of their studies. And even then, it was argued, only if lecturers were adequately trained in the use of English as a language of instruction; otherwise there is a danger of losing educational quality. The discussion did conclude that it would be useful for students to follow a compulsory module in 'academic English' from the start of their studies – because no-one disputes that good reading, speaking and written skills in the English language are of great importance for a future scientist.

Virtually all these arguments, and more besides, are discussed in the memorandum that the Academy has devoted to the future of Dutch as a language of science. The memorandum analyses the present situation on the basis of a number of factual data, both quantitative and qualitative. Trends in recent decades are explained on the basis of the changes as outlined above. The memorandum then adopts a standpoint. What that standpoint is becomes clear as soon as one reads the title: *Nederlands tenzij...* (Dutch unless...); the Academy thus accepts all the arguments presented above on this point.

The reasoning underlying the memorandum would have carried more weight, however, if the core notions had been defined somewhat more clearly. 'Science' is too diffuse a term to incorporate both science as an academic discipline and the nuts-and-bolts practice of scientific endeavour: the actual research, the products of that research and academic education.

If these three meanings had been distinguished more clearly, it would also have become clear which conflicts of interests need to be resolved. For example, it is in the interests of individual scientists and the furtherance of their careers to publish exclusively in refereed English-language journals. But the variation in the differentiated development of disciplines themselves, and the way in which they relate to social developments, require a much more careful approach to the choice language. And universities, as institutes of both research and teaching, find themselves with a foot in both camps. As *research* institutes, it is in their interest to adopt an increasingly international profile, and in this respect a visible presence in the most important English-language publications is of great importance. As *educational* institutes, however, universities cannot simply isolate themselves from the national education landscape. Although the importance of striving for a European system of higher education is widely espoused as a principle, a more important consideration at present in virtually all European countries is the fact that higher education is part of an education system which is constructed entirely in the official language of that country. Simply switching to a different language of instruction at the upper end of the system is not a practical proposition. This is even more the case now that virtually all European countries have in reality become multilingual countries of immigration, where the importance of a good command of the national language is – rightly – emphasised as being an essential condition for a successful educational career.

To summarise, then: when discussing Dutch as a language of science, a distinction needs to be made between the language in which scientific research is conducted, the language in which science is taught and the language in which the results of scientific research are made accessible to a wider public of highly educated readers. These distinctions dovetail seamlessly with the three functions of Dutch universities as institutions: research, education and 'serving society'.

In passing, the KNAW memorandum notes that it is not only the Netherlands, but also other European countries which are wrestling with this problem. The final recommendation is, accordingly: '*This report must be translated into English*'. My own recommendation would go further: it should also be translated into German and French, and perhaps also Spanish and Italian. Because this is indeed an issue which goes to the very heart of European scientific activity. And so it is in the interests of Europe, with all its language differences, to find good solutions.

GREETJE VAN DEN BERGH
Translated by Julian Ross.

www.knaw.nl

Loss, Longing and Lamentation
The Work of Oscar van den Boogaard

Since the publication in 1995 of his great novel *Julia's Delight* (De heerlijkheid van Julia), the Dutch writer Oscar van den Boogaard, who was born in 1964, has been considered to be one of the finest literary talents in the Dutch-speaking world. The novel depicts the life of Julia Callebaut, a woman married to an older man, whose greatest delight is what a seventeenth-century text so beautifully termed '*pretiosissimum donum Dei*', the coupling of man and woman, and the associated ecstasy. What she cannot find with her husband she gets from an even older, but randier, farmer who lives a hundred yards up the road. Or, when the fire seems to be going out there too, from the sandy beaches of Brazil. This is much more than a regional novel; it can also be regarded as a novel of ideas, in which the author makes his character into the vehicle for his view that you must make your imagination accord with reality and vice versa. For Van den Boogaard ecstasy is the greatest good.

Julia's Delight was nominated for three major literary awards, comparable to the Booker Prize. The light tone of the work was rightly praised, together with the supple, associative language, rich in imagery and the astounding composition. These qualities are to be found in all Van den Boogaard's books. They are studies in passion and longing such as Dutch literature has rarely produced. In his empathy for female characters and their emotional life, and in the expressive power of his prose, the author is the equal of his predecessors, Hugo Claus, of Catholic origin, and Jan Siebelink, born into the Calvinist faith. Yet he is free from the religious past that played such a great part in their lives. His writing was shaped by his youth which, because of his father's mobility (he was a professional soldier) and his mother's alcoholism, lacked stability and security. Born in the small town of Harderwijk, on the IJselmeer, he spent his early years in the former Dutch colony of Surinam and subsequently grew up, with his two sisters, in the little town of Deventer. After studying law he established himself as a solicitor in Brussels, but after a year opted for writing. In Brussels, so he said, he felt at home for the first time in his life. Yet presently he lives in Berlin.

For all their '*oceanic*' longing, his characters are always looking for security. They are incapable of forming lasting relationships, but remain optimistic in their striving for unity of body and soul. The paradox in all Van den Boogaard's work is that characters want to feel safe in strong relationships while at the same time claiming considerable independence in those relationships. It looks to us very like the paradox of the present generation of young Europeans, those in their thirties and early forties, often without children, many of them divorced or never married, but seriously searching.

Oscar van den Boogaard (1964-). Photo by Bart Michiels.

In the novels that preceded *Julia's Delight* Van den Boogaard also examined family relationships. In his first novel, *Dentz*, (1990) he concentrated on a narcissistic widow from Amsterdam-South, who cannot let her son go. *Fremdkörper* (1991), set in Brussels, has three characters who test the boundaries of the possible with regard to love. In *Bruno's Optimism* (Bruno's optimisme, 1993) the homosexual, Bruno Blanski, tries to escape from his life in the Alps; particularly in the relationship between the title character and his friend, the novel shows all kinds of other nuances of passion.

In the novel *Love's Death* (Liefdesdood, 1997), which also appeared in an English translation, the passion has to be repressed, while it develops relentlessly in the shadow cast by the death of a little girl. A woman is there when the little eight-year-old girl who lives next door to her overdoes her game of holding her breath under water for as long as she can, and drowns. The woman is called Inez, and she has a relationship with Hans. The drowned girl, Vera, is the daughter of Oda and Paul, a big cheese in the army. This Oda, as we readers immediately suspect, has every reason to feel guilty over her daughter's drowning, but precisely *why* this is we only find out at the end of the novel. And then again an older colleague of her husband, one Emile, has something to do with it.

Love's Death is composed of four parts. The action takes place in periods far separate from each other in time: 10 August 1973, November 1980, no date i.e. probably also in 1980, and 1987. And this is for a reason. *Love's Death* begins with a sentence which draws its significance from repetition. *'Once there was a sailor who swallowed the end of a rope and through the convolutions of his intestines was run up the mast'*. One could see this image as a metaphor for the life that one brings upon oneself. Such a death by guilt is a life-sentence, however much the four main characters try to get away from the fact – Inez and Hans, for instance, by taking in a foster-daughter, Paul by going to Surinam, his wife by seeking escape in adultery. Hanged with the rope they swallowed. The remarkable thing about the composition is that Inez, the woman on whom the spotlight falls at the beginning, and her husband Hans, virtually vanish from the story after the first part. They briefly reappear to lend, as it were, the little American girl who is staying with them to the couple who have lost their daughter through drowning.

Daisy, for that is the little girl's name, seems to fit the role of substitute daughter for a while, but when it comes to it she disappears as inconspicuously as she arrived. And then the fourth and final part tells us who is the real father of the drowned girl. With hindsight, this explains why, from the time she drowned, her mother, Oda, has more or less banished her husband Paul from her bed and her vagina.

These people wallow in their grief, particularly the mother, but not because they had loved the child so very much. At least, one only feels that at one point, with the father. And it is precisely the relationship between Vera's parents that explains the book's title. The fact that Vera's death means the end of Oda's love for her husband – so great and unending is her grief, so seemingly impossible to share – can only be explained by the secret Oda shared with, again, the even older general, Emile; note the parallel here with *Julia's Delight*. The book also contains beautifully written pages that are worth enjoying in themselves, where commas replace full stops and string sentences together to form lyrical passages.

Since *Love's Death* Van den Boogaard has developed into a highly versatile author, whose ability to write lively and witty dialogue has led not only to a quartet of plays, but also to the beautiful, intimate novel *A Bed Full of Foam* (Een bed vol schuim, 2002). This work adds another dimension to the interpretation of *Love's Death*: the longing for a degree of self-containment, for the maintenance of one's own domain in whatever loving relationship, which is still unexpressed in the earlier novel but made explicit here. In this the prose of Oscar van den Boogaard transcends the everyday realism so typical of Dutch prose and takes on a broader meaning.

WAM DE MOOR
Translated by Sheila M. Dale.

Oscar van den Boogaard, *Love's Death*. New York: Farrar, Straus & Giroux, 2001; 152 pp. ISBN 0-374185-85-9.

A Sailor's Grave for Captain Jan
Dutch and American writer Jan de Hartog

The Dutch novelist and playwright Jan de Hartog, who died in Houston, Texas, in September 2002, was born in Haarlem in 1914, the son of a professor of Calvinist theology and a Quaker mother. A born rebel, he ran away to sea at the age of ten. In the thirties he held a variety of odd jobs in Amsterdam, while publishing detective stories (under the pen name F.R. Eckmar) and plays.

Then in October 1940, shortly after the Germans had occupied the Netherlands, he published what was to become his greatest success: the novel *Hollands Glorie* (1940), a tale of Dutch derring-do on the high seas. Buying this novel with its defiant title quickly became an act of symbolic resistance, and turned it into one of the great bestsellers of twentieth-century Dutch literature. When 300,000 copies had been sold, De Hartog had to go into hiding because he refused to join the Kultuurkamer, the Nazi-led writers' guild. In 1943 he managed to escape from occupied Holland via France and Switzerland to Spain and freedom in England. The story of this dangerous journey went untold until 1999, when he published *The Escape* (De Vlucht), written with the help of his wife Marjorie.

Hollands Glorie is the story of Captain Jan Wandelaar and his ocean-going tug and how they transported the cranes, dredgers, hoppers, docks and sluice gates which the Dutch used to build harbours and dams all over the world, in Argentina and the Falklands, in the Middle East and the Dutch East Indies. The novel, written in a vigorous and salty, non-literary style, follows Jan Wandelaar's career from common sailor to captain of his own ship and his epic struggle with the arch-capitalist Kwel, who exploits and abuses the sailors who work for him. Like the socialist playwright Herman Heijermans in his play *The Good Hope* (Op hoop van zegen, 1900), De Hartog's novel paints a sharply critical portrait of the class divide in pre-war Dutch society, pitting honest Dutch sailors against the dirty tricks of the greedy company owners. In the end Wandelaar wins and takes over from Kwel, with the aim of protecting the interests of the sailors and especially of the Dutch tugboat industry against foreign competitors.

After the war De Hartog scored a second bestseller with his trilogy *God's Beggars* (Gods geuzen). First published in 1947-49, it had been reprinted ten times by 1967, was translated into English in 1957 and made into a Hollywood movie, *The Spiral Road,* in 1962. It tells the story of young Dr Anton Zorgdrager and his heroic adventures in the Colonial Health Service of the Dutch East Indies (present-day Indonesia). Zorgdrager's first assignment is to fight a plague epidemic in Borneo, and around him De Hartog paints a whole world of colonial characters and episodes – the old Sultan playing billiards in his palace; Dr Brits-Jansen, the subject of many tall stories, an outspoken atheist and the world's greatest authority on leprosy; and the heroic Captain Willem Waterreus of the Salvation Army whose wife, once a prostitute in Amsterdam, is now a leper dying in Java. In the course of the novel Zorgdrager goes through a soul-wrenching, existentialist battle with religious doubt. Its climax is the gripping tale of tropical madness in the closing chapters, which was separately published as 'Duel with a Witch Doctor' in *Reader's Digest Condensed Books* in 1961. Set on the wild coast of New Guinea, it recounts the spiritual battle between young Zorgdrager and the Papuan witch doctor Burubi whose black magic slowly drives Zorgdrager insane, causing him to run off into the jungle and degenerate into a naked apeman, until he is, finally, saved by the white magic, the true religion, of his friend the Salvation Army Captain.

Despite these two great successes, or perhaps because of them, De Hartog – whose model had been the American novelist and social critic Upton Sinclair (1878-1968) – was seen as 'just' a popular storyteller.

His novels received little critical acclaim in the Netherlands, not least because his heroic romanticism and passionate religious concerns were perceived as simplistic in the prevailing intellectual climate of post-war Holland. In retaliation, in 1950 De Hartog, defending his own craftsmanship and '*unrelenting, shameless honesty*', launched a scathing attack on what he called the pathological degeneration of the Dutch highbrows of the day – writers like Simon Vestdijk, Anna Blaman and W.F. Hermans, no less – whom he described as a bunch of '*psychopaths, spotty adolescents, lesbian women....and bloated masturbators.*'

After this clash De Hartog left the Netherlands and – like other Dutch authors such as Dola de Jong, Leo Vroman and Hans Koning – settled in the United States. He decided to write in English, and from the start this was a great success. In 1951 his play *The Fourposter* – about his love affair with Dutch actress Lily Bouwmeester – was turned into a musical, *I Do, I Do*, and became a hit on Broadway, where in 1952 it was chosen as best play of the New York season. That same year *The Fourposter* was made into a movie, and in Minneapolis *I Do, I Do* began a successful run of 22 years. Another of his plays, *Skipper next to God*, was also made into a film, *The Inspector* (1961); in it, after the war, a Dutch policeman rescues a Jewish girl from an ex-Nazi and helps to smuggle her to Palestine.

Jan de Hartog (1914-2002), as portrayed by Paul Citroen in 1974. Collection

Letterkundig Museum, The Hague / © SABAM Belgium 2003.

But what really made him famous was his novel *The Hospital* (1964), which offered a hard-hitting critique, inspired by his Quaker beliefs, of the scandalous conditions in the Houston hospital for poor and black people. Eventually, De Hartog's campaign for healthcare reform led to his appointment as extraordinary professor of gerontology and, early in 2002, to an honorary doctorate of the University of Houston. In 1969, in a Quaker protest against the Vietnam war, he launched a campaign for the adoption of the countless war orphans from that country with his book *The Children*. In the seventies this was followed by his great four-volume historical novel about the Quakers in the United States, *The Peaceable Kingdom* (1972-1975).

But the sea was really his first love, and it always played a central role in his work, both in fiction and in film. In *The Lost Sea* (1951) he wrote of his adventures when as a ten-year-old he ran away to sea. In 1952 the English translation of *Hollands Glorie* came out as *Captain Jan. A Story of Ocean Tugboats*. His sailors' novel *Stella* (1950) was made into the film *The Key* (1958), starring William Holden and Sophia Loren. In the sixties his novel *The Captain* (1966) sold more than one million copies. In 1971, his fifth Hollywood film, *The Little Ark*, told the story of two war orphans and their pets who are trapped in a flood, but sail to safety in a houseboat. The film was based on his novel of 1953, the year of the great floods that devastated the Netherlands.

In December 2002, De Hartog's ashes were scattered in the North Sea, not far from the coast of his native Holland.

REINIER SALVERDA

Music

A Sound Spectacular? Hooverphonic's Musical Adventure

In 1996, a good song and a beautiful young girl in the Tuscan countryside launched the Flemish group Hoover onto the world music scene. The beautiful young girl was Liv Tyler, who starred in Bernardo Bertolucci's film *Stealing Beauty*. The soundtrack of the film includes *2Wicky*, the Hoover single that was frequently to be heard on European and American radio. *2Wicky* was highly reminiscent of the Bristol trip-hop scene in Britain that was extremely popular at the time, represented by groups like Portishead and Massive Attack.

By the time *Stealing Beauty* arrived in the cinemas Hoover had already released their first album, *A New Stereophonic Sound Spectacular* (1996), which included *2Wicky* and ten other trip-hop tracks. Clearly influenced by the electronic music of the 1980s and the retro-futuristic atmosphere that accompanied it, *A New Stereophonic Sound Spectacular* was a soundscape

rather than an album made up of neatly separated songs. Nevertheless, *2Wicky* is still by far the best track on the album, if only thanks to the memorable sample from Isaac Hayes' version of Burt Bacharach's *Walk On By*, which sets the whole tone of the track. Jim Gillespie also used *2Wicky* in his film *I Know What You Did Last Summer* (1997), where it provided the background music for a murder. The chorus of *2Wicky* begins with the appropriate lines '*I can hurt you / you can hurt me*'.

After the release of the debut album, the name and composition of the group changed. Alex Callier, bass player and the brains behind the group, renamed the group Hooverphonic when he discovered that there were other bands in Germany and England called Hoover. A hectic tour schedule followed the success of the first album. This took its toll on singer Liesje Sadonius, and she left the group. Her place on tour was initially taken by Kyoko Baertsoen, and for the recording of the second album by Geike Arnaert, who is still the group's vocalist today. Guitarist Raymond Geerts has remained with the group, while keyboard player Frank Duchêne left Hooverphonic after the second album.

This second album, *Blue Wonder Power Milk*, was released in 1998. Musically it derived largely from *Sound Spectacular*, but had more of a pop feel and was slightly less diffuse. *Blue Wonder Power Milk* too was popular with film directors. The haunting *Eden* was used in *I Still Know What You Did Last Summer* (1998), the sequel to the 1997 Jim Gillespie film mentioned above. The first single released from the album, *This Strange Effect*, was a cover version of Dave Berry's popular 1960s song (written by Ray Davies). It was included in the soundtrack of *Shades* (1999), a film by the Flemish director Erik van Looy starring Mickey Rourke, for which Alex Callier wrote the music. Hooverphonic are remarkably good at taking a number written by someone else and transforming it to produce their own unique sound. The gaunt, frail voice of Geike Arnaert, the sonorous, predominantly electronic soundscape and the deep, dark bass tones are now the band's hallmark.

Hooverphonic's music is also characterised by extremely polished and professional production techniques, which were already evident in their debut album. This is due not only to Alex Callier, an experienced sound technician with an excellent ear for mixes, but also to the respective producers of the albums. *A New Stereophonic Sound Spectacular* was mixed by Roland Harrington (Björk, Soul II Soul, Simply Red) and *Blue Wonder Power Milk* was produced by Mark Plati (David Bowie, The Cure).

Hooverphonic's third album, *The Magnificent Tree,* was released in 2000 and certainly lived up to the expectations of the public and the media. Perfectly composed and orchestrated songs such as *Vinegar & Salt* and *Mad about You* have a light, sing-along feel, but at the same time they are poignant and leave a lasting impression. *The Magnificent Tree* is Geike Arnaert at her best; here she reveals her remarkable vocal range,

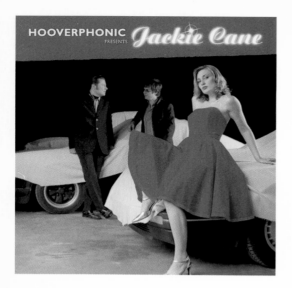

ten overshadowed by the unforgettable voice of Geike Arnaert, who is utterly convincing in the role of a fading pop star. Despite these reservations, *Hooverphonic Presents Jackie Cane* is an interesting album. We should have nothing but praise for the fact that an established group such as Hooverphonic dares to embark on such a musical adventure. In the meantime, we shall look forward to future releases. It will be interesting to see where the group's musical journey takes them next.

BART VAN DER STRAETEN
Translated by Yvette Mead.

DISCOGRAPHY

A New Stereophonic Sound Spectacular, 1996 (as Hoover).
Blue Wonder Power Milk, 1998.
The Magnificent Tree, 2000.
Hooverphonic Presents Jackie Cane, 2002.

www.hooverphonic.com and www.hooverphonicusa.com

moving easily between extremes. Until this third album Hooverphonic had established their reputation mainly in the studio and there were very few reviews of live concerts. During the tour that followed the release of *The Magnificent Tree* Hooverphonic proved themselves to be excellent live performers, able to create an ambience that completely captivates their audiences. In 2001 Hooverphonic became the first-ever Belgian band to close Rock Werchter, Belgium's top rock festival. No mean feat, at a time when Flemish music is flourishing on the international stage.

Jackie Cane was the last single released from *The Magnificent Tree*. The song tells of the rise and fall of a fictitious pop diva. The story was developed in the album *Hooverphonic Presents Jackie Cane*, released at the end of September 2002. This is a true concept album, a soundtrack for a non-existent film about the life of Jackie Cane told by her equally fictitious twin sister. Hooverphonic have pulled out all the stops on this album. The cocktail kitsch of the opening number *Sometimes*, with its striking big-band arrangements, contrasts with the subdued and oppressive *Others Delight*, which is a sensitive, intriguing song. The first five tracks of the album relate Jackie Cane's rise to fame, culminating in the swinging number *The World Is Mine*, which was released as a first single. Thereafter things go downhill fast, with her delirium in the seventh track bringing her to *The Kiss* (of death) in the final song on the album.

I cannot quite decide whether the musical adventure *Hooverphonic Presents Jackie Cane* is a success or not. It is, in any case, an intriguing album that – even for Hooverphonic – is a rich patchwork of sound. It has a number of enjoyable songs such as *The World Is Mine* and *Others Delight* (see above). Here and there, however, it becomes somewhat corny, as musicals tend to. This is partly due to the lyrics, which sometimes lack meaning and are often simply bad – a sensitive subject for the group. But the forgettable lyrics are of-

Weightless Music The Work of Simeon ten Holt

Simeon ten Holt found himself in Classic FM's 'All-Time Top Ten' ahead of Richard Wagner, the only living composer in the list. How can such a thing happen? It is a mystery to the composer himself. He has no kindred spirits in the Netherlands. He is a typical 'loner'.

Simeon ten Holt (1923-) was twelve when he became a pupil of Jakob van Domselaer. Ten Holt senior, Henri Friso, a painter as was Simeon's brother Friso, knew the Van Domselaers well and Simeon was a friend of Jaap, Jakob van Domselaer's son. Ten Holt's first pieces, which are still tonal, were written under the influence of Van Domselaer: *Kompositie I-IV* (1942-1946) and *Sonate* (1953) for piano and a *Suite* (1953) for string quartet. One can also trace influences from Janáček and Bartók.

In 1949 Ten Holt went to Paris, without a cent in his pocket and with nowhere to stay. He was helped by a painter, and through him was put in touch with Honegger at the Ecole Normale. He also had lessons from the French composer Darius Milhaud, but Ten Holt was too individualistic to submit to a strict discipline and he thumbed a lift to the South of France. There he fell in love (with the daughter of a millionaire, no less), and there his music was appreciated. In an interview Ten Holt said: '*I was actually catapulted to maestro by the French, while I was really still a child. After a couple of years I burst that bubble. I longed for the forbidding Dutch climate and character, and I went back.*'

When he returned to Bergen in 1954 he lived in a converted Second World War bunker. The bunker, in the countryside, had no water and no light, but the composer had no money either for rent, and he wanted to be able to compose in peace and quiet.

As for his music: in the 1950s Ten Holt invented

a system of his own which he called 'Diagonal thought', a kind of music built on tritonal relationships. *Diagonal Music for Strings* (Diagonaalmuziek voor strijkers, 1958) and *Sonate diagonaal* marked the beginning of a period during which Ten Holt eliminated the tonic. This system culminated in the piece studied by many avant-garde musicians: *..A/.TA-LON for Mezzosoprano and 36 Instrumentalists* (..A/.TA-LON voor mezzosopraan en 36 spelende instrumenten, 1967-68), in which strongly serialist influences from Pierre Boulez played a considerable part. At the same time Ten Holt developed a theoretically interesting substructure, which he could sell to the journal *Raster*.

From then on the tonality that played a part in his most successful romantic-minimalist period was doomed: '*In a composition written in a tonal system we can always hear a suppressed memory, a guilty conscience, and the desire to be associated with the use of power by an underprivileged group.*'

Tripticon for Six Percussionists (Tripticon voor zes slagwerkers) was created in 1965, under the influence of the German composer Karlheinz Stockhausen. Ten Holt borrowed the idea of the time octave from Stockhausen, in a strict ordering of twelve metronomically determined tempi applied as a series like the parameters of pitch, length, intensity, and dynamics. *Tripticon* is a play of sound colours, in which the silences are as important as the sounds. However contrived this might appear, the result was a music that was very much alive. That was evident, among other things, at a concert on 15 March 2000 when *Diagonal Music for Strings* was first heard, and in the Paradijskerk in Rotterdam the Mayor of Bergen invested Ten Holt with the regalia of a Knight of the Order of the Lion of the Netherlands. At that time Ten Holt had already acquired a multitude of admirers with his romantic-minimalist music in the styles of Schumann and Chopin, and in the case of *Natalon in E* even in that of Schubert. After that followed the endlessly expanding music of the last twenty years, such as the now famous *Canto Ostinato* and *Lemniscaat*, in which music plays and grinds like the sea, in which time is crystallised.

Shortly before the beginning of this last phase, Ten Holt worked at the Institute for Sonology, in Utrecht (1969-1975). In the interim he had outgrown his hermit-like existence. He established the 'Bergen Work Group for Contemporary Music' and organised quite outstanding concerts, at first in a cinema and later in the Ruïnekerk. He continued to play the piano and created a furore with typical ' bunker pieces' such as *Solo Devil Dance* (Soloduiveldans, 1959), *Cycle to Madness* (Cyclus aan de waanzin, 1961-62) and later with *Inferno I and II* for tape (1971). Meanwhile he also taught at the Academy for Plastic Arts in Arnhem (1970-1987), where he experimented with group improvisations. In the same period Ten Holt made his real breakthrough with *Canto Ostinato* (1976-1979), of variable duration and with a variable orchestra (mostly of four pianos). Chords or groups of chords are hidden in bars and sections and take on a life of their own, the melodic binding becomes looser, bars and sections are given a repeat mark so that the performers make their own decision on the number of repetitions, time becomes space in which the notes float freely. It is weightless music, unfettered by form. Its première, on 25 April 1979 in the Ruïnekerk in Bergen, was of historical significance and assured the work an unprecedented success.

There are four more works for a variable orchestra (two to four pianos) which will fill an evening: *Lemniscaat* (1982-1983), *Horizon* (1983-1985), *Incantatie IV* (1990) and *Méandres* (1997). Time and again the music outstrips the intended time span: the performance of *Lemniscaat* in 1983 went on for thirty hours; different groups of pianists kept changing places with each other. Ten Holt: '*My hands grope for something I cannot "grasp" with my mind: I believe in my hands. With them I feel around in the dark and reach for a reality that I (the personification of that reality) experience only as a patch of mist, a sensation.*' After hardly touching a piano for years, something began to come to life under his hands: '*quite morbid, tonal things, bordering on the banal, the decadent. "Canto Ostinato" grew from this. "Canto" is bordering on the banal. If you don't listen carefully, you find it banal. But when you realise what the form is, the structure, and how the tensions work, then you get quite another story.*'

Nowadays CDs of his music are often played at baptisms and funerals. Music that brings peace, frequently performed in the octagonal hall of the Vredenburg Music Centre in Utrecht, which has become more or less a 'Ten Holt Centre'. When in 2001 a golden disk was presented to Ten Holt at the Vredenburg Centre for more than fifteen thousand sales of a recording of *Canto Ostinato* by Polo de Haas and Kees Wieringa, it was evident that never before had a Dutch classical composer achieved such a success. Ten Holt has become a pop idol of classical music.

ERNST VERMEULEN
Translated by Sheila M. Dale.

SELECTIVE DISCOGRAPHY

Horizon. Donemus Records, 1995.
Canto Ostinato. Donemus Records, 1995.
Palimpsest. Donemus Records, 2000.

Philosophy and Science

Be Glad that Life has no Meaning
On the Essays of Jaap van Heerden

Who wouldn't give his right arm for a title like that? It stands at the head of an essay by Jaap van Heerden (1940-), who studied philosophy in Amsterdam, was one of the editors of the student paper *Propria Cures* which was a nursery for a good many pointed Dutch pens, and is now a professor at the Psychology Laboratory of Amsterdam University. Van Heerden has other such splendid titles in stock, including *Prose to Catch Girls With* (Proza waarmee je meisjes vangt), *The Tyranny of Fabrications* (Schrikbewind der verzinsels), *Traumas Ancient and Modern* (Van oude en nieuwe trauma's) and *If 2+2=5, 4+4=10. On Consistency in Nonsense* (Als 2+2=5, dan 4+4=10. Over samenhang in onzin). Every few years he collects up the pieces he has written for newspapers (mainly *NRC Handelsblad*) and journals and publishes them.

What is an essay? Not a rough draft or a provisional version of a 'definitive' piece that one can't at present be bothered to write, a *'shaving from a scholar's workbench'*, for that, as Robert Musil says, is a paper or a treatise, but *'the unique and immutable form assumed in a decisive thought by the inner life of an individual'* (Musil again). The essay can be about anything and everything, according to Van Heerden it doesn't have to be reasonable, it can argue the most absurd case, it has *'the strength of the writer who refuses to abide by all those rules that mask his personality'* and – last but not least – *'above all, an essayist must not be boring'*.

If there really is a 'Dutch School' of laconic, down-to-earth, unintentionally humorous essayists of a rather positivist stamp which includes such writers as Karel van het Reve and Rudy Kousbroek, then surely Jaap van Heerden is a member too. Common sense plays a major role in these essays from the polder where the ditches mutter *'just act normal'* to each other as they go their own sweet way. In an article on Russell and Wittgenstein that takes as its text the famous final sentence of the *Tractatus*: *'What we cannot speak about we must pass over in silence'* (referring among other things to ethics) Van Heerden at first seems to agree with Wittgenstein, who found Russell's pronouncements about his horror of violence, dogmatism and tyranny vulgar and repulsive. Because one *shows* one's ethical convictions, one doesn't shout them from the rooftops. The perfectionist Wittgenstein had an irascible contempt for a lack of seriousness in other people, but in Van Heerden's view he went too far when, as the anonymous patron of Viennese artists, he condemned as tasteless the letters of thanks he received from them via an intermediary. Van Heerden wonders why Wittgenstein should have been so excessively irritated by this display of common decency, and turns back to the more civilised Russell.

Decency and basic civilisation pervade these essays, but Van Heerden is also adept at the *'salutary superficiality ... which keeps us going'*. The best of his writings have that Lightness which Calvino demanded of literature, without it ever sliding into levity. Take, for example, the essay whose title I have borrowed for this piece. Van Heerden starts by remarking that while anyone who says that life has no meaning is accorded respect (*'an acknowledged moralist who bears an existential disillusionment with distinction'*), someone who says that he is glad of it is *'requested to keep his strange ideas to himself until the children are in bed,*

and if there are no children I am bluntly told that any delight at the fact that life has no meaning leads to genocide, racism, criminal assault, moonlighting, benefit fraud, broken election promises, land-grabs and homicide'. Van Heerden looks at various arguments. At the end he turns the question around: suppose that life did have a meaning, and we knew what it was. And then he ends like this: *'That would be an utter catastrophe. The disastrous consequences which immediately spring to mind would be shattering. We should sink into a gigantic trough of cold porridge. The dictates of knowing that meaning would hamper every movement, block every initiative and blight every new idea because of the obligatory, unavoidable checking to see how far it contributes to the all-embracing purpose of this life. We should be able to experience the meaning of life only as a doom. Every step could be a deviation. Life would come to a standstill. And nobody wants that. Be glad that life has no meaning.'*

Cheerful and categorical statements which briefly throw the windows of our worrisome existence wide open.

Ultimately, what Van Heerden argues for is *'in the absence of a higher goal, to start doing something oneself'*, *'to arrange existence so it's half-way pleasant'*. Humanity has never done anything else. And in the process has produced religions, ideologies, weapons, laws and textile paintings – all of them creations of the human spirit. In another essay he returns to the question of meaning, and gives a laconic answer: "Life has meaning when you feel like it". Actually, this works better in Dutch (*'Het leven heeft zin als je er zin in hebt'*); sadly, the play on *'zin'*, meaning, and *'ergens zin in hebben'*, to feel like something, is untranslatable. Perhaps that fact gives the Dutch a head start when it comes to answering the question of meaning, Van Heerden comments: *'You could say that everything's fine if at least we, the Dutch, have got it sorted.'* The professional psychologist always has something to say in these essays. Van Heerden decided very early on that any clear distinction between psychology and philosophy was uninteresting and imaginary. In his view psychoanalysis is not a science, at most it is a therapy whose success cannot always be demonstrated unambiguously. Concepts like the slip of the tongue or repression are actually part of the cultural heritage of a cultivated individual. The unconscious is not, but the explanation of how it works is, according to the essayist, Freud's legacy. Moreover, Van Heerden thinks that psychologists should not leave psychoanalysis to the Freudians but continue to subject unconscious processes, for example, to experimental testing.

Van Heerden has no very high opinion of Dutch philosophers. They are too modest. '*People sit up straight when they hear there's a philosopher in the room, itching to ask him something about the meaning of life, while he himself would prefer his expertise to be restricted to the logic of conjunctions or the problem of how a woman can become a grandmother before her mother.*' He hasn't much time, either, for Derrida and his ilk. In *The Tyranny of Fabrications* he wonders rather apocalyptically whether we really are adequately prepared – obviously not, then – for the approaching collapse of postmodernism, narratology, the appalling dogma '*Everything is text*', the mantra '*In the final analysis, readers are themselves the authors of the text they are reading*' and other stuff in the same vein: '*Just try to imagine sometime what a great filthy mess and economic inefficiency we shall find in the faculties of arts and philosophy when they finally manage to throw off the yoke of Foucault, Derrida, Marx, Freud, Mieke Bal, Lacan, Heidegger and Lyotard. We shall need a kind of cultural Marshall Plan to make all those intellectual areas more or less habitable again.*' The withering humour is in the fifth name, that of a Dutch lady professor of the Theory of Literature not quite at ease among those male giants. '*Who is going to have to manage that painful archive which will reveal that everyone spied on everyone else and interpreted them in an incriminating way? People have collaborated uncritically in a tyranny of fabrications. If you didn't join in your life wasn't worth living. You were accused of ducking the issues, incest, lack of subjectivity, hostility to fictionality, of secretly listening to scholarship. You had to be very sure of yourself not to bend under that pressure. And so almost everyone became "inoffizieller Mitarbeiter" of the State Bureau for Textual Exegesis.*'

After all this, it is hardly surprising that Van Heerden steers his bicycle well clear of philosophers like Heidegger and Levinas. That he himself is a cyclist is apparent from a splendid, archetypically Dutch piece: 'Underworld Types Do Not Ride Bikes' ('De penoze fietst principieel niet'). The essay starts with the remark that Sartre couldn't ride a bike. Van Heerden believes that today's philosophy must take account of the cyclist, the least powerful road-user, hated though he is by criminals and psychopaths. There then follows an anecdote from his own experience. At a crossroads the cycling essayist gets away first, to the grave displeasure of a Honda containing three trendy youths. A furious chase ensues, and the essayist narrowly escapes being assaulted. Then come some reflections on psychopaths who cannot tolerate any hesitation, on U-turns that are seen as a proof of guilt and a good reason to embark on a manhunt. Sartre turns up again at the end of the piece: only through mad rage can the outcasts of the earth become human, says the existentialist; only through blind violence can they recreate themselves. Van Heerden opts for decency and concludes, mildly and lethally: '*But I think it would have been better if Sartre had stayed on his bike a bit longer.*' Would Wittgenstein have been a cyclist? Is Roger Scruton? Be glad that essay-writing has meaning. Particularly if, like Van Heerden, you feel like doing it.

LUC DEVOLDERE
Translated by Tanis Guest

Trailblazers in PGD Twenty Years of Genetic Medicine at the University of Brussels

The Centre for Genetic Medicine at the University of Brussels celebrated its twentieth birthday in 2002. It is the youngest of eight centres that Belgium can boast; nonetheless this baby of the family leads them all in one very specific technique: pre-implantation genetic diagnosis (PGD) or, in plain English, making sure that only healthy embryos are implanted in the womb. Even at international level the centre is playing a pioneering role in this field. Patients from all over the world come to Jette in the hope of holding a healthy baby in their arms nine months later.

In the early years the centre was mainly engaged in carrying out the classic tests during pregnancy, such as amniocentesis which can show whether there is anything wrong with the foetus during pregnancy. Even today this is still their most important function, but in 1993 they introduced PGD. Until then the technique was only known in the United Kingdom, where it had been practised for three or four years. The University of Brussels centre has made up the ground quickly. At present 117 of the 1,000 babies that have been born in the whole world by this method were 'Made in Belgium'.

The great advantage of PGD is that congenital abnormalities can be excluded at the beginning rather than identified only when pregnancy is already established. The method of working is more or less as follows: the doctors take ova from the mother and fertilise them in a test-tube with sperm from the father, just as in classic *in vitro* fertilisation (IVF). The embryo that is created must then mature for three days before a cell is extracted. That one tiny cell will allow the doctors to say whether that embryo will develop into a healthy baby.

After almost ten years of experience with this technique, the Centre for Genetic Medicine at the University of Brussels can detect an impressive number of hereditary diseases up front. More than that, no other centre anywhere in the world can identify so many genetic deviations. The researchers can identify not only conditions which are apparent at birth, such as Down's syndrome, but also afflictions which only show up later in life, such as hereditary forms of breast cancer, or certain diseases of the muscles. Anyone who thinks that the investigators in Jette are giving a free hand to parents who would like a so-called 'designer baby', a baby that looks exactly as they would wish and has no defects, has got it all wrong. They only check for hereditary, and therefore genetically-determined abnormalities, and no one embryo is tested for a whole spectrum of conditions. In each case, the investigation relates to a specific affliction which has shown up in the family of one of the prospective parents.

The largest group of patients are therefore people who are faced with a hereditary disease in their immediate family, and who want to spare themselves the pain and mental suffering of an abortion; PGD can ensure that only healthy embryos are implanted. In Jette they also get a lot of parents who already have a child with a genetic abnormality and who wish to avoid running the same risk with a second child. In addition a fair number of people from abroad come to the centre, in the first instance because the staff of the University of Brussels have built up a cast-iron reputation for this pioneering technique, but also because in some countries this method is highly controversial. In Germany, for example, an embryo is protected by law, hence a method such as PGD is also illegal. So quite a number of Germans come to the University of Brussels.

Sadly, PGD is not for everyone. The treatment is expensive and physically very demanding. Patients have to shell out some 1,500 euro for each attempt, and although the centre has a high success rate, the parents-to-be must take into account that at least three sessions are necessary to give any real chance of success. Moreover, although the procedure is exactly the same, PGD is more tiring than IVF, because it is much more intensive. The aim is to take as many ova as possible, to increase the chance of a healthy embryo.

It is doubtful whether these discomforts can be got rid of in the future; but in any event the chances of success will continue to increase, and the range of abnormalities that can be detected will be further extended.

KIM HERBOTS
Translated by Sheila M. Dale.

Centre for Genetic Medicine AZ-VUB: Laarbeeklaan 101 / 1090 Brussels / Belgium / Tel. +32 2 477 60 71 / fax +32 2 477 60 72

A Wider Perception of 'Science'

At the beginning of the seventeenth century the Netherlands were regarded as a hotbed of Copernicanism. Many academics and scholars there were quite familiar with the idea that the sun did not move round the earth but the earth round the sun. When the French canon Pierre Gassendi toured the Northern Netherlands in 1629 he was amazed to discover that '*they all think the earth moves*'. A further striking feature of Copernicanism in the Republic is that from the 1640s it became hopelessly entangled with the debate on Descartes' philosophy. Anyone who supported Copernicus was assumed to be a Cartesian and could therefore bank on attracting forceful criticism from orthodox Calvinist ministers. All in all, this gave the history of Copernicanism in the Dutch Republic a unique flavour, making it a fascinating variant in the history of the construction of the new world-picture.

Nevertheless, only quite recently Rienk Vermij, a well-known Dutch historian of science, found it virtually impossible to find an international publisher for his voluminous study of the subject, despite its being written in English. He was up against the perception, which still prevails, that scientific development was primarily an Anglo-Saxon achievement. Although Italy with Galileo and France with Descartes could obviously not be ignored, the Scientific Revolution of the seventeenth century did, after all, culminate in the work of the Englishman Isaac Newton. British science is therefore considered, even retrospectively, as having led the way. This Anglo-Saxon prejudice has been reinforced both by the growing dominance of English as the language of science, and by the financial power of Anglo-American publishers. In the United States, the main centre for work on the history of science, knowledge of other languages is limited, even among younger historians; and if a language has to be learned, preference is given to French, German or Italian rather than to Dutch. No wonder, therefore, that the Dutch contribution to the history of science has been structurally undervalued. It also partly explains why a book, even one written in English, will not always easily find a publisher outside the Netherlands. Vermij himself was faced with an impossible choice between drastically shortening his book (by omitting most of the theological debate), or publishing the work in Dutch. In the first case one of the most characteristic elements of Dutch Copernicanism would have been lost, and in the second he would merely have confirmed the Anglo-Saxon bias by default.

Fortunately there was one other possibility. Just when Vermij was casting around for a solution to his dilemma, the Royal Netherlands Academy of Arts and Sciences (KNAW) changed its publication policy. Traditionally the Academy had published work in every conceivable field of scholarship in the form of reports and proceedings, treatises and abstracts, even its own journals. There was a time when publication by an up-and-coming researcher in, for example, the Proceedings of the Physics Section was a prestigious debut, and even well-established scholars have in the past chosen to have their most important work published by the Academy. But those days have now passed. Commercial publishers dominate the market, and it is simply no longer possible to cover every field effectively in a world where scholarship is now so specialised and fragmented. So in about 1995 the Academy decided to focus its publishing activities more narrowly. But focus on what? Why astronomy, say, and not biology? Why linguistics and not economics? Its solution was to opt for the history of scholarship, of *scientia* in the broadest sense, so as to in-

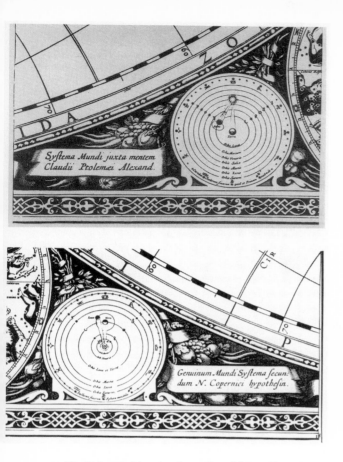

ures too, and thus avoids the presumption that even here in the Netherlands scientific activity merely reflected the spread of Newtonianism, which would only have strengthened the aforementioned Anglo-Saxon bias. The third volume in the series, which quite coincidentally covers more or less the same historical period, is Rina Knoeff's *Herman Boerhaave (1668-1738). Calvinist Chemist and Physician.* This work too pursues the line that Dutch science had no reason to hide its light under a bushel. Knoeff departs from the standard interpretation of the great physician Boerhaave in taking his Calvinist convictions seriously, not just in his private life but also as a formative influence on his scientific work. The fourth and, for the time being, last volume in the series is Johanna Levelt Stengers' fairly technical study, *How Fluids Unmix. Discoveries by the School of Van der Waals and Kamerlingh Onnes.* Though this work takes us outside the Golden Age, there is a tenuous link with the other volumes in that both the Amsterdam professor Van der Waals and his younger Leiden colleague Kamerlingh Onnes figured prominently in the so-called *Second* Golden Age of Dutch history.

Like the first three volumes, Levelt Stengers' study also happens to deal with the history of science. However, there is no intention of limiting this series to 'science' in the English use of the word. To abandon the original guidelines of *scientia* (or in Dutch, '*wetenschappen*') in its wider continental sense would be to deny its very *raison d'être*. So we may look forward in the future to studies that cover the whole spectrum of scholarship in the arts and sciences. A start has been made.

K. VAN BERKEL
Translated by Chris Emery.

Rienk Vermij, *The Calvinist Copernicans. The Reception of the New Astronomy in the Dutch Republic, 1575-1750.* KNAW / Edita, 2002; 433 pp. ISBN 90-6984-340-3.

Gerhard Wiesenfeldt, *Leerer Raum in Minervas Haus. Experimentelle Naturlehre an der Universität Leiden, 1675-1715.* KNAW / Edita, 2002; 464 pp. ISBN 90-6984-339-0.

Rina Knoeff, *Herman Boerhaave (1668-1738). Calvinist Chemist and Physician.* KNAW / Edita, 2002; 237 pp. ISBN 90-6894-342-0.

Johanna Levelt Sengers, *How Fluids Unmix. Discoveries by the School of Van der Waals and Kamerlingh Onnes.* KNAW / Edita, 2002; 302 pp. ISBN 90-6984-357-9.

The Ptolemaic (above) and the 'true' Copernican (below) systems of the world as depicted by Nicolaas Visscher on his 1669 edition of the world map by Jodocus Hondius. Photo from *The Calvinist Copernicans* (Rienk Vermij, 2002).

clude the humanities and the social sciences. Every field of scholarship would be admissible, but only in a historical context. And so it was that Edita (the name of the Academy's publishing division) initiated the series 'History of Science and Scholarship in the Netherlands'. Rienk Vermij's *The Calvinist Copernicans. The Reception of the New Astronomy in the Dutch Republic, 1575-1750* was the first volume in the series and appeared in the bookshops in mid-2002.

And Edita has not been idle since then, for three more volumes have already been published. The second volume is Gerhard Wiesenfeldt's *Leerer Raum in Minervas Haus. Experimentelle Naturlehre an der Universität Leiden, 1675-1715,* a study of the experimental philosophy that spread from Leiden and conquered continental Europe at the start of the eighteenth century. The experimental tradition has frequently been associated with the Dutch Newtonians 's Gravesande and Musschenbroek. But Wiesenfeldt deliberately focuses on older influences and lesser-known fig-

Society

The Netherlands and the Tragedy of Srebrenica

Some events should never be forgotten. Among them are those that took place on 11 July 1995. On that day, the Bosnian Serb army overran the 'safe haven' of Srebrenica, a Muslim enclave in Bosnia that was under the protection of the United Nations. In the days that followed, 7,500 Muslim men and boys were brutally murdered. Dutchbat, the Dutch UN peacekeeping force, was powerless to intervene. The troops were not equipped to fight off an attack and, worse still, their rules of engagement made no provision for such action. Even their requests for air strikes to deter the Serbian forces were repeatedly turned down. The Dutch peacekeepers withdrew from the area a few days later.

But simply recalling these events will not tell us who was responsible for them. It has taken several years to establish who was to blame, because the Dutch government was reluctant to face up to what happened. That is why the Netherlands Institute for War Documentation (NIOD), an independent body, was commissioned to investigate the fall of Srebrenica. NIOD took its time reporting its findings, which were finally published on 10 April 2002. The NIOD report and appendices, published under the title *Srebrenica, a Safe Haven* (Srebrenica, een veilig gebied), run to several thousand pages; 3,400, to be precise. Once the report had been published it was no longer possible to avoid the question of who was to blame – a question that was raised repeatedly during the ensuing months. It was raised following the resignation of the entire Dutch cabinet, in Dutch parliamentary debates, in yet another Dutch parliamentary enquiry, and in a public enquiry broadcast on Dutch television.

To understand how this process unfolded we first need to consider the main conclusions of the NIOD report:

- The government must carry the largest share of blame. In 1993, the Lubbers cabinet dispatched troops on a mission with a '*very unclear mandate*' to a UN Muslim enclave that was virtually impossible to defend. The government's decision was based on '*a combination of humanitarian concern and political ambitions*' and it involved '*enormous risks*'. The Lubbers cabinet was succeeded by that of Wim Kok, which was equally responsible. By the end of 1994 the United Nations as well as the Dutch Minister of Defence Joris Voorhoeve had reached the conclusion that defending Srebrenica was an impossible task. The Dutchbat troops and the Muslim population they were assigned to protect were sitting targets. But the international community would not take action, and Minister Voorhoeve resigned himself to the fact that the situation was '*untenable*'.

- The report was lenient towards the members of Dutchbat, who have often been criticised for not fighting back. According to NIOD, '*armed resistance was not an option*'. The Dutch troops were heavily outnumbered. Their requests for air support were turned down. Moreover, their rules of engagement allowed them to fire only in self-defence. Nor is it true that the Muslim men were slaughtered '*in full view*' of the 'Blue Helmets'. No-one could have predicted this atrocity, which took place out of sight of the Dutch troops. Although they did, reluctantly, co-operate in an evacuation in which the men were separated from the women and children, the Dutchbat peacekeepers had been forced to choose the lesser of two evils and could not be held responsible for the separation.

- In the aftermath of the fall of Srebrenica, senior military figures made serious errors. Army generals attempted to disguise the truth about the tragedy. NIOD describes their secrecy as '*a cover-up that rebounded on the army like a boomerang*'.

In the days immediately following the publication of the report it was not clear how the Dutch cabinet – and Prime Minister Wim Kok in particular – would react. Kok was, after all, the only member of the government apart from Defence Minister Pronk who had been involved in every stage of the Srebrenica drama. As such he could be held accountable for dispatching the Dutchbat troops and for the course of events during the fall of Srebrenica, and also for the way in which the aftermath was dealt with. Kok's response was also influenced by the report of the Netherlands Interchurch Peace Council (IKV), which had been published prior to the NIOD report. In contrast to NIOD's findings, the IKV concluded that given more decisive action by the Dutch cabinet Dutchbat could have prevented the massacre. Minister Pronk took this conclusion very much to heart.

Thus far the government had defended itself by claiming that it had had to do *something*; doing nothing had not been an option. In other words, the Netherlands and the international community had tried to make the best of a bad job. That was all they could do. Would it have been better if we had stayed at home? It was the Bosnian Serbs – and General Mladic in particular – who were to blame for the tragic culmination of events. But such justifications cannot conceal the fact that the international community and the Netherlands had failed miserably. The United Nations acknowledged this in a critical report and an enquiry by the French government drew similar conclusions.

Prime Minister Kok too accepted that disastrous mistakes had been made. He differed from the United Nations, however, in that rather than taking refuge in the anonymity of '*the international community*', he took upon himself the successive cabinets' responsibility for the debacle. Given the report's conclusions, the Prime Minister felt he had no alternative but to resign. The other ministers also took this as a signal to step down, and Kok's second cabinet fell shortly before the general election scheduled for 15 May 2002 (see p. 299). Kok's dramatic gesture won him respect not only in the Netherlands, but also worldwide: he had personally acknowledged the failure of the international community.

But the poisoned chalice had not yet been drained. Kok had settled his own account, but Parliament wanted to take the matter further. It wanted the whole matter sorted out, and so a public enquiry was launched – a step that should have been taken much earlier. After

NIOD's thorough investigation this move was seen as rather pointless, but that was not how it turned out. Although few new facts emerged, the public hearings held in November 2002 created a deep impression. For the first time commanding officers, generals on the home front and government ministers had the opportunity to give their version of events in full – in front of the cameras and the people of the Netherlands. The whole country was drawn into the many dilemmas confronting the decision-makers and the issues they had to wrestle with.

The enquiry's findings were published in January 2003. This report – which is particularly critical of the attitude of ex-General Hans Couzy, then Commander-in-Chief of the Dutch ground forces – does not contain a great deal of new information, but it has at least brought the dilemmas of the Srebrenica tragedy out into the open and, via the television cameras, into the homes of the people of the Netherlands. That, after all, is where the drama began. The overwhelming majority of Dutch people did not want to stand idly by while ethnic cleansing was taking place in Bosnia. But neither they nor the politicians representing them had really grasped all the implications of intervening in the conflict. And we have learned to our consternation that half measures are not enough to prevent a tragedy.

WILLEM BREEDVELD
Translated by Yvette Mead.

Jan Willem Honig & Norbert Both, *Srebrenica: Record of a War Crime*. New York, 1997.

The Vlaams Blok

The electoral success in 2002 of Jean-Marie Le Pen in France and the Pim Fortuyn List (LPF) in the Netherlands has, in spite of the huge differences between them, again focused attention on Flanders and its extreme right-wing party, the Vlaams Blok or Flemish Bloc. In a display of total ignorance and disturbing over-simplification, Le Pen, Fortuyn and Vlaams Blok leader Filip Dewinter have all been tarred with the same brush. In some quarters Flanders has once again been portrayed as a region virtually synonymous with neo-Fascism and the extreme right. In Flanders itself, however, the events in France and the Netherlands caused some wry amusement when it became their neighbours' turn to be faced with unusual and extremist voting behaviour.

France, Austria, Denmark, Italy and now the Netherlands have all proved just as susceptible as Flanders to the virus of the extreme right. Dozens of Flemish politicians, journalists, political commentators and artists have been arguing for years that the rise of the Vlaams Blok should not be regarded as a typically Flemish phenomenon, but their analyses and warnings have not always been taken seriously. After all, there are quite a few people who have a vested interest in associating Flanders with the extreme right.

Because Wallonia has never had an extreme right-wing party worthy of the name, and also because Flanders has produced a number of Fascist supporters in the past, it has been all too easy for political opponents to pigeonhole Flanders as a hotbed of right-wing extremism. Only since Le Pen's spectacular breakthrough has it become obvious, especially among Belgium's French speakers, that the success of the extreme right is a Europe-wide phenomenon that cannot simply be linked to a single region.

The chief reason why Flanders is often associated with the Vlaams Blok is the fact that the Blok presents itself as the sole successor to the Flemish Movement and the only Flemish nationalist party. It spares neither money nor effort in projecting the image of being the only radical Flemish party that resolutely defends Flemish interests. It has adopted the Lion of Flanders – the emblem of 'official' Flanders – as the party's symbol and sings the official Flemish anthem at its meetings.

In order to distance itself from the democratic pro-Flemish parties and movements who support a federal Belgium with the greatest possible cultural autonomy for Flanders, the Vlaams Blok has from the start adopted the most radical political programme possible. Its aim is to destroy the Belgian state and achieve total independence for Flanders. However, the history of its birth and evolution provides ample evidence that at heart the Blok's motives are rooted more deeply in radical right-wing attitudes than in Flemish nationalism.

After the Second World War, during which many Flemish Nationalists had been tarnished by political and military collaboration with Nazi Germany, the founders of the newly-resurrected Flemish nationalist political organisations opted firmly for democracy. The ill-fated totalitarian principles and ultra-right assumptions were thrown overboard. In 1954 the Volksunie, the Flemish People's Union, was set up as the party of Flemish nationalism with a federal state as its principle objective. Its founder, Frans van der Elst, was later to emphasise that: '*We did not want any kind of neo-fascist, right-wing, anti-democratic party. We opted wholeheartedly for a democratic party, and accepted parliamentary democracy. We knew that the Flemish people are democratic at heart, with no inclination for revolution.*' But as the party grew and began to attract younger members, internal divisions started to appear. In the 1960s society was becoming increasingly vocal, traditional religious and socio-political structures were breaking down, and new concerns about such things as the environment and pacifism were moving to centre stage. Some of the older members began to feel alienated from the younger centre-left leadership which they felt had abandoned the party's conservative traditions, and in 1971 the party finally split. One of those who believed that the party had moved much too far to the left was Karel Dillen. The final straw came when the Volksunie joined the national government and was inevitably forced to accept compromises. In 1978 Dillen founded the Vlaams Blok.

With his new party Dillen's main target was the Volksunie, whom he accused of following a course that was too left-wing and too pragmatist. He and the Vlaams Blok stood for an uncompromising policy of right-wing Flemish nationalism. In his electoral challenge to the Volksunie, which was cooperating in the federalisation of Belgium, Flemish independence was placed at the top of the agenda. Federalism did not go far enough. Political interest at that time was mainly concerned with the Flemish-Walloon conflict and the gradual transformation of Belgium into a federal state. But Dillen's policies did not attract much support. Between 1978 and 1987 he sat lonely and alone in the Chamber, the Blok's sole representative. Within the party itself, there was growing discontent at this stagnation. In particular, the Vlaams Blok Jongeren, the youth party led by Filip Dewinter which maintained close contacts with foreign right-wing extremists such as Le Pen's Front National, argued that '*it has become quite clear that few people are going to leave the Volksunie to join the Vlaams Blok ... The younger generation is starting to rebel against the left-wing establishment.*' Under the influence of Dewinter and profiting from Le Pen's first electoral breakthrough in March 1983, it was decided to hold a proper congress in 1984 to discuss the theme of foreigners and immigrants. The Vlaams Blok had radically changed its tactics and was now targeting voters who were totally uninterested in the demands of Flemish radicalism. From that moment on, the party's prime topic was the presence of North African immigrants who, in leaflets and posters, were held responsible for the high level of unemployment. From 1987 on, it was the younger members who called the tune. Dillen was shipped off to the European Parliament and Gerolf Annemans and, in particular, Filip Dewinter took over the reins. Almost immediately a number of Flemish nationalist demonstrations which did not accord with the Blok's right-wing nationalism were disrupted by violence. At the Flanders Day celebrations on 11 July one of the presenters, a Surinamese lady, was booed, while at the Pilgrimage to the IJzer Tower, the chief symbol of Flemish emancipation, the Chairman was prevented from speaking. In Antwerp there were demonstrations against the opening of a mosque. The tone was now set: the Blok had opted publicly for a radical right-wing approach and even Flemish symbols were no longer sacrosanct. In the European Parliament the Vlaams Blok formed a working alliance with Le Pen's Front National. Le Pen then joined Dewinter on a 'city walk' in Antwerp. Subsequently, the Blok published its official position on foreigners which faithfully echoed Le Pen's 70-point plan. From being a Flemish Nationalist party the Vlaams Blok has turned itself into an ultra-right party whose programme largely consists of radical right-wing attitudes to crime, immigration, security and drugs, together with conservative views on abortion, gay marriages etc.

The Blok's electoral success was a direct result of this change of direction: it succeeded in attracting new voters with no interest in Flemish nationalism. In particular, it was able to penetrate the impoverished districts of large and medium-sized cities – often traditionally socialist strongholds – and to spread out from there into the rural areas of Flanders. In this the Blok reflected a European trend: its message appeals particularly to voters who are not well educated and whose chances in life are few – precisely the voters who previously would have supported the left. In Flanders, the traditional Flemish nationalist comes from the better educated and financially more secure middle classes, which is one of the reasons why Flemish nationalism never became a mass movement. The Blok has managed to reach those voters who were immune to the complicated democratic-nationalist programme of federalism and restructuring.

As the Blok enjoyed increasing electoral success, so the democratic parties grew more and more hostile to it. On 10 May 1989 all the Flemish parties agreed to create a protective barrier, a *cordon sanitaire*, around their ultra-right rival. They all signed a protocol in which they formally engaged themselves '*not to make any arrangements or enter into any agreement whatsoever with the Vlaams Blok, either in the framework of democratically elected bodies at the district, provincial, regional, national or European level, or in the context of elections at the said levels*'. The Vlaams Blok was thereby isolated. From then on, any vote for the Blok would at most be a protest vote; it would have no influence on the actual conduct of policy.

The Blok's political isolation also extends to the social sphere. In spite of the Blok's efforts, Flanders continues to develop slowly but surely into a multicultural society in which second and third generation immigrants play an important part. Cultural life in Flanders has never been affected by the Blok's self-centredness and its rejection of foreign cultures. Antwerp, the Blok's 'home town' where it achieves its best results, continues to pursue an internationally oriented cultural policy.

Flanders has also introduced a whole battery of measures to deal with the dissatisfaction and social problems which provided such fertile soil for the ideas of the extreme right. In this process a distinction has rightly been made between those who vote for the Blok and the party's representatives. Voters who support the Blok because they feel themselves to be sidelined and socially excluded should not be stigmatised. Their problems must be taken seriously and every effort must be made to resolve them, even if this can only be done in the medium or long term. Furthermore, over 80% of Flemish voters have deliberately *not* voted for the Vlaams Blok, and recent polls indicate that even those who support it do not actually believe that the party's programme is practicable. They vote for the Blok out of frustration, resentment and anger, and to send a signal to the other parties that serious social problems still have to be addressed in prosperous Flanders. The other parties' sensitivity to these problems has significantly increased in recent years, and not least because the situation is commonplace throughout Europe. Flanders is not an island and the Blok is by no means a typically Flemish phenomenon. One indirect effect of its successes has been to give an extra stimulus to democracy in Flanders. Parties and groupings have come to realise that they should not be working against each other but should rather be endeavouring to collaborate more closely. Recent studies show that increasing numbers of people are becoming involved in societies and organisations. Between 1991 and 1998 the figure rose from 38% to 50%. And it is not only the traditional social and cultural organisations that are growing. The so-called 'new' social movements with an interest in issues like the environment, peace and third-world development are also attracting more members. The hundreds of thousands of volunteers in the clubs and societies of Flanders are the best safeguard against the extreme right, and probably the most efficient means of combating it.

Probably the most important lesson that leading figures in Flanders have learned from the successes of the Vlaams Blok is that material progress does not in itself create a healthy society. The massive individualisation and atomisation of society brought about by economic liberalisation is not without its dangers.

The Blok has put its finger on many of society's wounds. But after several years of despondency and failure to analyse and tackle the problems, the healing process has begun. It will be a long-term operation. So Flanders will have to sweat it out with the Vlaams Blok for a while yet.

JOS BOUVEROUX
Translated by Chris Emery.

An *Annus Horribilis* for Dutch Politics

The autumn and winter of 2001 were mild in the Netherlands, and so was the political climate. The economy was booming, and that autumn Prime Minister Wim Kok of the social-democratic Labour Party (Partij van de Arbeid or PvdA), whose second four-year term of office was moving to a successful end, was voted the most popular Dutch prime minister since World War II.

True, the attack on the Twin Towers in New York had sparked a vigorous debate in the country about the place and the degree of integration of Dutch citizens of foreign origin and Islam's role in this, but that debate never exceeded the bounds of decorum. When members of parliament left The Hague in December 2001 for their Christmas recess, friend and foe alike still assumed that the coming year – with two elections scheduled – would bring little change in the stability that characterised the Dutch model of political consensus.

Until, early in 2002, a brand-new phenomenon appeared in the political arena.

'Professor' Pim Fortuyn joined the discussion about the role of Islam in Dutch society in flamboyant style, at the same time contrasting himself with what he called the stubborn inflexibility of the political establishment in The Hague. Fortuyn gained more and more support, and it soon became apparent that there was a very definite and widening gulf between sizeable sections of the Dutch population and the politicians in The Hague, where the established parties had absolutely no idea how to deal with xenophobia in various forms and noisy public dissatisfaction with the existing policies on integration and asylum.

Fortuyn – a sociologist by profession – was at the time a publicist and columnist on *Elsevier*, the largest weekly paper in the Netherlands. The former extraordinary professor had already experimented with a variety of political parties. As a student he had been a committed Marxist, but over the years he had tried the Social Democrats, then the Christian Democrats, before finally ending up as a liberal-conservative. But his explosive and intransigent personality meant that in none of those parties had he managed to attain the prominent position he so ardently desired. For years Fortuyn had been preaching against the political establishment in his columns, and in those same columns he never shrank from saying that his aim was to become prime minister of the Netherlands and then, as an enlightened leader, to restore the nation to the orderly society of standards and values that it had still been in the 1950s, in Fortuyn's early youth.

Pim Fortuyn began to make his presence felt more and more forcefully. And the Dutch media, the electronic media in particular, gave him every opportunity to do so. His popularity increased with every television appearance. This flamboyant figure possessed enormous charisma – that quickly became apparent – and he played on the themes of the failing asylum policy, immigrant crime and fundamentalist Islam with verve and without mincing his words. The result was that he rapidly gained a reputation for saying out loud what the man in the street was forbidden to say by the politically-correct establishment. Partly because of this, his popularity grew at lightning speed. And that is even more remarkable given that he openly paraded his homosexuality and publicly stated that he visited darkrooms in sex clubs with some regularity.

Initially the established parties reacted to 'Professor Pim''s carryings-on with slightly disparaging amusement; but as the months passed they failed to come up with any effective answer to Fortuyn, who had in the meantime decided to take an active part in politics by standing in the upcoming council and parliamentary elections.

Because he played entirely by his own rules when debating with political opponents, time and again he succeeded – in the public's eyes, at least – in winning those debates. And ignoring him did not help either, because he became more and more popular.

On 6 March 2002 Fortuyn and his political faction Leefbaar Rotterdam (Livable Rotterdam) achieved a staggering result. Coming from nowhere, he won 17 of the 45 seats on Rotterdam City Council. At a stroke his group thus became the largest in the traditionally hard-left port city. Fortuyn himself was elected to the council; but he made clear that his ambitions did not stop there. Opinion polls suggested that he personally

People mourning and placing floral tributes in front of the house of Pim Fortuyn in the Dutch city of Rotterdam yesterday   *Michael Sohn/AP*

Anger, remorse and confusion in a country famed for its tolerance

– by now he had quarrelled with Leefbaar Rotterdam and been thrown out – might be good for perhaps as many as 40 parliamentary seats, which would make his the largest political grouping in the country.

There then ensued an unprecedently acrimonious election campaign, with accusations and threats vigorously bandied back and forth. But everything seemed to indicate that the advance of the Pim Fortuyn List (LPF) was unstoppable.

Then, in the early evening of 6 May, Pim Fortuyn was shot dead as he left a studio in Hilversum after a radio broadcast. The suspected killer turned out to be fanatical environmental activist named Volkert van der Graaf; he has since made a full confession and is undergoing psychiatric investigation prior to his trial. According to reports, he wanted to save the fatherland from the menace of Pim Fortuyn.

The Netherlands was swept by a wave of grief and rage without precedent in that country and the mood became more and more vicious. Politicians and journalists were threatened and had to be provided with round-the-clock bodyguards. But the elections of 15 May 2002 went ahead, with astonishing results. The parties of the so-called Purple Coalition, the PvdA (social democrats; party colour red), VVD (liberals; blue) and D'66 (democrats; green) were virtually wiped out, while the Christian Democrats of the opposition CDA

Newspaper clipping from *The Independent* of 8 May 2002, two days after the Fortuyn murder.

won 14 seats and the LPF, the List of the murdered Pim Fortuyn, came from nowhere to take 26 parliamentary seats out of 150.

As a constitutional monarch Queen Beatrix had no option but to invite the leader of the Christian Democrats, the relatively inexperienced Jan Peter Balkenende, to form a majority cabinet consisting of the CDA, the LPF and a third party. After the mandatory dickering the Liberals agreed to join such a cabinet; but they demanded and got a splendid reward for doing so – the almost total inclusion of everything they wanted in a newly-created so-called strategic accord.

The new cabinet was greeted with considerable scepticism, largely because of those of its members who belonged to the Pim Fortuyn List. Ministers and State Secretaries were recruited from here, there and everywhere and seemed to belong to every possible political party, while not one of them had any political experience. The same went for the LPF group in parliament. From the moment they were installed the group was plagued by uncontrollable quarrels, which sometimes even ended in blows. One Deputy after another was sacked from his job or from the party, and the squabbling even spread to the party's cabinet members. There two LPF ministers – the unworldly professor Bomhof and the multimillionaire recording industry boss Heinsbroek – were dismissed for literally fighting each other, while their party colleague Nawijn (minister for integration at the Department of Justice) caused a nationwide furore by calling in no uncertain terms for the reintroduction of the death penalty. And while all this was going on the LPF's party organisation was riven by schisms between rival members who dragged each other before the courts at the drop of a hat.

Finally, in October 2002, the young and inexperienced Minister-President Jan Peter Balkenende came to the end of his tether. After exactly 87 days in office he tendered his cabinet's resignation to Queen Beatrix. New elections were called for 22 January 2003, the earliest date they could legally be held.

During the first three weeks of 2003 the Dutch media were totally obsessed with politics. Hardly a radio or television programme was broadcast without politicians appearing in it somewhere. It seemed that for the Dutch media politics was sexy. The innumerable opinion polls indicated a neck-and-neck race between Jan Peter Balkenende's CDA and the resurgent PvdA under its new leader Wouter Bos, who was portrayed as the Dutch Kennedy. There were two main issues in the campaign: who would win the most seats, and whether the CDA and VVD together be able to gain the majority they both desired and so quickly form a government.

The result of the elections of 22 January is complicated. The CDA remains the largest party with 44 parliamentary seats, followed by the PvdA with 42. But the CDA and VVD combined failed to gain a majority; the latter increased its seats by four – from 24 to 28 – but this fell short of the number needed. The Pim Fortuyn List still holds 8 of the stunning 26 seats it won the year before.

After a few days' consideration Balkenende came to the conclusion that only one option was open to him: a coalition with the PvdA. But forming such a government may prove a lengthy business. It will be some time yet before the traditional tranquillity of the Dutch political arena is restored. Not to mention the old cosy relationships.

RUTGER VAN SANTEN (1 March 2003)
Translated by Tanis Guest.

Fashion for the People MoMu: Antwerp's New Fashion Museum

Fashion is the pop music of the visual arts. The typical intellectual, for whom meaning, *gravitas* and substance are of paramount importance, tends to regard fashion as superficial, frivolous and pointless – a preconceived notion which ignores Oscar Wilde's obser-

vation that *'a well-tied tie is the first serious step in life'*.

As the media were informed at a briefing by the Antwerp Fashion Museum (MoMu), which opened its doors to the public on 21 September 2002, getting rid of such preconceptions is one of the museum's aims. MoMu was not to be an ivory tower for designers and their aficionados but an accessible museum and documentation centre. Linda Loppa, MoMu's curator, wants to attract visitors to the museum – and in large numbers, according to the press information. The programme of activities is geared to a wide range of target groups and includes exhibitions, tours, studio sessions, workshops, animation for children, evening events, previews, lectures, debates, study days and round-table meetings. An open-plan restoration workshop allows visitors a backstage glimpse of the work carried out at the museum. Designers should be able to discuss their work with writers, artists, and directors etc. The extensive collection will be registered in the Museum System, so that it will be available in digital form in word and image. Companies can organise evening visits for groups of at least 50, and there are 'hands-on' birthday tours for children – complete with cake and soft drinks.

The temple of fashion as a multifunctional People's Palace: this appears to be the message underlying the museum's ambitious plans. ModeNatie, the beautifully renovated premises in Nationalestraat, houses not only the fashion museum but also the Flanders Fashion Institute and the renowned fashion department of Antwerp's Academy of Fine Arts. There is also a conference room, a bookshop and a brasserie.

Architect M. José Van Hee (see p. 267) was commissioned to adapt the original 1910 building to its new purpose. She restored the basic structure to its former glory, adding a public corridor through the building and a glass dome. Transparency and accessibility, then, are key elements in the design. Van Hee believes that bringing together a number of separate yet interrelated functions within the same building guarantees *'a permanent dynamic'*. This aligns perfectly with the museum's own policy, which is to create a dynamic exhibition environment.

The provincial council's plans to put the city of Antwerp on the fashion map go back more than thirty years. In 1967, following a lace exhibition, the Sterckshof in Deurne set up its own costume and textile department. In 1977 the expanding collection was transferred to the Vrieselhof in Oelegem, but public interest proved disappointing. The provincial council briefly considered halting the initiative, but it was too late: fashion had become a serious matter in Antwerp. Six young designers, collectively dubbed the 'Antwerp Six', took the fashion world by storm in the early 1990s. Not entirely unexpectedly; during the first half of the previous decade their work had gone largely unnoticed, but in 1986 the Six (Ann Demeulemeester, Marina Yee, Dries van Noten, Dirk Bikkembergs, Dirk van Saene and Walter van Beirendonck) captivated the British fashion press at the British Designer Show in London. With few resources but a great deal of nerve,

The 'Red' section of *Selectie 1: Backstage / Achter de schermen*, the opening exhibition of the MoMu. Photo by Koen de Waal.

they fired the enthusiasm of press and international buyers alike. And they certainly knew how to get themselves noticed. Walter van Beirendonck, dressed as a gnome and seated on a toadstool, took down orders in a large story-book ledger. In 1988 the Six conquered Paris and since then that *succes fou* has continued. And it does not stop at the Six. Since their initial success, two new generations of designers are attracting interest and making a name for themselves internationally. In March 2003, no fewer than twenty Belgian designers travelled to Paris to present their collections for women. In the midst of all this frenetic activity, the powers that be had no choice but to join the crusade: Antwerp had to have its own fashion museum.

The result is certainly impressive. MoMu has three exhibition spaces: the White Box for permanent exhibits, the Gallery for smaller monographic exhibitions reflecting the latest trends, and the main space, which will house two major themed exhibitions a year. The exhibition *Patterns* (Patronen) opened on 14 March 2003. In September 2003, in association with Europalia Italy, there will be an exhibition on Genoa as a city of fashion. The first themed exhibition was *Selectie 1: Backstage / Achter de schermen*, a first selection from MoMu's wide collection. Most of the items in the collection were inherited from the Textile and Costume Museum in Oelegem, consisting of West-European clothing, lace, textiles and costumes from the sixteenth century to the present day. The Oelegem collection had

focused on the nineteenth century, but MoMu's vision and Linda Loppa's passion for acquisitions are adding a new contemporary chapter to the collection. The museum's well-stocked library (some 15,000 volumes and a vast archive on medieval needlework, together with countless portfolios of documents, patterns, picture postcards, etc.) consists of two complementary collections. The library at the Vrieselhof focuses on the history of costume, fashion and textiles, while the second collection is the recently acquired Stodel library. Over a period of thirty years, Dutchman Wiebe Stodel built up a collection of books on traditional costumes from all over the world; by 1993 he had more than 6,000 books on traditional dress, jewellery, body-decoration and hairstyles.

Selectie 1 was regarded as a showcase for the MoMu collection and an expression of the museum's exhibition policy. Items from the various sub-collections were exhibited in a striking yet restrained setting designed by Bob Verhelst. His inspiration for the design was the museum's 'warehouse' function. In the museum storerooms each item is wrapped in acid-free paper to protect it from light, moisture and dust. In the past the items were then placed in cardboard boxes, but since June 2002 a more modern storage system has been used. Verhelst incorporated the redundant cardboard boxes in his design. Storage acts as a 'leveller': items are placed together and no one item is more important than the rest. Verhelst chose to present them to the public in the same way, still in their 'democratic' cardboard boxes. The approach was not a didactic one and the exhibits in *Selectie 1* were not presented chronologically: a black general's tricorne from 1880 was placed next to a *Kiss the Future* scarf by Walter van Beirendonck, and a white cotton corset from 1900 could be seen next to a once futuristic nylon steel-ribbed corset from the 1950s. In this way visitors were encouraged to discover how the new incorporates the old and *vice versa*. In a deliberate break with convention, items of men's and women's clothing were exhibited together. *Selectie 1* was a 'subdued' exhibition: visitors could find their own way through the softly-lit displays, between the islands of boxes and palettes, and be delighted by a child's Zouave uniform jacket (1850-1880), the stiletto-heels-without-shoes by Jurgi Persoons that were designed to be worn during shows and photo shoots, and a yellowing book on handicrafts in northern France.

The texts accompanying the exhibits in *Selectie 1* were deliberately kept as concise as possible. This was a wise decision, given that the obvious Achilles' heel of the fashion world is the verbosity that surrounds it. Here we come up against a different breed of intellectual. This one too is looking for *gravitas* and meaning, but is very reluctant to admit it and is driven by post-post-modern intellectual annexationism to plant his flag on new territory. Fashion has consequently become the pop music of the visual arts in another sense: everything has suddenly become sociologically relevant and/or of psychological interest. Reference must be made to other forms of art, sources must be quoted, connections must be discovered, in an irritating quest for intellectual credibility that produces painfully superfluous texts. This was obvious during the Landed / Geland festivities in 2001. During that year, Antwerp's 'Year of Fashion', there were a number of interesting exhibitions and a couple of new fashion publications appeared. The catalogues and the new (untitled) magazine contain excruciatingly woolly articles that appear to have been written with the blood, sweat and tears of the authors, and have doubtless produced a similar effect in many readers. Sadly, the same verbal pomposity is to some extent evident in the book accompanying the *Selectie 1* exhibition, *Het ModeMuseum / The Fashion Museum: Backstage*, which was published in Dutch and English. The book is not an exhibition catalogue but an introduction to the MoMu and the vision of those who run it. Although most of the texts are very readable – and at the same time *worth* reading – the decision was taken to include a '*general philosophical context for the fashion phenomenon*' (intellectual credibility again!), intended to anchor fashion in our perception of culture. Unfortunately, the author's style is so obscure and high-flown as to be virtually unreadable. If it wants to introduce alternative exhibition techniques, avoid clichés and stimulate a dialogue on fashion with a wide range of target groups, MoMu will have to keep the white noise of this laboured discourse to a minimum. It managed to do this with the opening exhibition, but it will need to do so also in other areas of communication where the volume still needs to be turned down.

FILIP MATTHIJS
Translated by Yvette Mead

Kaat Deboo *et al.*, *Selectie 1. Het ModeMuseum / The Fashion Museum: Backstage*. Ludion: Ghent, 2002; 192 pp.
ISBN 90-5544-423-5.

MoMu: Nationalestraat 28 / 2000 Antwerp. Tel. +32 (0)3 470 27 70 / info@momu.be
www.momu.be en www.modenatie.com

Honoré δ'O: Playing Marbles with Art

It could only happen to an art critic. Summer 1995, in the monastery of San Francesco della Vigna. The exhibition *Onder Anderen / Among Others* is the Flemish-Dutch contribution to that year's Venice Biennale. The curators were the Fleming Bart de Baere and the Dutchman Lex ter Braak. One of the artists they selected was the then virtually unknown Fleming Honoré δ'O. Not only did his artistic offerings slightly shock most visitors, but from that day on a renowned Flemish art critic would never be the same again. Wim van Mulders had written an article for the catalogue, in which he interpreted δ'O's work. Van Mulders was known as an extremely capable and erudite, but decidedly hermetic critic. Anyone reading one of his pieces had to sit down and really concentrate on it. Honoré δ'O had apparently done this too, because the article appeared in the catalogue in an utterly unprecedented form: the artist had drawn a circle or an oval around every word Van Mulders had written. This made the article literally unreadable, because the human eye could not cope with reading the circled and thereby isolated words as sentences. With this Honoré δ'O pulled off the sort of rather mischievous *tour de force* that characterises all his work: stripping something of its meaning and giving it a new one. On the understanding that this 'something' is not thereby automatically improved: it may be interpreted differently, but not necessarily on the same level.

This was also the case in the monastery garden in Venice: Honoré δ'O had built a complicated construction out of plastic piping, had scattered countless apparently trivial objects throughout *and* set the statue of St Francis on a pedestal that slowly revolved. What did all this mean? No one really knew, probably including De Baere and Ter Braak. After all, in the catalogue they themselves wrote: '*we draw the positions, lines and circles that are ideal for our ideas on serviettes. Not a balanced distribution but concentration and scattering: contraction and extraction, a rhythm that is not related to the visitor's haste. We want to compel attention and contemplation – not directly through the monastery and St Francis but indirectly, summoned up by the nature and grouping of the work. Honoré immediately deprives us of the possibility of comfortably*

slumping back into our previous thoughts. He always goes a few steps further than the course that would put you at your ease ... He repeatedly refuses to develop his certainties any further. ... the complexity that there was will be replaced by another, and of this we can for the moment only experience the wildness.'

At the time Honoré δ'O had only just emerged as an artist. He was born in Oudenaarde in 1969 with the prosaic name of Raf van Ommeslaeghe, and in 1984 he rechristened himself Honoré δ'O. He started as a painter, but soon found this too limiting: for him, it was not the work of art that counted but the artist and the public itself, which is not such an obvious position to take in this fundamentally conceptual era. How should the artist behave and/or manifest himself in the public space; can one be anything other than a public artist? And how ought the public to behave and/or manifest itself? Or should, rather, both the artist and the public remain strictly in the private space? In short: is art pointless?

These are all difficult questions; and so after taking part in such 1994-1995 exhibitions as *Images Outside* (Beelden Buiten) in Tielt, *This Is the Show and the Show is Many Things* in Ghent and the above-mentioned *Onder Anderen / Among Others*, Honoré δ'O retreated from the world to reflect properly on things. He did this in the *Oh!*, a space above the *Dolle Mol* café in Spoormakersstraat in Brussels. For almost a year in 1996 he withdrew to the room above this now defunct

anarchist establishment. There he drew up an inventory of himself: hundreds of photos and slides, of his work or his presence, were processed into a computer archive. Anyone who wanted could visit him, but not as easily as all that: if the visitor succeeded in blowing a marble through a system of pipes (from the café to the first floor), the artist might perhaps open the door to have a good talk.

The marble is a characteristic 'object' for Honoré δ'O. In the beginning it was one you could play marbles with or blow through a tube. It was also an eye through which you could look inside, and it was a *'symbol of a thought that ran recklessly around, was extremely mobile and above all transparent'* (Hilde Kuijken in an article in the catalogue for the exhibition *Fascinating Facets of Flanders* – Fascinerende Facetten van Vlaanderen). More definitions were to follow: at *Over the Edges* in Ghent in 2000, for example, one such marble became a motionless glass ball, suspended here and there around the city as if floating in the air. These small pearls turned perception upside down, and suddenly everything was projected in miniature, and this in the city of the Mystic Lamb. And at the *Octopus* contemporary art event during Brugge 2002, Honoré δ'O 'decorated' the houses on a square with big glass

Honoré δ'O and Franciska Lambrechts, *Sinking Test.* Middelheim, Antwerp, 2002.

marbles, whose flickering broke up the dullness of the workmen's homes, while at the same time here too the gaze was turned inward.

From the small, individual marbles, which he also stuck together to create proper little sculptures, to the complex constructions of ropes and pipes: Honoré δ'O turned what was fragmentary into a new whole, which then briefly looked like a work of art. Just as he had once made an image of his mother using bottles of cleaning fluid, brushes, buckets and floor-cloths. But by making more changes this sculpture can again become something else. This is what Honoré δ'O has always done: even in the most complicated constructions that appear to definitively mark off a space (museum room, gallery, outdoors), he also built in their disappearance, because after all an artist does not create one-off works, and the viewer does not look at a work just once. To do so is an utterly pointless occupation. Rather, δ'O creates a setting in which anything can happen, including the unexpected, and so the viewer is obliged to seek things out.

In fact this seems to be the heart of Honoré δ'O's work: you seek it out. This is very clear in the installation at the exhibition called *Fascinating Facets of Flanders* held in 1988, first at the Centro Cultural de Bélem in Lisbon and later in the Museum of Fine Art in Antwerp: the viewer himself had to capture a whole stock of images from a slide projector on a sheet of white paper and focus them himself. And at the 1998 Sao Paolo Biennale he installed two carousels full of objects: one was purely sculptural, while visitors could add items to or remove them from the other.

Creating, destroying, growing, recreating, it seems like a game. And this is quite right: Honoré δ'O likes to play with the viewer, tries to involve him in his work and thinking. To this end he uses poetic language: not one of his constructions or works, not one change or movement looks hard, sombre or ugly, everything seems light and sublime. Honoré δ'O shows that this is deliberate in the installation that was to be seen in Rheims in early 2001 and in an adapted version at MUHKA in Antwerp last year. It was as a result of a heart operation that the artist built a large and complex construction at the FRAC in Rheims, with numerous references to the medical world, with a hovering operating table (suspended from the ceiling) as the *pièce de résistance*. Very heavy stuff at first sight, but the whole work was composed in such a way that it radiated an almost unbearable lightness, '*as if the elements were elevated from life to another, higher level. And this is an almost literal translation of what Honoré δ'O considers the significance or value of art to be: the elevation of the soul.*' (Els Roelandt in her review of this exhibition in the *Financieel-Economische Tijd*).

The way he deals with art means that the work of Honoré δ'O often comes across as completely hermetic and literally incomprehensible. It has seemed like that to me several times. In his Himalaya project, for example, a 'report' on his stay in those mountains, which takes the most diverse forms and turns up regularly, and the work he created with Francisca Lambrechts at the Middelheim Open-Air Museum in Antwerp in Autumn 2002: I did not understand much of it, and judging by the reviews I read nor did the other critics and reporters (So Wim van Mulders may have been the first, but he was certainly not the only one). This is something which present-day art lovers have for some time had to learn to live with: they must be prepared to submit entirely to the proposal, to the artist's game. Sometimes it works, sometimes it doesn't. It is a trend that has been around for several decades, but which has become stronger again in the last few years, and not only in the case of Honoré δ'O. Artists create works that sound out the environment in which they are placed, examine the history of the place, seek interaction with the viewer and raise fundamental questions of meaning. In this case, the phenomenon of 'time', in the sense of 'here and now', is entirely pushed aside: the moment of experience will always be different, because the artist, the work and the public are constantly exchanging new information and/or points of view.

The paradox is that the artist lowers the threshold for the public drastically, but that public still has to find its way to his work. This is because the attitude of 'looking at fine art' has held good for centuries. Honoré δ'O is one of those who wants to put an end to this, for, as he himself once put it: '*art should not be worshipped, it can be used.*'

MARC RUYTERS
Translated by Gregory Ball.

Short Takes

Always the same H_2O indeed: *The Sublime Song of Maybe* is a collection of translated poems by Arjen Duinker (1956-) with such titles as 'Let me have the rain with the right amount of droplets' and 'The river that runs past my house is cheerful' and lines like 'The wind has a blue tail / Water has a blue tail'. In 'Where are my tears, where are they' we even have water in its saltiest form.

On the back flap of this anthology it says: '*His poetry is very much about the reality of things as separate, self-contained entities, about flowers, stones, mountains, wind, and water.*' Duinker is indeed not a great fan of abstractions. His work is light-hearted, witty, and profound in a pleasantly unostentatious way. The poet wants to look without preconceived perspectives and write without being constrained by theories. The result is wonder and modesty, as in these lines from *Loose Poems* (Losse gedichten, 1990):

On the one hand is the thing.
On the other is the mystery.
More of the thing and the mystery I don't know.

How in whatever name,
How can I know more about it?
And this knowing is a slight knowing, I must add,
A slight idea at most.

Arjen Duinker, *The Sublime Song of Maybe* (Tr. Willem Groenewegen). Todmorden (Lancs): Arc Publications, 2002; 143 pp. ISBN 1-900072-77-7.

The Sublime Song of Maybe appeared in the series *Visible Poets*. Series Editor Jean Boase-Beier writes: '*There is a prevailing view of translated poetry, especially in England, which maintains that it should be read as though it had been originally written in English*'. However, this attitude can also mean that some poetry simply never gets translated. This is certainly not the fault of Rotterdam's Poetry International Foundation, where for many years poetry from all over the world has been lovingly translated and promoted. At the core of the Foundation is its annual festival, which was first held in 1970 and has since grown into one of the leading platforms for poetry in the world, and one of the largest. Every year in June some forty poets from all corners of the earth come to Rotterdam, where during the week-long festival they give readings from their work in many languages in the Muncipal Theatre. Famous names and new talents alike take the stage. On the occasion of the festival the poets are translated into Dutch, some of them for the first time. English translations too are provided, to cater for the international audience.

On 6 November 2002, with financial support from the European Commission, the Foundation launched Poetry International Web, a unique collaboration with editors and literary organisations abroad. This splendid site has not only poetry by famous contemporary poets in the original and in English translation, but also news about poetry, reviews, essays, interviews and columns. On the site each country has its own domain with '*national poetry facts and news*', while the central section is internationally oriented. The intention is to add at least four countries a year to the site.

www.poetryinternational.org

Since 1987 the Academy Award for Best Foreign Language Film has gone to a Dutch film on no fewer than three occasions, the winners being successively *The Assault* (De aanslag, 1986), *Antonia* (1995) and *Character* (Karakter, 1997). And this year there was a nomination for Paula van der Oest's *Zus & zo*, a lively comedy of manners about three sisters who want to prevent their brother's marriage. A fine second chance for a film whose world première in Toronto coincided with the attack on the Twin Towers, while in the

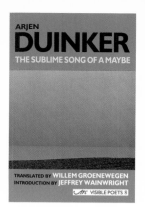

ARJEN DUINKER
THE SUBLIME SONG OF A MAYBE

TRANSLATED BY WILLEM GROENEWEGEN
INTRODUCTION BY JEFFREY WAINWRIGHT
Arc VISIBLE POETS 8

Netherlands itself it was released on the day after Pim Fortuyn's murder. A real double whammy for a film which according to those involved is '*screamingly funny*' and '*universally recognisable*'. After all, what family doesn't sometimes find itself quarrelling violently? But in *Zus & zo* a real family war breaks out when Nino announces that he intends to marry the art critic Bo. His three elder sisters can't understand it, for surely their brother was homosexual? When it turns out that his conversion to heterosexuality is a deliberate ploy to get his hands on a legacy the sisters decide that it is time to act.

Sections of the Dutch press branded the film corny. American film magazines like *Variety* ('*Paula van der Oest brings a whimsical vigor to her script*') and *Celebrity* ('*hilarious*'), on the other hand, were highly enthusiastic. Van der Oest herself, who already has a new film, *Moonlight*, showing in Dutch cinemas, says that she wanted to make a comedy for the *Bridget Jones* target group, in which '*the feel-good factor was all-important*'. Whether it will win her an Oscar is still unkown at the time of writing. In any case, though, the somewhat tepid Dutch reactions to *Zus & zo* have not discouraged the American market. In May 2002 it was already known that the film rights had been sold to the American producers Renee Missel and Jonathan Dana, who want to make an American version of the film.

Flanders too has an Oscar nomination. *Gridlock* (Fait D'Hiver) by Dirk Beliën and Anja Daelemans is one of the lucky five in the Best Live Action Short Film category. In this seven-minute film, which has already gained an Honorable Mention for Cinematography at the Woodstock Film Festival in 2002, a young man wreaks irreparable havoc when, stuck in the traffic-jam, he decides to call his wife on his new mobile phone.

Nor is this all; in November 2002 Belgian film was the subject of special attention at the Lincoln Center in New York under the label *Transcendent Realism*. Three recent Flemish full-length films were to be seen there. *Hop*, the first film by Dominique Standaert, tells the story of Burundian illegal aliens in Belgium with a mix of *faits divers* and warm humour. In *A Girl* (Meisje) Dorothée van den Berge sketches the coming-of-age of a young woman who, in an attempt to find herself, leaves her boy-friend and her job in order to settle in Brussels. And Frank van Passel's *Villa des Roses* is a colourful film version of Willem Elsschot's novel of the same name, described by the organisers of the Lincoln Center festival as '*a wonderful period piece, evocative of a Europe poised right on the brink of war*'.

Villa des Roses – the novel itself, which was better than the film, but what else is new? – was published by Penguin in the early nineties in an excellent translation by Paul Vincent, but soon after its appearance was consigned to the pulping machine. Happily, in 2002 Vincent was able to take his revenge with a well-received translation of Elsschot's *Cheese* (Kaas, 1933). And in 2002 the Willem Elsschot Genootschap brought out *Poems from the Past*. They have created a beautiful little volume in a limited edition, containing English translations by Paul Vincent and others of the ten *Verzen van vroeger* and two other poems. A work of love; and it could not be otherwise, with such marvellous lines as '*Can one of you, some learned sir, / most wisely and ingeniously / contend with plausibility / that worms will never feed on her?*' ('At a Child's Deathbed').

In this yearbook you can find an excerpt from Anne Provoost's novel *Voyagers on the Ark* (De arkvaarders, 2001). The English translation of the book will be published by Levine in the course of 2003. Provoost took the subject-matter for her novel from the Bible, more specifically from the story of the Flood. It is the tale of the girl Re Jana, who with her family leaves the rising waters of the marshes and heads into the desert. There the greatest ship of all time is built. Provoost's is a tale of adventure, but it is also a love story and a metaphor for contemporary society. For what is one to think of a god who picks some people as his chosen ones, while all the rest are condemned to a terrible fate?

We have still more translations of Flemish and Dutch novels to announce. For instance, Farrar, Straus and Giroux is planning a translation of Peter Verhelst's *Tonguecat* (Tongkat, 1999), described in *The Low Countries* 2001 as '*a phenomenal and chaotic explosion of half-mythical, half fairy-tale stories about terrorism and viruses*'. Canongate (UK) and Grove Atlantic (USA) have bought the rights to Karel Glastra van Loon's *De passievrucht* (1999). This novel, in which the father of a thirteen-year-old son discovers that he has been sterile all his life, has been published under the title *A Father's Affair*. Ballantine Books have published Maya Rasker's *Unknown Destination* (Met onbekende bestemming, 2000), described by *Kirkus Reviews* as '*a cerebral but riveting narrative about love and parenthood, wondrously denuded of the usual sap and sentimentality*'. Marcel Möring's novelle *Modelvliegen* (2000) is about a family man who gives up his job and with his family earns a living making up model aircraft kits for the owner of a toy shop.

The book was published by Morrow (USA) as *The Dream Room* and was praised by *Publishers Weekly* as a *'deftly woven story, subtly but beautifully written'*. And Renate Dorrestein, whose earlier novel *A Heart of Stone* (Hart van steen) was highly acclaimed by reviewers in the *Wall Street Journal* and *Washington Post*, has had her *Without Mercy* (Zonder genade, 2001) published by Doubleday / Penguin; the press release described it as *'a modern tragedy that lingers in the mind long after the book is closed'*. Indeed, Dorrestein sold the English-language rights to the book even before it appeared in Dutch.

Willem Elsschot, *Cheese* (Tr. Paul Vincent). London: Granta Books, 2002; 153 pp. ISBN 1-86207-481-X / Willem Elsschot, *Poems from the Past*. Amsterdam / Leuven: Willem Elsschot Genootschap, 2002. 30 pp. / Karel Glastra van Loon, *A Father's Affair* (Tr. Sam Garrett). Edinburgh: Canongate, 2002 / Maya Rasker, *Unknown Destination* (Tr. Barbara Fasting). New York: Ballantine, 2002. ISBN 0345446763 / Marcel Möring, The Dream Room (Tr. Stacey Knecht). London: Flamingo, 2002; 128 pp. ISBN 0007129688 / Renate Dorrestein, *Without Mercy* (Tr. Hester Velmans). London: Doubleday, 2002; 293 pp. ISBN 0385603533.

The Flemish visual artist and theatrical producer Jan Fabre has long had a particular fascination with dance. In March 2002, as part of 'Bruges – Cultural Capital of Europe', he created a new production of *Swan Lake* with the Royal Ballet of Flanders. Fabre works on the principle that the classical language of ballet is the starting-point for redefining dance, and with evident success: his *Swan Lake* drew full houses wherever it was performed, both in his own country and in Paris, Amsterdam and Reggio Emilia. In August 2002 Fabre's version of this classic of the ballet repertoire was also danced six times at the Edinburgh Festival, where it won the Herald Angel, given by the daily paper *The Herald* for the most striking production at the festival. The 12,000 people who attended the performances in Edinburgh apparently had few problems with the introduction of Fabre's fantastical universe into *Swan Lake*, but the reviewers' reactions were mixed. Some thought Fabre a brilliant visionary, while others could find not one worthwhile moment in the two and a half hours of the performance. In any event, it won the Flemish Royal Ballet's dancers an ovation lasting several minutes, and Kenneth Spiers went so far as to write in the *Daily Mail* that Fabre had reinvented *Swan Lake*.

Another Flemish 'reinventor' in the field of dance is Anne Teresa de Keersmaeker. Nearly ten years ago now Deborah Jowitt of *The Village Voice* described her in the 1994 edition of *The Low Countries* as an '*adventuress in the thickets of postmodernism*'. In 2002 De Keersmaeker's company, Rosas, was exactly 20 years old. The anniversary was celebrated with a exhibition in Brussels' Palais des Beaux-Arts. Videos, paintings, sculptures and installations illuminated De Keersmaeker's work with Rosas from a variety of angles. In addition there was a whole room filled with

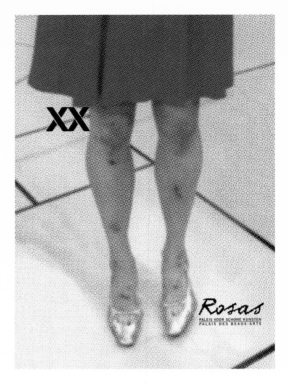

documentation from the choreographer's personal archive: notebooks, diaries, annotated diagrams, sheets of paper with dance notation and books and other sources which provided inspiration for her choreographic activities. The exhibition also contained an impressive chronological overview of all De Keersmaeker's performances, both solo and with Rosas, since 1980: a total of 1760, from Douai to Malmo, from Johannesburg to Mexico City. The exhibition has finished now, but there is also a commemorative book, and while stocks last one can even buy a Rosas XX T-shirt.

Jan Fabre: www.troubleyn.be
Royal Ballet of Flanders: www.koninklijkballetvanvlaanderen.be
Anne Teresa de Keersmaeker: www.rosas.be

Dutch actors trying their luck in Hollywood have not uncommonly found themselves playing bad guys. Jeroen Krabbé, for instance, as the duplicitous Soviet general Georgi Koskov who tries to put a spoke in James Bond's wheel in *The Living Daylights* (1987), or Rutger Hauer as the international terrorist Wulfgar confronting Sylvester Stallone in *Nighthawks* (1981). Hauer was also in the classic *Blade Runner*, but now works mainly in the straight-to-video circuit with parts in films like *Turbulence 3: Heavy Metal* (2001).

Hans Toonen's book *The First Dutch Hollywood Star* (Nederlands eerste Hollywood-ster, 2002) shows that the transition to Tinsel Town has always been a difficult one for Dutch actors. The book tells the life-story of Philip Dorn alias Frits van Dongen alias Hein van der Niet. In the 1930s Van der Niet (1901-1975) played the hero in five Dutch films under the name Frits van Dongen. One of these films was directed by the German director Hermann Kosterlitz, who had left Berlin for the Netherlands because he was Jewish and subsequently made a career for himself in the American film industry as Henry Koster. It was Koster who brought Van der Niet to Hollywood. As Philip Dorn he made his first film there in 1940: *Ski Patrol*, in which he portrayed a Norwegian athlete. In the years that followed he was, among other things, a German doctor, a Yugoslav partisan, a French colonel, a Dutch pilot and a German resistance fighter. As a popular actor he frequently took part in the Freedom War Bond Shows, the tours by film stars designed to maintain morale in American army bases. He played opposite such stars as Joan Crawford, John Wayne and Johnny Weismuller but, sadly, always in films which were never going to become classics. He almost got a part in *Casablanca*; but that chance of enduring fame passed him by when MGM, who held his contract, refused to lend him to Warner Brothers.

Tragically, it was a visit to the Netherlands that put an end to his career. He was walking along the beach at Scheveningen when a gust of wind blew a plank onto his head, leaving him with concussion. He seemed to make a quick recovery, but on his return to Los Angeles it became apparent that his balance and speech had been irrevocably affected.

Jaap Harskamp, Head of Dutch and Flemish Collections at the British Library, is the compiler of 'The Low Countries: a Selective Catalogue of Reference Works': an impressive survey, running to over 180 pages, of bibliographies, encyclopedias and reference books on the most diverse aspects of the Low Countries. All the works listed are in the British Library, and the survey can be found on its website: from 'Animals' via 'Carpets' to 'Zionism'.

In addition, he has recently been responsible for the electronic listing of all the Elzevier books (so called from the Dutch publishing and printing dynasty which produced them) in the University of London Library and the British Library. Although the Elzeviers did not publish in English, they were responsible for the Latin works of a number of English and Scottish authors. By the last quarter of the seventeenth-century Elzevier books were widely available in England and such eminent figures as Sir Walter Raleigh, Robert Burton, Thomas Browne, John Milton and John Dryden had Elzeviers in their collections. As a consequence, excellent Elzevier holdings are to be found in, for example, the Bodleian Library in Oxford and the National Library of Scotland in Edinburgh. The Elsevier in Central London site is a cooperative effort by the British Library (Dutch/Flemish Section), the Koninklijke Bibliotheek (STCN), University College London (Department of Dutch Studies) and the University of

London Library (Rare Books). Now, more than half a century after these Elzeviers were received at this university library, the entire collection has been made available, both through the ULL and STCN catalogues, and also through COPAC, the combined catalogue of major British research libraries.

Harskamp also worked on the new Dutch and Flemish internet resources page, which is produced in co-operation with University College London Dutch Department. This page is aimed at a wide audience; the editors have no specific target group in mind. It should function as a first resource for supplying information on the Low Countries and on the Dutch presence in the UK. This page is a point of departure for those seeking their way through an overwhelming number of websites.

www.bl.uk/collections/westeuropean/dutchflemish.html.

Since September 2002 the Fleming Johan Duijck has held the post of permanent conductor of the Choir of the Academy of Saint-Martin-in-the-Fields in London. The Choir was founded in 1975 by the Hungarian conductor László Heltay, since when it has acquired a world-wide reputation. Duijck, since 1999 chief conductor of the Flemish Radio Choir, intends to give Flemish music a prominent place in the repertoire. An initial series of concerts in England (in October-November 2002) included, along with *Psalms* by Jules van Nuffel, the English première of Vic Nees' *Concerto per la beata Virgine* (for oboe and choir). In London in December Duijck conducted the Choir and Orchestra of the Academy of Saint-Martin-in-the-Fields in his own *Cantate Domino*, a large-scale cantata for soprano, double choir and orchestra.

More music from Flanders, but of a very different kind. In 2003 the Logos Foundation celebrates 35 years of existence. This Ghent Foundation describes itself as '*Flanders' unique professional organisation for the promotion of new musics and audio related arts by means of new music production, concerts, performances, composition, technological research projects and other contemporary music-related activitities*'. Which gives it plenty to get its teeth into, for anyone wanting to make new and experimental music is looking for new sounds and so also needs new instruments. Logos sees instrument-making is a natural and vital part of its activities. As early at the beginning of last century the Italian futurists were saying that the old instruments were inadequate for the musical representation of the 'century of the motor'.

Godfrid-Willem Raes of Logos is a zealous creator of instruments. Among his creations are a 'Dudaphone', an 'Optorgophone', a series of fingerboards and fingerboxes, 'Synthelogs' (portable synthesizers), 'Singing Bicycles', real remotely-controlled cannon, automata of various kinds and even a radar-controlled instrument like the 'Virtual Jews Harp'. And all of them put together with great love and dedication, for as Raes himself says: '*Nothing is as human as the ma-*

chine. Besides, didn't man invent tools so as to be able to transcend the many limitations of his body's mechanics?'

Saint-Martin-in-the-Fields: www.academysmif.co.uk

Logos Foundation: www.ping.be/logos

On 31 January 2003 Werenfried van Straaten, perhaps the Low Countries' best-known cleric after Father Damiaan, died. His biography appeared in English as *They Call me the Bacon Priest* (1991). 'Bacon priest' was a nickname which the Dutch Norbertine priest would bear until his death. In 1947 he wrote an article for the news-sheet of the Flemish abbey of Tongerloo, where he was the Abbot's secretary, and that article changed his life. Van Straaten had been deeply affected by the appalling plight of the refugees and displaced persons in post-war Germany and argued fervently for reconciliation. He also organised relief measures. Flanders reacted by collecting massive quantities of bacon.

But things did not stop with this one-off collection of what would later be called 'Oostpriesterhulp' (Priestly Aid to the East). As early as 1950 Van Straaten was able to buy freight wagons from Dutch Railways for next to nothing, and these he had converted into mobile churches. In this way he could combine the useful (concrete material aid) with the spiritual (preaching the faith). Incidentally, Van Straaten was not infrequently criticised for being 'conservative'. In concrete terms that meant that he made no secret of the fact that he regarded the Church as a bulwark against communism, atheism and the increasing secularisation of society. He also created the 'Bouworde' (Building Order): thousands of young Flemings spent two or three weeks of their vacation in Germany or Eastern Europe helping to build new homes for war victims and refugees. From the 1960s on Oostpriesterhulp became a real international organisation; it now operates under the name 'Kerk in Nood' (Church in Need), has headquarters near Frankfurt and springs into action anywhere in the world where the Faith is being oppressed.

www.kerkinnood.nl

On 25 August 1914 soldiers of the German invasion force murdered 248 civilians in Leuven. In other Belgian towns too there were many civilian victims. In *German Atrocities, 1914. A History of Denial* John Horne and Alan Kramer have written a penetrating survey of events during that brutal summer of war. By no coincidence, the book was presented in the Graduation Hall of the University Building in Leuven, in 1914 the site of the University Library; the Germans burned that to the ground.

The German violence was in part due to the myth of the *franc-tireurs*: Belgian civilians-turned-snipers, lying in wait to give as many German soldiers as possible a dose of lead poisoning. Now it is true that here

and there some stout-hearted Belgian did indeed lie hidden with a gun; but there was certainly no question of the kind of organised *Volkskrieg* described in the German papers. But the Germans' nervousness meant that the slightest provocation attracted disproportionate punishment. And these reprisals were in turn exaggerated so as to inflame hatred of the Germans or draw neutral states such as the US into the war. In that sense the book demonstrates perfectly how the modern media, which were developing rapidly at the beginning of last century, could serve as war propaganda: within a very short time a repulsive image of the enemy could be created and circulated far and wide, an image which would still stick to them years later.

John Horne & Alan Kramer, *German Atrocities, 1914. A History of Denial*. New Haven (CT) / London: Yale University Press, 2001; 623 pp. ISBN 0300089759.

The Netherlands may have just endured a turbulent political year (see p. 299), but the history of the Dutch political system and the culture of consultation still catches the imagination. The Dutch States-General are among the oldest representative institutions in Europe which can claim a more or less continuous history. For almost six hundred years, almost without interruption, the States-General have been the principle arena within which Dutch politics has taken shape.

In *Monarchies, States Generals and Parliaments* the historian H.G. Koenigsberger has written a history of the childhood years of this political instrument. The States-General definitively established itself as a representative body in 1464, but until 1576 its history is rather elusive: its meetings were held *ad hoc*, it had no permanent members, kept no minutes or resolutions, it did not even establish an archive. In his thorough study Koenigsberger gives a lively account of the constantly shifting balance of power between ruler and subjects in the fifteenth and sixteenth centuries, with particular attention to the role of the States-General, set against a broad background of cooperation and conflict in Europe.

Benjamin Schmidt's *Innocence Abroad. The Dutch Imagination and the New World, 1570-1670* is another fascinating historical study, but of a very different kind. It is an example of 'representation history', focusing not so much on what happened in the past as on the images and ideas which people in a particular period had of events or individuals.

Here Schmidt is concerned with Dutch perceptions of America in the period 1570-1670. We see that from about 1560, in the early years of the Revolt against Spanish rule, the image of America in the Netherlands evolves in line with the political circumstances. Hispanophilia becomes Hispanophobia, drawing a parallel between the oppressed Dutch and the native Americans, also oppressed and robbed of their land. When the Dutch first set foot there, shortly before 1600, America is to them a continent of wonders. But when they also settle there, disillusion sets in; the Indians

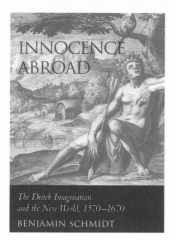

Vanessa Bezemer-Sellers, *Courtly Gardens in Holland, 1600-1650. The House of Orange and the Hortus Batavus*. Amsterdam / Woodbridge: Architectura & Natura Press / Garden Art Press, 2001; 424 pp. ISBN 90-7157-078-9.

In December 2002 the new Fotomuseum in the former Schamhart-Heijligers Building in the Hague opened with the exhibition *Fotografen in Nederland – Een anthologie*. This exhibition of 225 Dutch photographers from 1850 to the present has also been preserved in a splendid book of the same title. So now the Netherlands has three museums of photography; as well as this new one there are also the Nederlands Fotomuseum in Rotterdam and the FOAM in Amsterdam.

As it happens, the Schamhart-Heijliger Building nearly became the abode of a very different museum. The original intention was to house the Escher Museum there. But the work of the Dutch master of spatial illusions, repeating geometric patterns and impossible buildings has now found a home in the Museum Het Paleis in The Hague. The upper floor of Queen Beatrix's former working palace now even has a room where visitors can sit on chairs, put on 3-D spectacles, and feel that they are flying right through Escher's buildings.

You will also find 3-D on Kees Kalderbach's website, where you can pay a virtual visit to the house and studio of the famous Delft painter Vermeer. You also get a guided tour of his painting *View of Delft* and Quicktime movies about the southern gates of Vermeer's Delft or the ships to be seen in *View of Delft*. And Kaldenbach hasn't finished yet; on 24 February 2003 his website said: '*More Vermeer projects coming up – stay tuned!*'.

Pieter Bruegel too has recently inspired an interactive approach, but this time in book form. In *The Little Bruegel* Catherine de Duve has produced an attractive activity book for children, with the motto '*a great idea for discovering art while having fun*'. And fun it certainly is: there are old engravings to be coloured in, the young readers can hunt for Icarus in the famous painting *The Fall of Icarus*, and a few pages further on they are encouraged to try their hands at drawing monsters in the Bruegel fashion.

Fotomuseum Den Haag: Stadhouderskade 43 / 2517 HV The Hague / The Netherlands / www.fotomuseumdenhaag.nl

Escher in het Paleis: Lange Voorhout 74 / 2514 HV The Hague / The Netherlands / www.escherinhetpaleis.nl

Kees Kaldenbach's Vermeer site: www.johannesvermeer.info

Catherine de Duve, *The Little Bruegel*. Kate'Art Editions / www.happymuseum.com, 2002; 32 pp. ISBN 2-9600263-5-7.

The Van Gogh Letters Project, which got under way in 1994, anticipates that by about 2008 it will have published the painter's complete correspondence in probably a round dozen hefty volumes. Meanwhile Van Gogh is still a source of inspiration, as a couple of London theatres showed in 2002. Nicholas Wright's

turn out to be far from the noble savages they had imagined. And when after the Peace of Munster (1648) the quarrel with Spain was settled, the English and the French were the scapegoats. After their failed colonial adventures in Brazil and the New Netherlands the Dutch largely lost interest in America. It had again become a remote continent.

H.H. Koenigsberger, *Monarchies, States Generals and Parliaments. The Netherlands in the Fifteenth and Sixteenth Centuries*. Cambridge: Cambridge University Press, 2002; 401 pp. ISBN 0-521-80330-6. Benjamin Schmidt, *Innocence Abroad. The Dutch Imagination and the New World, 1570-1670*. Cambridge: Cambridge University Press, 2002; 450 pp. ISBN 0-521-80408-6.

'*This spot must breathe coastline. A sort of transition from water to land. Liveliness, energy.*' So here's the water again, and yes, it's a Dutchman talking. Garden designer Piet Oudolf is setting to work in New York. He has been asked to replant Battery Park, not far from Ground Zero. In May 2003 the plants will go into the ground, the beginning of his 'horticultural masterplan' in which annuals will give way to perennials which '*come back every year stronger and more beautiful, thus creating a sense of renewal and return.*'

The Dutch have something when it comes to gardens. As early as the seventeenth century travellers were feasting their eyes on the many beautiful gardens and country estates in the Republic. In *Courtly Gardens in Holland, 1600-1650* Vanessa Bezemer-Sellers gives a systematic account of the gardens of Stadholder Frederik Hendrik. We know these gardens only in their completed form from paintings and prints, but Bezemer-Sellers has also reconstructed the design stages and their execution. These were gigantic projects, spread among subcontractors who employed countless local craftsmen. You can find it all in this book. For example, the major and minor concerns of garden designers of the time – how are the ditches to be filled in, but also: what does a grotto cost, and who is to supply the shells for it?

play *Vincent in Brixton* deals with a relatively unknown period in the artist's life: the years before he started painting, when he was working for his uncle in London as an art dealer. In the play we watch Van Gogh fall in love with his landlady's daughter; but the young lady is already spoken for. No problem; the landlady herself becomes his love interest. The role was played by Clare Higgins, who won an Evening Standard Theatre Award for her performance, beating among others the Oscar-winner Gwynneth Paltrow to the prize.

Vincent in Brixton had its première in early May 2002 at the National Theatre. Later it played to full houses in the West End and was showered with favourable reviews. Michael Billington in *The Guardian* compared the figure of Van Gogh as portrayed in the play with '*the display of crazed genius interspersed with a few token stabs at a canvas*' in the well-known Van Gogh biopic *Lust for Life*: '*Forget Kirk Douglas as the jaw-jutting screen Van Gogh. Wright and Company give us the artist as he genuinely might have been*'. And on 13 February 2003 the play was among the prizes again, carrying off two Olivier Awards (London's equivalent of the Tony Awards): Best Actress in a Play (Clare Higgins again) and Best New Play. Until 4 May 2003 the play can be seen with its original London cast (including the Dutchman Jochum ten Haaf) at New York's Golden Theatre.

Golden Theatre: 252 West 45th Street / New York, NY 10036 / USA

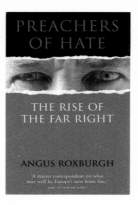

'*I have never heard anyone use the words "moderate" and "tolerance" as negative concepts before, but Dewinter said the words mockingly. "Multicultural" he said with a sneer*'. Thus Angus Roxburgh on Vlaams Blok big-shot Filip Dewinter in his *Preachers of Hate. The Rise of the Far Right*, in which he charts the success of extreme right-wing ideas in Western Europe. In smoothly-written personal pieces the author clearly demonstrates that throughout Europe army boots and shaven heads have given way to a neat-and-tidy, bespoke-suited fascism.

The quotation above comes from the chapter 'Belgium – Europe's Hole in the Head'. As a BBC correspondent Roxburgh had already narrowly escaped being shot by Chechen rebels and been kicked out of Russia on suspicion of spying. So a barbecue and a conference with the Vlaams Blok (see p. 297) was not a problem.

While in the Low Countries Roxburgh not only probes the motivations of '*the ultranationalist Vlaams Blok*', in 'Holland's Dead Souls' he also examines the Pim Fortuyn effect (see p. 299). There too his analysis is merciless; he describes the murdered Fortuyn's contribution to Dutch politics as follows: '*(…) to have legitimised racism and xenophobia by exaggerating the danger posed to Dutch society by Islam. He personally may have had the intellectual ability to distinguish between racism per se and his very particular, closely focused arguments. But his followers, and others influenced by his policies (not to mention the government, now implementing them), may be less sophisticated, turning Holland away from its decades-long traditions of tolerance and enlightenment for the sake of fighting a non-existent threat.*'

Meanwhile the intercultural outcry in the Low Countries continues unabated. Oddly enough, the strongest attack on Islam in the Netherlands after the death of Fortuyn came from the liberal VVD politician and MP Ayann Hirsi Ali, a Somalian political refugee and ex-Muslim. She described Islam as '*a backward religion*' and the prophet Mohammed as '*a perverted man*'. That brought her death-threats, and shushing noises from her own party.

'*She should keep her mouth shut*', was also the view of Dyab Abou Jahjah. A couple of years ago this Belgian of Lebanese origin set up the European Arab League (AEL); he dreams of a pan-European coalition of Arab Muslims. The AEL has three demands: '*Bilingual education for Arab-speaking kids, hiring quotas that protect Muslims, and the right to keep one's own cultural customs*'. In February 2003 Jahjah gave a lecture in London, where he was introduced as the '*Arab Malcolm X*'. And in *Time Europe Magazine* John Miller wrote: '*Civil-rights activist or self-interested agitator? Abou Jahjah may be a little bit of both. But Belgians shouldn't expect him to quiet down anytime soon – he's running for Parliament in 2003*'.

Angus Roxburgh, *Preachers of Hate. The Rise of the Far Right*. London: Gibson Square Books Ltd, 2002; 312 pp. ISBN 1-903933-21-8.

FILIP MATTHIJS
Translated by Tanis Guest.

Bibliography

of selected Dutch-Language Publications translated into English (traced November 22, 2001 - November 21, 2002)

Amstel
The Amstel / Peter-Paul de Baar ... [et al.; ed. d'ARTS, Paul Spies; transl. from the Dutch Rachel Esner ... et al.; literary extracts Marco Daane (ed.) ... et al.; interviews Marcella van der Weg; final ed. Wieneke 't Hoen]. Amsterdam: Lubberhuizen, cop. 2002. 330 p.
Transl. of: De Amstel. 2002.

Amstelkring
Amstelkring Museum, Our Lord in the Attic, Amsterdam / Marco Blokhuis ... [et al.; with photos by Peter Mookhoek, Gert-Jan van Rooij; transl. from the Dutch: Sam Herman]. Amsterdam [etc.]: Ludion, cop. 2002. 64 p.: (Ludion guides)
Transl. of: Museum Amstelkring, Ons' Lieve Heer op Solder, 2002.

Asselt, Willem J. van
The federal theology of Johannes Cocceius (1603-1669) / by Willem J. van Asselt; transl. [from the Dutch] by Raymond A. Blacketer. Leiden [etc.]: Brill, 2001. XI, 360 p. (Studies in the history of Christian thought; vol. 100)
Transl. of: Amicitia Dei: een onderzoek naar de structuur van de theologie van Johannes Coccejus (1603-1669). 1988.

Bie, Ceciel de
In the sunny south of France: Paul Gauguin and Vincent van Gogh art activity book / [transl. from the Dutch by: Martin Cleaver; concept, text, ill. and graphic design: Ceciel de Bie and Martijn Leenen]. Amsterdam: Van Gogh Museum, 2000. [40] p.
Transl. of: In het zonnige zuiden: Paul Gauguin en Van Gogh werkboek. 2000.

Blockmans, Wim
Emperor Charles V, 1500-1558 / Wim Blockmans; transl. [from the Dutch] by Isola van den Hoven-Vardon. London: Arnold; New York: Oxford University Press, 2001. XI, [6], 193 p.
Transl. of: Keizer Karel V, 1500-1558: de utopie van het keizerschap. 2000.

Blok, Diana
Ay dios / photogr. Diana Blok; text Jan Brokken; [transl. from the Dutch by Sam Garrett; ed. Bas Vroege ... et al.]. Edam: Paradox; Ede: Veenman; Amsterdam [etc.]: Voetnoot, cop. 2001. [96] p.
Transl. of: Ay dios. 2001.

Blok, F.F.
Isaac Vossius and his circle: his life until his farewell to Queen Christina of Sweden, 1618-1655 / F.F. Blok; [transl. from the Dutch by Cis van Heertum]. Groningen: Forsten, cop. 2000. 520 p.
Transl. of: Isaac Vossius en zijn kring. 1999.

Blotkamp, Carel
Mondrian: the art of destruction / Carel Blotkamp; [transl. from the Dutch by Barbara Potter Fasting]. London: Reaktion Books, 2001. 264 p.
First English ed.: 1994.
Transl. of: Mondriaan: destructie als kunst. 1994.

Blussé, Leonard
Bitter bonds: a colonial divorce drama of the seventeenth century / Leonard Blussé; transl. [from the Dutch] by Diana Webb. Princeton NJ: Wiener Publ, 2002.
Transl. of: Bitters bruid: een koloniaal huwelijksdrama in de Gouden Eeuw. 1997.

Boogaard, Oscar van den
Love's death / Oscar van den Boogaard; transl. from the Dutch by Ina Rilke. 1st ed. New York: Farrar, Straus and Giroux, 2001. 152 p.
Transl. of: Liefdesdood. 1999.

Bos, Burny
Good times with the Molesons / stories by Burny Bos; ill. by Hans de Beer; transl. [from the German] by J. Alison James. New York [etc.]: North-South Books, 2001. 46 p.
Transl. of: Familie Maulwurf: herzlichen Glückwunsch!. 2001. (Ich lese selber).
Original Dutch ed.: Familie Mol-de Mol: hartelijk gefeliciteerd. 2001. (Hoera, ik kan lezen).

Brouwers, Jan
It did not end with three beguines: history of the Congregation of the Sisters of Charity of Our Lady Mother of Mercy: foundations outside the Netherlands / by Jan Brouwers; [transl. from the Dutch: Anne Johnson]. 's-Hertogenbosch: Congregation of the Sisters of Charity of Our Lady, Mother of Mercy, 2001. X, 123 p.
Transl. of: Na de drie begijnen ging het verder. 2000.

Civil
The civil code of the Netherlands Antilles and Aruba / transl. by Peter Haanappel ... [et al.]. The Hague [etc.]: Kluwer Law International, cop. 2002. X, 466 p.
(Series of legislation in translation; 17) Contains: Book 3: Patrimonial law (law of property, rights and interests) in general; Book 5: Real rights; Book 6 General part of the law of obligations; Book 7 Special (specific) contracts.

Claus, Felix
IJburg: haveneiland and rieteilanden / Felix Claus, Frits van Dongen, Ton Schaap; [with the cooperation of Leo van den Burg ... et al.; ed. by Nienke Huizinga; transl. from the Dutch by John Kirkpatrick; drawings by Leo van den Burg ... et al.]. Rotterdam: 010 Publishers, 2001. 155 p.
Transl. of: IJburg: haveneiland en rieteilanden. 2001.

Colourful
The colourful world of the VOC: national anniversary book VOC, 1602-2002 / ed. by Leo Akveld and Els M. Jacobs; [with the cooperation of Peter Sigmond; with contributions by Leo Akveld ... et al.; transl. from the Dutch Don Mader]. Bussum: THOTH; Amsterdam: Netherlands Maritime Museum Amsterdam; Amsterdam: Rijksmuseum Amsterdam; Rotterdam: Maritime Museum Rotterdam, cop. 2002. 191 p.
Publ. appears simultaneously with the National Anniversary Exhibition "The colourful world of the VOC 1602-2002" in the Netherlands Maritime Museum Amsterdam, from March 16 through October 27, 2002 and in the Maritime Museum Rotterdam, from March 16 through September 15, 2002, it also accompanies the exhibition "The Dutch Encounter with Asia 1600-1950" at the Rijksmuseum Amsterdam, from October 12, 2002 through February 9, 2003.
Transl. of: De kleurrijke wereld van de VOC. 2002.

Dekkers, Midas
The way of all flesh: a celebration of decay / Midas Dekkers; transl. from the Dutch by Sherry Marx-Macdonald. London: Harvill, 2001. 280 p.
First English ed.: London: Harvill, 2000.
Transl. of: De vergankelijkheid. 1997.

Doets, Cees
A life long of learning: elements for a policy agenda: the six key messages of the European memorandum in a Dutch perspective / Cees Doets and Anneke Westerhuis; [transl. from the Dutch: Barry Hake].
's-Hertogenbosch: cinop, 2001. 134 p.
(Expertisecentrum-reeks)
Transl. of: Een leven lang leren: elementen voor een beleidsagenda. 2001.

Dorrestein, Renate
A heart of stone / Renate Dorrestein; transl. from the Dutch by Hester Velmans.
London: Black Swan, 2001. 251 p.
First English ed.: London: Doubleday, 2000.
Transl. of: Een hart van steen. 1998.
Other ed.: Thorndike, ME: Thorndike Press, 2001.
Large print book.
Other ed.: New York: Penguin USA, 2002.

Dorrestein, Renate
Without mercy / Renate Dorrestein; transl. from the Dutch by Hester Velmans.
London [etc.]: Doubleday, 2002. 293 p.
Transl. of: Zonder genade. 2001.

Duuren, David van
Krisses: a critical bibliography / David van Duuren; [photogr.: Irene de Groot ... et al.; transl. from the Dutch: Karin Beks; ed. of English text: Timothy Rogers; ill.: Tropenmuseum ... et al.]. Wijk en Aalburg: Pictures Publishers, cop. 2002. 192 p.
Transl. of: Krissen: een beredeneerde bibliografie. 1998.

Duyns, Don
Tunnel warrior(s) / Don Duyns; transl. [from the Dutch] by Carin van Rijswoud. Amsterdam: International Theatre & Film Books, 2002. 58 p.
(Theatre in translation)
Transl. of: De tunnelbouwer(s), 1998. Publ. in: Meer toneel. 2001.

Elsschot, Willem (pseud. of Alphonsus Josephus De Ridder)
Cheese / Willem Elsschot; transl. [from the Dutch] and with a pref. by Paul Vincent.
London [etc.]: Granta Books, 2002. XVI, 134 p.
Transl. of: Kaas. 1933.

Euwe, Max
Fischer world champion! / Max Euwe & Jan Timman; transl. [from the Dutch] by Piet Verhagen.
Alkmaar: New In Chess, 2002. 159 p.
Transl. of: De tweekamp Spasski-Fischer 1972. 1972.

Everything
Everything you should know about Zeeland / [ed.: Province of Zeeland, Office of Information; ill.: Kees de Jonge; photos: Jaap Wolterbeek; transl. from the Dutch].
2nd ed. [Middelburg]: Province of Zeeland, 2002. 48 p.
First English ed. entitled: Everything you need to know about Zeeland. 1999.
Transl. of: Wat je gewoon moet weten over Zeeland. 3th rev. ed. 1999.

Fisscher, Tiny
The princess gift book / Tiny Fisscher [text]; and Barbara de Wolff [ill.; transl. from the Dutch].
London: Bloomsbury Children's, 2001.
[50] p. + 1 card crown + 1 sheet of stickers
Transl. of: En dan was ik de prinses. 1999.

Frank, Anne
The diary of a young girl / Anne Frank; ed. by Otto H. Frank and Mirjam Pressler; transl. [from the Dutch] by Susan Massotty; ill. by Harry Brockway. London [etc.] : Puffin Books, 2002. 426 p. (Puffin modern classics)
First English ed.: New York [etc.]: Doubleday, 1995.
Transl. of: Het Achterhuis: dagboekbrieven 14 juni 1942-1 augustus 1944. Rev. and enl. ed. 1991.

Geyl, Pieter
History of the Dutch-speaking peoples, 1555-1648 / Pieter Geyl; [transl. from the Dutch]. London: Phoenix Press, 2001. 589 p.
First English ed. publ. in 2 vol. entitled: The revolt of the Netherlands, 1555-1609. London: Williams & Norgate, 1932.
Transl. of: Geschiedenis van de Nederlandsche stam. Vol. 1: Tot 1609. 1930. (Nederlandsche bibliotheek; 562) (Encyclopædie in monographieën), and: The Netherlands divided, 1609-1648. London: Williams & Norgate, 1936.
Based on a part of: Geschiedenis van de Nederlandsche stam. Vol. 2: 1609-1688. 1934. (Nederlandsche bibliotheek; 562) (Encyclopædie in monographieën).

Geyl, Pieter
Orange and Stuart, 1641-72 / Pieter Geyl; transl. [from the Dutch] by Arnold Pomerans.
London: Phoenix, 2001. XI, 443 p.
First English ed.: London: Weidenfeld & Nicolson, 1969.
Transl. of: Oranje en Stuart, 1641-1672. 1939.

Glastra van Loon, Karel van
A father's affair / Karel van Loon; transl. from the Dutch by Sam Garrett.
Edinburgh: Canongate, 2002. 199 p.
Transl. of: De passievrucht. 1999.

Growing
Growing strong: the development of the Dutch agricultural sector: background and prospects / ed. by Leo Douw and Jaap Post; [photogr. Wim te Brake; ill. IMAG ... et al.; transl. from the Dutch]. The Hague: LEI, cop. 2000. 184 p.
Publication on the occasion of the 60th anniversary of the Agricultural Economics Research Institute (LEI), December 2000.

Transl. of: Kracht door verandering: de ontwikkeling van de Nederlandse agrosector: achtergronden en perspectief. 2000.

Grünhagen, Harm
A century in review: a look at fifty highlights from a hundred years of social housing / [text Harm Grünhagen, Hans Ibelings; transl. from the Dutch Bonnie Beekman; photogr. Mick Palarczyk ... et al.].
Hilversum: Aedes vereniging van woningcorporaties, [2001]. 67 p.
Transl. of: Een beeld van een eeuw. 2000.

Grunberg, Arnon
Silent extras / by Arnon Grunberg; transl. from the Dutch by Sam Garrett.
London [etc.]: Vintage, 2001. 368 p.
First English ed.: London: Secker & Warburg, 2000.
Transl. of: Figuranten. 1997.

Guit, André
Discover Amsterdam: city of bicycles / [compilation of route, text: André Guit; ed.: Peter Janssen ... et al; photo's: Petterik Wiggen ... et al.; transl. from the Dutch].
[S.l.: s.n., 2000] ([S.l.: De Volharding). 15 p.
Provided by Amsterdam city council's Department of Infrastructure, Traffic and Transportation (Dienst Infrastructuur, Verkeer en Vervoer), in collab. with the Amsterdam branche of the Cyclists' Union (Fietsersbond) to mark the occasion of Vélo Mondial 2000 and Fietsfeest 2000 on June 18, 2000 in the Vondelpark.
Transl. of: Ontdek Amsterdam: de stad van fietsers. 2000.

Haan, Linda de
King & king / Linda de Haan & Stern Nijland; [transl. from the Dutch].
1st print.
Berkeley [etc.]: Tricycle Press, 2002. [32] p.
Transl. of: Koning & koning. 2000.

History
The history of the Jews in the Netherlands / ed. by J.C.H. Blom, R.G. Fuks-Mansfeld, I. Schöffer; transl. [from the Dutch] by Arnold J. Pomerans and Erica Pomerans. Oxford [etc.]: Littman Library of Jewish Civilization, 2002. XV, 508 p., [52] p. pl. (Littman library of Jewish civilization)
Transl. of: Geschiedenis van de joden in Nederland. 1995.

Huizinga, Johan
Erasmus and the Age of Reformation / Johan Huizinga; transl. from the Dutch by F. Hopman; [pref. by G.N. Clark]. London: Phoenix Press, 2002. 288 p.
First English ed. entitled: Erasmus of Rotterdam. London: Phaidon Press, 1952.
First American ed. entitled: Erasmus. New York [etc.]: Scribner, 1924.
Transl. of: Erasmus. 1924.

Huygens, Constantijn
Holy days: a verse translation of Constantijn Huygens' Heilighe Daghen / transl. [from the Dutch] by Koos Daley. Lewiston, NY [etc.]: Mellen Poetry Press, cop. 2001. VIII, 19 p.
Text in English and Dutch.
Transl. of: Heilighe Daghen. 1645.

In
In a different light: fourteen contemporary Dutch-language poets / ed. Rob Schouten and Robert Minhinnick; transl. from the Dutch by Lloyd Haft, P.C. Evans, James Brockway [... et al.] Bridgend, Wales: Seren; Poetry Wales Press, 2002. 140 p.
Contains poems of: H.H. ter Balkt, Remco Campert, Hugo Claus, J. Eijkelboom, Anna Enquist, Eva Gerlach, Judith Herzberg, Esther Jansma, Rutger Kopland, Gerrit Kouwenaar, K. Michel, Leonard Nolens, Willem van Toorn and Hans R. Vlek.

Jacobs, M.G.P.A.
The magic of Heineken / M.G.P.A. Jacobs, W.H.G. Maas; [transl. from the Dutch: Mark Baker ... et al.]. Amsterdam: Heineken, 2001. [454] p.
Publ. in cooperation with: Historion.
Transl. of: De magie van Heineken. 2001.

Jagtenberg, Yvonne
The first day at school / Yvonne Jagtenberg; [transl. from the Dutch]. London: Cat's Whiskers, 2002. 24 p.
First English ed. entitled: Jack the Wolf. Brookfield, Connecticut: Roaring Brook Press, 2002.
Transl. of: Een bijzondere dag. 2001.

Jagtenberg, Yvonne
Jack the Wolf / Yvonne Jagtenberg; [transl. from the Dutch]. 1st ed. Brookfield, Connecticut: Roaring Brook Press, 2002. [20] p.
Transl. of: Een bijzondere dag. 2001.

Japin, Arthur
The two hearts of Kwasi Boachi / Arthur Japin; transl. [from the Dutch] by Ina Rilke. New York: Random House, 2002. 400p.
First English ed.: London: Chatto & Windus, 2000.
Transl. of: De zwarte met het witte hart. 1997.

Jong, Erik de
Nature and art: Dutch garden and landscape architecture, 1650-1740 / Erik de Jong; transl. [from the Dutch] by Ann Langenakens. Philadelphia, Pa.: University of Pennsylvania Press, 2001. XII, 228 p. (Penn studies in landscape architecture)
Transl. of: Natuur en kunst: Nederlandse tuin- en landschapsarchitectuur, 1650-1740. 1993.

Kat, Otto de (pseud. of Jan Geurt Gaarlandt)
The figure in the distance / Otto de Kat; transl. from the Dutch by Arnold and Erica Pomerans. London: Harvill, 2002. 128 p.

Transl. of: Man in de verte. 1998.

Komrij, Gerrit
Forgotten city & other poems / Gerrit Komrij; transl. from the Dutch by John Irons. Plumstead: The Snail Press/Queillerie, 2001.
Transl. of a choice of his work.

Kopland, Rutger (pseud. of Rutger Hendrik van den Hoofdakker)
Memories of the unknown / Rutger Kopland; transl. from the Dutch and with an introd. by James Brockway; with a forew. by J.M. Coetzee. London: Harvill, 2001. XIV, 111 p.
Text in English and Dutch.
Transl. of a choice of his work from: Onder het vee. 1996, Het orgeltje van yesterday. 1968, Alles op de fiets. 1969, Wie wat vindt, heeft slecht gezocht. 1972, Een lege plek om te blijven. 1975, Al die mooie beloften. 1978, Dit uitzicht. 1982, Voor het verdwijnt en daarna. 1985, Dankzij de dingen. 1989, Geduldig gereedschap. 1993, Tot het ons loslaat. 1997, and uncollected poems.

Krabbé, Tim
The cave / Tim Krabbé; transl. from the Dutch by Sam Garrett. London: Bloomsbury, 2001. 211 p.
First English ed.: New York: Farrar, Straus and Giroux, 2000.
Transl. of: De grot. 1997.

Krabbé, Tim
The rider / Tim Krabbé; transl. from the Dutch by Sam Garrett. London: Bloomsbury, 2002. 148 p.
Transl. of: De renner. Baarn: Rap, 1978.
Other ed.: New York: St. Martin's Press.

Kurpershoek, Marcel
Arabia of the Bedouins / Marcel Kurpershoek; transl. [from the Dutch] by Paul Vincent. London: Saqi Books, 2001. 312 p.

Transl. of: Diep in Arabië & De laatste bedoeïen. 1996.
Original Dutch editions entitled: Diep in Arabië. 1992. (Meulenhoff editie; E 1247) and: De laatste bedoeïn. 1995. (Meulenhoff editie; 1439).

Lebacs, Diana
Caimin's secret / Diana Lebacs; [transl. from the Dutch by Laura Quast]. Amsterdam: Leopold; Amsterdam: N.A.N.A., 2001.
Publ. by order of the Stichting Culturele Manifestaties N.A.N.A. on the occasion of the Kinderboekenfestival 2001.
Transl. of: Caimins geheim. 2001.

Linschoten, Jan Huygen van
Civil and corrupt Asia: images and text in the Itinerario and the Icones of Jan Huygen van Linschoten / Ernst van den Boogaart; [transl. from the Dutch]. Chicago: University of Chicago Press, 2002. 128 p.
Transl. of: Het verheven en verdorven Azië: woord en beeld in het Itinerario en de Icones van Jan Huygen van Linschoten. 2000.

Loo, Tessa de (pseud. of J.M. Duyvené de Wit)
A bed in heaven / Tessa de Loo; transl. from the Dutch by Ina Rilke. London: Arcadia Books, 2002. 120 p.
Transl. of: Een bed in de hemel. 2000.

Luijten, Jan A.F.M.
Canada and Noord-Brabant: an eternal bond / Jan A.F.M. Luijten; [transl. from the Dutch].
Soesterberg: Aspekt, 2002. 76 p.
Transl. of: Canada en Noord-Brabant: een band voor altijd. 2002.

Melet, Ed
The architectural detail: Dutch architects visualise their concepts: Wiel Arets ... Koen van Velzen / Ed Melet; [ed.: Els Brinkman ... et al.; transl. from the

Dutch: Robyn de Jong-Dalziel ... et al.].
Rotterdam: NAi Publishers, 2002. 192 p.
Transl. of: Het architectonische detail. 2002.

Metz, Tracy
Fun!: leisure and landscape / Tracy Metz; photogr. Janine Schrijver and Otto Snoek; [transl. from the Dutch Peter Mason; ed. Els Brinkman ... et al.].
Rotterdam: NAi Publishers, cop. 2002. 284 p.
Transl. of: Pret!: leisure en landschap. 2002.

Möring, Marcel
The dream room / Marcel Möring; [transl. from the Dutch]. London: Flamingo, 2002. 118 p.
Transl. of: Modelvliegen. 2000.

Möring, Marcel
In Babylon / Marcel Möring; transl. from the Dutch by Stacey Knecht. New York: Perennial; HarperCollins, 2001. 432 p.
First English ed.: London: Flamingo, 1999.
Transl. of: In Babylon. 1997.

Moeyaert, Bart
It's love we don't understand / Bart Moeyaert; transl. from the Dutch by Wanda Boeke. Asheville, North Carolina: Front Street, 2002. 160 p.
Transl. of: Het is de liefde die we niet begrijpen. 1999.

Moor, Margriet de
Duke of Egypt / Margriet de Moor; transl. from the Dutch by Paul Vincent. London: Picador, 2002. 256 p.
First English ed.: 2001.
Transl. of: Hertog van Egypte. 1996.

Moor, Margriet de
First gray, then white, then blue / Margriet de Moor; transl. from the Dutch by Paul Vincent.
1st ed. Woodstock [etc.]: Overlook Press, 2001. 218 p.
First English ed.: London [etc.]: Picador, 1994.

Transl. of: Eerst grijs dan wit dan blauw. 1991.

Münninghoff, Alexander
Max Euwe: the biography / Alexander Münninghoff; including 50 games with the original analysis by the Dutch world champion; [transl. from the Dutch by Piet Verhagen; photogr.: Euwe family collection ... et al.].
Alkmaar: New in Chess, 2001. 351 p.
Transl. of: Max Euwe: biografie van een wereldkampioen. 1976.

Mulisch, Harry
The procedure / Harry Mulisch; transl. [from the Dutch] by Paul Vincent. London [etc.]: Penguin Books, 2002. 240 p.
First English ed.: London [etc.]: Viking, 2001.
Transl. of: De procedure. 1998.

Nooteboom, Cees
All souls' day / Cees Nooteboom; transl. from the Dutch by Susan Massotty. London [etc.]: Pan Macmillan, 2002. 200 p.
First English ed.: New York: Harcourt, 2001.
Transl. of: Allerzielen. 1998.

Perrée, Rob
Cover to cover: the artist's book in perspective / Rob Perrée; [transl. from the Dutch: Mari Shields; reproduction photogr.: Edo Kuipers]. Rotterdam: NAi Publishers; Breda: De Beyerd, cop. 2002. 141 p. (Fascinations)
Publ. on the occasion of the Exhibition: "Cover to cover, kunstenaarsboeken uit de Collectie Becht" in De Beyerd, Breda (September 8, 2002 – November 10, 2002).
Transl. of: Cover to cover: het kunstenaarsboek in perspectief. 2002. (Fascinaties; 12).

Pietersma, A.
The townhall of Utrecht / [by A. Pietersma and C.C.S. Wilmer; transl. from

the Dutch Donald Gardner; ed. by Jean Vaughan; photogr.: Photography Department Het Utrechts Archief].
Utrecht: Stichting Publikaties Oud-Utrecht, 2000. 31 p. (Utrechtse monumenten; 6 [i.e. 5])
Publ. in co-operation with Het Utrechts Archief.
Transl. of: Het stadhuis van Utrecht. 2000.
(Utrechtse monumenten; 5).

Rasker, Maya
Unknown destination / Maya Rasker; [transl. from the Dutch by Barbara Fasting]. New York: Ballantine Books, 2002. 215 p.
Transl. of: Met onbekende bestemming. 2000.

Rearranging
Rearranging the world / ed. Josephine Balmer; introd.: Michèle Roberts; transl. from the Dutch by Sam Garrett and Ruth Levitt. Norwich: The British Centre for Literary Translation, 2001.
Contains transl. of a selection from work of among others Arnon Grunberg and Tessa de Loo.

Roekel, Chris van
The torn horizon: the airborne chaplains at Arnhem / by Chris van Roekel; transl. [from the Dutch] by Jan Arriens and John Chipperfield. [Oosterbeek: Vereniging Vrienden van het Airborne Museum], [2001]. 134 p.
Transl. of: Verscheurde horizon: de airborne chaplains van Arnhem. 1998.

Rouweler, Hannie
Garden of longing / Hannie Rouweler; [transl. from the Dutch: John Irons]. [Bergen op Zoom]: Kleinood & Grootzeer, cop. 2000.
Concertina-type book, [18] p.
Pages are printed on one side.
Transl. of: Tuin van verlangen. 2000.

Rouweler, Hannie
A timeless tide: poems / Hannie Rouweler; transl. [from the Dutch] by John Irons.
Groningen: Passage, cop. 2001. 44 p.

Ruebsamen, Helga
The song and the truth / Helga Ruebsamen; transl. from the Dutch by Paul Vincent. 1st ed. New York: Vintage International, 2002. 355 p.
First English ed.: New York: Knopf, 2000.
Transl. of: Het lied en de waarheid. 1997.

Rutgers, A. van der Loeff
Children on the Oregon trail / A. Rutgers van der Loeff; [transl. from the Dutch by Roy Edwards]. London: Hodder Children's, 2000. 220 p. (Hodder modern classics)
First English ed.: London: University of London Press, 1961.
Transl. of: De kinderkaravaan. 1949.

Schogt, Philibert
The wild numbers / by Philibert Schogt; [transl. from the Dutch]. London: Phoenix, 2002. 176 p.
First English ed.: New York: Four Walls Eight Windows, 2000.
Transl. of: De wilde getallen. 1998.

Schubert, Ingrid
Bear's eggs / Ingrid and Dieter Schubert; [transl. from the Dutch by Susanne Padberg].
London: Andersen, 2002, [i.e. 2001]. [28] p.
First English ed.: Asheville, North Carolina: Front Street, Lemniscaat, 1999.
Transl. of: Dat komt er nou van ... 1999.

Schubert, Ingrid
Room for one more / Ingrid and Dieter Schubert; [transl. from the Dutch]. London: Andersen Front Street [etc.], 2002. [32] p.
Transl. of: Er kan nog meer bij. 2001.

Schubert, Ingrid
There's always room for one more / Ingrid and Dieter Schubert; [transl. from the Dutch].
1st ed. Asheville NC: Front Street Lemniscaat, cop. 2002. [28] p.
Transl. of: Er kan nog meer bij. 2001.

Simoen, Jan
What about Anna? / Jan Simoen; transl. from the Dutch by John Nieuwenhuizen. Crows Nest, NSW.: Allen & Unwin, 2001. 254 p.; 20 cm
Transl. of: En met Anna? 1999.
Other ed.: New York: Walker, 2002.

Snoek, Paul
Hercules, Richelieu, and Nostradamus / Paul Snoek; transl. from the Dutch with an introd. by Kendall Dunkelberg. København: Green Integer, 2000. 175 p.; 16 cm. (Green Integer; 65)
Transl. of a selection of his poems from: Hercules: gedichten. 1960, Richelieu: gedichten. 1961, and: Nostradamus: gedichten. 1964.

Story
The story boat: stories from island travel over the water; now they are taking a boat to you / ill. of Annemarie van Haeringen; transl. from the Dutch by Greta Kilburn, Jan Michael, Wycliffe Smith ... et al. Amsterdam: Leopold; Amsterdam: N.A.N.A., 2002.
Contains a selection from work of: Toon Tellegen, Hans Hagen, Loeki Morales, Sjoerd Kuyper and Joke van Leeuwen.

Suchtelen, Ariane van
Holland, frozen in time: the Dutch winter landscape in the Golden Age / Ariane van Suchtelen; with contributions by Frederik J. Duparc, Peter van der Ploeg, Epco Runia; [transl. from the Dutch Michael Hoyle ... et al.; ed. Peter van der Ploeg ... et al.].
Zwolle: Waanders, cop.

2001. 176 p.
Catalogue, publ. on the occasion of the Exhibition: "Winters van weleer: sneeuw en ijs in het Mauritshuis" in the Mauritshuis, The Hague, November 24, 2001 – February 25, 2002.

Swaan, Abram de
Human societies: an introduction / Abram de Swaan; transl. [from the Dutch] by Beverley Jackson.
Cambridge: Polity, 2001. XI, 160 p.
Publ. in association with Blackwell Publ., Malden, MA.
Transl. of: ensenmaatschappij. 1996.

Too
Too blessed to be depressed: Crimson architectural historians 1994-2002 / [ed. Crimson; Ewout Dorman ... et al.; transl. from the Dutch John Kirkpatrick ... et al.].
Rotterdam: 010 Publishers; Rotterdam: Rotterdam-Maaskant Foundation, 2002. 312 p.
Publ. under the auspices of the Rotterdam-Maaskant Foundation on the occasion of the presentation of the 9th Rotterdam-Maaskant Award for Young Architects to Wouter Vanstiphout on May 17, 2002 in the Burgerzaal of Rotterdam's City Hall. Original Dutch texts published on: www.010publishers.nl and: www.crimsonweb.org.

Towards
Towards a library of bits and bytes: the DUTL as centre of knowledge for science and innovation / report of the DUTL visiting committee; [transl. from the Dutch]. Delft: Delft University Press, cop. 2000. 61 p.
Transl. of: Naar een bibliotheek van bits en bytes: de BTUD als kennisknooppunt voor wetenschap en innovatie. 1999.

Ubachs, P.J.H.
Masters from Maastricht: historical sketch of the

Brothers of Maastricht 1840-2000 / P.J.H. Ubachs; [English transl. from the Dutch Th.M. van Schaick; pictures: J.B.M. Smit; maps: N. Bosman].
1st ed. Maastricht: Stichting Historische Reeks Maastricht, 2001. 140 p. (Vierkant Maastricht; 31)
Transl. of: Meesters uit Maastricht: historische schets van de Broeders van Maastricht, 1840-2000. 1999.

Van Genechten, Guido
Flop-Ear / Guido Van Genechten; [transl. from the Dutch]. Hauppauge, NY: Barron's Educational Series, cop. 2001. [32] p.
First English ed.: London: Cat's Whiskers, 1999.
Transl. of: Rikki. 1999.

Van Genechten, Guido
Flop-ear is brave! / Guido van Genechten; [transl. from the Dutch]. London: Cat's Whisken, 2002. [24] p.
Transl. of: Rikki durft. 2001.

Van Genechten, Guido
Potty time / Guido Van Genechten; [transl. from the Dutch]. London: Cat's Whiskers, 2000. [25] p.
Transl. of: Het grote billenboek. 2000.

Veenendaal, Augustus J. (jr.)
Railways in the Netherlands: a brief history, 1834-1994 / Augustus J. Veenendaal, Jr. Stanford, CA.: Stanford University Press, 2001. X, 235 p.
Enl. English version of: De ijzeren weg in een land vol water. 1998.

Veldman, Ilja M.
Crispijn de Passe and his progeny (1564-1670): a century of print production / Ilja M. Veldman; transl. from the Dutch by Michael Hoyle. Rotterdam: Sound & Vision Publishers, cop. 2001. 505 p. (Studies in prints and printmaking; vol. 3).

Veldman, Ilja M.
Profit and pleasure: print books by Crispijn de

Passe / Ilja M. Veldman; transl. from the Dutch by Michael Hoyle; the Latin transl. into Dutch by Clara Klein. Rotterdam: Sound & Vision Publishers, cop. 2001. 421 p. (Studies in prints and printmaking; vol. 4).

Velthuijs, Max
Crocodile's masterpiece / Max Velthuijs; [transl. from the Dutch]. London: Andersen Press, 2001. [28] p.
First English ed.: 1991.
Transl. of: Krokodil en het meesterwerk. 1991.
First Dutch ed.: 1988.

Verbeek, Hans
Travels through town and country: Dutch and Flemish landscape drawings 1550-1830 / Hans Verbeek; with contributions by Robert-Jan te Rijdt; [transl. from the Dutch by: Kist & Kilian; photogr.: Bob Goedewaagen]. [Willemstad]: BCD Holdings, cop. 2000. 219 p.
Catalogue of the Exhibition: "Travels through town and country: Dutch and Flemish landscape drawings 1550-1830", (October 7, 2000 – December 3, 2000) in the Teyler Museum at Haarlem on the occasion of the 25th anniversary of the BCD Holdings.

Verweerd, Johanna
The winter garden: a novel / by Johanna Verweerd; [transl. from the Dutch into English by Helen Richardson-Hewitt]. Minneapolis, Minnesota: BethanyHouse, [2001]. 269 p.
Transl. of: De wintertuin: roman. Zoetermeer: Boekencentrum, 1995. (L-label).

Vincent
Vincent van Gogh. Amsterdam: Van Gogh Museum; Blaricum: V+K Publishing; [Wormer]: Inmerc, 1999-.... .. vol.
Later publ.: London: Lund Humphries Publishers, 2001.
Drawings. Vol. 3. Antwerp

& Paris 1885-1888 /
Marije Vellekoop, Sjaar
van Heugten; [transl. from
the Dutch]. 2001. 342 p.
Transl. of: Vincent van
Gogh. Tekeningen: 3:
Antwerpen & Parijs 1885-
1888, 2001.

Westera, Bette
Sleep tight, Baboon Bear /
Bette Westera; ill. by
Suzanne Diederen; [transl.
from the Dutch with the as-
sistance of John
Nieuwenhuizen].
London [etc.] : Allan &
Unwin, 2002. [20] p.
Transl. of: Welterusten,
Beer Baboen. 2001.

Wiedijk, Fr.M.
Wooden shoes of Holland /
[text: Fr.M. Wiedijk;
research J. Kooijman; pho-
togr. Bas van Buuren
... *et al.*; transl. from the
Dutch Special Translations
BV; ill. Tjasker Design
BNO 2000]. [Koog aan de
Zaan: Kooijman Souvenirs
& Gifts], [2001]. 33 p.
Transl. of: Klompen in
Nederland. 2001.

Will, Chris
Hieronymus Bosch: be-
tween heaven & hell /
Chris Will; [transl. from the
Dutch: Ruth Koenig].
Amsterdam: PlanPlan, cop.
2001. 120 p.
Transl. of: Jeroen Bosch:
tussen hemel & hel. 2001.

Woerden, Henk van
A mouthful of glass: the
man who killed the
father of apartheid / Henk
van Woerden; transl. from
the Dutch and ed. by Dan
Jacobson.
London: Granta, 2001. 168 p.
1st English ed.: 2000.
Transl. of: Een mond vol
glas. 1998.

Woud, Auke van der
The art of building: from
classicism to modernity: the
Dutch architectural debate
1840-1900 / Auke van der
Woud; [transl. from the
Dutch]. Aldershot: Ashgate,
cop. 2001. XI, 240 p.
(Reinterpreting classicism)
Transl. of: Waarheid en
karakter: het debat over de

bouwkunst, 1840-1900.
1997.

Zandvliet, Robert
Brushwood / Robert
Zandvliet; mit Texten von,
with contributions by
Leontine Coelewij, Andreas
Fiedler, Rudi Fuchs; [Über-
setz. aus dem Nieder-
ländischen Beth O'Brien ...
et al.; Photogr. Henk
Geraedts ... et al.].
Amsterdam: Stedelijk
Museum Amsterdam;
Luzern: Kunstmuseum
Luzern; Rotterdam: NAi
Uitgevers, cop. 2001. 115 p.
([Catalogus] / Stedelijk
Museum Amsterdam;
nr. 854A)
Text in German and English
Publ. on the occasion of
the Exhibition:
"Brushwood" in the
Stedelijk Museum at
Amsterdam (May 12, 2001
– July 22, 2001)
and the Kunstmuseum
Luzern (September 21,
2001 – November 25,
2001).

Zee, Henri van der
"Bound to the sea": Peter J.
Sterkenburg, a painter of
seascapes (1955-2000) / by
Henri van der Zee [biogra-
phy] and Ton van der Werf
[captions]; [English transl.
from the Dutch: Willem
Proost; photogr.: Gert
Fopma]. Harlingen: Peter J.
Sterkenburg Maritime
Paintings Foundation, 2001.
128 p.
Transl. of: "Met de zee ver-
bonden": Peter J. Sterkenburg: een maritiem schilder
(1955-2000). 2001.

Editor:
Dutch Book in Translation
Koninklijke Bibliotheek
The Hague
The Netherlands

Contributors

Dirk van Assche (1955-)
Deputy editor
'Stichting Ons Erfdeel'
Murissonstraat 260,
8930 Rekkem, Belgium

Boudewijn Bakker (1938-)
Chief Curator Gemeente-
archief Amsterdam
Beulingstraat 19,
1017 BA Amsterdam,
The Netherlands

W.J. van Bekkum (1954-)
Lecturer in Post-Bible
Hebrew (University of
Groningen) / Professor of
Modern Judaism,
University of Amsterdam)
Holstek 36,
9713 DC Groningen,
The Netherlands

*Greetje van den Bergh
(1947-)*
Vice-President of the
University of Amsterdam's
Board of Directors
Johan de Wittstraat 13,
2334 AM Leiden,
The Netherlands

K. van Berkel (1953-)
Professor of the History of
Natural Sciences
(University of Groningen)
Fonteinkruid 8,
9801 LE Zuidhorn,
The Netherlands

Leonard Blussé (1946-)
Professor of Overseas
History (University of
Leiden)
De Lairessestraat 106-2,
1071 PK Amsterdam,
The Netherlands

Jos Borré (1948-)
Teacher / Literary critic
Vredelaan 8, 2500 Lier,
Belgium

Kristiaan Borret (1966-)
Researcher (Dept. of
Architecture and Urban
Development, University
of Ghent)
Eden City 17,
1190 Brussels, Belgium

Jos Bouveroux (1947-)
Chief editor News (VRT
Radio)
A. Reyerslaan 52,
1043 Brussels, Belgium

Piet Boyens (1947-)
Official for Culture
(Council of Sint-Martens-
Latem)
c/o Dorp 1,
9830 Sint-Martens-Latem,
Belgium

Willem Breedveld (1945-)
Journalist *Trouw* / Lecturer
in Mass Communication
and Politics (University of
Leiden)
Waardsedijk 102,
3421 NH Oudewater,
The Netherlands

Jeroen Brouwers (1940-)
Writer
c/o Atlas Publishers,
P.O. Box 13,
1000 AA Amsterdam,
The Netherlands

Guido Burggraeve (1940-)
Curator The Zwin
Graaf Léon Lippensdreef 8,
8300 Knokke-Heist,
Belgium

Anton Claessens (1936-)
Member of the editorial
board *Ons Erfdeel*
Honkersven 29,
2440 Geel, Belgium

Kamiel D'Hooghe (1929-)
Organ player / Writer
Beiaardlaan 1,
1850 Grimbergen, Belgium

Marco Daane (1959-)
Editor / Literary critic
Dreeslaan 25,
2641 TH Pijnacker,
The Netherlands

Mark Delaere (1958-)
Professor of Musicology
(Catholic University of
Leuven)
Sint-Annastraat 30,
3050 Oud-Heverlee,
Belgium

Jozef Deleu (1937-)
Writer / Editor
Het Liegend Konijn
Murissonstraat 220,
8930 Rekkem, Belgium

Daniël Depenbrock (1978-)
Environmental Planning
staff member (City Council,
Groningen)
Bleekveld 11,
9711 XS Groningen,
The Netherlands

Luc Devoldere (1956-)
Chief Editor
'Stichting Ons Erfdeel'
Murissonstraat 260,
8930 Rekkem, Belgium

Bernard Dewulf (1960-)
Editor *De Morgen*
Sint-Laureisstraat 89,
2018 Antwerp, Belgium

P.C. Emmer (1944-)
Professor of the History of
European Expansion and
Related Migrations
(University of Leiden)
Van Beuningenlaan 32,
2334 CC Leiden,
The Netherlands

J.P. Guépin (1929-)
Writer
Stadionweg 114,
1077 SV Amsterdam,
The Netherlands

Kim Herbots (1978-)
Freelance journalist
Augustijnenstraat 57,
2800 Mechelen, Belgium

Marc Hooghe (1964-)
Lecturer in Sociology
(University Institute
Antwerp) / FWO Researcher
Breendonkstraat 24,
9000 Ghent, Belgium

Hans Ibelings (1963-)
Architecture critic
Javakade 542,
1019 SE Amsterdam,
The Netherlands

Peter Karstkarel (1945-)
Writer / Editor Friese Pers
Boekerij
Gysbert Japicxstraat 9,
8933 AZ Leeuwarden,
The Netherlands

Isabella Lanz (1953-)
Dance critic / Art historian
Binnenkadijk 306,
1018 AZ Amsterdam,
The Netherlands

Pieter Leroy (1954-)
Professor at the Faculty of
Political Science, section
'Environment, Nature and
Landscape' (University of
Nijmegen)
Grameystraat 4,
6525 DP Nijmegen,
The Netherlands

Annemie Leysen (1948-)
Lecturer (Katholieke
Hogeschool, Leuven)
Bertemstraat 7,
3001 Heverlee, Belgium

Erik Martens (1962-)
Film critic
Mellinetplein 11,
2600 Berchem, Belgium

Filip Matthijs (1966-)
Editorial secretary *The Low
Countries*
Murissonstraat 260,
8930 Rekkem, Belgium

Ludo Meyvis (1956-)
Editor *Campuskrant*
(Catholic University of
Leuven)
Oude Markt 13,
3000 Leuven, Belgium

Wam de Moor (1936-)
Literary critic
Postweg 32,
6523 LC Nijmegen,
The Netherlands

Jos Nijhof (1952-)
Theatre critic / Teacher
Berkenkade 14,
2351 NB Leiderdorp,
The Netherlands

Herman Pleij (1943-)
Professor of Medieval
Dutch Literature
(University of Amsterdam)
Nieuwe Hilversumseweg 36,
1406 TG Bussum,
The Netherlands

Anne Provoost (1964-)
Writer
c/o Atlas Publishers,
P.O. Box 13,
1000 AA Amsterdam,
The Netherlands

Friederike de Raat (1953-)
Editor *NRC Handelsblad*

P.O. Box 8987,
3000 TH Rotterdam,
The Netherlands

Tineke Reijnders
Art critic
Zuideinde 116,
1121 DH Amsterdam,
The Netherlands

Marc Ruyters (1952-)
Editor *De Financieel-
Economische Tijd* /
Art critic
Koning Albertlei 15,
2650 Edegem, Belgium

Reinier Salverda (1948-)
Professor of Dutch
Language and Literature
University College London,
Gower Street,
London WC1E 6 BT,
United Kingdom

Rutger van Santen (1953-)
Editor Wereldomroep
Nederland
Theresiaplein 9,
5041 BJ Tilburg,
The Netherlands

G.J. Schutte (1940-)
Professor of the History of
Dutch Protestantism (Free
University of Amsterdam)
Roeltjesweg 10,
1217 TD Hilversum,
The Netherlands

Gary Schwartz (1940-)
Director Codart /
Researcher
P.O. Box 162,
3600 AD Maarssen,
The Netherlands

Marie Christine van der
Sman (1957-)
Director Museum Meer-
manno-Westreenianum
Prinsessegracht 30,
2514 AP The Hague,
The Netherlands

Kees Snoek (1952-)
Researcher / Literary critic
Boogjes 46,
3311 VC Dordrecht,
The Netherlands

Bart van der Straeten
(1979-)
Editorial secretary *Ons
Erfdeel*
Murissonstraat 260,
8930 Rekkem, Belgium

Koen Vergeer (1962-)
Literary critic / Writer
Abel Tasmanstraat 63,
3531 GT Utrecht,
The Netherlands

Ernst Vermeulen (1933-)
Music critic
Albrecht Thaerlaan 63,
3571 EH Utrecht,
The Netherlands

Jozef de Vos (1945-)
Professor of English
Literature (University of
Ghent)
Ossenstraat 38,
9000 Ghent, Belgium

Jan Wauters (1939-)
Sports journalist
G. van Kerckhovenstraat 120,
2880 Bornem, Belgium

Translators

Franz de Backer
Gregory Ball
E.D. Blodgett
James Brockway
Sheila M. Dale
Derek Denné
Lindsay Edwards
Chris Emery
Peter Flynn
Nancy Forest-Flier
Tanis Guest
Theo Hermans
James S Holmes
John Irons

Peter van de Kamp
S.J. Leinbach
Yvette Mead
Elizabeth Mollison
Alison Mouthaan-Gwillim
John Nieuwenhuizen
Sonja Prescod
Julian Ross

ADVISOR ON ENGLISH USAGE
Tanis Guest (UK)

As well as the yearbook *The Low Countries*, the Flemish Netherlands foundation 'Stichting Ons Erfdeel' publishes a number of books covering various aspects of the culture of Flanders and the Netherlands.

O. Vandeputte / P. Vincent /
T. Hermans
*Dutch. The Language of
Twenty Million Dutch and
Flemish People.*
Illustrated; 64 pp.

J.A. Kossmann-Putto &
E.H. Kossmann
*The Low Countries.
History of the Northern and
Southern Netherlands.*
Illustrated; 64 pp.

Jaap Goedegebuure &
Anne Marie Musschoot
*Contemporary Fiction of
the Low Countries.*
Illustrated and with
translated extracts from
15 novels; 128 pp.

Hugo Brems &
Ad Zuiderent
*Contemporary Poetry of the
Low Countries.*
With 52 translated poems;
112 pp.

Elly Stegeman &
Marc Ruyters
*Contemporary Sculptors of
the Low Countries.*
Illustrated in four colour
printing; 128 pp.

Hans Ibelings &
Francis Strauven
*Contemporary Architects of
the Low Countries.*
Illustrated in four colour
printing; 128 pp.

Isabella Lanz &
Katie Verstockt,
*Contemporary Dance in
the Low Countries.*
Illustrated; 128 pp.

Between 1993 and 2002
the first ten issues
of the yearbook *The Low
Countries* were published.